Management Across Cultures

Developing Global Competencies

SECOND EDITION

RICHARD M. STEERS
LUCIARA NARDON
CARLOS J. SANCHEZ-RUNDE

CAMBRIDGE
UNIVERSITY PRESS

CAMBRIDGE
UNIVERSITY PRESS

University Printing House, Cambridge CB2 8BS, United Kingdom

Published in the United States of America by Cambridge University Press, New York

Cambridge University Press is part of the University of Cambridge.

It furthers the University's mission by disseminating knowledge in the pursuit of education, learning and research at the highest international levels of excellence.

www.cambridge.org
Information on this title: www.cambridge.org/9781107645912

© Richard M. Steers, Luciara Nardon and Carlos J. Sanchez-Runde 2013

First published 2013
Reprinted 2013

Printed in the United Kingdom by T. J. International Ltd, Padstow

A catalog record for this publication is available from the British Library

Library of Congress Cataloging in Publication data
Steers, Richard M.
Management across cultures : developing global competencies / Richard M. Steers,
Carlos J. Sanchez-Runde, Luciara Nardon. – 2nd ed.
    p.   cm.
ISBN 978-1-107-64591-2 (pbk.)
1. Management – Cross-cultural studies.   2. International business enterprises – Management.
I. Sanchez – Runde, Carlos.   II. Nardon, Luciara, 1972–   III. Title.
HD62.4.S735   2013
658'.049–dc23   2012015417

ISBN 978-1-107-03012-1 Hardback
ISBN 978-1-107-64591-2 Paperback

Management Across Cultures

The second edition of this popular textbook explores the latest approaches to cross-cultural management, as well as presenting strategies and tactics for managing international assignments and global teams. With a clear emphasis on learning and development, the text encourages students to acquire skills in multicultural competence that will be highly valued by their future employers. This has never been as important as now, in a world where, increasingly, all managers are global managers and where management practices and processes can differ significantly across national and regional boundaries. This new edition has been updated after extensive market feedback to include new features: a new chapter on working and living abroad; applications boxes showing how theories and key concepts can be applied to solve real-life management problems; student questions to encourage critical thinking; and updated examples and references.

Supplementary teaching and learning materials are available on a companion website at www.cambridge.org/steers.

RICHARD M. STEERS is Professor Emeritus of Organization and Management in the Lundquist College of Business, University of Oregon, United States.

LUCIARA NARDON is Assistant Professor of International Business at the Sprott School of Business, Carleton University, Ottawa, Canada.

CARLOS J. SANCHEZ-RUNDE is Professor and Director in the Department of Managing People in Organizations at IESE Business School, Barcelona, Spain.

Contents

Exhibits

Guided tour

Guided tour

Learning strategy for the book

This book is divided into three parts

GLOBAL CHALLENGES
Part I sets the stage for our analysis by discussing both the challenges facing managers and how various global management roles can differ across organizational boundaries and cultural settings.

GLOBAL UNDERSTANDING
Part II focuses on developing a deeper awareness and understanding of the global environment in which managers will increasingly find themselves.

GLOBAL MANAGEMENT
Part III builds on this foundation to focus on developing specific skills managers will need to survive and succeed in the future.

Global challenges . . .

Part I CHALLENGES FOR GLOBAL MANAGERS

1 The new global realities
2 The new global managers

Global understanding . . .

Part II DEVELOPING GLOBAL UNDERSTANDING

3 The cultural environment
4 The organizational environment
5 The situational environment

Global management . . .

Part III DEVELOPING GLOBAL MANAGEMENT SKILLS

6 Communicating across cultures
7 Negotiating global agreements
8 Leading global organizations
9 Managing a global workforce
10 Working with global teams
11 Living and working globally
12 Epilogue

Learning strategy for the chapters

Each chapter likewise follows a learning strategy aimed at building bridges between theory and practice using a range of interesting real-world applications and examples.

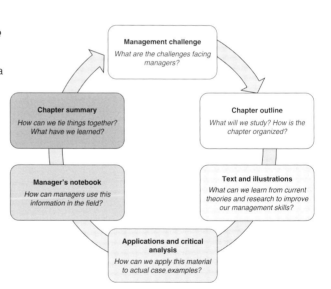

Management challenge
What are the challenges facing managers?

Chapter outline
What will we study? How is the chapter organized?

Text and illustrations
What can we learn from current theories and research to improve our management skills?

Applications and critical analysis
How can we apply this material to actual case examples?

Manager's notebook
How can managers use this information in the field?

Chapter summary
How can we tie things together? What have we learned?

GLOBAL CHALLENGES

Each chapter begins by discussing the **management challenges** that serve as the basis for the chapter. **Chapter outlines** organize the text.

The text brings together what we currently know – and, in some cases, what we don't know – about the problems global managers may face in the field and the global skills they will need to survive and succeed. These materials are based on current theory and research.

GLOBAL UNDERSTANDING

Applications are interspersed throughout each chapter to illustrate how the concepts under study apply in practice. Discussion questions encourage students to develop an understanding of what managers did in particular situations and how they might have done it better.

GLOBAL MANAGEMENT SKILLS

Manager's notebooks summarize the key implications and lessons for managers.

A **summary points** section concludes each chapter to complete the learning cycle.

Learning strategy online

An **instructor's guide** is available at www.cambridge.org/steers that demonstrates how best to use the book and PowerPoint slides in the classroom.

Instructors will find a comprehensive package of PowerPoint slides for every chapter, clearly structured to introduce the topic, summarize key concepts, the applications and manager's notebooks and encourage discussion and reflection.

A range of exercises to test student learning is also provided.

In addition recommended in-depth cases for each chapter are available at www.iveycases.com/CaseMateBrowse.aspx

Introduction

When facts are lacking, rumors abound.

Alberto Moravia[1]
Novelist and journalist, Italy

Success in the global economy requires a number of ingredients, including innovative ideas and products, access to raw materials and competitive labor, savvy marketing strategies, solid financing, sustainable supply chains, and predictable logistical support. The central driver in this endeavor, however, is the manager – who is perpetually caught in the middle. Indeed, no one ever said being a manager was easy, but it seems to get more difficult with each passing year. As competitive pressures increase across most industries and services, so too do the pressures on managers to deliver results. Succeeding against the odds often catapults a manager into the higher echelons of the organization, with a concomitant increase in personal rewards. Failure to deliver often slows one's career advancement, though, if it doesn't stop it altogether. The stakes are very high for managers and organizations alike.

With this in mind, what do managers need to know to survive and succeed in this complex and turbulent environment? Certainly, they need to understand both micro- and macroeconomics. They need to understand the fundamentals of business practices, including strategy, marketing, operations and logistics, finance, and accounting. They also need to understand issues such as outsourcing, political risk, legal institutions, and the application of emerging technologies to organizational operations. In addition to this knowledge, however, managers must understand how to work with other people and organizations around the world to get their jobs done. We refer to this as *multicultural competence*, and it is the focus of this book.

Throughout this volume, our emphasis is on learning and development, not drawing arbitrary conclusions or selecting favorites. This is done in the belief that successful global managers will focus more on understanding and flexibility than evaluation and dogmatism. This understanding can facilitate a manager's ability both to prepare and to act in ways that are more in tune with local environments. As a result, managers who are better prepared for future events are more likely to succeed – full stop. There are fewer surprises and more time to develop winning strategies on the ground, and, in the realm of managerial effectiveness, this is crucial. By integrating these two perspectives – explorations into the cultural drivers underlying managerial action and the common management strategies used in the field – it is our intention to present a more process-oriented look at global managers at work.

This book is aimed at managers from around the world. It is not intended to be a North American book, a European book, a Latin American book, and so forth. Rather, it aims to explore managerial processes and practices from the standpoint of managers from all regions of the globe – China and Brazil, India and Germany, Australia and Singapore – as they pursue their goals and objectives in the field. This is done in the belief that the fundamental managerial role around the world is a relative constant, even though the details and specifics of managerial cognitions and actions may often vary – sometimes significantly – across cultures. Taken together, our goal in this book is to help managers develop an enhanced behavioral repertoire of cross-cultural management skills that can be used in a timely fashion by managers when they are confronted with challenging and often confusing situations. It is our hope that future managers, by better understanding cultural realities on the ground, and then using this understanding to develop improved coping strategies, will succeed when many of their predecessors did not.

Global challenges facing managers

In view of the myriad challenges facing today's organizations, managers viewing global assignments – or even global travel – would do well to learn as much as they can about the world in which they are going to work. The same also holds true for local managers working in their home countries, where the global business world is increasingly challenging them on their own turf. Like it or not, with both globalization and competition intensifying almost everywhere, the challenge for managers is to outperform their competitors, whether individually or collectively. This can be attempted either by focusing exclusively on one's own self-interests or by building mutually beneficial strategic alliances with global partners. Either way, the challenges and pitfalls can be significant.

Another important factor to take into consideration here is a fundamental shift in the nature of geopolitics. The days of hegemony – East or West – are over. No longer will global business leaders focus on one or two stock markets, currencies, economies, or political leaders. Today's business environment is far too complex and interrelated for that. Contrary to some predictions, nation states and multinational corporations will remain both powerful and important; we are not, in fact, moving towards a "borderless society." Global networks, comprising technological, entrepreneurial, social welfare, and environmental interest groups, will also remain powerful. Indeed, networks and relationships will increasingly represent power, not traditional or historic institutions. Future economic and business endeavors, like future political, social, and environmental endeavors, will be increasingly characterized by a search for common ground, productive partnerships, and mutual benefit.

When faced with this rising global challenge, managers have two choices: first, in international transactions, they can assume that they are who they are and the world should adapt to them ("I am a Dutch manager with Dutch traits, and everyone understands this and will make allowances"); or, second, they can work to develop greater multicultural competencies that allow them either to adapt to others, when possible, or at least to understand why others behave as they do ("I am a Dutch manager who is working to understand the cultural context in which my counterparts operate"). While both approaches can work – especially if these managers and their firms possess critical resources – the second strategy of working to develop increased multicultural competencies clearly offers greater potential benefits in the long run.

In this endeavor, managers cannot find help by simply reaching for a book called something along the lines of *Global Management for Dummies*. Indeed, if it existed, such a book title would be an oxymoron. Global managers cannot afford to be "dummies" (perhaps "uneducated" is a better word here). Simply put, they and their companies would fail if such were the case – full stop. Instead, successful managers view working across borders as a long-term developmental process requiring intelligence and insight, not just a fancy title. It is a strategic process, not just a tactical one.

Goals of the book

As a result, this book focuses on developing a deeper understanding of how management practices and processes can often differ around the world, and why. It draws heavily on recent research in cultural anthropology, psychology, economics, and management as it relates to how managers structure their enterprises and pursue the day-to-day work necessary to make a venture succeed. It emphasizes both differences and similarities across cultures, since we believe that this approach mirrors reality. It attempts to explore the psychological underpinnings that help shape the attitudes and behaviors of managers, as well as their approaches to people from other regions of the world. Most of all, though, this book is about learning. It introduces a learning model early in the text to serve as a guide in the intellectual and practical development of managers seeking global experience. Further, it assumes a lifelong learning approach to global encounters, managerial performance, and career success.

The title of this book, *Management Across Cultures: Developing Global Competencies*, reflects our twin goals in writing it. First, we wanted to examine how management practices and processes can frequently differ – often significantly – across national and regional boundaries. Managers in different cultures often see their roles and responsibilities in different ways. They often organize themselves and make decisions differently. They often communicate, negotiate, and motivate employees in different ways. Understanding these differences is the first step in developing global management capabilities. Second, we wanted to identify and discuss realistic strategies and tactics that can be used by global managers as they work to succeed across cultures. In other words, we wanted to explore how people can work and manage across cultures – and how they can overcome many of the hurdles along the way. We see these two goals as not just mutually compatible but indispensable for meeting the business challenges ahead.

Like most authors who seek an interested audience, we wrote this book primarily to express our own views, ideas, and frustrations. As both teachers and researchers in the field, we have grown increasingly impatient with books in this general area that seem to aim somewhat below the readers' intelligence in the presentation of materials. In our view, managers and would-be managers alike are intelligent consumers of behavioral information. To do their jobs better, they seek useful information and dialogue about the uncertain environments in which they work; they are not seeking unwarranted or simplistic conclusions or narrow rulebooks. Moreover, in our view, managers are looking for learning strategies, not prescriptions, and understand that becoming a global manager is a long-term pursuit – a marathon, not a sprint.

We have likewise been dismayed seeing books that assume one world view, whether it be British, American, French, or whatever, in interpreting both global business challenges and managerial behavior. Instead, we have tried diligently to cast our net a bit wider and incorporate divergent viewpoints when exploring various topics, such as communication, negotiation, and leadership. For example, asking how Chinese or Indian management practices differ from Australian or Canadian practices assumes a largely Western bias as a starting point: "How are *they* different from us?" Instead, why not ask a simpler and more useful question, to find out how Chinese, Indian, Australian, and Canadian management styles in general differ: "How are we *all* different from each another?" Moreover, we might add a further, also useful, question concerning managerial similarities across cultures: "How are we *all* similar to each other?" To achieve this end, we have resisted a "one-size-fits-all" approach to management, locally or globally, in the belief that such an approach limits both understanding and success in the field. Rather, our goal here is to develop multicultural competence through the development of learning strategies in which managers can draw on their own personal experiences, combined with outside information such as that provided in this book and elsewhere, to develop cross-cultural understanding and "theories-in-use" that can guide them in the pursuit of their managerial activities.

In writing this book, we were also able to draw on our research and teaching experiences in various countries and regions of the world, including Argentina, Belgium, Brazil, Canada, Chile, China, Denmark, Germany, Japan, Mexico, Norway, Netherlands, Peru, South Africa, South Korea, Spain, the United Kingdom, the United States, and Uruguay. In doing so, we learned from our colleagues and students in various parts of the world, and we believe that these experiences have made this a better book than it might otherwise have been. Our aim here is not to write a bias-free book, as we believe this would have been an impossible task. Indeed, the decision to write this book in English, largely for reasons of audience, market, and personal competence, does itself introduce some bias into the end result. Rather, our intent was to write a book that simultaneously reflects differing national, cultural, and personal viewpoints, in which biases are identified and discussed openly instead of being hidden or rationalized. As a result, this book contains few certainties and many contradictions, reflecting our views on the life of global managers.

Global management model

We view management success in the global arena as consisting of three interrelated components: understanding global challenges; understanding global environments; and developing global management skills.

- *Understanding global challenges*. Managers must first understand the challenges and obstacles they face, as well as the opportunities. They must understand their jobs and how their efforts fit into the larger organizational objectives.
- *Understanding the global environment*. Managers must next understand how to assess the local environments in which they work and make suitable choices among available alternatives. While there are many ways to break up this environment for the purposes of analysis and understanding, we suggest that a productive approach is to visualize three interrelated environments: cultural, organizational, and situational; that is, to accomplish their tasks and responsibilities, managers must succeed in all

Exhibit A Global management model

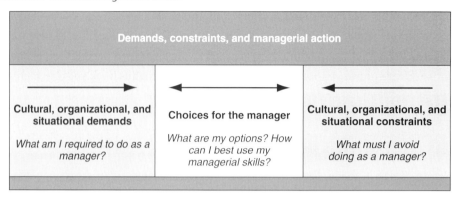

three environments simultaneously. Taken together, this environment creates both *demands* and *constraints* on managerial *action* (see Exhibit A). These limitations raise two pertinent questions for global managers: what must I do as a manager – that is, what is expected of me to succeed – and, second, what must I avoid doing as a manager? What actions should I avoid in order not to offend others or lose opportunities? Within these two limitations, managers are free to make informed choices among their available 'options concerning their present and future actions. The question here is: what are my options, and how can I best use my managerial skills on behalf of the organization? A model outlining this process, based on the classic work of Oxford University professor Rosemary Stewart, is discussed in detail in Chapter 5 for use as a guide to managerial assessment and action.

- *Developing global management skills.* Once the local environment is better understood and choices have been made, managers must have (or develop) suitable global managerial skills to carry out their actions. As discussed in this book, we view these skills as including cross-cultural communication, negotiation, leadership, workforce management, team management, and living and working successfully abroad.

Few projects of this magnitude can be successful without the support of families. This is especially true in our case, with all three of our families joining together to help make this project a reality. In particular, Richard would like to thank the four generations of women who surround and support him: Pat, Sheila, Kathleen, and Allison; Luciara would like to thank her mother, Jussara, for her unconditional support, and her son, Caio, for his inspiration; and Carlos would like to thank his wife, Carol, and daughters, Clara and Isabel, for their continued support and encouragement. Throughout, our families have been there for us in every way possible, and for this we are grateful.

Any successful book is a joint venture between authors, instructors, students, and publishers. In this regard, we were fortunate to have received useful comments from instructors and outside reviewers alike aimed at making this edition superior to the last. Student comments, both in our own classes and those of others, have also helped us improve on the first edition. Finally, we are indebted to the people at Cambridge University Press for their help and support throughout the revision and production process. They lived up to their reputation as a first-class group of people to work with. In particular, we wish to thank Paula Parish, Raihanah Begum, and Jo Lane for their advice, patience, and support through the project. We are indebted to them all.

Note

1 Alberto Moravia, *Gli Indifferenti* [*The Indifferent Ones*] (trans. Aida Mastrangelo). New York: E. P. Dutton, 1932.

PART I

CHALLENGES FOR GLOBAL MANAGERS

CHAPTER 1

The new global realities

MANAGEMENT CHALLENGE

No one said being a manager is easy, and this opening chapter illustrates why. With increasing globalization comes increased pressure for both change and competitiveness. Understanding this changing environment is our first challenge. The second is building mutually beneficial interpersonal and multicultural relationships with people in different parts of the globe in order to overcome these challenges and take advantage of the opportunities presented by the turbulent global environment. We argue here that an important key to succeeding in the global business environment is developing sufficient multicultural competence to work and manage successfully across cultures.

Chapter outline

Applications

A competitive world offers two possibilities. You can lose. Or, if you want to win, you can change.

Lester Thurow
Sloan School of Management, Massachusetts Institute of Technology,
United States

In the future, the ability to learn faster than your competitors may be the only sustainable competitive advantage.

Arie de Geus
Corporate planning director, Royal Dutch Shell, the Netherlands

We live in a turbulent and contradictory world, in which there are few certainties and change is constant. Over time, we increasingly come to realize that much of what we think we see around us can, in reality, be something entirely different. We require greater perceptual accuracy just as the horizons become more and more cloudy. Business cycles are becoming more dynamic and unpredictable, and companies, institutions, and employees come and go with increasing regularity. Much of this uncertainty is the result of economic forces that are beyond the control of individuals and major corporations. Much results from recent waves of technological change that resist pressures for stability or predictability. Much also results from the failures of individuals and corporates to understand the realities on the ground when they pit themselves against local institutions, competitors, and cultures. Knowledge is definitely power when it comes to global business, and, as our knowledge base becomes more uncertain, companies and their managers seek help wherever they can find it.

Considering the amount of knowledge required to succeed in today's global business environment and the speed with which this knowledge becomes obsolete, it is the thesis of this book that mastering learning skills and developing an ability to work successfully with partners in different parts of the world may well be the best strategy available to managers who want to succeed. Business and institutional knowledge is transmitted through interpersonal interactions. If managers are able to build mutually beneficial interpersonal and multicultural relationships with partners around the world, they may be able to overcome their knowledge gaps. Our aim in this book, then, is to develop information and learning models that managers can build upon to pursue their careers and corporate missions.

As managers increasingly find themselves working across borders, their list of cultural contradictions continues to grow. Consider just a few examples. Most French and Germans refer to the European Union as "we," while many British refer to it as "they"; all are members. To some Europeans, Japan is part of the "Far East," while, to some Japanese, Europe is part of the "Far East"; it all depends on where you are standing. Criticizing heads of state is a favorite pastime in many countries around the world, but criticizing the king in Thailand is a felony punishable by fifteen years in jail. Every time Nigerian-born oncologist Nkechi Mba fills in her name on a form somewhere, she is politely told to write her name, not her degree. In South Korea, a world leader in IT networks, supervisors often assume employees are not working unless they are sitting at their desks in the office. Moreover, in a recent marketing survey among US college students, only 7 percent could identify the national origins of many of their favorite brands, including Adidas, Samsung, Nokia, Lego, and Ericsson. In particular, quality ratings of Nokia cellphones soared after students concluded, incorrectly, that they were made in Japan.

There is more. Germany's Bavarian Radio Symphony Orchestra recently deleted part of its classical repertoire from a concert tour because it violated the European Union's new noise at work limitations. US telecommunications giant AT&T has been successfully sued in class action suits for gender discrimination against both its female and male employees. When you sink a hole in one while playing golf with friends in North America and Europe, it is often customary for your partners to pay you a cash prize; in Japan, you pay them. The head of Nigeria's Niger Delta Development Corporation was fired from his job after it was discovered that he had paid millions of dollars of public money to a local witch doctor to vanquish a rival. The penalty for a first offense of smuggling a small quantity of recreational drugs into western Europe is usually a stern lecture or a warning; in Singapore, it is death. Finally, dressing for global business meetings can be challenging: wearing anything made of leather can be offensive to many Hindus in India; wearing yellow is reserved for the royal family in Malaysia; and white is the color of mourning in many parts of Asia.

Serious? Silly? Absurd? Perhaps the correct answer here is that it is all in the eye of the beholder. When confronted by such examples, many observers are dismissive, suggesting that the world is getting smaller and that many of these troublesome habits and customs will likely disappear over time as globalization pressures work to homogenize how business is done – properly, they believe – across national boundaries. The world is not getting smaller, however; it is getting faster.[1] Many globalization pressures are currently bypassing – and, indeed, in some cases actually accentuating – divergent local customs, conventions, and business practices, if for no other reason than to protect local societies from the ravages of economic warfare. What this means for managers is that many of these and other local customs will likely be around for a long time, and wise managers will prepare themselves to capitalize on these differences, not ignore them.

Globalization, change, and competitiveness

Although there are many ways to conceptualize globalization, most definitions share common roots. For our purposes here, and following the work of *New York Times* columnist Thomas Friedman, we define *globalization* as the inexorable integration of markets, capital, nation states, and technologies in ways that allow individuals, groups, corporations, and countries to reach around the world farther, faster, more deeply, and more cheaply than ever before.[2] This process is increasingly creating a powerful backlash from those left behind by the new economic and political system. In essence, this new global reality represents a major paradigm shift in international politics, economics, and business that impacts corporations and their managers, as well as society at large – and, as experience teaches us, few such changes occur without winners and losers.

Economic historians have suggested that, as a world-changing phenomenon, globalization has passed through three reasonably distinct phases.[3] Phase one involved the globalization of countries and ran roughly from the 1400s through the early 1900s. In this phase, nations tried with varying degree of success to define their relationships with other nations. The age of imperialism in the seventeenth and eighteenth centuries, when several of Europe's largest countries tried to divide up much of the rest of the world as colonies, provides a good example of this. Phase two involved the globalization of companies and ran throughout most of the twentieth century. This was the age when many well-known multinational corporations were born and companies began seeing their markets in global terms. Phase three – the current phase – began roughly with the new twenty-first century and involves the globalization of individuals. This is when globalization is experienced on a personal level; it affects individuals, as, for example, when an Indian entrepreneur hires young people trained in Hindu temple art to make computer-assisted character designs for global computer game companies. This is a global application of a traditional Hindu art form, and it indicates just how personal globalization can become. Globalization can also be felt on a personal level when outsourced or imported products, ranging from automobiles to toothpaste, lead to downsizing and job losses for individuals in the local economies. The recent economic meltdown has only added to these troubles.

Moreover, because of a decline in the cost of both transportation and telecommunications, combined with the proliferation of personal computers (PCs) and the bandwidth and common software applications that connect them, global companies are now able to build *global workflow platforms*. These platforms can divide up almost any job and, with scanning and digitization, outsource each of its components to teams of skilled knowledge workers around the globe, based on which team can perform the function with the highest skill at the lowest cost. Jobs ranging from clothing manufacturing to accounting to radiology are examples of this. Thus, the advice to large and small countries alike around the world seems to be to get on board the global train and find a place to add value; otherwise you risk being left behind.

Application 1.1 **Canada Post**

To see what can happen here, consider a recent example from Canada. In a dispute over wages and working conditions, unionized Canada Post workers went on strike. Their goal was to create sufficient frustrations for customers that management would be forced into a quick settlement. As a result of the strike, local and international mail delivery was halted for several weeks. In the old days this would have meant that people's bills would go unpaid, letters and other forms of correspondence would slow, and customers would be greatly inconvenienced, putting considerable pressure on the government. This time, however, the outcome was very different. Millions of people who used to mail their monthly bills simply converted to electronic bill paying. E-mail use increased as handwritten letters became increasingly slow and difficult. "Many find mail in paper form to be quaint; it no longer plays a central role in society," an editorial in *The Globe and Mail* daily newspaper concluded. "The strike will only accelerate that trend by making online converts of those who have hitherto been reluctant."[4] Union vice-president George Floresco took a different view, however. He argued that, instead of cutting wages, Canada Post should try to become more relevant to Canadians by expanding its service. "We know there's a move to online services, but we also know a lot of people don't want to go there," he observed. When the strike was finally settled, Canada Post had lost many of its long-term loyal customers, and the actual cost of delivering a letter increased because of the reduced volume of mail and increased delivery costs. Electronics had replaced people.

Think about it...

(1)   Canada Post is not the only national postal service having serious troubles in today's new electronic marketplace. What is the future of such national postal services?

(2)   Is there a similar problem in your own home country?

(3)   What, if anything, can postal services do to regain markets and their competitive edge?

(4)   In what other ways is the global economy changing in directions that threaten other businesses?

Exhibit 1.1 Globalization drivers

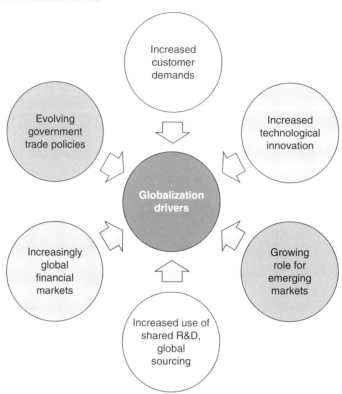

Many factors account for the new global economy. We refer to these as globalization drivers (see Exhibit 1.1). These include the various forces emerging from the global environment that, essentially, force countries, institutions, and companies to globalize or fail. Consider the following drivers.

- *Increased customer demands and access to competing products and services.* Customers around the world are increasingly demanding more for less. They are putting increased pressure on both the price and quality of the products and services that various firms offer. Customers increasingly prefer global brands over local products; they want Blackberries, iPads, or BMWs, not because they are Canadian, American, or German but because they are "branded." They see themselves as pacesetters, demanding only the latest in technologies, luxuries, products, and services. Moreover, customers increasingly have greater access to products and services that go beyond local distributors (e.g., e-business, television shopping).

- *Technological innovation and application.* Improved telecommunications and information technology (IT) facilitate increased access to global networks, markets, partners, and customers. Basic and applied research, often conducted by global strategic alliances or international joint ventures, is increasingly generating new products and services (e.g., new technologies, new medicines, new DNA or genetic applications), thereby creating new markets.

- *Increased power and influence of emerging markets and economies.* As many economic forces continue to globalize, the differences between haves and have-nots have tended to become accentuated. Emerging markets present traditional corporations with a particular challenge, while many emerging economies are demanding greater respect and greater access to global markets. Meanwhile, some economies and societies fall further into poverty and despair. Consider: Zimbabwe continues to sink in a world of official corruption and violence in which its inflation rate recently exceeded 250,000,000 percent and expiration dates are now printed on its national currency.

- *Shared research and development (R&D) and global sourcing.* Many companies are going global in order to spread their research and product development costs across multiple regional markets. Outsourcing is now the rule, not the exception. Consider: 70 percent of the components used in the manufacture of Boeing's 787 "Dreamliner" are sourced from foreign suppliers.[5] Global supply chains are becoming increasingly efficient, while transportation and logistical costs are often declining.

- *Increased interdependence of financial markets.* Global economies and financial markets have become more and more interdependent. Access to capital markets is becoming increasingly globalized. This trend has proven catastrophic in some cases when these intertwined markets have collapsed simultaneously.

- *Evolving government trade policies.* Governments are increasingly supporting local economic development initiatives to lure new (and often foreign) investments and create local employment. They are also increasingly supporting aggressive trade initiatives to support the global expansion of local companies. Trade barriers are being systematically reduced across much of the world through multilateral trade agreements (e.g., World Trade Organization, European Union, North American Free Trade Agreement). With increased recessionary pressures, however, it is anyone's guess whether this trend will continue or reverse itself.

Taken together, the results of these globalization drivers represent a sea change in the challenges facing businesses and the way in which they conduct themselves in the global economy, and they have a direct influence on the quality and effectiveness of management. Companies are under increasing pressure to achieve greater efficiencies and economies of scale. Local firms have no place to hide.

Looking to the future, what new and different globalization pressures are likely to emerge to challenge international (and national) companies and their managers? How will these new pressures affect the opportunities and threats faced by firms? How will these new pressures affect the management skills that will be required to succeed in the future?

Application 1.2 Hamburgers and A380s

A typical hamburger sold in New York, London, Beijing, Melbourne, or Moscow contains ingredients from at least a dozen different countries. It is truly a global product.[6] In the United States, for example, the hamburger buns include Canadian yeast, Chinese vitamin enrichments, Polish wheat gluten, and Dutch mold-inhibiting preservatives, while the tomatoes typically come from Mexico, Guatemala, Colombia, or New Zealand. The lettuce mostly comes from Canada, Mexico, or Peru, while the beef in one patty can contain meat from up to fifty cattle shipped from several countries. And don't forget the Canadian mustard seeds, Italian vinegar, and Australian garlic powder. Think about it. If you were in charge of food safety for the US Department of Agriculture (or similar operations in other countries), how might you begin to gain oversight over the quality and safety of a hamburger's – or any other product's – ingredients? In other words, how would you do your job?

Now think further. If the world of the humble hamburger is so complicated, imagine the world of global business. Imagine the world of software development, consumer electronics, financial instruments, aircraft manufacture, and so forth. An Airbus A380, for example, has over a million parts sourced from three dozen countries around the world. Imagine the world of the global manager, whose job it is to develop, source, transport, assemble, and distribute the products or services under his or her control. The world is indeed a complicated place – especially for today's managers.

Think about it...

(1) How is it possible to make money selling a 99 cent hamburger with ingredients from perhaps a dozen countries?

(2) As noted above, if you worked for the government overseeing food safety for such products, how would you do your job?

(3) Is a manager's job easier or more difficult at Airbus or McDonald's? Why?

The emerging global landscape

Much of what is being written today about doing business in the new global economy is characterized by a sense of energy, urgency, and opportunity. We hear about developing transformational leaders, building strategic alliances, launching global product platforms, leveraging technological breakthroughs, first-mover advantages, global venturing, outsourcing, sustainable supply chains, and, most of all, making money. Action – and winning – seem to be the operational words. Discussions about global business assume a sense of perpetual dynamic equilibrium. We are told that nothing is certain except change, and that winners are always prepared for change; we are also told that global business is like white water rafting – always on the edge; and so forth. Everything is in motion, and opportunities abound.

At the same time, however, there is another, somewhat more troublesome side to this story of globalization that is discussed far less often, yet it is equally important. This side is characterized by seemingly endless conflicts with partners, continual misunderstandings with suppliers and distributors, mutual distrust, perpetual delays, ongoing cost overruns, political and economic risks and setbacks, personal stress, and, in some cases, lost careers. Indeed, over 50 percent of international joint ventures fail within the first five years of operation. The principal reasons cited for these failures are cultural differences and conflicts between partners.[7]

This downside has several potentially severe consequences for organizational success, especially in the area of building workable global partnerships. Although it is not easy to get a handle on all the changes occurring in the global environment, three prominent changes stand out: the evolution from intermittent to continual change, from isolation to increasing interconnectedness, and from biculturalism to multiculturalism.

Application 1.3 Apple iPhone

Apple's iPhones are very popular worldwide. Apple does not actually make the phones, however. It neither manufactures the components nor assembles them into a finished product.[8] The components come from a variety of suppliers, while the assembly is carried out by Foxconn, a Taiwanese firm, at its plant in Shenzhen, China. Samsung Electronics turns out to be a particularly important supplier. It provides some of the phone's most important components, including the flash memory that holds the phone's apps, music and operating software, the working memory (or DRAM), and the applications processor that makes the whole thing work. Together, these account

Application 1.3   (cont.)

for over one-quarter of the component cost of an iPhone. This puts Samsung Electronics in the somewhat unusual position of supplying a significant proportion of one of its main rival's products, since Samsung also makes smartphones and tablet computers of its own. Apple is one of Samsung's largest customers, and Samsung is one of Apple's biggest suppliers. This is actually part of Samsung's business model: acting as a supplier of components for others gives it the scale to produce its own products more cheaply. For its part, Apple is happy to let other firms handle component production and assembly, because this leaves it free to concentrate on its strengths: designing elegant, easy-to-use combinations of hardware, software, and services. Stranger still, Apple sued Samsung recently over the design of its Galaxy handset (a smartphone that bears a strong resemblance to an iPhone) and its Galaxy Tab tablet computer (which looks rather like an iPad), claiming that they copied hardware and design features from Apple products. Samsung retaliated by counter-suing. In the latest twist, Apple has just gained injunctions to prevent the sale of Samsung's Galaxy Tab in Europe and Australia. The two firms' mutually beneficial trading relationship continues, however.

Think about it. . .

(1)   How is it possible for two companies to work closely together in a global strategic alliance when they are not only direct competitors in the marketplace, but also suing one another in court?

(2)   What does this global alliance tell you about the future of global strategies and competitiveness in highly dynamic industries?

(3)   What are the management challenges for Apple and Samsung in making this long-term relationship work?

(4)   Are there lessons from this strategic alliance for other global companies?

(5)   Is it easier or more difficult for companies to work with firms from other cultures (e.g., those in the United States and South Korea)? Why? What are the management implications of such differences?

From intermittent to continual change

Change is everywhere. Companies, products, and managers come and go. This turbulence increasingly requires almost everyone, from investors to consumers, to pay greater heed to the nature, scope, and speed of world events, both economically and politically.

Exhibit 1.2 The changing global economy

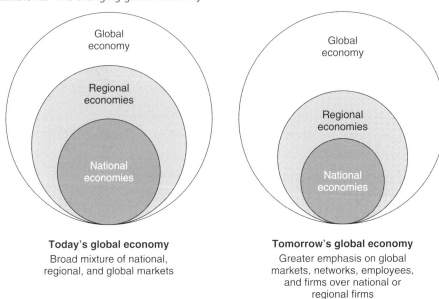

Today's global economy
Broad mixture of national,
regional, and global markets

Tomorrow's global economy
Greater emphasis on global
markets, networks, employees,
and firms over national or
regional firms

Details have become more important. Personal relationships, even though they are under increasing threat, remain one of the last safe havens in an otherwise largely unpredictable world.

Across this changing environment – indeed, as one of the principal causes of these changes – we can see the relentless development and application of new technologies, especially with regard to the digital revolution (see Exhibit 1.2). Technology is largely held to be a principal driver of globalization and the key to national economic development and competitiveness. Indeed, global business as we know it today would not be possible without technology. It was only with the emergence of affordable and reliable computer and communication technologies that coordination and collaboration across borders became possible. A few years ago subsidiaries were managed as independent organizations, and managers traveled around the globe for coordination purposes. Today electronic technologies facilitate the transfer of information and make communication through text, voice, and video simple and affordable.

At the same time, globalization has resulted in an increase in the transfer and diffusion of technological innovation across borders, as well as competition among nations to develop and adopt advanced technologies. As business becomes more and more global, the need for better and cheaper technology increases, pushing technological development to new heights. Computers are obsolete as soon as they are out of the box, smartphones integrate new functionalities for managers on the move, and we have cellphone coverage and internet access in almost every corner of the world. Managers cannot understand globalization or manage globally without understanding the influence of technology on business.

From isolation to interconnectedness

In today's increasingly turbulent and uncertain business environment, major changes occur with increasing regularity. The recent collapse of the global financial markets, accompanied by worldwide recession, has caused hardships around the world and has led to changes, both political and economic, in rich and poor countries alike . The economic and political power of India and China continues to grow exponentially, and both are struggling to manage the positive and negative consequences of growth and development. Russia is trying to reassert itself politically and economically in the world, overcome rampant corruption in its business sector, and reform its economic system in order to build local companies that can compete effectively in the global economy. Arab nations are struggling for greater democracy and human rights. Japan is trying to rebuild its economy after its recent catastrophic environmental disaster. France is trying to reinvigorate its economy by changing its historically uncompetitive labor policies. Turkey is trying to join the European Union so that its companies can gain greater access to world markets. South Africa continues to struggle to shed the vestiges of its old apartheid system and build a new, stronger economy based on more egalitarian principles. Throughout, there is a swelling consumer demand for higher-quality but lower-cost goods and services that challenge most governments and corporations. In a nutshell, welcome to today's increasingly global economy. In this new economy, globalization is not a debate; it is a reality.

This is not to say that the challenges and potential perils of globalization are a recent phenomenon. Indeed, quite the contrary is true; globalization has always been a major part of commerce. What is new, however, is the magnitude of globalization today and its impact on standards of living, international trade, social welfare, and environmental sustainability. In 1975 global foreign direct investment (FDI) totaled just $23 billion; by 1998, a little over twenty years later, it totaled $644 billion; and by 2008, just ten years after that, it totaled $1.5 trillion. It is estimated that, by 2020, global foreign direct investment will surpass $3 trillion. Despite regional and worldwide recessions and economic setbacks, global FDI continues to grow at a seemingly uncontrollable rate. What are the ramifications of this increase for organizations and their managers? What are the implications for developed and less developed countries? Is there a role for governments and public policy in this revolution?

Application 1.4 Ethanol and the price of tortillas in Mexico

Clearly, the degree of economic and social interconnectedness between both countries and companies has increased significantly in recent years – and not always in a positive direction. For example, when the use of ethanol as an additive to gasoline production increased significantly in American and European markets, corn prices around the world skyrocketed, and the price of tortillas in Mexico, a staple food among Mexico's poor, nearly doubled. A short time later, however, the bottom fell out of the ethanol market as oil prices dropped and the price of corn fell. Then, a year later, oil prices skyrocketed again, as did the price of corn. Caught in the middle of all of this was the Mexican peasant, just trying to survive: unintended, yet nonetheless very real, consequences.

Think about it...

(1) Do companies have an obligation, moral or otherwise, to consider the economic, social, or environmental ramifications of their actions beyond the confines of there own firms or countries?

(2) Realistically, what, if anything, can these companies do to be sensitive to these ramifications, while still complying with their legal obligations to their stockholders?

(3) Someone once said that everyone is an environmentalist – that is, no company intentionally sets out to destroy the environment. Do you believe this to be true? Why or why not?

(4) Who gets to decide who is socially or environmentally responsible and who is not?

From biculturalism to multiculturalism

The increasing intensity and diversity that characterize today's global business environment require managers to succeed simultaneously in multiple cultures, not just one. Gone are the days when a manager prepared for a long-term assignment in France or Germany – or even Europe. Today this same manager must deal simultaneously with partners from perhaps a dozen or more different cultures around the globe. As a result, learning one language and culture may no longer be enough, as it was in the past. In addition, the timeline for developing these business relationships has declined from years to months – and sometimes to weeks. To us, this requires a new approach to developing global managers. This evolution from a principally bicultural business environment to a more multicultural or global environment presents managers with at least three new challenges in attempting to adapt quickly to the new realities on the ground.

- *It is sometimes unclear to which culture we should adapt.* Suppose that your company has asked you to join a global project team to work on a six-month R&D project. The team includes one Brazilian, one Indian, one Portuguese, and one Russian. Every member of the team has a permanent appointment in his or her home country but is temporarily assigned to work at company headquarters (HQ) in Sweden for this project. Which culture should team members adapt to? In this case, there is no dominant cultural group to dictate the rules. Considering the multiple cultures involved, and the little exposure each manager has likely had with the other cultures, the traditional approach of adaptation is unlikely to be successful. Nevertheless, the group's members have to be able to work together quickly and effectively to produce results (and protect their careers), despite their differences. What would you do?

- *Many multicultural encounters happen on short notice, leaving little time to learn about the other culture.* Imagine that you have just returned from a week's stay in India, where you were negotiating an outsourcing agreement. As you arrive in your home office, you learn that an incredible acquisition opportunity has just turned up in South Africa and that you are supposed to leave in a week to explore the matter further. You have never been to South Africa, nor do you know anybody from there. What do you do?

- *Multicultural meetings increasingly occur virtually, by way of computers or video conferencing, instead of through more traditional face-to-face interactions.* Suppose that you were asked to build a partnership with a partner from Singapore who you have never met, and that you know little about the multiple cultures of Singapore. Suppose further that this task is to be completed online, without any face-to-face communication or interactions. Your boss is in a hurry for results. What would you do?

Taken together, these three challenges illustrate just how difficult it can be to work or manage across cultures in today's rapidly changing business environment. The old ways of communicating, negotiating, leading, and doing business are simply less effective than they were in the past. As such, the principal focus of this book will be on how to facilitate management success in global environments – how to become a global manager.

Management and multicultural competence

Globalization pressures represent a serious challenge facing businesses, and the way in which they conduct themselves in the global economy, and they have a direct influence on the quality and effectiveness of management. Even so, globalization presents companies with opportunities as well as challenges. The manner in which they respond – or fail to respond – to such challenges will in large measure determine who wins and who loses. Those that succeed will need to have sufficient managers with economic grounding, political and legal skills, and cultural awareness to decipher the complexities that characterize their surrounding environment. Tying this all together will be the management know-how to outsmart, outperform, or outlast the competition on a continuing basis. Although globalization seems to be inevitable, however, not all cultures and countries will react in the same way, and therein lies one of the principal challenges for managers working across cultures.

Application 1.5 Launching a new venture in India

Many observers have suggested that the future belongs to India. Everyone seems to be going there these days, and this developing nation has become a haven for outsourcing. For all its global assets, however, India can be a tough place for entrepreneurs. Indeed, the World Bank's "Ease of doing business" index ranks India 165th out of 183 countries in terms of the ease of launching a new business there. Furthermore, India scores 182nd out of 183 (behind Angola) in terms of the government or legal enforcement of contracts. Why? A large part of the answer to this question lies in a culture filled with red tape and, at times, non-sensical permits, policies, and procedures. Sometimes entrepreneurs cannot even discover what the rules are until they are snagged.[9] In Mumbai, for example, there are thirty-seven procedural hoops to jump through just to gain approval to build a warehouse. Meeting these requirements can routinely take up to a year to complete. Moreover, many of these rules differ across regions, increasing the confusion of foreigners. Added to this is India's endemic corruption, often exemplified by an unwillingness or inability of many recipients of a bribe to fulfill their side of the bargain even after being paid. Finally, new start-ups often have difficulty finding or retaining sufficient qualified employees to staff their operations. Employee turnover is rampant and companies are expected to invest

Application 1.5   (cont.)

heavily in training. This combination of multiple ambiguous and often conflict-ing rules, coupled with pervasive rule breaking, often leads to confusion among numerous would-be investors. In fact, foreign direct investment has fallen by one-third in just the last year. As with other countries experiencing rapid global-ization, the future may be bright but it is far from certain.

Think about it...

(1)   Many countries have strong and complex government bureaucracies that often serve to inhibit new investment – especially by foreigners. As an entrepreneur interested in foreign investment, how might you prepare your-self for dealing with such bureaucracies?

(2)   It is said that all countries have corruption; it is just the magnitude or nature that is different. Do you believe this is correct? If so, how would you determine the level of corruption that is "acceptable" for you to continue pursuing business affairs in a particular country?

(3)   How might an understanding of multicultural competence better prepare both entrepreneurs and global managers for the "realities on the ground" in international ventures?

(4)   As an entrepreneur looking to invest in developing economies, what steps might you take to protect yourself and your firm against the consequences of local corruption?

In view of the myriad challenges such as this, managers viewing global assignments – or even global travel – would do well to learn as much as they can about the world in which they will work. The same holds true for local managers working in their home countries, where the global business world is increasingly challenging them on their own turf. Like it or not, with globalization and competition both increasing almost everywhere, the challenge for managers is to outperform their competitors, individually or collectively. This can be attempted either by focusing exclusively on one's own self-interests or by building mutually beneficial strategic alliances with global partners. Either way, the challenges and pitfalls can be significant.

Another important factor to take into consideration here is a fundamental shift in the nature of geopolitics. The days of hegemony   East or West – are over. No longer will global business leaders focus on one or two stock markets, currencies, economies, or political leaders. Today's business environment is far too complex and interrelated for that. Contrary to some predictions, nation states and multinational corporations will remain both powerful and important; we are not, in fact, moving towards a "borderless society." Global networks, comprising technological, entrepreneurial, social welfare, and environmental interest groups, will also remain powerful. Indeed, networks and relationships will increasingly represent power, not traditional or historic institutions. Future economic and business endeavors, like future political, social, and environmental endeavors, will be increasingly characterized by a search for common ground, productive partnerships, and mutual benefit.

The plight of many of today's failed or mediocre managers is evident from the legion of stories about failures in cross-border enterprise. Managers are responsible for utilizing human, financial, informational, and physical resources in ways that facilitate their organization's overall objectives in turbulent and sometimes hostile environments about which they often understand very little. These challenges can be particularly problematic when operations cross national boundaries.

As globalization pressures increase and managers spend more time crossing borders to conduct business, the training and development community has increasingly advocated more intensive analyses of the criteria for managerial success in the global economy. As more attention is focused on this challenge, a growing cadre of management experts is zeroing in on the need for managers to develop perspectives that stretch beyond domestic borders. This concept is identified in many ways (e.g., "global mindset," "cultural intelligence," "global leadership"), but we refer to it simply as *multicultural competence* (see Chapter 2). Whatever it is called, its characteristics and skills are in increasing demand as firms large and small, established and entrepreneurial, strive for global competitiveness.

We suggest in this volume that endeavoring to meet these challenges is far more the result of hard work, clear thinking, serious reflection, and attentive behavior than any of the quick fixes that are so readily available. We suggest further that, to accomplish this, managers will need to develop some degree of multicultural competence as an important tool to guide their social interactions and business decisions and prevent themselves from repeating the intercultural and strategic mistakes made by so many of their predecessors. Clearly, working and managing in the global economy require more than cross-cultural understanding and skills, but we argue that, without such skills, the manager's job is all the more difficult to accomplish. If the world is truly moving towards greater complexity, interconnections, and corporate interrelationships, the new global manager will obviously need to play a role in order for organizations and their stakeholders to succeed.

Summary points

- Globalization is the inexorable integration of markets, capital, nation states, and technologies in ways that allow individuals, groups, corporations, and countries to reach around the world farther, faster, more deeply, and more cheaply than ever before. This process is increasingly creating a powerful backlash from those left behind by the new economic and political system.

- This new global reality represents a major paradigm shift in international politics, economics, and business that impacts corporations and their managers, as well as society at large. Moreover, as experience teaches us, few such changes occur without winners and losers.

- While it is not easy to get a handle on all the changes occurring in the global environment, three prominent changes stand out: the evolution from intermittent to continual change, from isolation to increasing interconnectedness, and from biculturalism to multiculturalism. The evolution from a principally bicultural business environment to a more multicultural or global environment presents managers with at least three new challenges in attempting to adapt quickly to the new realities on the ground: it is sometimes unclear to which culture we should adapt; many multicultural encounters happen on short notice, leaving little time to learn about the other culture; and multicultural meetings increasingly occur virtually, by way of computers or video conferencing, instead of through more traditional face-to-face interactions.

- As globalization pressures increase and managers spend more time crossing borders to conduct business, a growing cadre of management experts is zeroing in on the need for managers to develop perspectives that stretch beyond domestic borders. This concept is identified in many ways (e.g., "global mindset," "cultural intelligence," "global leadership"), but we refer to it simply as *multicultural competence*. Whatever it is called, its characteristics and skills are in increasing demand as firms large and small, established and entrepreneurial, strive for global competitiveness.

Notes

1 Personal communication, Norbert Reithofer, Munich, Germany, 2004.
2 Thomas Friedman, *The Lexus and the Olive Tree*. New York: Anchor Books, 2000.
3 Thomas Friedman, *The World Is Flat: A Brief History of the Twenty-First Century*, New York: Farrar, Straus and Giroux, 2005.

4 Anita Elash, "Canada Post strike: residents ask if they really need a postman," *Christian Science Monitor*, June 23, 2011, p. 1.

5 Keith Epstein and Judith Crown, "Globalization bites Boeing," *Business Week*, March 24, 2008, p. 32.

6 Elizabeth Dwoskin, "Your dinner has been touched by multitudes," *Bloomberg Business Week*, August 29, 2011, pp. 29–30.

7 See www.hewitt.com.

8 *The Economist*, "Slicing an Apple," *The Economist*, August 10, 2011, p. 46.

9 *The Economist*, "The Hindu rate of self-deception," *The Economist*, April 23, 2011, p. 47.

CHAPTER *2*

The new global managers

MANAGEMENT CHALLENGE

As companies face an increasingly turbulent and complex global business environment, a logical question arises: can organizations today be managed in the same way they were in the past? In other words, does a changed environment – one characterized by multiple economic and political systems, divergent social norms and values, and highly diverse educational and skill levels – require us to reassess both the managerial role in general and management practices in particular? Indeed, is the very definition of management itself changing? Moreover, how should today's managers best prepare themselves for greater involvement in global assignments in this new world? Key to success here will be their ability to develop new global management skills aimed at successfully doing business across cultures. To accomplish this, managers must first understand the role of continual on-the-job learning.

Chapter outline

Applications

In a time of drastic change, it is the learners who will inherit the future. The learned usually find themselves prepared for a world that no longer exists.

Eric Hoffer[1]
Moral philosopher, United States

We don't look so much at what and where people have studied, but rather at their drive, initiative, and cultural sensitivity.

Stephen Green[2]
Group chief executive officer (CEO), HSBC, United Kingdom

Many years ago a popular film making the rounds of the local movie theaters was *If It's Tuesday It Must Be Belgium*. The film used humor to highlight the plight of a typical American tourist who was overcome by the cultural differences across the countries included in her whirlwind tour of Europe. The film's underlying message was that tourists – at least, American tourists – seldom allow sufficient time in their travels to learn about cultural differences, preferring instead to race from one popular tourist site to another in search of good food, unique experiences, and photographs to show to their friends and family back home. The issue is one of having *been* there, not having *learned* anything. Today, despite a widespread recognition that we live and work in an increasingly interconnected global economy, it is curious that the dilemma posed in this old film is still salient for many contemporary managers and entrepreneurs alike. How serious are we about learning about other cultures? If we are serious, how do we accomplish this in meaningful ways as part of our busy work schedules?

A major challenge facing numerous managers and entrepreneurs today is how to deal with people abroad – both partners and competitors – who we simply do not understand. More often than not, the problem is not just language differences; it is *cultural* differences. Consider: how can we trust or do business with prospective foreign business partners who won't:

- "put their cards on the table" and say what they actually mean;
- work "24/7" and "stay on target" until the job is completed;
- "step up to the plate," make concrete commitments, and accept responsibility for their side of the partnership; or
- "let their hair down" and open up to us, so we can get to know each other.

In other words, how can we trust or do business with prospective foreign business partners when we know so little about them, their backgrounds, their approaches to business, and their future intents? The obvious question here is: what to do? Unfortunately, the answer to this question is not as simple as perhaps it once was. Gone are the days when prospective managers could learn French, or German, or Spanish in college and feel prepared for an international career. Learning foreign languages and foreign cultures is obviously very helpful, but it is often impractical in view of the rapidity with which business opportunities appear and disappear around the world. Besides, today's managers need much more than this.

This challenge of understanding people from other cultures is made more difficult by the increasing speed with which business often occurs. A key factor here is the way in which recent technological advancements have pushed both the pace and complexity of globalization to new heights. Communication and information technology makes it possible to collaborate – or compete – globally from anywhere in the world, regardless of one's country of origin or cultural background. As a growing number of organizations have established increased operations around the world, managers' exposure to both partners and competitors from significantly different cultural backgrounds has increased at a rate that has surprised economists and social scientists alike. The implication of this for managers of all types is clear: managers with a capability to think and understand business relationships from a global perspective in real time will more often than not succeed over those with more limited, nation-based mindsets.

Traditional views of management

Definitions of *management* abound. What is significant about these definitions, coming from all parts of the world, is their lack of any notable variance. Management is management – or so we are told. Dating from the early writings by Frederick Taylor, Henri Fayol, Max Weber, Mary Parker Follett, and others in the late nineteenth and early twentieth centuries and continuing through today, most writers have agreed that management involves the coordination and control of people, materiel, and processes in order to achieve specific organizational objectives as efficiently and effectively as possible. Indeed, business historian Claude George has discovered the roots of such a definition dating back to the ancient Samarians, Egyptians, Hebrews, and Chinese well over 3,000 years ago.[3] Neither the concept nor the profession of management is new; indeed, they are widely thought to form a central pillar of organized society: getting things done through coordinated efforts.

While the underlying definition remains the same, variations around this theme can easily be found. Industrial engineers, dating from the time of scientific management proponent Frederick Taylor, have long emphasized production or operations management and the necessity to structure jobs, people, and incentive systems in ways that maximized performance.[4] Similarly, French industrial engineer Henri Fayol, also writing at the beginning of the twentieth century, emphasized the importance of standardized "principles" of management, including the division of work, unity of command, unity of direction, and the subordination of individual interests to the general (i.e., the organization's) interest.[5] Although Taylor focused on workers and Fayol focused on administrative structures, their mantra was the same: organizations must be managed through strength, discipline, hierarchy, and logic (see Exhibit 2.1).

Around this same time, social scientists and other academicians were taking a different perspective on this same phenomenon. German-born, Harvard-educated psychologist Hugo Munsterberg launched investigations into the application of psychological principles to management and workers. In the process, he created the field of industrial psychology. In his 1913 book *Psychology and Industrial Efficiency*, he asserted that the aim of this new discipline was "to sketch the outlines of a new science, which is

Exhibit 2.1 Traditional "logic" of organization and management

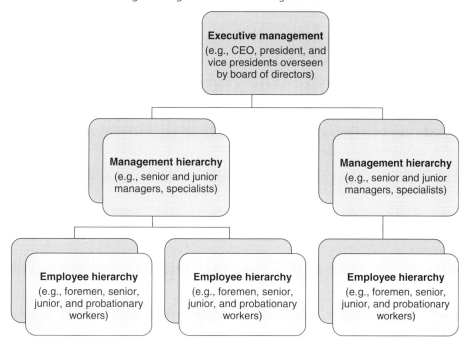

to intermediate between the modern laboratory psychology and the problem of eco-nomics."[6] Meanwhile, German sociologist Max Weber wrote extensively about how organizations organize and operate – or, more accurately, should organize and operate.[7] Weber introduced the concept of *bureaucracy* as the most perfect form of organization. (Obviously, this term has taken on very different and negative connotations in recent years, but this was its original meaning.) Rules governed everything and little was left to chance. People were hired and promoted on the basis of qualifications – not unlike the ancient Chinese civil service system at the time of Confucius. Power and authority were vested in offices, not individuals. Even here, however, the conclusion was the same: rules and standard operating procedures uniformly enforced by competent managers would lead to efficient operations. The goal remained unchanged.

Now fast-forward 100 years and consider the advice of contemporary writers on management, both Eastern and Western. While contemporary writers have added some depth to the ongoing dialog about the nature and role of management, they have not added much breadth. Consider two contemporary definitions of management: "Management involves coordinating and overseeing the work activities of others so that their activities are completed efficiently and effectively";[8] and: "Management is the process of assembling and using sets of resources in a goal-directed manner to accom-plish tasks in an organizational setting."[9] Once again, the desired end state remains unchanged.

Rethinking managerial roles

This stability in our conception of management – unchanged over the centuries – implies that all managers do essentially the same work. Indeed, in one of the most frequently cited studies of management, McGill professor Henry Mintzberg concludes that "managers' jobs are remarkably alike," whether we are looking at foremen, com-pany presidents, or government administrators.[10] In the end, "the primary purpose of the manager is to ensure that his or her organization serves its basic purpose – the efficient production of specific goods and services." Mintzberg goes a step further and suggests that all managers serve ten basic *managerial roles* in varying degrees. These are: figurehead, leader, liaison, monitor, disseminator, spokesperson, entrepreneur, disturb-ance handler, resource allocator, and negotiator.[11] These traits, in turn, can be organ-ized into three clusters – interpersonal, informational, and decisional – as illustrated in Exhibit 2.2.

Exhibit 2.2 Managerial roles

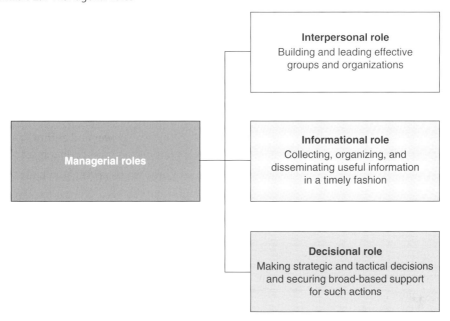

While all this may be correct as far as it goes, however, this line of reasoning seems to ignore, or at least downplay, the challenges facing global managers in performing these roles across cultures. As we discuss in the rest of this book, cultural differences can play an important role in both the conceptualization and practice of management around the world. People's conceptions of business management, as well as their application of management principles, often result from a combination of cultural backgrounds, personal experiences, and the situations confronting them. Thus, we must ask: would a typical Australian, Polish, or Indonesian manager approach business decisions and actions in the same way as their Indian, Bolivian, or French counterparts? If not, how might their approaches be different? How can global managers simultaneously deal with such diverse world views?

Intensifying globalization pressures only add to the problem. Like it or not, in today's increasingly turbulent and complex business environment, everyone is (or is rapidly becoming) a global manager, regardless of where he or she works. Ten years ago people focused considerable attention on the differences between British managers, Chinese managers, Mexican managers, and so forth. They were relatively comfortable with their well-intentioned cultural stereotypes. Today these stereotypes have become somewhat blurred, as the global economy becomes a reality and most business is international.

This is not to say that substantial differences no longer exist between managers from various countries or the ways in which they do business. Of course they do. Rather, it is to say that the very definition of effective management has changed in ways that have little to do with national origin. Most managers today have to engage with customers, business partners, and employees from various regions of the world. Success or failure depends on these managers' ability to communicate, negotiate, contract, lead, organize, coordinate, and control activities across borders.

Indeed, succeeding in today's demanding global economy requires a greater degree of international and cross-cultural communication, collaboration, and cooperation than ever before. Increasingly, companies must think in global terms, as national and even regional companies are progressively becoming a thing of the past. During the days of the old American frontier, in the middle of the nineteenth century, there was a popular saying: "Go west, young man." That was where the opportunities were. Today the advice is very different: "Go global." The future has shifted unequivocally and irreversibly, as have the opportunities, and smart companies and their managers respond accordingly.

The responsibility of managers in all this is to make things happen – to maximize consumer benefit and the company's bottom line. At the same time, society asks – and often demands – that managers pay fair wages, provide safe and equitable working conditions for their employees, follow the laws and regulations in the countries where they do business, protect the environment, act in socially responsible ways, and abide by ethical norms and professional standards. It is an understatement to point out that accomplishing these often conflicting goals is no easy task. In view of this, the question for today's managers is how they can best prepare themselves for this brave new world of international business.

Culture and the managerial role

The central thesis of this book is that understanding managerial roles and responsibilities by themselves and in the absence of cultural awareness or understanding is a highly suboptimal strategy for global managers. Successful managers must understand the context in which their managerial behavior transpired, and, in order to understand this, it is important to know the local environment. This challenge can be seen in two ways. First, how can cultural variations change managerial role expectations? Second, once this is understood, how are such changes possible – if at all?

Managerial role expectations

If people often vary across cultures in their thoughts and habits, so too can they vary in their expectations concerning appropriate managerial roles. Two related issues are relevant here: first, what is the ideal managerial role – the role people say they prefer to see in good managers – and, second, what is the "real" managerial role – the everyday roles that managers play out in real life, warts and all? Theoretically, these two roles should be highly correlated, but in reality significant differences are often found. Not surprisingly, taking these comparisons across borders only adds to the ambiguity.

First, consider how people in various cultures describe their ideal manager. INSEAD professor Andre Laurent conducted one of the more interesting studies on this topic.[12] He focused his attention on understanding the normative managerial role (that is, what is expected of managers) and discovered significant differences across cultures. He asked managers from different cultures a series of questions dealing with effective management. Laurent's results demonstrate wide variations in responses across cultures, as shown in Exhibit 2.3. For each set of responses, note how far apart typical managers are in responding to rather simple statements about appropriate managerial behavior. For each of the three questions, the percentage of managers in agreement

Exhibit 2.3 Perceptions of managerial roles

	Percentage of managers who agree with each statement		
Country	"Managers must have the answers to most questions asked by subordinates"	"The main reason for a chain of command is so people know who has authority"	"It is OK to bypass chain of command to get something done efficiently"
China	74	70	59
France	53	43	43
Germany	46	26	45
Indonesia	73	83	51
Italy	66	–	56
Japan	78	50	–
Netherlands	17	31	44
Spain	–	34	74
Sweden	10	30	26
United Kingdom	27	34	35
United States	18	17	32

Source: Data from Andre Laurent, reported in John Saee, *Managing Organizations in a Global Economy*. Mason, OH: Thompson/Southwestern, 2005, pp. 39–42.

ranges from 10 to 78 percent, 17 to 83 percent, and 26 to 74 percent, respectively. These percentages aren't even close. If managers from different countries differ so much in their descriptions of the correct managerial role, it is no wonder that significant differences can be found in actual management style across national boundaries.

A second study, conducted by Cambridge University professor Charles Hampden-Turner and Dutch management consultant Fons Trompenaars, also found significant differences across managers based on culture, as shown in Exhibit 2.4. For example, managers in the United States, Sweden, Japan, Finland, and South Korea showed more overall drive and initiative than leaders in Portugal, Norway, Greece, and the United

Exhibit 2.4 Perceptions of managerial practices

Country	Manager's sense of drive and initiative (percentage of agreement by managers)	Country	Manager's willingness to delegate authority (percentage of agreement by managers)
United States	74	Sweden	76
Sweden	72	Japan	69
Japan	72	Norway	69
Finland	70	United States	66
South Korea	68	Singapore	65
Netherlands	67	Denmark	65
Singapore	66	Canada	64
Switzerland	66	Finland	63
Belgium	65	Switzerland	62
Ireland	65	Netherlands	61
France	65	Australia	61
Austria	63	Germany	61
Denmark	63	New Zealand	61
Italy	62	Ireland	60
Australia	62	United Kingdom	59
Canada	62	Belgium	55
Spain	62	Austria	54
New Zealand	59	France	54
Greece	59	Italy	47
United Kingdom	58	Spain	44
Norway	55	Portugal	43
Portugal	49	Greece	38

Source: Charles Hampden-Turner and Fons Trompenaars, *The Seven Cultures of Capitalism*. New York: Doubleday, 1993, ch. 1.

Kingdom. Note also that Canadian managers placed less emphasis on managerial drive and initiative than their US counterparts. At the same time, managers in Sweden, Japan, Norway, Canada, and the United States tended to be more willing to delegate authority than leaders in Greece, Portugal, Spain, and Italy. These findings, along with those of Andre Laurent, suggest clearly that effective managerial behavior can easily vary across cultures.

Other studies confirm this conclusion. For example, one study found that British managers were more participative than their French and German counterparts.[13] Two possible reasons were suggested for this. First, the United Kingdom is more egalitarian than France, and the political environment supports this approach. Second, top British managers tend not to be involved in the day-to-day affairs of the business, and delegate many key decisions to middle and lower-level managers. The French and Germans, by contrast, tend to prefer a more work-centered, authoritarian approach. Although it is true that German co-determination leads to power sharing with employees throughout the organization, some have argued that this has resulted not from German culture but, rather, from German laws. By contrast, Scandinavian countries make wide use of participative leadership approaches, again following from their somewhat more egalitarian culture.

On the other side of the world, Japanese managers tend to be somewhat authoritarian, but at the same time listen to the opinions of their subordinates. One study found that Japanese managers place greater confidence in the skills and capabilities of their subordinates than their counterparts in other cultures.[14] Another feature of Japanese leadership is an inclination to give subordinates ambiguous goals instead of highly specific ones. In other words, many Japanese managers tell their workers what they want in a general way, but leave it to the workers to determine the details and the work plan. This practice is also commonplace in South Korea, and contrasts sharply with typical US managers, who often take a hands-on, management-by-objectives approach to project management.

To illustrate this point, let us return to Mintzberg's ten managerial roles. Although this model was designed around North American managers, it can also be useful in exploring on a conceptual level how culture and managerial roles can intersect. For the sake of example, Exhibit 2.5 illustrates how each of the ten managerial roles can be influenced by cultural differences. For instance, considerable research has indicated that most people in individualistic cultures prefer managers who take charge, while most people in collectivistic cultures prefer managers who are more consultative. Similarly, managers in high-context cultures frequently make extensive use of the context surrounding a message to get their point across, while managers in low-context cultures

Exhibit 2.5 Cultural influences on managerial roles

Managerial roles	Differences across cultures
Interpersonal roles	
Figurehead	Figureheads have considerable symbolic value in some cultures; in others, being described as a figurehead is not seen as a compliment.
Leader	Individualistic cultures prefer highly visible "take charge" leaders; collectivistic cultures prefer more consultative leaders.
Liaison	Some cultures prefer informal contacts based on long-standing personal relationships; others prefer to use official representatives.
Informational roles	
Monitor	Culture often influences both the extent of information monitoring and which specific information sources receive greatest attention.
Disseminator	In some cultures, the context surrounding a message is more important than the message itself; in others, the reverse is true.
Spokesperson	Culture often influences who is respected and seen as a legitimate spokesperson for an organization.
Decisional roles	
Entrepreneur	Some cultures are highly supportive of innovation and change; others prefer the status quo and resist change.
Disturbance handler	Some cultures resolve conflict quietly; others accept and at times encourage a more public approach.
Resource allocator	Hierarchical cultures support differential resource allocations; egalitarian cultures prefer greater equality or equity in distributions.
Negotiator	Some cultures negotiate all items in a proposed contract simultaneously; others negotiate each item sequentially.

Source: Based on Henry Mintzberg, *The Nature of Managerial Work*, New York: Harper & Row, 1972, pp. 54–94.

tend to rely almost exclusively on specific and detailed messages and ignore much of the message context. In short, the managerial role keeps changing – not necessarily in major ways, but certainly in important ways – as we move across borders.

Matching roles to local situations

It is important for managers to understand their own management style. The fundamental question here is: can you be the manager you are expected to be in your overseas assignment? How much do you understand this new environment and can you adapt your style to maximize your potential as a manager there? For example, if your management style is highly participative, can you become an autocrat overnight if you need to? And should you? Someone has suggested that self-awareness is one of the most important skills managers should have. As a result, knowing what others expect of you is of little value if you don't know what you can comfortably be. Hence, before addressing other issues, managers need to know what type of managers they are, what types of behaviors they are comfortable with or willing to learn, and how far they are willing and able to change and still be authentic to themselves and their values.

Considering the important influence of culture in determining what is expected of managers, how can a manager be successful across cultures? In many cases, successful managers are found to develop an awareness of cultural differences and adapt their management styles to the extent possible to match local conditions. This strategy is not always the best, however. In several cases, a manager is sent abroad to promote change, and not fitting the local culture may be the manager's most important competitive advantage. In these circumstances, "going native" may not be the best approach.

Rob Coffee and Gareth Jones suggest that the key to a manager's success lies in the ability to conform just enough to the local environment as not to be rejected by the local culture.[15] Conforming too much can undermine the manager's potential to make important changes in the organization, however. Frequently a manager is sent abroad or charged with global operations because of some personal characteristic and particular way of doing things that is linked to his or her cultural background. Losing these abilities may not be in the organization's or followers' best interests. Clearly, alienating the local culture is bound to bring some challenges, but going native may not be the best solution either. The success of global management lies in the fine balance of conforming enough to the key aspects of the cultural context, allowing managers to engage and gain leverage, which can then be used to promote change. The idea here is that managers must conform enough to the new cultural milieu, gaining acceptance as a member, in order to make the necessary connections to make changes. Effective managers understand what it is about the culture that can be changed – and what cannot – and operate within those constraints.

Application 2.1 Management trends: France and the United States

US managers have at times suggested that it is more difficult to get along with the French than any other people in Europe. Not surprisingly, many French managers feel the same about Americans. Why is this? According to Edward T. Hall and Mildred Reed Hall, many US managers criticize their French managerial counterparts for a number of reasons:[16] they won't delegate; they won't keep their subordinates informed; they don't feel a sense of responsibility towards their subordinates; they refuse to accept responsibility for things; they are not team players; they are overly sensitive to hierarchy and status; they are highly authoritarian; they are not interested in improving their job skills or knowledge; they are primarily concerned with their own self-interest; and they are less mobile than

Americans. Obviously, there are variations in such observations, but, according to these noted anthropologists, this is the gist of American opinion.

At the same time, Hall and Hall quote several French managers who hold similarly negative opinions about their US counterparts:[17] American managers in Europe are not creative – they are too tied to their checklists; success is not achieved by logic and procedure alone; American executives are reliable and hardworking, and often charming and innocent, but they are too narrow in their focus – they are not well rounded; they have no time for cultural interests and lack appreciation for art, music, and philosophy; too many American executives are preoccupied with financial reporting (this syndrome produces people who avoid decisions); and Americans don't know how to present themselves – they sprawl and slouch and have no finesse.

Who is right here? Perhaps perceptions by both sides are correct to some extent. Clearly, one factor that may help explain these differing perceptions is the fundamental difference between French and American cultures in terms of their time orientation. As noted above, most Americans are decidedly monochronic, meaning that they tend to stress a high degree of scheduling in their lives, with concentration of effort being on one activity at a time, and elaborate codes of behavior built around promptness in meeting obligations and appointments. Put more simply, many Americans tend to be a bit linear in their thinking and behavior, always focusing on the ultimate goal. By contrast, most French are polychronic, stressing human relationships and social interaction over arbitrary schedules and appointments, and engaging in several activities simultaneously, with frequent interruptions. To many French managers, the journey is probably more important than the ultimate destination. To many American managers, however, it is all about the goal.

Think about it...

(1) It has been said that the problem with both French and American managers is that they are both too self-centered. In other words, the fundamental problem is that, while there are certainly cultural differences, French and Americans are actually too much alike to get along well. Do you agree or disagree with this assertion? Why or why not?

(2) If you were building a new team consisting of French and American members, what strategies would you use to get people working together?

Types of global assignments

Global managers come in all shapes and sizes, as well as skills and abilities. Indeed, in today's global economy, almost all managers are involved in some form or another with global management. As such, it is difficult – if not impossible – to develop a precise definition that accurately encompasses all their activities and responsibilities. As a starting point, however, we define a *global manager* as someone who works with or through people across national boundaries to accomplish global corporate objectives. Inherent in this definition is the assumption that many – if not all – of these managers work with people from differing cultural backgrounds and, as such, must somehow accommodate or respond to these differences. Also inherent in this definition is the recognition that some of these cross-cultural interactions may be across countries with fewer cultural differences than others (e.g., Canada and the United States, versus Canada and Saudi Arabia). Indeed, some of these cultural differences can often be found within a single country.

Paramount to this definition is the assumption that global managers are – and must be – different from more traditional managers. They must have a world view, not a national one; they must understand not just cultural differences but also the ways in which to navigate such differences to achieve corporate objectives; they must seek partnerships, not domination; and, above all, they must have both the competence and the confidence to work with colleagues and partners from around the world. Included within this definition are managers who have very different corporate lifestyles. Some live abroad, some live in airplanes, and some live in virtual space. Some do all three.

For the sake of parsimony, and acknowledging that there are obvious risks in categorizations, we suggest that these global managers can be roughly divided into three somewhat overlapping categories: expatriates, frequent flyers, and virtual managers (see Exhibit 2.6). We suggest, further, that the characteristics and cultural challenges of each of these types of managers can be quite different (see Exhibit 2.7). While *expatriates* typically require deep knowledge of a particular country or region, *frequent flyers* more often require broad knowledge of cultural differences and cultural processes in general. One leads a somewhat stable life, albeit in a foreign country; the other leads a highly mobile existence. This is not to say that one approach is superior to the other, only that they are different and that each plays an important role in global commerce. Added to this is a category of other managers who work largely through computer and information technology and who essentially wander the globe in cyberspace to achieve their results. We refer to these individuals as *virtual managers*, in recognition of their basic patterns of

Exhibit 2.6 Types of global assignments

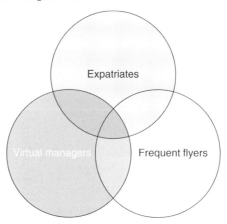

Exhibit 2.7 Challenges of global assignments

Characteristics and management challenges	Expatriates	Frequent flyers	Virtual managers
Principal management focus	Long-term face-to-face management, where managers are either assigned to reside in a foreign country to oversee company operations or hired to bring special expertise to a foreign firm.	Short-term face-to-face management, where managers with particular expertise (e.g., project management, financial controls) are flown in to plan, implement, or control specific operations.	Virtual (or remote) technical management in specialized areas (e.g., logistics, IT), where managers perform most of their tasks and responsibilities via information networks and digital technologies.
Degree of cultural embeddedness and technological dependence	High cultural embeddedness; low technological dependence.	Moderate cultural embeddedness and technological dependence.	Low cultural embeddedness; high technological dependence.
Primary mode of communication and interaction	Largely face to face.	Balance of face to face and virtual.	Largely virtual.
Key success factors for working across cultures	Typically requires deep knowledge of the culture(s) and culture–business relationships where they live and work; bilingual or multilingual skills important; understanding global issues – not just local ones – is also critical.	Typically requires moderate understanding of cultural differences and dynamics in general and culture business relationships around the globe; multilingual skills important; deep understanding of global issues critical.	Typically requires at least a modest understanding of cultural differences and variations in business practices around the globe, although a deeper understanding is preferred; multilingual skills often useful.
Typical cultural challenge (global management myopia)	*Regional myopia*: overemphasis on local or regional issues and business practices at the expense of global issues and overall corporate objectives.	*Global myopia*: overemphasis on global issues and overall corporate objectives at the expense of local customs and business practices.	*Technological myopia*: ignorance of the impact of cultural differences on the local uses, misuses, and applications of communication and information technology.

collegial and business interaction.[18] (Some have suggested that we need to add a fourth category of global managers, namely everyone else, since in fact most managerial positions require some degree of multicultural expertise even when sitting at corporate headquarters simply working with global clients.)

Expatriates

Traditionally, the most common foreign assignments have involved the long-term relocation of parent company managers to various countries in which the parent firm does, or wants to do, business. Firms have often preferred to use expatriate managers for a number of reasons, especially when they needed parent-company representation and control in a distant location, wanted to provide developmental opportunities for parent-country managers, or needed to fill skill gaps when locals did not have the skills to do the job themselves.[19] Today, however, the term "expatriate" has come to describe any person working in residence in a foreign country. This could include a Swiss manager working for a Swiss company in South Korea, or a Swiss manager working for a South Korean company in South Korea. Both face similar challenges of living abroad for lengthy periods.

Application 2.2 Expats at LG

LG's Nam Yong did not set out to hire a group of aggressive Western-style expatriate managers, but he knew LG needed change. The company's South Korean management team had built an engineering powerhouse that excelled at manufacturing high-quality goods, but the company realized that more than four-fifths of its revenue came from overseas and nearly 60 percent of its manufacturing was done outside South Korea. When Nam took over LG Electronics' top job, the company was coasting. It had become a top-five consumer electronics player globally, but had few major hits. Nam believed the company needed to be a trendsetter if it wanted to prosper in the digital age. To shake things up, he asked headhunters to find top talent from multinationals worldwide, regardless of nationality.

Irish-born Dermot Boden, chief marketing officer for LG, was the first non-Korean to be hired by LG as an internal change agent. Nam hired the veteran of Pfizer and Johnson & Johnson to help turn LG into a premium brand. The problem was that LG's marketing was uninspiring. So Boden determined to give the brand a more sophisticated image, with high-end products such as a cellphone co-branded with fashion house Prada and washing machines costing $1,500 or more. He also took a more organized approach to marketing, by hiring a single international advertising agency in London to handle advertising worldwide. Other foreign expatriates were asked to standardize the hodgepodge of processes and systems that LG had developed around the world. Purchasing, for example, was done by four different business units and was split between factories and subsidiaries in 110 countries. "I'm like a conductor, getting 2,000 purchasing officers to work in concert to make good music," says Tom Linton, a twenty-year veteran of IBM who joined LG as its first chief procurement officer in 2008. Nam said in 2010 that Linton's efforts to reshape the purchasing system had already saved the company hundreds of millions of dollars. Meanwhile, LG's supply chain was equally chaotic. Didier Chenneveau, a Swiss who left Hewlett-Packard (HP), also in 2008, to become LG's chief supply-chain officer, inherited more than ten warehouse management systems, five transportation operations, and four computer systems to monitor the movement of parts and finished products. His goal: to merge everything into a single global system.

Not unexpectedly, Boden and the other foreign managers were not entirely welcomed by local South Korean managers. "The biggest worry was the prospect of Western executives imposing a way of thinking that might not work in our Confucian culture," said marketing manager Choi Seung Hun. "The prospect of communicating with my boss in English gave me a headache," added Lee Kyo Weon, a purchasing manager. Over time, however, both Choi and Lee agreed that the newcomers had made an effort to bridge the cultural gap. The results of this experiment in internationalization are interesting. When an anticipated surge in global sales failed to materialize, LG decided not to renew the contracts of Boden and the other expats. The company announced that it had decided to pursue a different executive strategy, using mostly South Korean executives, not foreign ones. Meanwhile, across town, rival electronics giant Samsung continued to hire more expats.

Think about it. . .

(1) How do you explain the rapid buildup, and equally rapid termination, of the expatriate managers at LG?

(2)   What did LG gain – and possibly lose – from its three-year experiment with expatriate managers?

(3)   Overall, what lessons emerge from the LG experience for other managers entering into an expatriate experience?

While some of the advantages of expatriate assignments may be fairly obvious, finding people who can actually succeed in expatriate assignments can be problematic. Although traveling abroad (perhaps on a vacation or business trip) is often seen by people as an enjoyable experience, actually living abroad can be frustrating, stressful, and sometimes very unpleasant. For many, staying in a four-star hotel, eating in fine restaurants, seeing new sights, and knowing that soon they will be back in their own bed is far more preferable to setting up a household in a strange neighborhood where few people speak your language, finding new schools for the kids, shopping in local markets stocked with foods they can't identify, and using public transportation. For others, these same experiences provide a sense of adventure and learning. Clearly, the location of the assignment plays an important role as well. Some people will thrive in some locations and fail in others. The challenge for managers – and their companies – is to discover which type of person is fit to which type of assignment before getting on the airplane.

Many people see an international assignment as a great opportunity. It may be an opportunity to advance one's career, to make more money, or to learn new things. It may represent a personal challenge or a way to a more interesting life. Managers who take international assignments report learning new managerial skills, increasing their tolerance for ambiguity, learning new ways of seeing things, and improving their ability to work with others.[20] As noted above, however, living and working abroad is not easy. Long-term international assignments are particularly challenging for managers with family, when a partner may need to give up a career in the home country and may not find suitable employment in the host country, and when children require special attention such as international schooling. A recent survey suggests that 81 percent of workers declining an expatriate assignment cited family reasons.[21]

Frequent flyers

While extended expatriate assignments are often useful, some have suggested that the days when managers prepared for a long-term assignment in Italy, Russia, or Venezuela are rapidly being eclipsed by a new reality in which managers sometimes seem to spend more time in the air than on the ground. Global assignments of shorter duration – often accompanied by increased intensity – are usually focused on specific tasks or projects, and, as such, can often provide easier ways to assess results (see Exhibit 2.5).[22] In addition, there are many managers who would not consider uprooting the family for long-term expatriate assignments but would be interested in shorter international opportunities. This increases the pool of talent available for such postings – a big plus, since the demand for highly qualified international assignees is often higher than the supply.[23] Furthermore, employees often see short-term assignments as being easier on their friends and family, as well as their home-country career opportunities.

The main challenge facing managers on short-term assignments is that they often find themselves in a foreign country without family and friends, and with a very short time to develop relationships and become adjusted.[24] Since assignees are usually sent abroad for a short period in order to solve a specific problem or perform a specific task, they are not given the time to learn the ropes and adjust to the new locale, as would be the case in traditional long-term expatriate assignments. Instead, frequent flyers are often expected to perform as soon as they hit the ground, which increases the challenges of the assignment. Strong pressures to perform – quickly – coupled with a limited social and family life, frequently lead assignees to work long hours, enduring high levels of stress and, at times, a poor work–life balance.

Application 2.3 Frequent flyer at Frog Design

Jan Chipchase is the James Bond of design research.[25] "I just came back from six weeks on the road: Tokyo, London, Beirut, rural Uganda, Kenya, Spain, and New York," says the Brit, who is stationed in Shanghai as Frog Design's executive creative director of global insights. "I stayed in the Trump Tower, a $10 shack near the Sudanese border, and traveled with a Hezbollah fixer on a motorcycle." Chipchase, who originally studied interface design, gained his reputation as an extreme method researcher after spending almost a decade in Nokia's research center and design studio. Last year Frog hired Chipchase to apply sociology, ethnography, and psychology to product design for clients that include GE and Lenovo. Frog works with many of the world's leading companies, helping them to design, engineer, and bring to market meaningful products and services. With an interdisciplinary team of more than 1,600 designers, strategists, and software

Application 2.3   (cont.)

engineers, it delivers connected experiences that span multiple technologies, platforms, and media.

Originally based in Germany ("frog" is derived from the initial letters of the Federal Republic of Germany), and later in California, the company works across a broad spectrum of industries, including consumer electronics, telecommunications, healthcare, energy, automotive, media, entertainment, education, finance, retail, and fashion. It maintains offices in Amsterdam, Austin, Boston, Chennai, Bangalore, Gurgaon (India), Johannesburg, Kiev, Milan, Munich, New York, Seattle, Shanghai, and Vinnitsa (Ukraine). Clients include Disney, GE, HP, Intel, Microsoft, MTV, Qualcomm, Siemens, and other Fortune 500 brands. As part of this global project, Chipchase most recently ventured to Afghanistan to understand mobile banking for Frog's numerous telecom clients. "I could take my team anywhere in the world to research this," said Chipchase, who typically takes some 10,000 photos when he goes into the field. "But I know, when you go to the more extreme places, you're more likely to see things that exist elsewhere, but aren't quite as visible."

Think about it. . .

(1) While Frog Design has a long tradition of successful design work for major companies, it could be argued that the grueling work pace and travel demands could easily burn out many of its managers. In your view, what characteristics should a successful Frog Design manager have in order to survive in this fast-paced environment?

(2) What are the pluses and minuses of Jan Chipchase's job at Frog Design? Would you enjoy having such a job? Why or why not?

(3) What do you think Chipchase will be doing in five years? Why do you think so?

Virtual managers

The same communication technologies that are making globalization a reality and changing the nature of work are also influencing the lives and work habits of global managers. Many of these technologies are not new (e.g., cellphones). What has been different in recent years, however, has been the ways in which these communication technologies have increased both their operating powers and their interactive capabilities. Many of these technologies have merged into more powerful tools for busy managers. As it became possible to access e-mail and the Web through smartphones and tablets, it has also become possible to travel light and still be constantly connected. It is no longer necessary to carry a laptop and a bag full of cables; it is not even necessary to be in a specific location to connect. Wireless technology makes it possible to perform work anywhere and anytime with minimal equipment, making it possible to be a global manager without leaving one's home base. The key issue here is not having access to the technology, however; rather, it is a manager's ability to use such technology to build workable networks and relationships that collectively serve corporate interests.

Application 2.4 Virtual manager in Delhi

Adhira Iyengar, an entrepreneur from Delhi, is a good example of a virtual manager.[26] One recent morning Iyengar got up, prepared a cup of tea, and logged onto her PC. As expected, Debra Brown, her business partner in California, was already logged on and asking questions about Iyengar's latest report to her. As they finished their online Skype meeting, Iyengar looked at her calendar and realized that, again, it was going to be a long day. At 10:00 that morning she had a conference call with Xiang Bingwei (Mr. Xiang, or "Andrew," to use his Westernized name), a client from Shanghai, about some changes in their service contract. At 1:30 in the afternoon she had a videoconference meeting with a group of prospective Australian clients. Before the end of the day she had to complete a report and e-mail it to Gabriela Bedoya Cárdenas, a prospective partner in Monterrey, Mexico, and she still needed to prepare for her upcoming trip to Oslo the following week for her yearly face-to-face meeting with her co-workers.

Think about it. . .

(1) Adhira Iyengar clearly lives a busy life. What special qualities or skills does she possess – and what qualities or skills should other virtual workers possess – to survive and succeed in such a harried virtual existence?

(2) Iyengar spends a lot of time interacting with her colleagues across the globe, but very little time face to face with people. What do you think the challenges are of interacting mostly through technology?

Application 2.4   (cont.)

(3)   While we know very little about this case, speculate about what Iyengar's life might look like in five or ten years. What might be different? What might be the same?

Once again, it is important to remember that these three categories of global managers – expatriates, frequent flyers, and virtual managers – represent overlapping categories. Clearly, most expatriates today are heavy users of the Web and other communication technologies, while many virtual managers must travel at times to get their jobs done. Our purpose in differentiating between these three categories, even in terms of general trends, is to highlight differences in managerial responsibilities and challenges in doing business across national borders.

Global management myopia

Finally, we suggest that each type of global manager discussed above carries with it its own particular risk of shortsightedness, whereby managers may fail to see one or more aspects of the company's larger objectives and operations. We refer to this as *global management myopia*. At times, these blinders can be accompanied by an overprotectiveness or advocacy of one's own area of responsibility, often at the expense of the overall success of the firm. These myopias can be summarized as follows.

- *Regional myopia.* Expatriates can run a very real risk of regional myopia, whereby the country or region in which they work overshadows the rest of the world. While this perception may have an upside in terms of genuinely focusing on one country or region and its opportunities and needs, it also risks losing sight of the big picture facing the firm.
- *Global myopia.* At the same time, frequent flyers are often prone to experience global myopia, in which they focus so intently on global interconnectedness that they lose sight of the local challenges and opportunities upon which company success is built. In other words, while expatriates may focus too much on the trees, frequent flyers may focus too much on the forest.
- *Technological myopia.* Finally, virtual managers often run a risk of getting so carried away with their advanced technologies that they lose sight of the faces of the people who collectively comprise the enterprise. We refer to this as technological myopia. If organizations are comprised of individuals and groups who work together for a collective goal, an overemphasis on remote management through broadband and

the internet can at times overlook, ignore, offend, and threaten the organization's most precious resource: its people.

Developing global management skills

Becoming a global manager is the result of a process, a career path streaming through different assignments and cultures. It is a journey, not an end state. Indeed, instead of seeking an ideal (or idealized) global manager, we have examined various types of international assignments and international managers. We have explored the variety of the species, including expatriates, frequent flyers, and virtual managers. Global management is definitely not a one-size-fits-all paradigm. We have also examined the various challenges and opportunities associated with these assignments, and their impact on global managers and organizations.

Managerial and multicultural competence

Throughout, we suggest that what differentiates effective global managers is not so much their managerial skills – although this is obviously important – but the combination of these skills with additional multicultural or cross-cultural competencies that allow people to apply their managerial skills across a diverse spectrum of environments (see Exhibit 2.8). It is this synergistic integration of basic management skills working in tandem with a deep understanding of how organizations and management practices differ across cultures that differentiates the successful from the less successful global managers.

Whether relocating to a foreign country for a long stay, traveling around the world for short stints, or dealing with foreigners in one's home country, managers often face important cultural challenges. Different cultures have different assumptions, behaviors, communication styles, and expectations about management practice. The ability to deal

Exhibit 2.8 Building global management skills

Managerial competence
Planning, organizing, directing, coordinating, controlling

➕

Multicultural competence
Understanding and working effectively across cultures

🟰

Global management skills
Integration and application of management and cross-cultural skills

with these differences in ways that are both appropriate and effective goes by many names, but we refer to it simply as *multicultural competence*. It represents the capacity to work successfully across cultures. Being multiculturally competent is more than just being polite or empathetic to people from other cultures; it is getting things done through people by capitalizing on cultural diversity.

Multicultural competence can be seen as a way of viewing the world with a particular emphasis on broadening one's cultural perspective as it relates to cross-cultural behavior.[27] In other words, it asks the question: what can we learn from people around us from different cultures that can improve our ability to function effectively in a multicultural world? Multicultural competencies include elements of curiosity, awareness of diversity, and acceptance of complexity.[28] People with multicultural competence tend to open up themselves by rethinking boundaries and changing their behaviors. They are curious and concerned with context, possessing an ability to place current events and tasks into historical and probable future contexts alike. They accept inherent contradictions in everyday life, and have the ability to maintain their comfort level with continual change.

In addition, managers who possess multicultural competence have a commitment to diversity, consciousness and sensitivity, as well as valuing diversity itself. They exhibit a willingness to seek opportunities in surprises and uncertainties, including an ability to take moderate risks and make intuitive decisions. They focus on continuous improvement, with a capacity for self-improvement and helping others develop. They typically take a long-term perspective on activities and plans, focusing on long-term results and not obsessing on short-term problems or results. Finally, they frequently take a systems perspective, including an ability to seek out interdependencies and cause–effect relationships.

It seems clear that, as the world of business draws closer together, companies in all countries will require managers who can work in a truly global environment. In this environment, successful managers bring a depth and breadth of understanding of how to capitalize on cultural differences in ways that enhance corporate goals and employee welfare as well. In large measure, this is what distinguishes between managers who can succeed in their local surroundings and managers who can succeed in the global economy.

Developing multicultural competence

As noted earlier, developing global managers is no easy task. Indeed, a pivotal question facing both training directors and managers themselves is exactly how global managers can be developed. As a result, managers often turn for advice to those who specialize in cross-cultural training and development for help in preparing for foreign assignments. This over-reliance on others – instead of on oneself – can carry risks, however. When it comes to global business, it sometimes seems as if everyone is an expert. Indeed, when University of California, Los Angeles, professor William Ouchi was writing his classic book on what Western managers could learn from Japan, he noted that, in view of the collective lack of expertise on the topic, any Westerner who had flown over Tokyo could – and often did – claim to be an expert on Japan.[29] In point of fact, what many people fail to understand about being a global manager is that the view from 10,000 meters up is often very different from the view at ground level, where the challenges are immediate and very real.

Much has been written on the topic of developing global management skills, and much of what has been written is contradictory, simplistic, and sometimes simply incorrect. Successful global managers tend to rely on themselves, including their own perceptions and assessments of what is going on in the world. They often require personal insight more than outside advice. Indeed, what often differentiates successful global managers from unsuccessful ones is the fact that they have developed a way of thinking about the world that is flexible and inclusive and guides their behavior across cultures and national boundaries.

Application 2.5 Global training at Google

A "google" (also "googol") is a number followed by 100 zeros. It is a huge number, and, metaphorically, it captured the imagination of the founders of the company. They sought to build a nexus where millions and millions of people could cross paths. To accomplish this operationally, however, the company required a global reach and international expertise. This endeavor can be seen in a number of actions, but particularly in the company's global training program.

The example of Google's traveling managers illustrates how this company, and many others, search to find unique ways to educate their managers about both the global challenges facing them and the strategies that can help them succeed. To train a new generation of managers, search giant Google is now sending its young "brainiacs" on a worldwide mission.[30] One recent group of trainees began their journey in a small village outside Bangalore. There were no computers in the tiny village, only unpaved roads surrounded by open fields in which elephants roamed and trampled local crops at will. The visit was aimed at educating Google associate product managers about the humble, unwired ways of life experienced by billions of people around the world. Discussions with local villages began awkwardly, as the managers discover that the villagers had never heard of the company. As one young manager noted, the experience brought "a whole new meaning to what's on the back of [my] shirt," referring to a T-shirt with the company logo in front and, on the back, the now classic phrase from the company's home page: "I'm feeling lucky."

On their first day in Bangalore the visitors went to the Commercial Street shopping district for a bartering competition. Each Google manager was given 500 rupees (about $13) to spend on "items that don't suck," with a prize given to the one who attained the highest discount on the purchase. For most, it was the first time they had to bargain with street vendors. "I usually shop at Neiman Marcus," observed one manager, after she bargained the price of a necklace down from 375 rupees to 250. It was one of her colleagues who won the competition, however, by purchasing a deep burgundy *sherwani* – a traditional Indian outfit – for one-third of the original asking price.

From India, the group traveled to Japan, to visit the company's Shibuya head-quarters and network with fellow employees, learn about regional markets, and study the local culture. The visitors shared the product "road map" for the next year with their Japanese colleagues, answered questions, and then heard what the engineers and managers in each location were focusing on. They also got a sense of the local marketplace by talking to local Googlers, customers, and partners. In Tokyo, they learned that Yahoo! Japan was clobbering the competition – it's like Google and AOL and eBay rolled into one – but that Google had captured the imagination of the Japanese people. It was the no. 2 brand in the country, behind Toyota.

Tokyo's legendary electronics district, Akihabara, was chosen for another group competition, ostensibly to sharpen the product knowledge, business skills, and street smarts of the global travelers. They were divided into small teams and given $100 to buy the strangest gadgets they could find. Diving into stalls full of electronic gizmos, they found items such as a USB-powered smoke-removing ashtray and a stubby wand that, when waved back and forth, spells out words in LED lights.

Next the group traveled to China, and came face to face with the realities of doing business there. They immediately recognized the conflict of balancing the company's freewheeling management style with China's rigid government rules – and censorship. At Google headquarters in Beijing, the visiting managers interviewed local English-speaking consumers. Here they learned the stark realities of how effective the Chinese government can be at tilting the playing field to benefit the home team, Baidu.com, by occasionally blocking access to Google's site and by insinuating a nationalistic element into the choice. The lesson was clear to the visiting managers: Baidu knows more about China than Google. The journey continued, as did the learning.

In the case of Google, both learning strategies discussed here were used and both appeared to be successful. First, Google managers were intentionally placed into unfamiliar circumstances in which they quickly had to seek understanding and be aware of their first-hand experiences. They needed to reflect and make sense of these experiences and identify important lessons for the future. Second, at the same time these managers had to organize what they saw and develop theories-in-use for future actions that could be tried when they returned to the field. Note that Google went to great lengths to allow their managers to fail as well as succeed. Note, too, that there were few safety nets.

Think about it...

(1)   What, if anything, is unique about Google's approach to global management training?

(2)   Why do you think this program has been so successful for Google employees?

(3)   Would Google's approach work better at some types of organizations than others? Explain.

(4)   If you were in charge of Google's training program, what might you do to improve its effectiveness? Why?

The example of Google's traveling managers illustrates how many companies seek to find unique ways to educate their managers about both the global challenges facing them and the strategies that can help them succeed. In fact, the learning strategy at Google is actually rather simple. It is based on learning through comparisons – that is, what is your home culture like? How does it differ from the cultures you are currently experiencing? And what can you learn from these differences that can make you a better manager? The simplicity and relative cost-efficiency of such a strategy – particularly when combined with academic or in-class training – has proved to be effective in many companies and MBA programs.

Learning strategies for global managers

What have we learned in this chapter that can be of use to managers in the field? We close with a brief examination of two interrelated action steps that can help develop global skills in many managerial settings.

1 Understand the developmental process

Developing global management skills is the central theme of this book. The obvious question here is how these skills are developed and refined and then used effectively in the global arena. To answer this question, we are reminded of the observation of thirteenth-century Middle Eastern mullah Nasrudin: "Good judgment comes from experience; experience comes from bad judgment." In other words, people learn and develop largely on the basis of their past experiences and past mistakes. In our view, this is particularly noteworthy with regard to global managers. People try, make mistakes, and learn from those mistakes. This is the essence of experiential learning.

According to experiential learning theory, individual learning occurs over four stages that are collectively and interactively aimed at collecting and transforming knowledge: concrete experience, reflective observation, abstract conceptualization, and active experimentation.[31] This is illustrated in Exhibit 2.9.

In theory, a learning cycle begins with *concrete experiences* – how we feel about things that happen to us in everyday life. For example, let us imagine that you come from a culture that values direct and straightforward communication. You tell things how they are and don't pull your punches. As you engage in conversations with others, you may think that direct questioning is appropriate and will result in a straightforward answer. Now, let us imagine that an individual with whom you are

Exhibit 2.9 The experiential learning cycle

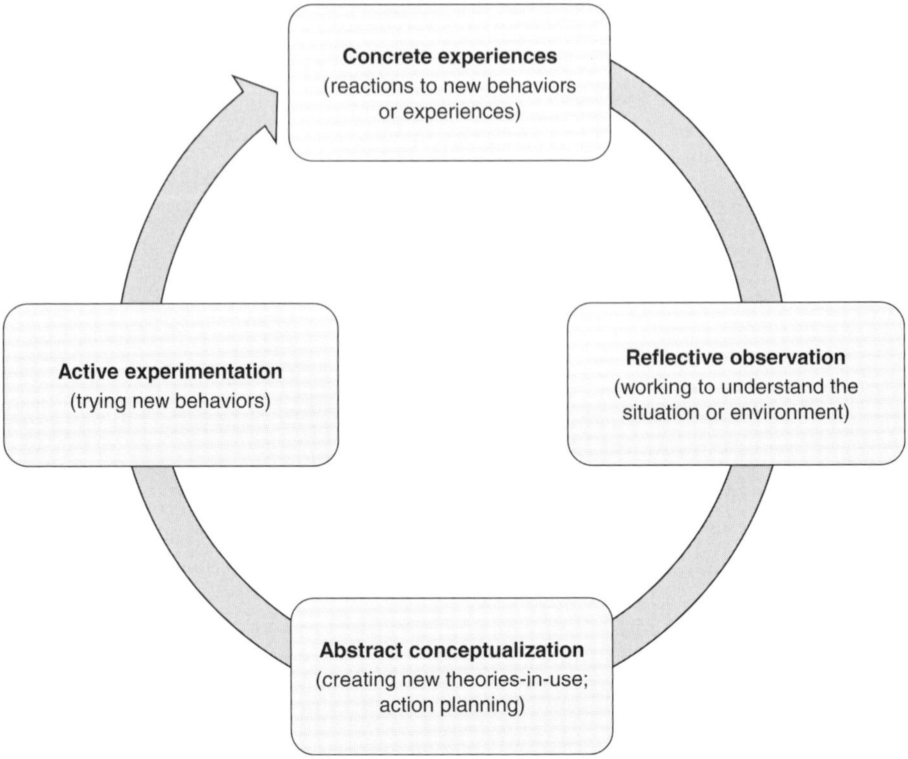

communicating comes from a culture that values indirect or subtle communication and the avoidance of public embarrassment. For this woman, direct questions may be inappropriate. Finally, consider that neither of you is sufficiently knowledgeable to adapt your communication styles to suit the other's culture. The most likely outcome of this scenario is that you will ask a direct question and will get what you perceive to be an unsatisfactory or evasive response. At this point, you are likely to experience an emotional reaction – discomfort, perplexity, offense, or surprise. This is your concrete experience.

These experiences or feelings, in turn, may then prompt you to try to understand what is happening. You may engage in *observation and reflection* – that is, once you realize that there is a disconnection between what is happening and what you thought would happen, you observe the other person and try to guess why she responded as she did. You may mentally run through a list of possible problems: maybe she did not hear you, maybe she did not understand the question, maybe she does not speak

English very well, maybe she is shy, maybe she is not comfortable with the question, and so forth. You then search for other clues to her behavior in the context of the situation that can help you understand her behavior. Simply put, you look for additional information that will help you make sense of the situation.

The observation and reflection then form the basis of *abstract conceptualization and generalizations*. As we think about it, we develop a theory of what is happening. We identify a plausible explanation for her behavior and begin searching for alternative solutions to your problem. Let us suppose that we conclude that your partner is uncomfortable with your question. Her body language suggests that she feels embarrassed to answer. Therefore, we theorize that you should pose the question in a different way.

Finally, this newly developed theory will guide any future actions you take to deal with this individual and others from the same culture. Here, we enter a stage of *active experimentation*. As we practice these new actions, we are developing new theories-in-use and testing the implications of what has been learned. You decide, for example, to formulate your questions in a different way, you observe the results, and start a new learning cycle. The cycle continues until you are able to identify successful behaviors. Learning through experience is a process of trial and error, in which we perceive a mismatch, reflect on it, identify solutions, and initiate new behaviors. When we identify successful behaviors, we incorporate them into our theories of how to behave. As such, the next time we engage in a similar situation, we draw upon our latest theory for guidance.[32]

2   *Develop management learning strategies*

This experiential learning model suggests that any developmental strategy for improving global managers' capabilities and skills should incorporate four variables:

- actual experiences in the field;
- the manner in which we try to understand, interpret, and analyze these experiences;
- theories-in-use, or action plans, we develop for future action based on our analyses; and
- attempts we make to try out new behavioral strategies.

Permeating this entire process are two critical learning strategies that aim to make learning and development easier: developing an awareness and an understanding of global interdependencies as they relate to cultural influences on human behavior; and developing theories-in-use, or action plans, to prepare for unforeseen events and the unanticipated actions of others (see Exhibit 2.10). (Cultural note: action plans such as

Exhibit 2.10 Action plans for cross-cultural learning

(1) Develop awareness and understanding	(2) Develop theories-in-use and action plans
• *Analysis and reflection*. Learn from observations, descriptions, actions, experiences, reflections, and analyses. Understand cultural differences and similarities and their consequences.	• *Conceptualization and action planning*. Adjust behavioral strategies or develop new strategies in response to what has been learned, and then experiment with these strategies in the field.
• *Management focus*. What have we learned about ourselves as managers and about the global environment in which we work?	• *Management focus*. How can we use what we have learned to become better global managers in the future?

these are often called "takeaways" in some countries, while other countries use this term to refer to fast-food restaurants. Thus, one person's classroom lessons may be another person's dinner!) Both these learning strategies have the same goal: developing the multicultural competencies necessary to work successfully across cultures. Moreover, both apply to a wide range of global managers, including expatriates, frequent flyers, and virtual managers. The jobs may be different, but the challenges remain the same.

The first learning strategy focuses on *developing awareness and understanding*. Here we want to learn from our and others' experiences, observations, descriptions, and analyses. We want to process and analyze the available information so as to achieve a better understanding of what occurred and why. What were the consequences – and how could the process have been handled better? The second learning strategy focuses on *developing theories-in-use, or action plans*. This includes adjusting our behavioral strategies and creating, and then experimenting with, new action plans in the field.

Learning strategies such as those developed by Google and similar firms have proved to be successful again and again as large and small companies work to improve and internationalize their human resources. With this learning model in mind, we turn now to exploring some of the cultural differences that can at times make working across cultures so problematic, as well as what managers can do to prepare themselves better for success in a turbulent and often contradictory environment.

Summary points

- A major challenge facing managers and entrepreneurs today is how to deal with both partners and competitors abroad who they simply don't understand. More often than not, the problem is not just language differences; it is cultural differences. This challenge is made more difficult by the increasing speed with which business often occurs. Communication and information technology makes it possible to collaborate – or compete – globally from anywhere in the world, regardless of one's country of origin or cultural background. The implication of this for managers of all types is clear: managers with a capability to think and understand business relationships from a global perspective in real time will more often than not succeed over those with more limited, nation-based mindsets.

- In today's increasingly turbulent and complex business environment, everyone is, or is rapidly becoming, a global manager, regardless of where he or she works. The very definition of effective management has changed in ways that have little to do with national origin. Today most managers must engage with customers, business partners, and employees from various regions of the world. Success or failure depends on managers' ability to communicate, negotiate, contract, lead, organize, coordinate, and control activities across borders.

- A global manager is someone who works with or through people across national boundaries to accomplish global corporate objectives. Inherent in this definition is the assumption that many – if not all – of these managers work with people from differing cultural backgrounds and, as such, somehow have to accommodate or respond to these differences. Also inherent in this definition is the recognition that some of these cross-cultural interactions may be across countries with fewer cultural differences than others (e.g., Canada and the United States versus Canada and Saudi Arabia). Indeed, some of these cultural differences can often be found within a single country.

- Global managers can be roughly divided into three somewhat overlapping categories: expatriates, frequent flyers, and virtual managers. The characteristics and cultural challenges of each of these types of managers can be quite different. While expatriates typically require deep knowledge of a particular country or region, frequent flyers more often require broad knowledge of cultural differences and cultural processes in general. One leads a somewhat stable life, albeit in a foreign country; the other leads a highly mobile existence. Added to this is a category of other managers who work largely through computer and information technology and who, essentially, wander the globe in cyberspace to achieve their results. We refer to these individuals as virtual managers in recognition of their basic patterns of collegial and business interaction

- Each type of global manager carries with it its own particular risk of shortsightedness, whereby managers may fail to see one or more aspects of the company's larger objectives and operations. We refer to this as global management myopia. At times, these blindnesses can be accompanied by an overprotectiveness or advocacy of one's own area of responsibility, often at the expense of the overall success of the firm.

- What differentiates effective global managers is not so much their managerial skills – important though this obviously is – but the combination of these skills with additional multicultural or cross-cultural competencies that allow people to apply their managerial skills across a diverse spectrum of environments. In other words: *global management skills = managerial competence + multicultural competence.*

- Different cultures have different assumptions, behaviors, communication styles, and expectations about management practice. The ability to deal with these differences in ways that are both appropriate and effective goes by many names (e.g., "cultural intelligence," "global mindset," etc.), but we refer to this simply as multicultural competence. It represents the capacity to work successfully across cultures. Being multiculturally competent is more than just being polite or empathetic to people from other cultures; it is getting things done through people by capitalizing on cultural diversity.

Notes

1 Eric Hoffer, *Reflections on the Human Condition*. Titusville, NJ: Hopewell Publications, 1973, p. 32.
2 Stephen Green, *Good Value: Reflections on Money, Morality, and an Uncertain World*. New York: Atlantic Monthly Press, 2010, p. 74.
3 Claude S. George, *The History of Management Thought*. Englewood Cliffs, NJ: Prentice Hall, 1972.
4 Frederick Taylor, *Scientific Management*. New York: Harper & Row, 1911.
5 Henri Fayol, *Administration Industrielle et Generale*. Paris: Dunod, 1916.
6 Hugo Munsterberg, *Psychology and Industrial Efficiency*. Cambridge, MA: Riverside Press, 1913.

7 Max Weber, *The Theory of Social and Economic Organization*. New York: Free Press, 1927.
8 Stephen Robbins and Mary Coulter, *Management*, 9th edn. Upper Saddle River, NJ: Pearson/ Prentice Hall, 2006, p. 7.
9 Michael Hitt, Stewart Black, and Lyman Porter, *Management*, 2nd edn. Upper Saddle River, NJ: Pearson/Prentice Hall, 2004, p. 8
10 Henry Mintzberg, *The Nature of Managerial Work*. New York: Harper & Row, 1973, p. 55.
11 Henry Mintzberg, *Structure in Fives: Designing Effective Organizations*. Englewood Cliffs, NJ: Prentice Hall, 1993.
12 Andre Laurent, "The cultural diversity of Western conceptions of management," *International Studies of Management and Organization*, 1983, 13(1/2), pp. 75–96.
13 Richard Hodgetts and Fred Luthans, *International Management: Culture, Strategy, and Behavior*, 5th edn. New York: McGraw-Hill-Irwin, 2003.
14 James Abbeglen and George Stalk, *Kaisha: The Japanese Corporation*. New York: Harper & Row, 1985.
15 Rob Goffee and Gareth Jones, *Why Should Anyone Be Led by You? What it Takes to Be an Authentic Leader*. Cambridge, MA: Harvard Business School Press, 2006, pp. 109–33.
16 Edward T. Hall and Mildred Reed Hall, *Understanding Cultural Differences: Germans, French and Americans*. Yarmouth, ME: Intercultural Press, 2000.
17 Hall and Hall, *Understanding Cultural Differences*.
18 We include *inpatriates* (foreign managers assigned to positions in the parent company's home country) in the same category as expatriates, since they share the same kinds of problems and challenges; the only difference is the reverse nature of their assignment. We also lump *telecommuters* (who work largely from home via networks) and digital nomads (who work via networks from anywhere in the world, depending upon where they happen to be) into the category of virtual managers, since both manage or do business largely using computer-mediated technologies.
19 Marja Tahvanainen, Denice Welch, and Verner Worm, "Implications of short-term international assignments," *European Management Journal*, 2005, 23(6), pp. 663–73.
20 Nancy Adler, *International Dimensions of Organizational Behavior*. Mason, OH: Thompson, 2008.
21 Martha J. Frase, "International commuters: are your overseas assignments creating risky stealth-pats?," *HR Magazine*, March, 2007, pp. 91–5.
22 Carla Joinson, "Cutting down the days: HR can make expat assignments short and sweet," *HR Magazine*, April 2000, pp. 93–7.
23 *The Economist*, "Traveling more lightly: staffing globalization," June 24, 2006, pp. 23–4.
24 Helene Mayerhofer, Linley Hartmann, Gabriela Michelitsch-Riedl, and Iris Kollinger, "Flexpatriate assignments: a neglected issue in global staffing," *International Journal of Human Resource Management*, 2004, 15(8), pp. 1371–89.
25 "Jan Chipchase," *Fast Company*, June 2011, p. 128.
26 Luciara Nardon and Richard M. Steers, "The new global manager: learning cultures on the fly," *Organizational Dynamics*, 2008, 37(1), pp. 47–59.

27 Mansour Javidan, Richard M. Steers, and Michael A. Hitt (eds.), *The Global Mindset*. Amsterdam: Elsevier, 2007; Orly Levy, Sully Taylor, Nakiye Boyacigiller, and Schon Beechler, "Global mindset: a review and proposed extensions," in Javidan *et al.*, *The Global Mindset*, pp. 11–41.

28 Kalburgi M. Srinivas, "Globalization of business and the third world," *Journal of Management Development*, 1995, 14(3), pp. 26–49.

29 William Ouchi, *Theory Z*. Reading, MA: Addison-Wesley, 1981.

30 Steven Levy, "Google goes globe-trotting," *Newsweek*, November 12, 2007, pp. 62–4.

31 Alice Y. Kolb and David A. Kolb, "Learning styles and learning spaces: enhancing experiential learning in higher education," *Academy of Management Learning and Education*, 2005, 4(2), pp. 193–212

32 Robert Hogan and Rodney Warrenfeltz, "Educating the modern manager," *Academy of Management Learning and Education*, 2003, 2(1), pp. 74–84; Kolb and Kolb, "Learning styles and learning spaces."

PART II

DEVELOPING GLOBAL UNDERSTANDING

CHAPTER 3

The cultural environment

While the success of global managers often rests on their ability to deal with cultural differences, the experts who advise them on this important topic are not always in agreement. In fact, sometimes they are in strong disagreement. What can managers do? Without understanding how to navigate diverse cultural beliefs, values, and traditions, managers are left to take their chances in this new, high-stakes, and ever-changing environment. The fact that most cultures incorporate multiple subcultures only exacerbates the problem. From a managerial standpoint, turning in one direction can lead to success; turning in the other can lead to failure. As a first step, managers can ask two questions. What is meant by the rather amorphous term "culture"? What is the relationship between culture, contexts, attitudes, and behaviors? Additionally, managers might wish to understand the answers to four further questions concerning the cultural and institutional environment in which they work. What are local beliefs, values, and social norms? What are local customs and traditions? How will local institutions (e.g., laws, government regulations) affect my work? What must I do and what must I avoid doing to be successful here? Managers who understand these issues are typically better prepared to compete and build successful partnerships in today's sometimes "winner takes all" global business arena. We begin with a model designed to identify and integrate the various demands and constraints placed on managerial action in the global environment.

Chapter outline

Applications

We do not see things as they are; we see things as we are.

Talmud Bavli[1]
Ancient book of wisdom, Babylonia

Ample evidence shows that the cultures of the world are getting more and more interconnected and that the business world is becoming increasingly global. As economic borders come down, cultural barriers will most likely go up and present new challenges and opportunities for business. When cultures come in contact, they may converge in some aspects, but their idiosyncrasies will likely amplify.

Robert J. House[2]
Wharton School, University of Pennsylvania, United States

In the previous two chapters, we set the stage for understanding the global management environment by examining both the changing nature of the global economy in general and the implications of these changes for global managers in particular. If managers are to change with the changing environment, however, they will have to possess two sets of skills. First, they must develop their conceptual skills. They must be able to develop a greater awareness and understanding of the environment – or, more accurately, environments – in which they work. This is the focus in Part II of this book, beginning with this chapter. Next, managers need to develop a repertoire of practical skills to respond to these changes in ways that facilitate their success. This is the focus in Part III.

Beginning with this chapter, we focus on developing an understanding of three interrelated environments in which managers find themselves: cultural, organizational, and situational (see Exhibit 3.1). What this means, in essence, is that when working across cultures there are at least three dynamics occurring simultaneously. In other words, people's attitudes and behaviors are influenced by the *cultures* in which they live, the *organizations* for which they work, and, finally, their own unique *situations* in which they find themselves. Each of these three often overlapping environments poses

Exhibit 3.1 Cultural, organizational, and situational environments of global management: a model

dilemmas and challenges for managers on both sides of the cultural fence. These challenges can be thought of as a series of questions – or information points – that managers need to know and understand before they set out on their assignments. Knowing the answers to these questions will make their job considerably easier. Each of these topics is discussed sequentially in the following three chapters. Following this, we turn our attention in Part III to discussing the development of specific and practical management skills for use in the field.

To see how these three environments work together to create a context for managerial action, suppose two managers are meeting to discuss a new contract that they hope will benefit both companies (see Exhibit 3.2). Company A is embedded in an individualistic culture and its managers believe in centralized decision making. By contrast, company B comes from a collectivistic culture and its managers believe in decentralized, or partici-pative, decision making. What happens when these two managers meet in their unique "situation"? There are many possibilities, but here is one example. Company A is a larger and more established firm. It has developed some proprietary technology that it protects diligently. When it looks at company B, it worries that its prospective partner may not be up to the challenge. At the same time, company B may be apprehensive about the power of company A, and worry that it might be taken over. This is just one example, but it illustrates how cultural and organizational environments help shape the situations in

Exhibit 3.2 Cultural, organizational, and situational environments of global management (example)

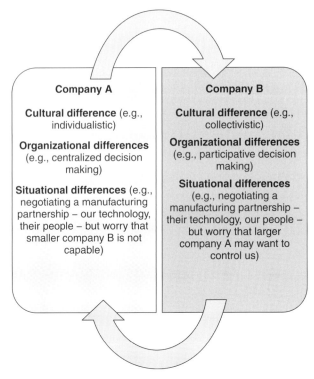

which managers find themselves. In the present chapter, we begin by exploring the *cultural environment* as it influences individual and corporate actions.

Managers working across borders face several *culture-specific questions* that can have a direct bearing on their success or failure in the field. These questions form the heart of this chapter, and include the following.

(1) How can we understand cultural differences (e.g., beliefs, values, norms) and their impact on social systems in ways that can help managers succeed?

(2) Is there a shorthand way to understanding these cultural differences, and, if so, what are the potential limitations of this approach?

(3) How can we understand the complexities and contradictions that permeate national and regional cultures?

(4) What is the relationship between cultural differences and national institutions (e.g., legal systems, government policies) that can constrain or shape global and local business?

To answer these questions, we need to step back and learn more about cultures and how they can differ – sometimes significantly – both across and within countries and regions. We begin with grasshoppers.

Cultures and subcultures

Grasshoppers are considered pests in North America, pets in China, and appetizers in Thailand. What does this suggest about the influence of cultural differences on perceptions of even the lowly insect? Indeed, what does this suggest about how and why tastes in general can differ so starkly across nations and regions? If cultures can have such differing views about grasshoppers, imagine what they can do with people. Philosophers and social scientists have long noted that, if you want to understand why people – including managers – behave as they do, a good place to begin is with a serious look at the cultural environment in which they work.

Think about the following three observations. First, Talmudic wisdom dates from well over 2,000 years ago, yet is as true today as it was when it was initially written. As noted in the first of the above quotations, culture influences our perceptions of world events and thereby influences our values, attitudes, and behaviors. It tells us what is acceptable and what is not. If cultures differ, though, so do our perceptions, values, and judgments. What may be pleasant, attractive, agreeable, or acceptable in one culture may not be in another. Second, more than 700 years ago Chinese scholar Wang Yinglin compiled a volume of ancient wisdom thought to be from Confucius and called the *Trimetric Classic* (or *Three Character Classic*), in which he observed that all people are basically the same; it is only their habits and environments that differ.[3] Third, Wharton professor Robert J. House recently observed that cultures around the world are getting increasingly interconnected and that the business world is becoming increasingly global. When these cultures come into contact, they may converge in some aspects, but their idiosyncrasies will likely amplify.

The Talmud, a Confucian scholar, and a modern-day business professor, each coming from a very different time and place in history, all understood what has too frequently eluded many contemporary managers: culture can make a difference in determining how we think and how we behave. This is equally true in our personal lives as it is in our work lives. Unfortunately, too many managers have ignored even the most rudimentary cross-national differences while working overseas, and, as a result, have missed significant opportunities both for themselves and their companies.

Learning about cultures

Culture is both simple and difficult to understand. It is simple because definitions abound that are easily understood by any reader. At the same time, however, culture can be difficult to comprehend, because of its subtleties and complexities. Moreover, most cultures incorporate, support, and are supported by various subcultures. The ancient Chinese Taoist philosopher Lao Tzu once observed that "[w]ater is the last thing a fish notices," using water as a metaphor for culture.[4] In other words, most people are so strongly immersed in their own culture that they often fail to see how it affects their patterns of thinking or their behavior; they are too close to it. It is only when we are "out of the water" that we become aware of our own cultural biases and assumptions. (If you don't believe this, try writing down ten adjectives that best describe your own culture. Then ask some friends from other cultures to write down ten adjectives that also describe your own culture. Compare the lists.)

In view of this dilemma, consider the challenge faced by Anna Håkansson, a Swedish investment banker from Stockholm, who was informed that she was being sent to Bahrain to negotiate a contract with Gulf One Investment Bank.[5] How would she prepare herself for the journey? Having never been to the Middle East, she first talked to colleagues who had some experience there. Next, she ran a Google search and discovered that there were over 400,000 hits on Arab culture alone. During this search she uncovered a number of recent articles in various respected sources that helped her to understand what to expect. For example, an article by Faiza Saleh Ambah in *The Washington Post* pointed out that the extended family was the single most important entity of Arab society, playing a pivotal role not only in social life but in economic and political life as well.[6] Even an individual's self-identity is based on a collective self. Each family member shares a collective ancestry, a collective respect for elders, and a collective obligation and responsibility for the welfare of the other family members. It is to the extended family, not to the government, that a person first turns for help.

Despite some modernization trends and the adoption of many superficial aspects of Western pop culture, the extended family still has been remarkably resilient to Westernization. With the move to the cities, members of Saudi extended families still tend to live in close proximity to one another whenever possible, and, when they cannot, they do a great deal of socializing with other members. In addition, many families retain homes in their hometowns as well as their place of work. A major reason for the resilience of the traditional extended family structure, however, is the extraordinary strength of traditional Islamic social, economic, and political values. Although some behavioral patterns have changed over time, Arab society's core values are deeply held and are likely to endure over time.

As Håkansson learned, three characteristics of Arab extended families stand out: gender roles, the role of elders, and the decision-making process.

- Arab societies are, typically, patriarchal societies, maintaining a respect for age and seniority that has largely disappeared in Western societies. The wisdom and authority of elders is seldom challenged, and younger men and women must wait their turn, often until their sixties or older, before they are accorded the role of family patriarchs and matriarchs.

- Traditional gender roles in Arab societies share a number of common characteristics with other traditional societies, the most notable of which is that men's roles are outside the home as family providers, protectors, and managers, and women's roles are in the home. Men are predominant outside the home – in business and public affairs – and women are to a large degree predominant within the home, particularly in parental decisions.

- The traditional method for reaching and legitimizing decisions in Arab society is through consultation (*shura*) among those within the group whose opinions are considered important.[7] From consultation emerges consensus (*ijma'*), which is binding on all members of the group.[8] Within the extended family, the principal consensus makers are senior male members or elders. This ancient process of consultation and consensus was given religious sanction in Islam. From texts in the Qur'an and the Sunna comes the belief that God would never permit a consensus of the Islamic community to be in error.[9] Consensual decision making is still the norm in family, government, or business decisions.

Based on what she learned, Håkansson next attempted to find a way to organize everything into a user-friendly format. She looked for a cultural model she could use to make some comparisons between Swedish and Arab societies to solidify what she had learned. She chose a model developed by Dutch management researcher Geert Hofstede and based on his classic book, *Culture's Consequences*.[10] Hofstede views culture as the "software of the mind" that differentiates one group or society from another. In other words, while people all have the same hardware, their brains and patterns of thinking and behaving can be very different (see also the Appendix).

Håkansson compared Hofstede's assessment of Arab cultures with his assessment of her native Sweden (see Exhibit 3.3). For Bahrain, she had found that people tend to be low on long-term orientation, high on uncertainty avoidance, moderately high on masculinity, moderately high on collectivism, and high in power distance – that is, a belief in rigid

Exhibit 3.3 Hofstede's cultural dimensions for Bahrain and Sweden

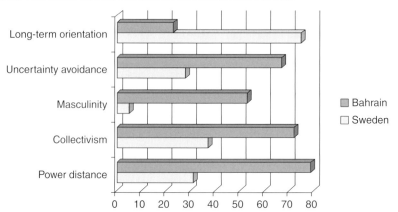

hierarchies. For Sweden, by contrast, she found very different scores. Specifically, Hofstede's scale indicates that Swedes tend to be high on long-term orientation, moderately low on uncertainty avoidance, very low on masculinity, moderately low on collectivism (that is, relatively high on individualism), and low on power distance. In other words, in Sweden we see a society in which egalitarianism is emphasized, including equality of gender and race. Power is widely shared and uncertainty is tolerated, in the belief that it helps facilitate creativity and innovation. Groups – and, indeed, society itself – are considered to be important by all, but so too is individualism.

Now Håkansson believed she had a concrete comparative framework on which to compare some of the basic differences between the two countries. Based on what she had learned, she further believed she was now prepared for her business trip to Bahrain. What she would learn later, however, as discussed below, was that she had only scratched the surface in preparing for her global encounter.

What is culture?

A key issue in dealing with culture relates to how we recognize culture when we see it. What do we mean by the term "culture"? One of the main challenges managers face when working across cultures is teasing out cultural influences from other phenomena in the world surrounding us. For example, where does culture end and personality begin? What is universal behavior and what is not? In this regard, finding a suitable working definition of culture can be challenging.

Hofstede defines culture as the collective programming of the mind that distinguishes the members of one human group from another.[11] Meanwhile, cultural anthropologist Clyde Kluckhohn defines culture as the collection of beliefs, values, behaviors, customs, and attitudes that distinguish the people of one society from another.[12] Researchers in the Global Leadership and Organizational Behavior Effectiveness (GLOBE) project define culture as shared motives, values, beliefs, identities, and interpretations or meanings of significant events that result from common experiences of members of collectives that are transmitted across generations.[13] Fons Trompenaars defines culture as the way in which a group of people solves problems and reconciles dilemmas.[14] Ann Swidler also took a problem-solving approach, viewing culture as a "toolkit" of symbols, stories, rituals, and world views that help the people of a culture survive and succeed.[15] Finally, cultural anthropologist Clifford Geertz defines culture as the means by which people communicate, perpetuate, and develop their knowledge about attitudes towards life.[16] Culture is the fabric of meaning in terms of which people interpret their experience and guide their actions.

While all these definitions are useful and share a great deal in common, they all have nuanced differences that may have more to say to academicians than managers. Taken together, these definitions suggest that, from the standpoint of global management, culture is perhaps best thought of as addressing three questions: who are we, how do we live, and how do we approach work? These three questions focus attention on individuals, environments, and work norms and values, and the answers to these questions allow us to draw some inferential conclusions about work and society and how managers in general should behave as they work across cultures.

Three aspects of these definitions are particularly salient for our discussion here.

- *Culture is shared by members of a group, and, indeed, sometimes defines the membership of the group itself.* As such, cultural preferences are neither universal around the world nor entirely personal; they are preferences that are commonly shared by a group of people, even if not by all members of the group. The fact that most Koreans and Mexicans like spicy food does not require that all of them prefer such cuisine, nor does it require that all Dutch and Canadians avoid it.

- *Culture is learned through membership in a group or community.* Cultures, in the form of normative social behavior, are learned from elders, teachers, officials, experiences, and society at large. We acquire values, assumptions, and behaviors by seeing how others behave, growing up in a community, going to school, and observing our family.

- *Culture influences the attitudes and behaviors of group members.* Many of our innate beliefs, values, and patterns of social behavior can be traced back to our particular cultural training and socialization. After we grow up, culture still tells us what is acceptable and unacceptable behavior, attractive and unattractive, and so forth. As a result, culture heavily influences socialization processes in terms of how we see ourselves and what we believe and hold dear. This, in turn, influences our *normative behavior*, or how we think those around us expect us to behave.

One intriguing study serves to illustrate the shared nature of cultures. This study found that shared values follow people throughout their life.[17] The study found that the anxieties and worries of elderly people were tied very closely to their national origin. That is, aging Germans tend to worry about losing their mental alertness, while their Dutch neighbors worry about gaining weight. Thais worry about losing their eyesight, while the more heterogeneous Americans tend to divide their anxieties between memory loss, weight gain, loss of energy, and an ability to care for themselves. Finally, Egyptians report that they worry about nothing as they age. The study authors suggest that perhaps the Egyptians concluded that, since problems associated with aging are inevitable, there is no need to worry about them – fate happens. The study concludes that an important aspect of studying aging is developing an understanding of cultural influences.

Cultures, beliefs, and normative behavior

Not long ago, a middle-aged woman in a village not far from Rio de Janeiro became very ill. She was convinced that she would die if she did not get proper treatment. So she took three actions: she went to the local medical clinic; she lit a candle in the local church; and she sacrificed a chicken following the local voodoo custom. She soon made a full recovery. Question: which of her three actions caused her recovery, or was it a combination of these actions, or was it simply good luck? It is such cause and effect connections in people's minds that are at the heart of understanding culture and cultural differences. Although we may disagree with how others see things, it is their perceptions, not ours, that help determine behavior.

Culture often sets the limits on what is considered acceptable and unacceptable behavior; it pressures individuals and groups into accepting and following *normative behavior*. In other words, culture determines the rules of the road that guide what people can do. Indeed, newspapers and periodicals are filled with examples of people who set out to break a "culture barrier." Rightly or wrongly, these barriers are typically established to ensure uniform practice among members of a society, and, as a result, societies often take a dim view of people who buck the system.

Application 3.1   What is truth?

One way to get to the heart of cultural differences and normative behavior is to ask a simple question: *what is truth?* What do people believe to be correct and true, beyond question, in this world? While we can easily see different responses to this question within a particular culture, imagine the differences we can see between cultures. Every day, managers are faced with moral or ethical dilemmas relating to conflicting personal and societal beliefs and values. This arena includes both societal norms in general, about right and wrong, and religious beliefs about what people "should" or "must" do. Many philosophers on this topic have been rather parochial in their conscious ignorance of other cultural traditions. They have routinely assumed the universal validity of their ethical values.[18] In other words, many of these writers have assumed that ethics represents a universal phenomenon, and that the challenge is to discover the "correct" set of values and social norms. Obviously, this approach is both naïve and unsatisfactory, as most successful global executives understand.

At the heart of this debate is people's conception of "truth." British communications consultant Richard Lewis has suggested, only partly in jest, "For a German and a Finn, the truth is the truth. In Japan and Britain, it is all right to tell the truth if it doesn't rock the boat. In China, there is no absolute truth. And in Italy, the truth is negotiable."[19] Similarly, British actor Peter Ustinov has observed, again only partly in jest, "In order to reach the truth the Germans add, the French subtract, and the British change the subject. I did not include the Americans, since they often give the impression that they already have the truth."[20] To the extent that these observations have merit, it would appear that truth is clearly in the eye of the beholder. In other words, the "truth" is not always "the truth." At the very least, we have to conclude that, at times, there are no universals when it comes to being truthful. What is your opinion?

    Think about it. . .

(1) Do you believe that, on a very fundamental level, there is a universal truth about some things that virtually all people would agree with, or are these truths situational or contingent in nature? Explain.

(2) When other people disagree with your conception of fundamental truths, how do you usually respond? Why?

(3) If there is no agreement on fundamental truths across cultures, how can managers do business in this arena?

Describing cultures

To understand the changes and challenges around the world, many researchers suggest we need some kind of tool or mechanism with which to compare cultural and sub-cultural differences and similarities. Such a mechanism can provide a heuristic to gain conceptual entry into why some people think and act differently from others. Many researchers – and many global managers – begin by comparing cultures on various cultural dimensions, such as hierarchical or egalitarian, individualistic or collectivistic, and so forth. Indeed, this is exactly what Håkansson did prior to her departure for the Middle East. Although comparing cultural dimensions may provide only a thumbnail sketch of some general trends between two or more cultures, it can be useful as a starting point for cross-cultural understanding.

Even this simple strategy is not without its problems, however. As noted cultural anthropologist Edward Hall once observed, "I have come to the conclusion that the analysis of culture could be likened to the task of identifying mushrooms. Because of the nature of the mushrooms, no two experts describe them in precisely the same way, which creates a problem for the rest of us when we are trying to decide whether the specimen in our hands is edible."[21]

Hall makes an important point here. While the success of global managers frequently rests on their understanding of cultures and cultural differences, the experts who advise them are not always in agreement. To apply Hall's metaphor, however, managers have to decide which mushrooms are edible and which are not. They need to know which practices or behaviors will create barriers to conducting business and which will open a path to partnership.

Culture theory jungle

A number of attempts have been made to capture the essence of cultural differences – and similarities – across borders, including the Hofstede model discussed earlier (see the Appendix). Each offers a different way to understand and measure culture. Four currently popular models are shown in Exhibit 3.4.

Taken together, these models attempt to accomplish two things. First, each model offers a well-reasoned set of dimensions along which various cultures can be compared. It offers us a form of shorthand for cultural analysis. We can break down assessments of various cultures into power distance, uncertainty avoidance, and so forth, allowing us to organize our thoughts and focus our attention on what otherwise would be a mon-umental task. Second, some of the models offer numeric scores for rating various

Exhibit 3.4 Selected models of cultural dimensions

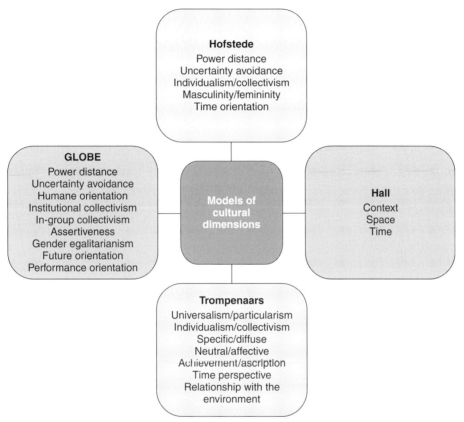

Source: Based on Edward T. Hall, *The Silent Language*. New York: Anchor Books, 1981; Edward T. Hall and Mildred Reed Hall, *Understanding Cultural Differences: Germans, French and Americans*. Yarmouth, ME: Intercultural Press, 1990; Geert Hofstede, *Culture's Consequence: International Differences in Work-Related Values*. Thousand Oaks, CA: Sage 2001; Fons Trompenaars, *Riding the Waves of Culture: Understanding Cultural Diversity in Global Business*. London: McGraw-Hill, 1993; Robert J. House, Paul J. Hanges, Mansour Javidan, Peter W. Dorfman, and Vipin Gupta. *Culture, Leadership, and Organizations: The GLOBE Study of 62 Societies*. Thousand Oaks, CA: Sage, 2004.

cultures. For example, we can use Hofstede's measures to say that Germany is more egalitarian than France. Regardless of whether these ratings are highly precise or only generally indicative of these countries, they nonetheless force managers to confront cultural differences and consider the managerial implications.

Unfortunately, these models frequently focus on different aspects of societal beliefs, norms, and values, and, as such, convergence across the models is therefore limited. From a managerial standpoint, it is logical to raise questions as to which model best suits the needs of organizations and their managers. This lack of agreement presents managers with a dilemma in terms of managerial understanding and action, which we refer to as the *culture theory jungle*. In other words, which model best serves managers' needs in the real world? For example, is it more important for managers to compare cultures on the basis of achievement versus ascription, as one model suggests, masculinity versus femininity, as another model suggests, or the use of time and space, as still another model suggests?

In addition, critics of this research point out – with some justification – that the theory and the research underlying the creation and use of such models both focus too much on comparing central tendencies between cultures and not enough on comparing the differences within each culture. In other words, are all Indonesians or Kenyans or Bulgarians alike? Obviously not. Moreover, it is inaccurate to suggest that there are few differences between the peoples of either east Asia (Chinese, Korean, Japanese) or western Europe (Dutch, French, Germans, Italians). Again, the answer is "No." Do these criticisms hold up? Do they change the basic argument about cultural differences influencing the way people see the world and respond to it? Probably not. As already noted, however, although the use of cultural dimensions is certainly helpful, it should be considered as only the beginning of a more detailed study.

Core cultural dimensions

Even so, while each of these models focuses on different aspects of culture, we believe that, taken together, they serve to amplify one another and reinforce their utility as critical evaluative components in better understanding global management and the world of international business. Each model has added something of value to this endeavor.

With this in mind, if we compare the various models of cultural dimensions, five dimensions emerge as being the most commonly used by researchers and managers alike (see Exhibit 3.5).[22] We refer to these as *core cultural dimensions* (or CCDs). Each focuses on one of five fundamental questions about cultures as they relate to social interaction and management practices in the global economy.

(1) *How are power and authority distributed in a society?* Is this distribution based on concepts of hierarchy or egalitarianism? What are societal beliefs concerning equality or privilege?

(2) *What is the fundamental building block of a society: individuals or groups?* How does a society organize for collective action?

Exhibit 3.5 Core cultural dimensions

(3) *On a societal level, how do people view their relationship with their surrounding environment?* Is their goal to control or master their environment or to live in harmony with it?

(4) *How do people in a society organize their time to carry out their work and non-work activities?* Do people approach work in a linear (i.e., one thing at a time) or a nonlinear (i.e., everything at once) fashion?

(5) *How do societies try to reduce uncertainties and control the behavior of their members?* Do they focus primarily on rules or relationships? In other words, do they work to control people through rules, policies, laws, and social norms that are uniformly applied across society, or do they attempt to control people through relationship and rules often tempered by personal relationships, in-group values, or unique circumstances?

The five core cultural dimensions that emerge from integrating existing models include the following: power distribution (hierarchical and egalitarian), social relationships (individualistic and collectivistic), environmental relationships (mastery-oriented and harmony-oriented), time and work patterns (monochronic and polychronic), and uncertainty and social control (rule-based and relationship-based; also called universalism/particularism). Taken together, these dimensions help build a broad-based portrait of how management and business practices in one culture differ from those in another (see Exhibit 3.6). In reviewing these dimensions, it is important to remember that country placement on dimensions is relative. For example, on the

Exhibit 3.6 Characteristics of core cultural dimensions

Hierarchical	Egalitarian
Centralized. Belief that power should be distributed hierarchically across society. Belief in ascribed or inherited power, with ultimate authority residing in institutions. Emphasis on organizing vertically and autocratic or centralized decision making. Emphasis on who is in charge. Acceptance of authority; reluctance to question authority.	*Decentralized.* Belief that power should be distributed relatively equally across society. Belief in shared or elected power, with ultimate authority residing in the people. Emphasis on organizing horizontally and participatory or decentralized decision making. Emphasis on who is best qualified. Rejection or skepticism of authority; willingness to question authority.

Individualistic	Collectivistic
Person-centered. Belief that people achieve self-identity through individual accomplishment. Focus on accomplishing individual goals. Sanctions reinforce independence and personal responsibility. Contract-based agreements. Tendency towards low-context (direct, frank) communication and individual decision making.	*Group-centered.* Belief that people achieve self-identity through group membership. Preference for preserving social harmony over individual rights. Focus on accomplishing group goals. Sanctions reinforce conformity to group norms. Relationship-based agreements. Tendency towards high-context (subtle, indirect) communication and group or participative decision making.

Mastery-oriented	Harmony-oriented
Dominance over nature. Focus on changing or controlling one's natural and social environment. Achievement valued over relationships. Emphasis on competition in the pursuit of personal or group goals. Embraces change and unquestioned innovation. Emphasis on material possessions as symbols of achievement. Emphasis on assertive, proactive, "masculine" approach. Preference for performance-based extrinsic rewards.	*Accommodation with nature.* Focus on living in harmony with nature and adjusting to the natural and social environment. Relationships valued over achievement. Emphasis on social progress, quality of life, and the welfare of others. Defends traditions; skepticism towards change. Emphasis on economy, harmony, and modesty. Emphasis on passive, reactive, "feminine" approach. Preference for seniority-based intrinsic rewards.

Monochronic	Polychronic
Linear. Sequential attention to individual tasks. Single-minded approach to work, planning, and implementation. Precise concept of time; punctual. Job-centered; commitment to the job, and often to the organization. Separation of work and personal life. Approach to work is focused and impatient.	*Nonlinear.* Simultaneous attention to multiple tasks. Interactive approach to work, planning, and implementation. Flexible concept of time; often late. People-centered; commitment to people and human relationships. Integration of work and personal life. Approach to work is at times unfocused and patient.

Rule-based	Relationship-based
Universalistic. Individual behavior should be largely regulated by rules, laws, formal policies, standard operating procedures, and social norms that are widely supported by societal members and applied uniformly to everyone. Emphasis on legal contracts and meticulous record keeping. Low tolerance for rule breaking. Decisions based largely on objective criteria (e.g., legal constraints, data, policies).	*Particularistic.* While rules and laws are important, they often require flexibility in their application or enforcement by influential people (e.g., parents, peers, superiors, government officials) or unique circumstances. Emphasis on interpersonal relationships and trust; less emphasis on record keeping. Moderate tolerance for rule breaking. Decisions often based on subjective criteria (e.g., hunches, personal connections).

hierarchy/equality dimension, while all cultures use hierarchies in various forms, some cultures make greater use of them than others and, as such, would rank higher on this dimension than would other cultures. Dimensions are thus viewed in terms of relative comparisons across cultures, not as metrics or absolute values.[23]

Taken together, these five core cultural dimensions highlight key aspects of cultural differences that can have a bearing on how business and management is conducted – or not conducted – around the world. Like the other models on which it is based, the core cultural dimensions described here provide only a quick cultural snapshot of the central tendencies in one country. They are a good starting point to investigate cultural differences between countries, but their utility will vary depending on the countries involved and the particular situation.

Application 3.2   Traffic fines in Finland

A good example of how cultures can differ using this CCD framework can be found in Finland, a country that stresses egalitarianism with a passion. Many Finnish laws are based on the principle of equity, not equality. For example, traffic fines vary based on personal income; the more you make, the more you can afford to pay. Police departments maintain direct computer access to internal revenue files to calculate the fines on the spot. Hence, when Jaako Rytsola, a young Finnish entrepreneur, was stopped driving his BMW at 43 miles per hour in a 25-mile-per-hour zone, his speeding ticket cost him $72,000. Similarly, when 27-year-old millionaire Jussi Salonoja, also in a BMW, was caught doing 40 miles per hour in a 25-mile-per-hour zone, he was fined $225,000. A government minister noted that this was a "Nordic tradition." They have both progressive taxation and progressive punishment.[24]

Think about it. . .

(1) What is your opinion of the fairness of tying traffic fines to personal income? Why might this be fair or unfair?

(2) Would you enjoy being a manager in a country that genuinely stresses equality – including equality with your subordinates?

(3) Do you think the kind of car you drive influences whether or not you get stopped by the police? Is this true in all cultures?

Cultural trends across regions

In order to operationalize the core cultural dimensions discussed here, it is helpful to have a means of classifying cultures so that country – or at least regional – comparisons can be made. Mindful of the limitations discussed above, we chose to estimate cultural differences within *country clusters* (as opposed to individual countries) by adapting a framework originally proposed by Simcha Ronan and Oded Shenkar,[25] and subsequently used by others with some modifications.[26] This framework focuses on identifying regions where ample anthropological data are available, and our use of these clusters reflects this imbalance. Because of this, some regions (e.g., central Asia, Polynesia) are not included, while others (e.g., Europe) are covered in considerable detail. In addition, according to these efforts, several countries (e.g., Brazil, India, and Israel) do not easily fit into such a framework, so, again, some caution is in order.

Based on this research, we can use this framework to identify nine country clusters for which sufficient data were available to estimate central tendencies in cultural characteristics: the Anglo cluster (e.g., Australia, Canada, the United Kingdom, the United States); the Arab cluster (e.g., Dubai, Egypt, Saudi Arabia); the eastern European cluster (e.g., Czech Republic, Hungary, Poland); the east/southeast Asian cluster (e.g., China, Japan, South Korea, Singapore, Thailand); the Germanic cluster (e.g., Austria, Germany); the Latin American cluster (e.g., Argentina, Costa Rica, Mexico); the Latin European cluster (e.g., France, Italy, Spain); the Nordic cluster (e.g., Denmark, Norway, Sweden); and the sub-Saharan African cluster (e.g., Ghana, Kenya, Nigeria). Culture ratings for regions were then estimated.[27]

The results are shown in Exhibit 3.7. Note that these are only rough estimates based on available research. Moreover, in making use of the information presented here, it is

Exhibit 3.7 Central tendencies of core cultural dimensions

Country clusters	Power distribution	Social relationships	Environmental relationships	Time and work patterns	Uncertainty and social control
Anglo	Moderately egalitarian	Strongly individualistic	Strongly mastery-oriented	Strongly monochronic	Moderately rule-based
Arab	Strongly hierarchical	Strongly collectivistic	Moderately harmony-oriented	Strongly polychronic	Strongly relationship-based
East European	Moderately hierarchical	Moderately collectivistic	Moderately mastery-oriented	Moderately monochronic	Moderately relationship-based
East/ southeast Asian	Strongly hierarchical	Strongly collectivistic	Strongly harmony-oriented	Moderately monochronic	Strongly relationship-based
Germanic	Moderately egalitarian	Moderately individualistic	Moderately mastery-oriented	Moderately monochronic	Strongly rule-based
Latin American	Moderately hierarchical	Moderately collectivistic	Moderately harmony-oriented	Strongly polychronic	Strongly relationship-based
Latin European	Moderately hierarchical	Moderately collectivistic	Moderately harmony-oriented	Moderately polychronic	Moderately relationship-based
Nordic	Strongly egalitarian	Moderately individualistic	Moderately harmony-oriented	Moderately monochronic	Strongly rule-based
Sub-Saharan African	Moderately hierarchical	Strongly collectivistic	Strongly harmony-oriented	Moderately polychronic	Strongly relationship-based

Notes: The CCD ratings represent central tendencies for selected country clusters (see text for details). Variations, sometimes substantial, around these central tendencies can be found in all clusters and countries. Some regions of the globe (e.g., central Asia) are not included here due to an absence of substantive data, while others (e.g., Europe) are represented in some detail due to the availability of sufficient data.
Sources: The country cluster categories used here are adapted from Simcha Ronan and Oded Shenkar, "Clustering cultures on attitudinal dimensions: a review and synthesis," *Academy of Management Review*, 1985, 10(3), pp. 435–54; and Robert J. House, Paul J. Hanges, Mansour Javidan, Peter W. Dorfman, and Vipin Gupta, *Culture, Leadership, and Organizations: The GLOBE Study of 62 Societies*. Thousand Oaks, CA: Sage, 2004.

important to recognize that no point on any assessment scale is preferred over any other; they are simply different, and significant within-cluster variance can often be found.

Although it is sometimes necessary to focus on central tendencies between cultures for purposes of general comparisons, the role of individual and regional differences as well as particular circumstances in determining attitudes and behaviors should not be overlooked. Even so, it should not be surprising that cultural ratings for countries in the same cluster of the world (e.g., Denmark, Norway, and Sweden) tend to be closer than ratings for countries located in a different cluster of the world (e.g., Italy, Spain, France). This is a natural consequence of contiguous countries in various regions living side by side with their neighbors over centuries and sometimes millennia. All the same, important cultural differences can be found across peoples inhabiting a particular region. Finally, it is important to remember that, while these core cultural dimensions may be a useful short cut for gaining conceptual entry into general cultural trends across countries and regions, they are in no way a substitute for more systematic in-depth analyses as they relate to the study of culture, work, and organizations.

Application 3.3   Stereotypes

Some people suggest that we can learn a great deal about cultures through humor, but this can be a risky pursuit. Consider the following tongue-in-cheek descriptions of behaviors of dairy farmers around the world.[28]

- *German farmer.* You have two cows. You engineer them so they are both blond, drink lots of beer, give excellent-quality milk, and can run at 50 kilometers an hour. Then you lose your competitive edge because your cows demand thirteen weeks of annual vacation.
- *Japanese farmer.* You have two cows. You redesign them so they are one-tenth the size of ordinary cows but can produce twenty times the milk. The cows learn to travel on unbelievably crowded trains. Both are at the top of their class at cow school.
- *French farmer.* You have two cows. You go on strike because you want three cows. After a month, you forget why you went on strike, but you know that, whatever it was, it was the Americans' fault.
- *Russian farmer.* You have two cows. You drink some vodka, count the cows again, and conclude that you now have five cows. You drink some more vodka, count the cows again, and conclude that you now have forty-two cows. The mafia shows up and steals however many cows you actually had.

Application 3.3   (cont.)

- *Brazilian farmer.* You have two cows, but you don't know where they are. Walking along a beach one day, you meet a beautiful woman. You break for lunch. Life is good.
- *American farmer (New York).* You have two cows. You sell the first cow, lease it back to yourself, and do an initial public offering on the second cow. You then force each cow to produce the milk of four cows. You are surprised when one cow drops dead. You spin an announcement to Wall Street analysts that you have downsized to reduce expenses. Your stock price goes up.
- *American farmer (California).* You have thousands of cows. Most are illegals.

Are these descriptions humorous? Are they helpful? Many argue that they are useful because such stories present realistic, if exaggerated, caricatures of the various cultures involved, and that we can learn a great deal about cultures from humor so long as we do not take things too seriously. Indeed, if cultures were not significantly different, such humor would not be so pervasive. Others argue that this type of humor represents the worst in cultural stereotyping and should be avoided. Either way, it must be recognized that cultures can, in fact, be very different and that many of these differences can be systematically observed and compared, with or without humor. If these comparisons are done with sufficient accuracy, valuable lessons can be learned that can help the international traveler. For this to happen in earnest, however, it is necessary to have more structured ways of comparison than simple humor. Such an understanding of culture and cultural differences is essential for managers working across national boundaries.

Think about it...

(1)   Are these descriptions humorous or simply in poor taste? Why?

(2)   Why are some cultures more easily offended by stereotypes than others? What causes this?

(3)   Is it acceptable to stereotype some cultures, but not others?

(4)   How do you respond when people from other cultures make fun of your own?

Cultural complexities and contradictions

The related concepts of culture and cultural differences were introduced above as a means of seeing beyond overt behaviors and better understanding why and how some people act differently from others. What is often missed in these generalizations, however, is that individuals within the same society may use different strategies to deal with identical challenges. As a result, it is often unwise to stereotype an entire culture. Instead, we need to look for nuances and counter-trends, not just the principal trends themselves. We also need to look for differences in *context* – the events and environments surrounding people as they form their attitudes and behavioral patterns. Failure to recognize this often leads to failed personal and business opportunities.

Think about the concept of equal opportunity in the workplace. The fight for equal opportunity has been a long and difficult struggle in many nations of the world, north, south, east, and west. For many, this struggle has been quite vociferous, because the underlying beliefs are so strong. What people often fail to recognize here, however, is that to a large extent societal and corporate practices regarding equal rights are embedded in our core beliefs and values. As a result, it is important to be able to compare such beliefs and practices across cultures, as well as within them. For example, some cultures stress sex role differentiation. In other words, men and women are expected to play different roles in society, and, as such, should be treated differently. Other cultures have increasingly stressed minimizing sex role differentiation, believing that men and women should share responsibilities both at home and at work. Still other cultures strive for flexibility and tolerance. As a result of these cultural differences, many people are quick to criticize the beliefs of others as being either overly paternalistic or overly indulgent. For the keen observer, though, differences can often be found just under the surface. To see how this works, we revisit Anna Håkansson as she arrives in Bahrain for her negotiations. Her first surprise is meeting her counterpart, Nahed Taher. Indeed, women executives in the MENA (Middle East and north Africa) region have increased significantly in recent years.

Application 3.4   Women executives in MENA

Nahed Taher is the first woman CEO of the Gulf One Investment Bank, based in Bahrain.[29] As a former senior economist at the National Commercial Bank, Taher has been immersed in plans for financing public sector projects, including expansion of the terminal that handles Mecca pilgrims at Jeddah's King Abdulaziz International Airport. She also oversees financing for a water desalination plant for Saudi Arabian Airlines, as well as Saudi copper, zinc, and gold mines. Taher may be an unusual example of an Arab executive, but she is increasingly becoming a common one. In fact, business leaders such as Taher are gaining power despite the odds. Ten women executives from the Middle East made the *Forbes* "World's 100 most powerful women" list.

How are women such as Taher managing to break through the global glass ceiling in the MENA region? In many cases, the increasing globalization of the world's economy has played an important role. The economic liberalization of several Muslim countries in recent years, along with the privatization of large parts of government-run companies, has helped Muslim businesswomen get a greater foothold. "Now opportunities are open to everyone," says Laura Osman, the first female president of the Arab Bankers Association of North America. "The private sector runs on meritocracy." In fact, banking in the Muslim world is populated by a growing number of women, even in the historically all-male executive suite. Sahar El-Sallab is second in command at Commercial International Bank, one of Egypt's largest private banks. Indeed, four out of ten Commercial International Bank employees and 70 percent of its management staff are women. Similarly, Maha Al-Ghunaim, chairman of Kuwait's Global Investment House, has steadily grown the investment bank she founded into more than $7 billion in assets. Recently it won permission to operate in Qatar, and next it wants to establish a presence in Saudi Arabia.

Muslim businesswomen also sit in the top ranks of mega-conglomerates. Imre Barmanbek runs one of Turkey's largest multinationals, Dogan Holding, which recently went through a shift in operational focus from finance to media and energy. Lubna Olayan helps oversee the Olayan Group of Saudi Arabia, one of the biggest multinationals in the Middle East, with investments in more than forty companies. The top ranks of the conglomerate run by the Khamis family of Egypt also include several women. Originally from India, Vidya Chhabria is chairman of the United Arab Emirates' Jumbo Group, a $2 billion multinational that operates in fifty countries, with interests in durables, chemicals, and machinery products. It also owns Jumbo Electronics, one of the Middle East's largest Sony distributors of consumer electronics, as well as worldwide brands in information technology and telecom products. Thus, while Muslim women may still have a long way to go to reach "equality" in the business world, progress can be seen. For a lucky and determined few, opportunities do exist. "Just being a woman in our part of the world is quite difficult," says El-Sallab of Egypt's Commercial International Bank; "but if you have the proper education, credibility, and integrity in the way you handle your job, intelligent men will always give you your due."

Think about it. . .

(1) How can we reconcile stereotypes about Arab and Muslim women with examples of successful businesswomen working in the MENA region such as those mentioned here?

(2) Do the women discussed here exhibit any common personal characteristics that may have helped them succeed?

(3) What other examples of cultural stereotypes from other parts of the world can you identify that are either overly simplistic or simply incorrect? Why do we have such stereotypes?

The examples of Taher and these other women managers raise an old dilemma. Even though cultural differences have been acknowledged across nation states and regions for centuries, there is no consensus regarding the role of cultural differences in global business. Do cultural constraints really matter if people operating in a global arena are able to overcome them? When dealing with this question, most people fall into one of two groups: believers and non-believers. Believers argue that, on the basis of available research evidence and practical experience, culture does matter, because what works in London will likely not work in Guangzhou, Bangalore, or Moscow. They point out that people who have worked abroad are well aware how different things can be in places around the world, and that much of this difference can be explained only by cultural characteristics. Non-believers, in turn, argue that people are different in general, and that no two Indians (or Chinese, or Russians, or Saudis) behave in exactly the same way. They argue further that organizations in one country can – and often must – operate very differently from those in another country. Finally, they argue that, from the standpoint of research, the variance explained by culture is often small, and numerous other factors may be equally (or perhaps more) important in explaining behavioral differences across borders, including legal, political, and economic differences and available technologies.

Which of these positions is a more accurate reflection of reality, and what are the implications for global managers? While both research and practical experience suggest that culture does matter, research and practical experience also suggest that culture alone is insufficient to explain the behavior of our foreign counterparts.[30] Otherwise, how can we explain the success of Taher in a male-dominated culture?

For this reason, we must be cautious in our interpretation of cultural phenomena. Strong preconceptions about the role (or lack thereof) of culture may blind us to the ways in which culture often does matter. Understanding the role of culture in management practice requires a way of thinking about culture that will help to identify cultural influences, and inform the best course of action to deal with them. In other words, we need to understand what culture is and what it does, how our own culture has influenced our way of thinking in terms of working assumptions and personal and group biases, and how to acquire a sufficient understanding of how culture works to be able to tease out culture influences on various situations in which we find ourselves. This is no easy task, clearly, but it may nonetheless be an important one for global managers.

Our two examples – Sweden's Håkansson and Bahrain's Tahler – highlight some important limitations of applying simplistic models to complex phenomena. On the one hand, such models provide a good starting point for understanding the influence of culture and the challenges posed by cultural differences. On the other hand, they focus our attention onto a limited set of parameters and may mislead our interpretation of reality. Instead, understanding culture influences on behavior requires us to seek out underlying complexities and contradictions, which, ultimately, aid us in our ability to act successfully in or across very different environments. We suggest five cultural complexities and contradictions that can be found in varying degrees in most cultures (see Exhibit 3.8):

(1) *Cultures are stable, but change over time.* One of the dangers in any attempt to categorize cultures into a set of fixed dimensions is that this implies that cultures are stable and remain unchanged. Although some aspects of culture are indeed stable and persistent, others evolve and change over time, however. In other words, at the same time that groups of people strive to remain faithful to what and who they are, they simultaneously accommodate change and evolve when necessary or desirable. The implication for managers is that the cultures they must work with – including their own – are in a constant state of flux. As they come in contact with other cultures (perhaps through global organization networks), they face new problems, apply their cultural frames in different ways, negotiate new behaviors, and change important aspects of their culture, leading to behaviors that may seem contradictory. Moreover, these changes take place within a cultural context, and the outcomes may be different from those originally anticipated. Take, for example, the implementation of performance-based rewards. In many Western countries merit pay and bonuses are based largely on individual performance, while in

Exhibit 3.8 Cultural complexities and contradictions

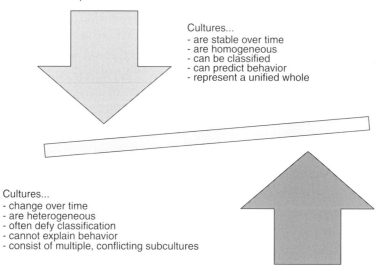

Cultures...
- are stable over time
- are homogeneous
- can be classified
- can predict behavior
- represent a unified whole

Cultures...
- change over time
- are heterogeneous
- often defy classification
- cannot explain behavior
- consist of multiple, conflicting subcultures

many Asian countries they are often distributed equally to an entire group or department. It is largely a matter of equity as opposed to equality.

(2) *Cultures are homogeneous, but allow for individuality.* A second problem in trying to categorize culture is that it implies a degree of homogeneity. When describing individual cultures (whether through simplified dimensions or deep descriptive analysis), we focus on shared aspects that are frequently found across the cultural group. Since cultures are shared, culture, by definition, includes what is common among members of a group. Members of a cultural group invest considerable time and effort in tying together the various strands that collectively represent and define social behavior. Cultures are also fragmented, however, in the sense that they often allow for internal variations – individuality – and even significant discrepancies in their midst. Despite people's tendency to stereotype, logic and personal experience suggest that variations – sometimes significant – can be found in all cultures. For example, while people often describe Australia as a highly individualistic culture and China as a highly collectivistic culture, there are, in fact, many collectivistic Australians and many individualistic Chinese. In fact, many cultures overlap considerably with those of their neighbors, having more in common than not. These differences – and similarities – must be clearly recognized when trying to make comparisons across cultures or nations. Although people often generalize about various cultures in order to facilitate a basic

understanding of cultural trends, it would be highly inaccurate to conclude that all members of a particular culture behave in the same way. Consider Commercial International Bank's Sahar El-Sallab's observation above that, "if you have the proper education, credibility, and integrity in the way you handle your job, intelligent men will always give you your due."[31] In other words, within a cultural context there are ways – perhaps transparent only to people within that culture – in which cultural constraints can be overcome. Only by understanding the cultural context in which behaviors occur can outsiders understand the behaviors that will be considered proper or acceptable across nation states and those that are likely to be very different in Cairo, London, and New York. In other words, we may find fragmentation of behaviors within cultures, but even these behaviors are imbued with cultural meaning.

(3) *Cultures are often classified into general categories that overlook subtle but important differences.* Descriptions of culture using a limited set of dimensions may lead to the impression that this limited set of adjectives can capture the essence of culture. Experience and observation tell us that culture is more complex and paradoxical, however, with many exceptions and qualifications to any general classification.[32] All cultures contain defining elements that defy universal qualifications. Examples include the Latino notion of *orgullo*, or pride for the accomplishments of their people; the Brazilian *jeitinho*, or flexible adaptability; and the Japanese concept of *kao*, or face (*kao o tateru* for saving face). These unique aspects of culture are enmeshed in, and derived from, unique historical experiences and responses and are not fully captured by general categories and descriptions, which fail to acknowledge the intricacies of the meaning underlying the concepts. Intelligent managers will avoid simple solutions and look for the nuances underlying categorizations, not just the rhetoric.

(4) *Cultures can explain, but not predict, behavior.* We have noted above that the use of several core cultural dimensions to describe a particular culture can be a useful way to begin the study of that culture. If this is not done with care or caution, however, this over-reliance on the use of cultural dimensions can lead to an exaggerated assumption of causality or determinism. It is easy to make connections between general cultural characteristics and actions, such as "People from collectivistic cultures prefer working in teams," or "Hierarchical cultures prefer authoritarian leaders." These types of conclusions are problematic, however, for several reasons. To begin with, as discussed above, fragmentation can result from the acceptance of cultural values within cultures. Second, cultures are composed of idiosyncratic

elements that can be combined in unique ways, leading to unpredictable consequences. Third, culture both constrains and enables behavior. Culture provides frameworks for making sense of the world around us, for learning and expanding our horizons. These frameworks are important for interpreting phenomena around us, communicating with others, and organizing social and psychological processes.[33] These cultural frameworks often limit the array of alternatives considered by members, however. Simply put, culture is an important source of biases in the way we interpret the world and choose to act. Understanding these biases may help us explain why people in different places make different decisions. This may help explain, for example, why women in the Arab world are less active in the workplace than Western women. Cultural biases may be overcome by individual effort, however, such as the examples of Taher and other Arab women who have been able to succeed in a male-dominated environment.[34]

(5) *Cultures represent a unified whole, but also consist of multiple and often conflicting subcultures.* Finally, as noted earlier, a key characteristic of culture is that it is learned. People acquire values, assumptions, and behaviors by seeing how others around them behave and by observing their families. Herein lies a major source for overgeneralizations and stereotypes about national cultures, however. This is because most people within one culture belong to multiple, and often conflicting, subcultures. Subcultures can include levels of education (intellectual culture), professions or specializations (professional culture), normative beliefs about right and wrong and organized religion (religious culture), places of work (organizational culture), geographic locations within a country (regional culture), and so forth. What this means is that people can also acquire additional cultural tools from the various subcultures to which they belong. Culture is a collective, socially constructed phenomenon that exists or emerges whenever a set of basic assumptions or beliefs is commonly held by a group of people.[35] Thus, multiple subcultures coexist within organizations, industries, and nations.[36] Cultural makeup is thus layered and influenced by varied group memberships. These subcultures may be overlapping, superimposed, or nested, and they may interact with each other. These multiple layers of culture shape individuals' attention, interpretations, and actions, and the cultural layer that is salient can vary over time.[37] As such, at a single point in time, people simultaneously belong to one culture and many cultures, making the study of cultural differences even more problematic.

Culture and institutional environments

At the height of the 2011 global economic crisis, Bank of America announced it would cut 30,000 jobs over three years in a bid to save $5 billion per year. The cost-cutting drive was part of a broader effort to reshape and shrink the bank as it coped with fallout from years of poor investments and what many considered to be poor management decisions. Shortly after the announcement, Bank of America's stock price increased significantly.[38] In difficult economic times, when demand declines for services or production, companies around the world face the same challenge: what to do with excess employees. While the challenge may be the same, however, corporate responses are not. In much of North America, like the situation at Bank of America, reduced demand for services often leads logically – and culturally consistently – to employee layoffs. Although widely recognized as causing hardship to people, layoffs are often deemed to be a prudent business and management response to a financial crisis.

In Germany or the Netherlands, however, long-standing social legislation makes it much more difficult – and more costly – to downsize employees. As a result, Dutch and German companies will often seek other remedies, such as seeking early retirements or job sharing. Finally, in Japan, layoffs are rare (although they still occur), since organizations risk losing their public reputation, which can affect their business and future hiring opportunities. Layoffs violate fundamental Japanese social norms regarding paternalism in the workplace. As a result, Japanese companies will frequently decide to transfer redundant employees to other parts of the organization or its subsidiaries, even if they too are overstaffed. Same problem, but very different responses – and it is all part of the institutional environment facing managers.

Culture and institutional environments go hand in hand. Indeed, they are frequently mutually reinforcing. The *institutional environment* generally consists of the legal-political environment, which either encourages or discourages companies from pursuing certain strategies that governments or society at large either support or oppose (see Exhibit 3.9). Governments obviously have considerable power to control organizations through the passage of laws and policies, technology transfers to favored companies, financial support, legal strictures on investment policies, import-export policies and constraints, and so forth. This arena is sometimes referred to as business–government relations, and a major debate in international business is the extent to which business and government should have an adversarial relationship or a cooperative one.

Exhibit 3.9 Institutional environment

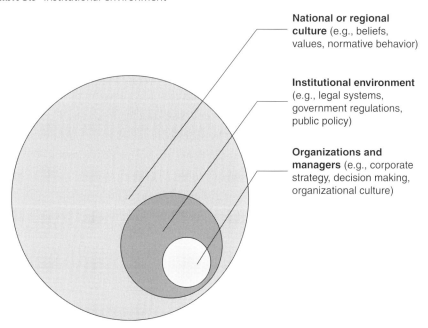

National or regional culture (e.g., beliefs, values, normative behavior)

Institutional environment (e.g., legal systems, government regulations, public policy)

Organizations and managers (e.g., corporate strategy, decision making, organizational culture)

Nowhere is this difference more notable than when comparing the institutional environments and business–government relationships between Japan and the United States. If there is a principal difference in the business strategies of Japanese and US firms, it is Japan's preoccupation with gaining market share, as opposed to the US preoccupation with achieving short-term net profits or higher stock prices. This fundamental difference results from several differences in the two business environments, which allow many Japanese firms to take a longer-term perspective than their US competitors.

First, consider the institutional environment in which most US firms operate. This environment is characterized by the following: distant and often adversarial business–government relations are common, including having the government as the principal regulator. The principal purpose of the company is to maximize stockholder wealth. Investors stress short-term transactions and returns on investment. A clear link exists between earnings per share and stock price. Managers are frequently offered stock options and large bonuses for superior performance. Finally, undervalued companies are frequently subject to hostile takeovers.

Now consider the very different institutional environment found in Japan. In contrast to much of the West, Japan's institutional environment is characterized by a strong and ongoing cooperative business–government relationship that permeates the core business environment, including government targeting of strategic industries and support for local industries. The principal purpose of a company is to build value over the long term to benefit investors, employees, and the nation. Investors stress long-term stock appreciation instead of earnings per share. Dividends are paid at a constant rate as a percentage of the par value of the stock, not as a percentage of profits. Managers are seldom offered stock options or large bonuses for superior performance. Few outside board members are present to defend stockholder interests. Finally, undervalued companies are typically protected by sister companies from outside takeovers.

As a result of these differences, Japanese firms are better positioned to focus their attention on attaining strategic objectives (such as beating competitors) instead of financial objectives (such as keeping stockholders happy). This competitive advantage occurs for three principal reasons. First, low profits and high retained earnings support growth. Second, close relationships with banks allow the use of high levels of debt to support growth. Finally, Japanese stockholders routinely accept low dividends and management's absolute control of the firm.

Application 3.5   Islamic legal systems

Columbia University anthropologist Lawrence Rosen has written extensively on the differences between Western and Islamic countries with respect to the functioning of the legal system.[39] According to Rosen, property in the West is viewed, for legal purposes, in terms of ownership ("Who owns this land?"); this is an objectivist approach. By contrast, under Islam, property is viewed in terms of its relationships to others ("Who is associated with this land?"); this is a subjectivist approach. Because the idea of a divisible self is unimaginable in Islam, power is both institutional and personal, with the implication that judges (and managers, we may add) are expected to rule without consciously trying to exclude their personal feelings and attitudes. Judges, then, will open widely the bounds of relevance to ascertain the ties of indebtedness of the various parties to a dispute, often getting people back to negotiate their own agreements with their kin rather than enunciating particular rights. Judges will assess witness reliability according to the nature and intensity of the witnesses' social ties rather than primarily relying on their objective expertise, and they will ascertain facts according more to their evaluation of the person and his or her past history than by observable circumstances. Rosen also stresses that, because of their greater effect on their networks of relationships, educated and wealthier people are also held to higher legal standards in Islamic cultures. For managers, the ethical landscape looks very much the same. Business contracts make heavy use of both personal contacts and networks and are largely transitory when conditions change in more particularistic cultures than in universalistic ones.

Think about it. . .

(1) How is the Islamic legal system different from the prevailing legal codes in the West?

(2) What is the impact of these differences on individual and group behavior?

(3) How can these differences impact non-Islamic businesspeople doing business in the Middle East?

(4) What might "foreigners" do to deal with these legal differences in ways that no one is offended?

MANAGER'S NOTEBOOK
The cultural environment

We have now come full circle, from looking for general dimensions with which to compare cultures to understanding that cultures are indeed complex and at times contradictory. Cultures are not easily pigeonholed into groups and categories. As Hall notes, "Culture hides much more than it reveals, and strangely enough what it hides, it hides most effectively from its own participants."[40] Caution is certainly in order.

Added to this is an understanding of the important role that culture and context play in influencing managerial action. These complexities and contradictions raise the intriguing question of how managers should act or react when they find themselves in the middle of cultural tension or change. A major challenge here is that different cultures often require very different behaviors from their managers, and what is acceptable in one country may be offensive in another. This is not surprising, but it nevertheless presents real challenges for managers when interacting with – and sometimes managing – a global workforce (see Chapter 9). How should managers behave, and will they be accepted when they are charged with accomplishing corporate objectives in a foreign culture? Should managers be themselves or try to adapt their management style to fit local customs and expectations? Fundamentally, how can they survive and succeed when they don't understand the rules of the game, and the rules that they do understand are often changing or do not apply to the specific individuals or contexts they are dealing with?

To aid in this understanding, we can summarize several interrelated coping strategies that may help managers as they try and make sense out of the "strange" behaviors of others (see Exhibit 3.10). More specifically, we discuss three management strategies: avoiding cultural stereotyping, seeing cultures in neutral terms, and preparing for the unexpected.

1 Avoid cultural stereotyping

To this end, understanding the influence of culture on management practices is an important first step. Managers who are able to understand the ways that culture can influence behavior and have knowledge of how cultures differ are better able to identify cultural phenomena and identify solutions to deal with them. In this regard, the role of *cultural stereotypes* is clearly relevant.

McGill professor Nancy Adler offers some sound advice on how to avoid making overgeneralizations or cultural stereotypes about the people from any culture.[41]

- Cultural descriptions, by their very nature, contain limited information. Keep in mind that such generalizations often mask other useful information about cultural diversity.

Exhibit 3.10 Action plans for working across cultures

(1) Avoid cultural stereotyping	(2) View cultural differences in neutral terms	(3) Prepare for the unexpected by enhancing your cognitive skills
• Cultural descriptions contain only limited in formation. • Be as objective as possible in describing cultures; avoid evaluations. • Focus on accurate descriptions of beliefs, values, and norms. • Cultural descriptions should be considered a first guess and a trigger to further exploration. • Cultural descriptions can change over time.	• Cultures are neither good nor bad; they are just different – and can have different behavioral implications. • Remember that most cultures are complex, and contradictions can often be found in attitudes and behaviors. • Use your expanded cultural knowledge to view situations through the eyes of others. • Look for subtleties and nuances in interpersonal interactions that explain what others are thinking.	• Self-awareness. • Empathy. • Information gathering and analysis. • Information integration and transformation. • Behavioral flexibility. • Mindfulness.

- Cultural descriptions should be limited to describing members of various groups as objectively as possible and should not include an evaluative component (e.g., "This is good," "That is bad").
- Cultural descriptions should provide an accurate description of the beliefs, values, and social norms of a group.
- Cultural descriptions should be considered a first best guess about the behaviors of a cultural group prior to developing more specific information about individual members of the group.
- Cultural descriptions should be modified over time, on the basis of new information gained through observation or experience.

When describing cultures and identifying cultural differences between two or more groups, some caution may be in order, for at least two reasons. First, while common sense would suggest that bigger cultural differences are harder to deal with than smaller ones, experience suggests that this is not always the case. In some situations, managers moving between countries perceived as culturally similar (e.g., the Netherlands and Belgium) find that "small" differences are just as hard to deal with as big ones. Worse, these small differences are frequently overlooked and not dealt with until some damage is done. Second, what may initially seem like a large cultural difference may be overcome by some smaller similarities. For instance, in a recent joint venture between a Brazilian company and a Chinese one (companies from two very different cultures), members found sources of similarity that facilitated the relationship, such as the similar levels of development and the importance of context and relationships in partnerships. In the words of one Brazilian managing director, "The Chinese are the Brazilians of Asia."[42]

2   View cultural differences in neutral terms

In addition, cultural differences are not a bad thing in the managerial world; they just require a bit more work at times. In many cases, depending on the task at hand, a degree of cultural difference is often seen as leading to improved managerial decision making and action. For example, a recent study found that Portuguese managers perceived business activities with Brazilians and Spaniards (with whom they are cultur-ally more similar) to be riskier and more difficult than business activities with Scandinavians (culturally very different). It is worth noting, however, that the same managers also felt more "at home" and preferred to socialize and make friends with Brazilians and Spaniards.[43]

What this suggests is that cultural differences are not inherently good or bad, but they can be perceived positively or negatively depending on the situation. Additionally, sometimes differences are not perceived the same way by the two parties. A manager from Portugal may appreciate Danish punctuality, while the Danish manager may find Portuguese tardiness annoying. On the other hand, the Danish manager may appreciate Portuguese flexibility (particularistic or low rule orientation), while the Portuguese manager may find the Danish obsession with rules frustrating.

Most importantly, it is difficult to predict how these identifiable differences will play out when two cultures meet. As a starting point, cultural frameworks create limitations on our ability to think and perceive the environment, suggesting that individuals from different cultures will have different understandings of the situation, and will probably act differently. As individuals interact with each other and the new environment around them, however, new understandings may emerge and new behaviors may be called for. It would be naïve to think that, in a cross-cultural situation, individuals will continue behaving in the same way they would at home for a long period of time. Over time, either they will negotiate a new way to relate or the relationship will not continue. Unfortunately, it is impossible to predict what will work for a particular context and relationship, since several other factors besides culture come into play. For example, who has power? Who are the majority? Who has the money? What is the personality of the ones in power? What is the goal of the relationship? Are there historical issues as well between both cultural groups that may lead to predispositions, or perceptions of superiority, inferiority, or sameness? Referring to the Chinese–Brazilian partnership above, a Chinese manager noted, "My opinion is that working with Brazilians is easier than working with North Americans, with French, or even with people from Singapore. It's amazing, because people from Singapore have the same cultural roots that we have. But, with Brazilians, it's easier because we treat each other as being on the same level. This may be more important than having the same cultural roots or speaking the same language."[44]

Simply put, when two or more cultures come into contact, the starting point for interaction is usually what these cultures bring to the table. The end result, though, will more likely depend on their interactions, the actors and organizations involved, the power differential, and the exchanges that take place. Management researchers Oded Shenkar, Yadong Luo, and Orly Yeheskel, coming from three very different cultures themselves, call this process *cultural friction*, in reference to the resistances and conflicts that need to be dealt with as two cultures come into contact, including issues of organizational identities, national identities, differences in resources and interests, and asymmetry in power and hierarchy.[45] These issues are dealt with and negotiated in a process of response and counter-response that will shape the relationship between the parties.

3   Prepare for the unexpected

Finally, when facing the complexities of cultural influences and the unpredictability of cultural encounters, an obvious question arises: what can global managers do? An often overlooked response to this difficult question rests on the speed with which managers can learn and adjust their behavior to fit each unique situation. Here, we do not mean adjusting the behavior to fit the other culture; we mean adjusting the behavior to fit the situation. Sometimes, what is in order is adjusting to the other culture as closely as possible. At other times, though, this behavior would be counterproductive (e.g., perhaps we really should avoid considering Nahed Taher as a traditional Arab woman). Knowing the difference is what separates successful global managers from the rest.

To this end, several important learning skills can be suggested for global managers.

- *Self-awareness*. Global managers need to understand that they are complex cultural beings and that their values, beliefs, assumptions, and communication preferences are a product of their cultural heritage (see Chapter 5).
- *Empathy*. Global managers must understand that others are also complex cultural beings, whose actions are a product of deep-seated cultural values and beliefs. When misunderstandings occur, competent global managers will search for cultural explanations of confusing or offensive behavior, before judging it (see Chapters 9).
- *Information gathering and analysis*. Managers have to uncover hidden cultural assumptions to become aware of how culture is shaping the perceptions, expectations, and behaviors of all involved parties (see Chapters 5).
- *Information integration and transformation*. Managers must assimilate the information gathered into a coherent theory of action (see Chapter 6).
- *Behavioral flexibility*. Managers need the ability to engage in different behaviors, to switch styles, and to accomplish tasks in more than one way (see Chapter 9).
- *Mindfulness*. Global managers must be mindful of themselves, the other, and the interaction. They must pay close attention to their feelings and actions, and others' actions and reactions (see Chapters 5).

In summary, managers must be keenly aware of their biases (and the biases of others) in their ways of looking at the world. This is not easy, because it requires a continual effort to move from our own perspective to the perspectives of others – or, at least, to try to do so. Understanding others requires and allows us to de-center our points of view, thereby expanding our personal worldviews. French philosopher Gilles Deleuze has referred to this concept as "being another thought in my thoughts, another possession in my possessions."[46] Throughout the remainder of the book, we discuss in detail several ways in which culture matters, highlighting how culture leads to different perspectives and understandings, and drawing out their implications for management practice. It is our hope that these discussions will help managers identify their own biases in management understanding and facilitate the recognition of potential cultural problems on the ground.

Summary points

- From a managerial standpoint, culture is perhaps best thought of as addressing three questions: who are we, how do we live, and how do we approach work? These questions focus attention on individuals, environments, and work norms and values. The answers to the questions allow us to draw some conclusions about work and society, as well as how managers in general should behave as they work across cultures.
- Culture often sets the limits on what is considered acceptable and unacceptable behavior. It pressures individuals and groups into accepting and following normative behavior. In other words, culture determines the rules of the road that guide what people can do. Rightly or wrongly, these barriers are typically established to ensure uniform practice among members of a society, and, as a result, societies often take a dim view of people who ignore or fight the system.
- Five core cultural dimensions are put forward to provide a broad-based portrait of how management and business practices in one culture differ from those in another: hierarchical and egalitarian, individualistic and collectivistic, mastery-oriented and harmony-oriented, monochronic and polychronic, and rule-based and relationship-based (also called universalism/particularism).
- While it is sometimes useful to focus on central tendencies between cultures for purposes of general comparisons (e.g., using the core cultural dimensions), these are only a general starting point. The role of individual and regional differences in determining attitudes and behaviors should not be overlooked.

The related concepts of culture and cultural differences were introduced as a means of seeing beyond overt behaviors and better understanding why and how some people act differently from others. What is often missed in these generalizations, however, is the fact that individuals within the same society may use different strategies to deal with identical challenges. As a result, it is generally unwise to stereotype an entire culture. Instead, managers need to look for nuances and counter-trends, not just the principal trends themselves.

Notes

1 The Talmud is a record of rabbinical discussions pertaining to Jewish law, ethics, customs, and history. Two versions exist from the two ancient centers of Jewish scholarship, Palestine and Babylonia. Correspondingly, two bodies of analysis developed, and two works of the Talmud were created. The older compilation is called the Jerusalem Talmud (Talmud Yerushalmi) and was compiled sometime during the fourth century BCE in the land of Israel. The Babylonian Talmud (Talmud Bavli) was compiled around the year 500 CE, although it continued to be edited over time. The word "Talmud," when used without qualification, usually refers to the Babylonian Talmud.

2 Robert J. House, "Introduction," in Robert J. House, Paul J. Hanges, Mansour Javidan, Peter W. Dorfman, and Vipin Gupta, *Culture, Leadership, and Organizations: The GLOBE Study of 62 Societies*. Thousand Oaks, CA: Sage, 2004, pp. 1–2, p. 1.

3 Wang Yinglin, *Trimetric Classic* (trans. Herbert Giles). Shanghai: Kelly & Walsh, 1910. The *Three Character Classic*, *Trimetric Classic*, or *San Zi Ji* is one of the classic Chinese texts. It was probably written in the thirteenth century and attributed to Wang Yinglin (1223–1296) during the Song Dynasty, but has also been attributed to Ou Shizi (1234–1324). Some writers have attributed the original wisdom collected in this volume to Confucius, although there is no conclusive evidence on this.

4 Lao-Tzu, or Laozi, was a philosopher of ancient China and is a central figure in Taoism. Laozi literally means "Old Master" and is generally considered an honorific. Laozi is revered as a god in religious forms of Taoism. Taishang Laojun is a title for Laozi in the Taoist religion, which refers to him as "One of the Three Pure Ones."

5 Elizabeth MacDonald and Megha Bahree, "Muslim women in charge," *Forbes*, July 30, 2008.

6 Faiza Saleh Ambah, "Saudi women rise in defense of the veil," *Washington Post*, June 1, 2006, p. A12.

7 *Shura* is Arabic for "consultation." It is believed to be the method by which pre-Islamic Arabian tribes selected leaders and made major decisions. *Shura* is mentioned twice in the Qur'an as a praiseworthy activity, and is a word often used in the name of parliaments in Muslim-majority countries.

8 *Ijma`* is an Arabic term referring ideally to the consensus of the *ummah*, the community of Muslims or followers of Islam.

9 The Qur'an, literally "the Recitation" in Arabic and sometimes transliterated as Quran, Qur'ān, Koran, Alcoran, or Al-Qur'ān`, is the central religious text of Islam. Muslims believe the Qur'an to be the book of divine guidance and direction for mankind, and consider the original Arabic text to be the final revelation of God. *Sunnah* literally means "trodden path," and therefore the *sunnah* of the prophet means "the way and the manners of the prophet." The

word in Sunni Islam means those religious achievements that were instituted by the Islamic prophet Muhammad during the twenty-three years of his ministry and that Muslims initially obtained through the consensus of companions of Muhammad, and further through generation-to-generation transmission.

10 Geert Hofstede, *Culture's Consequences: International Differences in Work-Related Values*. Thousand Oaks, CA: Sage, 2001.

11 Hofstede, *Culture's Consequences*.

12 Clyde Kluckhohn, "Culture and behavior," in Gardner Lindzey (ed.), *Handbook of Social Psychology*. New York: McGraw-Hill, 1951, pp. 921–76.

13 House *et al.*, *Culture, Leadership, and Organizations*.

14 Fons Trompenaars, *Riding the Waves of Culture: Understanding Cultural Diversity in Global Business*. London: McGraw-Hill, 1993.

15 Ann Swidler, "Culture in action: symbols and strategies," *American Sociological Review*, 1986, 51(2), pp. 273–86.

16 Clifford Geertz, *The Interpretation of Cultures*. New York: Basic Books, 1973.

17 Alice Dembner, "Fears of aging vary by nation," *Register-Guard*, November 6, 2007, p. A12.

18 Even situational approaches to ethics (of the type "When in Rome, behave as the Romans do") are not situational in the sense of mandating the applicability or non-applicability of their provisos depending on whether one is in Rome or Romania, and they issue their "When in Rome" command both from Rome and Romania, universally.

19 Richard D. Lewis, *When Cultures Collide*. London: Nicholas Brealey Publishing, 1999, p. 8.

20 Peter Ustinov, quoted in Richard D. Hill, *EuroManagers*, Brussels: Europublications, 1998, p. 230.

21 Edward T. Hall, *An Anthropology of Everyday Life: An Autobiography*. New York: Anchor Books, 1992, p. 210.

22 See Luciara Nardon and Richard M. Steers, "The culture theory jungle: divergence and convergence in models of national culture," in Rabi S. Bhagat and Richard M. Steers (eds.), *Cambridge Handbook of Culture, Organizations, and Work*. Cambridge University Press, 2009, pp. 3–22.

23 Nardon and Steers, "The culture theory jungle."

24 Steve Stecklow, "Helsinki on wheels: fast Finns find fines fit their finances," *Wall Street Journal*, January 2, 2001, p. A1; "Rich Finn gets hefty fine for speeding," *Register-Guard*, February 11, 2004, p. A3.

25 Simcha Ronan and Oded Shenkar, "Clustering cultures on attitudinal dimensions: a review and synthesis," *Academy of Management Review*, 1985, **10**(3), pp. 435–54.

26 House *et al.*, *Culture, Leadership, and Organizations*.

27 Based on the country clusters, and using multiple measures and multiple methods to the extent possible, we assessed and then integrated a combination of quantitative and qualitative measures from available research in order to categorize cultures along the five dimensions. First, existing quantitative measures from such researchers as Hofstede, Trompenaars, and House and his GLOBE associates were examined and compared. Next, ethnographic data compiled largely from cultural anthropology focusing on specific cultures

or geographic regions were incorporated into the analysis and compared against the quantitative findings. Finally, remaining points of disagreement were discussed between the co-authors and other researchers in an effort to reach a consensus on the final ratings. Although it is not claimed that this procedure eliminated all errors, it is felt that it represents a superior method to the previous reliance on single-source data. All the same, room for error persists, particularly because of the potential rater bias of the authors, and readers are cautioned to use their own judgment in interpreting results. In making our assessments, we chose to develop a more conservative ordinal rating scale, clustering cultures into four categories (e.g., strongly individualistic, moderately individualistic, moderately collectivistic, and strongly collectivistic) on the basis of the relative strength of the various dimensions compared to other cultures, instead of attempting to calculate specific numeric (or cardinal) ratings that may appear to be more precise than they actually are.

28 Personal communication from Daria Snezko, 2004.

29 MacDonald and Bahree, "Muslim women in charge."

30 Kwok Leung, Rabi Bhagat, Nancy Buchan, Miriam Erez, and Cristina B. Gibson, "Culture and international business: recent advances and their implications for future research," *Journal of International Business Studies*, 2005, **36**(4), pp. 357–78.

31 MacDonald and Bahree, "Muslim women in charge."

32 Alan Bird and Joyce S. Osland, "Teaching cultural sense-making", in Nakiye Boyacigiller, Richard Goodman, and Margaret Phillips (eds.), *Crossing Cultures: Insights from Master Teachers*. London: Routledge, 2003, pp. 89–100.

33 Seyla Benhabib, *The Claims of Culture: Equality and Diversity in the Global Era*. Princeton University Press, 2002, p. 15.

34 Luciara Nardon and Richard M. Steers, "The new global manager: learning cultures on the fly," *Organizational Dynamics*, 2008, **37**(1), pp. 47–59.

35 Edgar Schein, *Organizational Culture and Leadership*. San Francisco: Jossey-Bass, 2004.

36 Sonja Sackmann and Margaret E. Phillips, "Contextual influences on culture research," *International Journal of Cross Cultural Management*, 2004, **4**(3), pp. 370–90.

37 Susan Schneider and Jean-Louis Barsoux, *Managing Across Cultures*. London: Financial Times/Prentice Hall, 2003.

38 Huffington Post, "Bank of America to cut 30,000 jobs as part of restructuring plan," *Huffington Post*, December 14, 2011, p. 1.

39 Lawrence Rosen, *Law as Culture: An Invitation*. Princeton University Press, 2006, pp. 98–100.

40 Edward T. Hall, *The Silent Language*. New York: Anchor Books, 1990, p. 29.

41 Nancy J. Adler, *International Dimensions of Organizational Behavior*, 5th edn. Mason, OH: Thompson, 2008.

42 Guilherme Azevedo, "Brazilian management in China and a theory of the formation of hybrid organizational cultures," paper presented at the European Group of Organizations Studies (EGOS) conference, Amsterdam, July 12, 2008.

43 Susana Costa e Silva and Luciara Nardon, "An exploratory study of cultural differences and perceptions of relational risk," paper presented at the European International Business Academy conference, Catania, Italy, December 15, 2007.

44 Azevedo, "Brazilian management in China."

45 Oded Shenkar, Yadong Luo, and Orly Yeheskel, "From distance to friction: substituting metaphors and redirecting intercultural research," *Academy of Management Review*, 2008, **33** (4), pp. 905–22.

46 Martín Hopenhayn, "La aldea global entre la utopía transcultural y el ratio mercantil: paradojas de la globalización cultural," in Ramón Pajuelo and Pablo Sandoval, *Globalización y Diversidad Cultural: Una Mirada desde America Latina*. Lima: Instituto de Estudios Peruanos, pp. 423–4.

CHAPTER 4

The organizational environment

MANAGEMENT CHALLENGE

As discussed in the previous chapter, the external environment exerts a variety of pressures on organizations and their managers. Chapter 3 explored the cultural environment. In this chapter, we examine a second major area in which global awareness and understanding are critical for managers: the organizational environment. Organizations come in many shapes, sizes, and forms. Nothing is simple. Some organizations adapt, some resist, and many find their own creative solutions for dealing with local pressures. Managers need to understand the type of organizations they are working with, the types of solutions they have found to deal with their environments, and the implications of these solutions for managers. In other words, organizations themselves put pressures on managers by defining what is expected or required. Some of the more common challenges managers face with regard to the organization concern the organization's global strategy, organization design, control and decision-making processes, and organizational culture. These topics are discussed in this chapter, along with the implications for the managers, who are often caught in the middle.

Chapter outline

Applications

There are no universal solutions to organizational and management problems.
Organizations are symbolic entities; they function according to implicit models in the
minds of their members, and these are culturally determined.

Geert Hofstede[1]
Maastricht University, the Netherlands

Globalization does not mean imposing homogeneous solutions in a pluralistic world. It
means having a global vision and strategy, but it also means cultivating roots
and individual identities.

Gucharan Das[2]
Former chairman, Procter & Gamble (P&G), India

Many years ago (in the late 1930s, to be precise) Chester Barnard, then CEO of what would become telecom giant AT&T, wrote the first authoritative book on the executive role. His book, *Functions of the Executive*, went on to become a classic management reference that is still widely read and applied today.[3] Barnard defined an *organization* as a system of consciously coordinated activities of two or more persons aiming to achieve common objectives. He argued that organizations prosper or fail in line with the extent to which they – and their managers – are successful in achieving both effectiveness and efficiency in the common pursuit of these goals. In the intervening decades, in our view, no one has come up with a better definition. Organizations are not just about how to put people into boxes – or cubicles. Instead, they serve as a principal command and control system for focusing human, financial, and physical resources on the accomplishment of valued tasks. Organization designs live or die on the basis of their ability to assist managers with their responsibilities.

While Barnard was thinking about US firms in the 1930s, with a fairly narrow business focus, his observations still apply today when considering firms, large and small, doing business around the world. What has changed is not the fundamental challenges facing companies and their managers but, rather, the magnitude of these challenges, as well as the manner in which firms organize, coordinate, and control their talents to accomplish their core mission. Organizations vary in how embedded they are in their environments. For example, a domestic organization that has all its assets in one country likely faces more pressures to comply with local norms and beliefs than an organization that has, say, 5 percent of its assets in the country. Likewise, the pressures facing headquarters are often different from the pressures facing subsidiaries. Thus, for managers, knowing where they are in the organization and its environment is a critical success factor.

To succeed in any of these jobs, it seems imperative that managers would need to understand as much as possible about the *organizational environment* in which they work (see Exhibit 4.1). In particular, four important *organization-specific questions* arise.

(1) Global strategy usually comes from the top. As managers in the field, what do we need to understand about strategy that will help us perform our own jobs better?

(2) How can an understanding of differences in organizational design and management practices help us do business more effectively in foreign environments?

(3) How are decisions made in various organizations, and how can we use this information to reach suitable bilateral agreements more smoothly?

(4) How can we understand local organizational cultures and the role they play in building mutually beneficial partnerships?

These questions are the focus of the present chapter. Specifically, we examine four aspects of organizations as they relate to managerial performance in the field: global

Exhibit 4.1 The organizational environment

Exhibit 4.2 Context of organizational environments

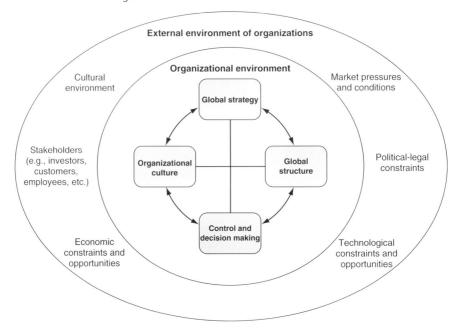

strategy, organizational structure, organizational decision making, and organizational culture. Throughout, the role of stakeholders, market pressures, and economic constraints in helping shape the organizational environment will become evident (see Exhibit 4.2).

Global strategy and structure

One of the best ways to learn about good strategic decisions is to look at bad ones. In 2007 Apple offered Vodafone a deal to become the exclusive British operator of the iPhone. Vodafone's then CEO was of the opinion, however, that the iPhone would be so costly that it would never take off. With little discussion, the board dismissed the proposal. Today, the iPhone is a major player in the British cellphone market, but it is sold through Madrid-based Telefónica, which saw the opportunity and seized upon it. Subsequently, Vodafone has worked to be a leader in Android technology in Europe, but it missed a sizable opportunity as a result of a narrow vision of technology and poor business strategy.[4]

P&G's Gucharan Das was speaking from experience when he observed (above) that globalization requires a diversity of answers, not a one-size-fits-all approach to organization and management. This includes having a global vision and strategy, but it also means tailoring corporate strategies to fit both local conditions and available resources. In this endeavor, the principal stakeholders of an organization (e.g., investors, employees, customers, governments, etc.) play a major role. The message here is simple: different stakeholders, different strategies.

Stakeholders and global strategies

A firm's *global strategy* is its unique solution to manage the challenges that arise by operating across borders. At its heart, these strategies provide conceptual entry into what the principal stakeholders of the firm (e.g., investors, employees, customers) want. It is a statement of investor and market power, as well as government power in some instances (see below). The challenge for company managers and executives is to develop strategies that will receive the support of the major stakeholders, while the challenge for major stakeholders is to discover or develop ways in which they can work together for a common end. None of this is easy, and companies routinely fail as a result of unsuccessful – or confused – strategies.

Strategy making usually begins with questions of mission and goals, and often costs as well. In fact, most companies operating in a global market initially have to deal with two opposing forces.

- *Pressures for cost reduction.* Companies face pressures for cost reduction, as customers want high-quality products at low price. This suggests that firms should manufacture global products that can maximize the company's economies of scale.
- *Pressures for local adaptation.* At the same time, companies face pressures for local adaptation, as customer tastes vary across geographic regions. Customers in Mexico, Canada, and Thailand often prefer very different versions of the same basic product (e.g., smaller cars versus bigger cars).

These two opposing forces lie at the heart of decisions about strategic planning and implementation. Based on this tension, IESE Professor Pankaj Ghemawat[5] suggests three principal global strategies that are available to firms, referred to as the *AAA strategic triangle* (see Exhibit 4.3).

Adaptation strategy

First, firms may choose an *adaptation strategy*, adjusting products to fit various local environments in an attempt to boost revenue and gain market share in the host country.

Exhibit 4.3 AAA strategic triangle

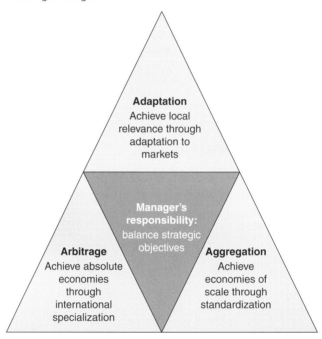

These firms often view themselves as a collection of relatively independent operating subsidiaries, each focusing on a specific local market. Each subsidiary is free to customize its products, marketing campaigns, and operating techniques to meet local needs. Consider Unilever, with $59 billion in global sales.

Application 4.1 Adaptation strategy at Unilever

There used to be one way to sell a product in developing markets, if you bothered to sell there at all: slap on a local label and market to the elite.[6] Unilever changed that. The Anglo-Dutch maker of such brands as Dove, Lipton, and Vaseline built a following among the world's poorest consumers by upending some of the basic rules of marketing. Instead of focusing on value for money, it shrunk packages to set a price even consumers living on $2 a day could afford. It helped people make money to buy its products. "It's not about doing good," but about tapping new markets, says chief executive Patrick Cescau. "Unilever was among the first to prove you can build brands at the bottom of the pyramid," says Martin Roll, head of Singapore branding consultancy Venture Republic. Companies from Nokia to

Application 4.1   (cont.)

Royal Philips Electronics have followed suit. The strategy was forged about twenty-five years ago, when Indian subsidiary Hindustan Lever (HLL) found its products out of reach for millions of Indians. HLL came up with a strategy to lower the price while making a profit: single-use packets for everything from shampoo to laundry detergent, costing pennies a pack. In doing so, it put marquee brands within reach. Unilever continues to woo cash-strapped customers. In India, it has trained rural women to sell products to their neighbors. "What Unilever does well is get inside these communities, understand their needs, and adapt its business model accordingly," says Joan E. Ricart, a professor at IESE Business School in Barcelona. Three years ago the company built a free community laundry in the biggest slum in São Paulo. Named after its Omo detergent brand, the laundry created an oasis of cleanliness that helps explain why Unilever has 70 percent of the Brazil detergent market – despite charging 20 percent more than Procter & Gamble's Ariel brand.

   Think about it. . .

(1)   How did Unilever use an adaptation strategy to capture global markets? Based on what you know, is this the most appropriate strategy for a global brands company?

(2)   Unilever could have remained in the rich markets of east Asia, North America, and western Europe and made considerable income. Why do you think it sought markets in poorer countries where customers often could not afford their products?

(3)   Unilever's CEO has commented that the company's strategy is "not about doing good." In your view, is the company exploiting people in poorer countries or providing a useful service there? Explain.

Aggregation strategy

Second, firms may choose an *aggregation strategy*, focusing on achieving economies of scale by standardizing products or services as much as possible. For example, a Mercedes-Benz is a Mercedes-Benz, and most people want it made in Germany – or at least made somewhere under tight German control – and not in some third world country. Using this strategy, firms try to create standardized products or services that will meet world demand. Another example is the Apple iPad. Designed in the United States and made in China, there is little need to tailor this product to meet various local needs, except for variations in the apps that are available, which are largely privately developed and sold. Manufacturing economies of scale are important here, however, so as to keep prices down and possible competitors out of the market. A third example of this strategy, using premium brands to differentiate one product from others and create demand for a relatively homogeneous product worldwide, is provided by Germany's Playmobil.

Application 4.2   Aggregation strategy at Playmobil

The application of the aggregation strategy can be seen in many German manufacturers. These firms often have a significant competitive disadvantage in the marketplace due to their unusually high-cost structure levels and government regulations. Even so, they are routinely successful. Why? Because they compete on the basis of quality, innovation, and reputation, not price. They make common products that are sold around the world. Take, for example, Playmobil, a maker of educational toys. Playmobil's strategy follows a pattern that can be found in many of Germany's small and medium-sized companies (referred to in German as *Mittelstand* firms). Specifically, because of its high-cost structure, it ignores low-price markets and instead focuses on markets where quality and its product uniqueness can command a high price. Within these markets, it focuses on making superior products using advanced technologies and/or superior craftsmanship. It then competes on the basis of customer satisfaction and repeat business, not short-term profit maximization. To supplement this effort, Playmobil hires and trains the best workers it can find, not the cheapest. It makes extensive use of apprenticeship programs as a competitive weapon. All employees, regardless of their level in the organization, are empowered to an extent seldom seen elsewhere, to help achieve the company's mission. This is largely done through co-determination and employee involvement (see below). Finally, Playmobil prefers to take a long-term perspective on market development and can be patient when necessary. This is largely possible because it has close ties with major German banks, which are relatively patient about getting a return on their investment, unlike in North America, where investors often require a shorter payback period. In short, Playmobil has developed an approach to competing in highly competitive global markets that blends both corporate strategy and organization structure with local prevailing work and social norms. It is a highly successful strategy.

Application 4.2   (cont.)

Think about it. . .

(1) If you could select one factor to explain the success of Playmobil's strategy over the past several years, what would it be?

(2) What are the implications of Playmobil's overall strategy for management and decision-making practices?

(3) Would you expect Playmobil to apply the same strategies and management practices when the company establishes subsidiary plants in other countries (e.g., Brazil, the United States, India)? Explain.

(4) Do you think these companies will continue to be successful in the coming years as price competition increases around the globe? Why?

Arbitrage strategy

A third strategic option for global firms is an *arbitrage strategy*. This is the exploitation of differences between markets by locating different parts of the supply chain in different places. In other words, firms can seek absolute economies of scale through international specialization. For example, an Australian firm may choose to locate its headquarters in Australia, a research and development center in South Korea, and a manufacturing facility in China. As a result, at least in theory, the company gets better and cheaper products to the market and creates a relative competitive advantage over its competitors.

Arbitrage strategies are commonplace in global companies because resources and talent are now spread so widely around the globe. Banks often prefer offshoring call centers to deal with the time-consuming clerical and customer service functions that characterize banking services. Pharmaceutical firms often outsource their basic and applied research to countries that have highly educated people who work for less than the required wages at home. Hospitals often have part of the radiology labs sourced in India or Thailand, where X-rays, for example, can be read quickly and less expensively. Most car companies now use arbitrage when having their design work done in one country, engines and transmissions made in another, electronics made in a third, and final assembly carried out in many countries.

Application 4.3   Arbitrage strategy at Ford

The Ford Fiesta is a global car. It is sourced and assembled in almost two dozen countries and sold in more than half the countries of the world. It is the brand of an

American company, but is not made there. Most of the engineering and design work is done in Germany, Spain, and the United Kingdom. Most of the electronics come from Japan. Assembly plants can be found in such diverse countries as Brazil, China, Germany, India, Mexico, South Africa, Thailand, and the United Kingdom. As a result, a typical Fiesta can have parts from at least a dozen countries.

Think about it. . .

(1) Do examples such as the Ford Fiesta suggest that the old national origin labels (e.g., "Made in USA," "Made in Brazil," etc.) are becoming archaic?

(2) Why does Ford use an arbitrage global strategy for its Fiesta, while Mercedes-Benz uses an aggregation strategy?

(3) What are the principal management challenges of using an arbitrage global strategy? Explain.

At its core, strategic choice is about prioritization. Companies may choose one or more of these strategic options depending on their specific circumstances. Some organizations may choose to focus on one of those strategies, for example by prioritizing adaptation and focusing on individual markets at the expense of economies of scale or the exploitation of differences. Others may be able to combine two – or even three – of the strategies, for example by simultaneously adapting to the local market and looking for opportunities to exploit those differences in ways that may benefit the whole organization. The fundamental issue here is to know what the priorities are and make sure there is a workable fit between the elements.

Global organization designs

For many firms, the choice of an appropriate organization design for conducting global business typically evolves over time as firms increase their involvement in global activities. This evolutionary process often begins with some form of *domestic organization design*, in which international activities are largely an appendage to the more central domestic activities, and evolves over time into a more integrated global organization design that places international business at the center of the organization's strategy. Domestic organization designs are most commonly found when a national firm initially begins to export a product that it has long made for the home market. This endeavor requires some structure to oversee successful implementation, but, because the venture is new and may not be successful, most organizations approach it with caution, using trusted local managers.

When a firm decides to sell its products abroad, or when its overseas sales volume increases, it frequently establishes an export department. This is a separate department within the home company's headquarters that is assigned specific responsibility for overseas transactions. Again, this is simple to establish and run. As companies become more sophisticated in differentiating among their global markets, they soon realize that localized expertise represents a strategic asset for satisfying local customer demands. In such cases, firms frequently establish international divisions. While export departments are usually located in corporate headquarters in the home country, international divisions are most often located overseas near the firm's principal global markets. Local managers are hired, again to get close to principal customers and markets, and to provide a world view for headquarters on future business opportunities abroad.

When international activities become a more prominent aspect of the total business, most companies reorganize in order to capitalize on this growing business sector. They then often select one of the typical *global organization designs* (see Exhibit 4.4). Companies go to great lengths to identify a design that will provide the best combination of such knowledge and support the firm's strategic objectives. An appropriate organization design should help the firm integrate four types of strategic information in order to facilitate successful competition: (1) area knowledge, involving an understanding of the local area's culture, economics, and social conditions; (2) product knowledge, involving an understanding of local customer needs and possible markets for company products; (3) functional knowledge, involving local access to expertise in the various functional areas of business, such as finance, production, etc.; and (4) customer knowledge, involving an understanding of each customer's particular needs for sales and service.

Most of these organization designs are straightforward. Two may need further explanation, however: global matrix and global network designs. *Global matrix organizations* represent a blend of two of the other global designs working in tandem (e.g., integrating a global functional design with a global product design). As with any matrix organization, each manager would have two supervisors, leading to improved communications and flexibility but reduced accountability and job clarity. In addition, driven by an increasingly dynamic environment, some organizations use *global network designs* to break the organization into groups with loose links, relying on regional groupings and regional headquarters and the creation of teams and projects that link different units around the world. Global networks are also popular in coordinating the

Exhibit 4.4 Global organization designs

Global organization design	Basis of organization	Principal applications
Global product	Worldwide responsibility for specific product groups (e.g., laundry products, baby products) assigned to different global operating units.	Establish separate worldwide divisions (possibly at corporate HQ) for each principal product group. Popular design for companies that emphasize relatively standardized product development and marketing of global products (e.g., baby products in one division, laundry products in another).
Global area design	Geographic regions of the world (e.g., Asia-Pacific, Latin American, Europe).	Establish several regional HQs around world that are each responsible for development and marketing of tailored products in various regions (e.g., selling different candies in the United Kingdom and the United States). Popular design when products require localization to suit different tastes.
Global function	Functional areas (e.g., finance, operations, marketing).	Establish global units for various functional responsibilities (e.g., divisions for global marketing, global finance, etc.). Popular design when company has relatively narrow product line that is easily transferred around the world (e.g., global airline).
Global customer	Unique needs of customers (e.g., business-to-business transactions, franchise business).	Establish separate worldwide divisions for similar products but different consumer groups (e.g., selling tires in bulk to automobile manufacturers and to local tire replacement companies). Popular design when building customer relations in competitive markets is critical.
Global matrix	Combination of two global designs (e.g., integrating global area with global product design).	Establish dual reporting lines for managers in various product or services groups (e.g., reporting to a manufacturing manager on production and quality specifications and to a marketing manager on number of units sold). Popular design in mass assembly or mass services companies (e.g., automobiles, chemicals).
Global network	Loosely coupled groups and teams (e.g., global R&D consortium).	Establish a cluster of business units from around the world (perhaps from different companies) to conduct R&D or build globalized products. Popular design in high-technology industry for new product development requiring multiple and interrelated technologies (e.g., cellphone tablets).

efforts of multiple companies coordinating their technologies and patents to create single products (e.g., high-tech products). These teams are often highly dynamic, thus changing the relationship between the units over time. This design is flexible and allows for strategy diversity and fast learning, but may be difficult to control and may generate high levels of ambiguity.

Beyond these standardized forms of organization, many companies develop their own unique *hybrid organization design* to suit their own particular global needs. The global auto giant Nissan, for example, uses a global area design to sell and service its cars around the world. Its US market is so large, however, that Nissan uses a functional organization design here to meet market demand successfully.

Understanding the relationship between global strategy and organizational design is critical for managers, as it provides information as to what the priorities of the organization are (product standardization versus country adaptation) and, as such, influences the degree of managerial discretion. For example, an organization following a global strategy and structure may wish to replicate the home organizational culture and processes in the foreign location and allow little room for adaptations. Headquarters may monitor the foreign manager's actions and attend to behavior that indicates a deviation from the home country's way of doing things. On the other hand, an organization following an adaptation strategy and global area design may grant the foreign manager considerable discretion with regard to how to manage the organization so long as the financial goals of the subsidiary are met. Likewise, understanding where one fits into the organization structure provides managers with key information regarding the perceived importance of their role and the types of pressures they are likely to face, whether locally or from headquarters.

Regional models of organization

Managers can learn a great deal about both strategy and structure by studying *local* trends in organization design. These designs can tell us who the primary beneficiaries of an organization are, who holds power and influence, the rights and privileges of rank-and-file employees, managerial role obligations, and how decisions are made. In many ways, a company's unique organization design is like its own personal fingerprint. It can provide insights into a company's character, values, ambitions, management systems, and operating procedures. Comparing these designs can help us understand how cultural differences can influence how businesses operate and how management is conducted. This can also help managers who have to work with highly diverse organizations from multiple countries.

While a country-by-country discussion is beyond the scope of this book, it is possible to identify four of the more common models based on the central question of who derives the greatest benefit from an organization's operations. This is often referred to (in Latin) as the issue of *Cui bono?* ("Who benefits?"). We refer to these as *regional models* (see Exhibit 4.5). Obviously, all regional organizations have multiple stakeholders, and many major or minor groups benefit in various ways (e.g., investor returns, employment, local community development). The question here, however, is: who stands to gain the most as a general trend? What we find when we begin exploring the role of cultural differences in organization design is that there are systematic differences across regions in principal beneficiaries. This is not to say that all organizations within a single culture share

Exhibit 4.5 Regional models of organization

Characteristics	Investor model	Family model	Network model	Mutual benefit model
Country examples	American, Australian, British, and Canadian companies.	Chinese *gong-si*, South Korean *chaebol*, Mexican *grupo*.	Japanese *kaisha* and *keiretsu*.	German *konzern*, Danish *selskabet*, Dutch *bedrijf*, and Swedish *företag*.
Primary beneficiaries (*Cui bono?*)	Principal emphasis on stockholders and investors as principal beneficiaries.	Principal emphasis on extended family members as both investors and principal beneficiaries.	Sequential emphasis on corporate network, individual company shareholders, and permanent employees.	Relative balance between stockholders and investors, most employees, local community, and public-at-large.
Center of power and influence	Centralized power largely held by investors and stockholders and delegated to top executives.	Centralized power held by family with government backing and tightly controlled through family management.	Moderately distributed power held by investors, sister companies, key banks, unions, and government.	Widely distributed power held by investors, partners, managers, works councils, unions, and government.
Trends in management selection	Professional education.	Family membership.	Seniority.	Technical mastery.
Trends in decision making	Top-down centralized management common, but not universal.	Top-down centralized management, often with government involvement and support.	Consultation with employees up, down, and across hierarchy, but final decisions typically made at top.	Collaboration between managers, works councils, and unions on key decisions.
Employee rights and job security	Weak legal protection of employee rights and job security for all employees.	Weak legal protection of employee rights and job security for all employees.	Weak legal, but strong social, protection of employee rights and job security for all "permanent" employees.	Strong legal protection of employee rights and job security for almost all employees.
Variability in basic model	Wide variations within basic model.	Few variations in basic model.	Moderate variations in basic model.	Few variations in basic model.

common objectives and principal beneficiaries – they don't – but trends can nevertheless be discovered that can help us understand why companies look different and operate in different ways across various regions of the world.

Investor models of organization

Many books on the topic of organization design and management structure assume that managers organize their resources in fairly similar ways. Typically, what they are talking about here is what may be described as an *investor model* (also called a traditional or stockholder model). A good example of this approach to organization and control can be found in what are often described as predominantly "Anglo" cultures, including Australia, Canada, New Zealand, the United Kingdom, and the United States. Most companies in this cluster make use of some type of investor structure as their chief organizing framework. In other words, the investors typically exert significant power and influence over the organization, management, and ultimate destiny of the firm, and recoup most of the profits or return on investment for themselves as owners. Indeed, in the United States, for example, commercial law requires that executives manage the firm for the exclusive benefit of investors (within legal and regulatory limits). They are not therefore allowed, for example, to provide greater benefits to employees or customers unless they can demonstrate that such actions clearly benefit investors. It is simply against the law.

At the same time, these companies typically make use of so-called "professional management." This is not to imply that other forms of management are not professional; rather, it is to emphasize that such companies rely heavily on outside, professionally trained, and presumably impartial managers (e.g., free from nepotism) to run their companies.

Identifying a "typical" company in any culture is a challenge, but perhaps nowhere is this challenge greater than with respect to US firms. As elsewhere, US companies reflect the culture(s) in which they do business, and since the United States is strongly multicultural it is not surprising to find major differences across companies – even in similar industries. All the same, it is possible to develop a general portrait of what such a company looks like in terms of its basic organization structure and management processes (see Exhibit 4.6). Based on what we know about prevailing American cultural patterns, consider how we might describe a typical US firm.

Exhibit 4.6 Investor model of a US corporation (example)

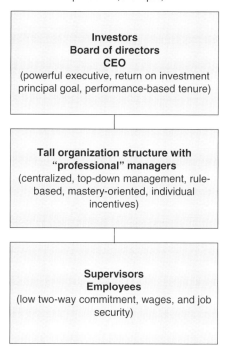

- *Mastery-oriented.* Many investor organizations stress individual or group achievement and responsibility, control over the environment, a linear approach to decision making, respect for rules and policies and a sense of order, and a belief that, at least in theory, anyone can rise to the top.

- *Powerful CEOs.* CEOs and company presidents often get most of the credit for company successes and much of the blame for failure; they also get much of the money, regardless. US CEOs tend to have considerable power as decision makers and leaders so long as they succeed. Indeed, we often hear about the "imperial CEO." If they do not succeed, however, they tend to disappear rather quickly.

- *Fluid organization design.* Organization design in typical US firms tends to be rather fluid. They tend to have many alliances and partners and frequently reinvent themselves when the need arises (e.g., under conditions of financial exigency). When they need capital to expand the business, market research for a new product, or in-depth legal advice, most US firms typically go outside the company. Likewise, manufacturing and service companies alike often rely on outside suppliers and distributors that have only a tenuous relationship with the company.

- *Low job security.* Employees on *all* levels are often viewed as factors of production, rather than valued members of the organization. Indeed, in some US companies, so-called "permanent" employees are routinely hired and fired on the basis of variations in workloads. From an accounting perspective, they are considered as part of a firm's variable costs, not fixed costs. Moreover, the use of contingent workers is on the rise, partly to save money and partly to increase operating efficiency. Not surprisingly, employee commitment to organizations is on the wane.

It is important to note here that it would be a mistake to assume that organization and management practices are identical – or even similar, in some cases – across the broad so-called "Anglo" cluster. For example, London Business School professor Nigel Nicholson has noted that typical governance rules in the United Kingdom are quite different from those in the United States. As a rule, British companies are far less tolerant of power aggregation than are their American counterparts. For example, they tend to oppose unitary boards of directors and strongly prefer the separation of the roles of chairman and CEO between two people, unlike the tendency in the United States to integrate these two roles into one person. They also dislike dual-share voting systems, and have rules that prevent banks from owning major shares in companies. British firms are also far less encumbered with layers of lawyers, spend far less money on government lobbying, and have generally weak trade associations. In general, then, Nicholson notes that British firms tend to be more liberal than their US counterparts and maintain more liquidity and fluidity in ownership. If British firms are more liberal in ownership and governance, however, they tend to be more conservative in management policies and practices. The ethos of British management is highly pragmatic, achievement-oriented, and entrepreneurial, but is often opposed to "out-of-the-box" thinking, weak on leadership, strong on financial management, and frequently poor on vision, community, and integration.

At the same time, systematic differences between the United States and Canada can also be noted. Adler offers the following observations. Compared to Americans, Canadians tend to understate their strengths and perhaps overstate their weaknesses.[7] They do not usually claim to be the best at something. Canadians strongly believe in collegiality. For example, Canada is one of the leaders in creating middle-country initiatives, whereby a group of countries in the world tries to get something done (instead of trying to go it alone). Canadians tend to be more formal than Americans – titles and family names are important. Canadians are generally more polite and less confrontational than their American counterparts. Canadians are also less explicitly and publicly religious. Finally, Canadians believe in more collective responsibility across society in such areas as education and healthcare. All this is not to say that overlaps do not occur; obviously, they do. Assuming that Americans and Canadians live identical lifestyles or share identical values can only lead to lost opportunities for global managers, however.

In summary, some might argue that, in making comparisons between American and British firms, and, indeed, firms in Australia, Canada, and New Zealand, the key issue is whether within-group variance is larger or smaller than between-group variance. In other words, commonalities can be found among all the countries that comprise the so-called "Anglo" cluster. Part of the reason for these similarities can be found in the historic British influences in all these cultures. Even so, in recognition of the strong individualism found in this cluster, it is not surprising to find that it is difficult to make generalizations about organization design and management practice. At the same time, part of the difference here can be found in the increasing cultural heterogeneity of people inhabiting all these countries. Diversity is increasing throughout. Indeed, as these two countries, along with their Australian, Canadian, and New Zealand counterparts, become increasingly multicultural, perhaps the term "Anglo" will lose much of its meaning as a descriptor of this cluster of countries.[8] In fact, these countries and cultures may begin evolving in very different directions in the future. For now, however, the evidence suggests that this country cluster retains much of its utility as characterizing central trends in this cluster.

Family models of organization

A distinguishing characteristic of the *family model* of organization is the centrality of family members in the routine operations of the firm. Frequently, multiple family members hold different positions in the corporate hierarchy. Such firms are typically run by the head of the family – often, although not exclusively, male. Moreover, family members are the principal beneficiaries of corporate operations and success. The family model can be seen in numerous variations. We focus here on the example of China, although this model can be found in many places throughout the world (e.g., South America, southeast Asia, the Middle East).[9]

When Westerners attempt to describe Chinese culture, they invariably begin – correctly or incorrectly – with *Confucianism*.[10] Confucius promulgated a code of ethical behavior that was meant to guide interpersonal relationships in everyday life. This code was summed up in the so-called *five cardinal virtues*. These consist of filial piety, absolute loyalty to one's superiors, strict observance of seniority, subservience to superiors, and mutual trust between friends and colleagues. Although these principles suggest a way of living in the broader society, they also have implications for business practices today. Confucius and his followers saw the universe – and hence society – as a hierarchical system ruled by an educated aristocratic elite. Concepts such as democracy and equality were disdained, while learning and education were highly prized. Confucian society stressed the virtues of self-discipline, hard work, diligence, and frugality.[11] Hence the fundamental nature of human relationships is not interactions among equals but, rather, interactions among unequals. In other words, correct interpersonal behavior is determined by one's age, gender, and position in society, and a breach in this social etiquette carries with it severe penalties.

These five cardinal virtues are reinforced by several social patterns that characterize traditional Chinese society, as well as business practices.

- *Guānxi.* This represents a strong personal relationship between two people with implications of a continual exchange of favors.[12] Two people have *guānxi* when they can assume that each is conscientiously committed to the other regardless of what happens. This bond is based on the exchange of favors (i.e., social capital), not necessarily friendship or sympathy, and it does not have to involve friends. It is more utilitarian than emotional. Failure to meet one's obligations under this arrangement causes a severe loss of face, however, and creates the appearance of being untrustworthy.

- *Face*. Face is largely interpreted to mean dignity, self-respect, and prestige. A central tenet of Confucianism is the maintenance of long-term social harmony.[13] This is based both on the upholding of correct relationships between individuals and on the protection of one's face. All social interactions must be conducted in a manner in which no party loses face. Hence, if an individual cannot keep a commitment, however small, he or she loses face. Similarly, a person loses face when he or she is not treated in accordance with his or her station or position in society. Thus, a senior manager will lose face if it becomes known that a junior colleague is earning a higher salary or was promoted ahead of him or her.

- *Rank*. Confucian principles were designed to recognize hierarchy and differences between class members. As a result, the behavioral requirements of individuals differed according to who was involved in the relationship. Among equals, certain patterns of prescribed behavior existed. You can see this today when two strangers discover upon meeting for the first time that they both attended the same high school or college. An instant bond emerges and there is a sense of immediate camaraderie. On the other hand, for people from outside this common background or clan, frequently there is hostility or distrust. Foreign observers note that some people can be very blunt and impolite when talking with total strangers, yet very hospitable and generous when dealing with friends or acquaintances. It is a question of belonging.

- *Harmony*. Within one's broad circle of acquaintances, there is a clear responsibility for maintaining group harmony. Again, this principle stresses harmony between unequals – that is, it links persons of unequal rank in power, prestige, or position. Since strong personal relationships outside the family tend to occur only between persons of equal rank, age, or prestige, harmony is the means of defining all other necessarily more formal relationships. It is everyone's responsibility to maintain this harmony continually among one's acquaintances and family members, and considerable effort is invested in doing so, including gift giving.

In view of China's strong cultural traditions, it is not surprising that its companies, both large and small, reflect this heritage. Chinese companies are generally called *gong-si* (pronounced "gong-suh"). Although the term originally referred to private family-owned enterprises, recent Chinese corporate law now uses this term to refer to all companies, regardless of whether they are large or small, family-owned or state-owned. To clarify this difference, smaller and medium-sized family-run enterprises are now often called *jia zu gong-si*. An illustration of a typical family-run company is shown in Exhibit 4.7. In brief, its characteristics are as follows.

Exhibit 4.7 Family model of a Chinese *gong-si* (example)

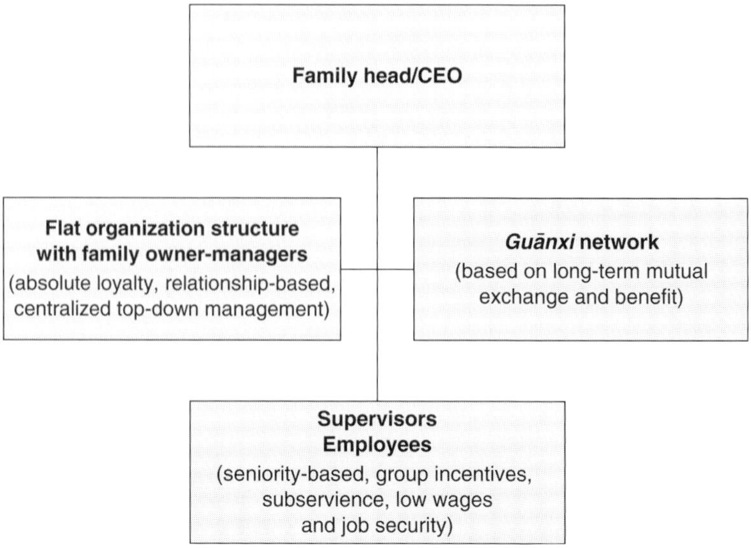

- *Flat, informal structure. Gong-si* companies have little formal structure, few standard operating procedures, and little specialization.[14] While they lack formal structure and procedures, personal relationships are likely to take precedence over more objectively defined concerns, such as organizational efficiency. Who one knows is often more important than what one knows, and employee loyalty is often preferred over actual performance.
- *Relationship-based.* Decisions are frequently based either on intuition or on longstanding business exchange relationships. According to Darden business professor Ming-Jer Chen, if these family firms have a competitive advantage, it lies in their small size, flexibility, network of connections, and negotiation skills.[15]
- *Family management.* Top management positions are often filled with family members, sometimes despite a lack of managerial competence.[16]
- *Business as private property.* Business owners tend to regard the business as the private property of the core family (not an individual), and are therefore reluctant to share ownership with outsiders or to borrow from individuals or organizations unrelated to the family in some way.
- *Family revenue.* Following from Confucian thought, the family is the most fundamental revenue and expenditure unit. Within a family, each member contributes his or her income to a common family fund. Each member then has a right to a

portion of this money, while the remainder belongs to the family as a whole. The interests of the entire family take precedence over individual members and others outside the family.

Network models of organization

Next, we turn to a look at the *network model*, frequently found in Japan. An overview of Japanese culture includes a strong belief in hierarchy, strong collectivism, a strong harmony orientation, moderate monochronism, and strong particularism. Hierarchy beliefs in Japan can be seen in the deep respect shown to elders and people in positions of authority. In many circumstances, their directives are to be obeyed immediately and without question. This belief follows from early Confucian teachings (see above). Indeed, the concept of authority in Japan differs from that typically found in the West. Western views of authority see power generally flowing in one direction: down. The supervisor or manager gives directions; those below him or her follow them. Authority is a one-way concept. In Japan and many other Asian countries, by contrast, power still flows downwards, but those exercising power must also look after the welfare and well-being of those they manage. In other words, a supervisor expects his or her directives to be followed without question, but will also spend considerable time guiding, coaching, and teaching subordinates so that they can progress in their careers. Subordinates – and in many cases their families too – will be looked after. Thus, authority here is seen as a two-way street; both sides (superiors and subordinates) have a role to play. By deferring to those above you, you are in essence asking them to look after you.

Japan is also a highly collectivistic nation. Groups generally take precedence over individuals, and people gain their personal identity through their group membership. An old saying, "The nail that sticks out will be hammered down," best exemplifies the importance of this belief. Contrast this to the old American and British saying, "The squeaky wheel gets the grease." As a result, employees naturally gravitate towards groups at work, and group achievement surpasses individual achievement on the job. Seniority-based or group-based rewards are frequently preferred over performance-based individual rewards.

Harmony – both with other people and with nature – is also a strong characteristic. Japan's respect for its surrounding environment is legendary. This is not to say they refrain from changing or challenging nature; rather, they typically attempt this in ways that do as little harm as possible to the environment. Likewise, most Japanese will go to great lengths not to offend anyone or create open conflict or argumentation. As a result, communications in Japan tends to emphasize context at least as much as content. Nonverbal signs and signals are frequently used to convey thoughts in cases when words may be inappropriate. Finally, many observers have noted that Japanese society tends to be highly particularistic: while clear rules of law pervade society, exceptions are routinely made for friends and family or for powerful and influential people.

Japan's large and highly diversified companies represent a unique approach to organization that has served their members and their country well over the years.[17] These organizations are generally referred to as *keiretsu*. A *keiretsu* refers to a uniquely Japanese form of corporate organization, consisting of a network of affiliated companies (*kaisha*) that form a tight-knit alliance to work towards each other's mutual success (see Exhibit 4.8). The design of these organizations is rooted in Japanese history and is successful largely because it is congruent with the national culture.[18] Japanese *keiretsu* typically consist of a group of interlocking companies clustered around one or more

Exhibit 4.8 Network model of a Japanese *keiretsu* (Kirin Holdings *kaisha*, Mitsubishi *keiretsu*)

banks, a lead manufacturer, and a trading company, overseen by a president's council consisting of the presidents of the major group companies.

Common features of *keiretsu* include the following.

- *Internal financing.* Financing is more likely to come from inside the Japanese conglomerate's own financial institutions (e.g., company-owned banks or insurance companies), while marketing research and even legal advice is frequently carried out within the group. Within each horizontal *keiretsu*, a company-owned bank or banks perform several functions, including internal financing for company operations and new ventures.

- *Trading companies.* Japanese companies tend to have large and highly competent trading companies (*sogoshosha*). These organizations provide member companies with ready access to global markets and distribution networks, and maintain offices throughout the world to continually look out for new or expanded markets. At the same time, their field offices collect and analyze market and economic intelligence that can be used by member companies to develop new products or otherwise get a jump on the competition. They frequently assist member companies with various marketing activities as well, and facilitate imports into Japan for their business customers.

- *Weak executives.* Compared to many other companies around the world, executives have less power, and decision making is distributed throughout the firm. Executives are prized for being consensus builders more than autocratic decision makers.

- *Long-term employees.* In contrast to many of their Western counterparts, Japanese firms tend to treat their employees as a fixed cost, not a variable cost, and relationships with suppliers tend to be closer and more stable over time.

- *Enterprise unions.* Japanese unions, called *enterprise unions*, tend to be company unions and are more closely associated with company interests than is the case in the West.

Mutual benefit models of organization

A fourth approach to organization and management can be seen in the *mutual benefit model*. This model is common in Germany, the Netherlands, and the Scandinavian countries and, once again, it is derived from the long-standing cultural traditions found in this region of the world. We focus here on Germany as one variation on this model.

A number of social scientists have attempted to describe German culture in general terms. Hofstede, for example, has described the typical German as relatively individualistic (although not so extreme as Americans), high on uncertainty avoidance and masculinity, and relatively low on power distance.[19] Hall and Hall add that Germans tend to be very punctual about time, follow schedules closely, demand order, value their personal space, respect power and position, and seek detailed information prior to decision making. Indeed, Hall and Hall quote a French executive as saying that "Germans are too busy managing to think creatively."[20] As discussed in Chapter 3, cultural anthropologists suggest that the dominant German culture includes a mastery orientation, moderate individualism and egalitarianism, a strong rule-based orientation, and a monochronic approach to time.

To foreign observers, Germans tend to be conservative, formal, and polite.[21] Formal titles are important in conversations, and privacy and protocol are valued. In business, Germans tend to be assertive, but not aggressive. Although firms are often characterized by strict departmentalization, decisions tend to be made on the basis of broad-based discussion and consensus building among key stakeholders. Negotiations are based on extensive assessments of data and plans, and, since Germany is a low-context culture (where message clarity counts – see Chapter 6), communication is explicit and easily understood by foreigners.

As with companies in any country, it is difficult to generalize about the nature or structure of the typical large German company (*Konzern* in German). A representative model is nevertheless presented in Exhibit 4.9.

- *Supervisory and management boards.* German firms are typically led from the top by two boards. At the very top is the *supervisory board (Aufsichtsrat)*, which, much like a board of directors in US firms, is responsible for ensuring that the principal corporate objectives are met over the long term. Its members are typically elected for five years and can only be changed by a vote of 75 percent of the voting shares. The supervisory board, in turn, oversees the activities of the *management board (Vorstand)*, which consists of the top management team of the firm and is responsible for its actual strategic and operational management.

- *Co-determination and works councils.* A major feature of mutual benefit structures is the enhanced power that employees at various levels of the organization have in decisions affecting the future of the organization. In Germany, this is called *co-determination (Mitbestimmung)*. As part of this, *works councils*, elected from rank-and-file employees, are represented on company supervisory boards and participate significantly in both strategy formulation and management practice.

- *Meister.* From the first-line supervisor (usually held by a *Meister*, or master technician) on up, managers are respected for what they know rather than who they are. They tend to be less controlling than many of their US counterparts. Instead, it is

Exhibit 4.9 Mutual benefit model of a German *Konzern* (example)

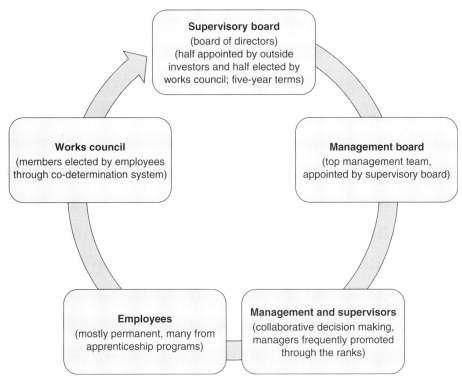

assumed that workers and supervisors will meet deadlines, guarantee quality and service, and do not require close supervision. Independence within agreed-upon parameters characterizes the working relationship between managers and the managed.

- *Technik*. Behind the organizational facade of German firms is a particular notion of technical competence commonly referred to as *Technik*. This describes the knowledge and skills required for work.[22] It is the science and art of manufacturing high-quality and technologically advanced products. The success of *Technik* in German manufacturing is evidenced by the fact that over 40 percent of Germany's gross domestic product (GDP) is derived from manufacturing. Indeed, Germany is responsible for over a half of all EU manufactured exports. It is for this reason that knowledge of *Technik* represents a principal determinant in the selection of supervisors and managers.

Control, participation, and decision making

Making timely, relevant, and – hopefully – wise decisions concerning the future directions of a firm is clearly a principal function of management. Critical to this process is where, when, and how information is sourced for optimum results. In other words, who has useful and important information or viewpoints that can lead to better decisions and who can be ignored, for reasons either of confidentiality or efficiency? Clearly, there are considerable and often heated disagreements on this issue. At the heart of this disagreement are the twin issues of management control and employee involvement or participation in decision making.

While many heuristics are available to examine the extent of organizational control and employee involvement in managerial decision making, we make use of a long-standing and simple framework.[23] This approach has seen widespread use among scholars and managers, due in part to its strong empirical base and in part to its down-to-earth approach to understanding how problems are actually addressed and resolved up and down the organizational hierarchy. This model offers a three-level classification scheme based on the amount of employee participation that is generally allowed by managers and organizations, allowing for variations around each (see Exhibit 4.10): centralized, consultative, and collaborative.[24]

Centralized decision making

If we look at a typical decision-making process in many of the so-called "Anglo" countries (e.g., Australia, Canada, New Zealand, the United Kingdom, the United States), we often find a process that centralizes power squarely in the hands of line managers. Here, the initial problem identification is largely a managerial or supervisory responsibility; workers' opinions are often ignored or not offered in the first place. Once a problem or issue has been identified, it is management's responsibility to analyze and resolve it, often with the help of senior managers or outside specialists and consultants. Decisions are then passed down to lower-level employees in the form of changed work procedures. Not surprisingly, since the people at the bottom of the hierarchy often have little understanding of management's conclusions or intents, decision implementation tends to be slow, as management now has to persuade workers to go along with the decision. Frequently, extrinsic rewards (i.e., externally administered rewards, such as pay or bonuses) need to be used instead of intrinsic rewards (i.e., internally administered rewards, such as pride in accomplishment or job satisfaction) as a result of this process.

Exhibit 4.10 Employee involvement in managerial decision making

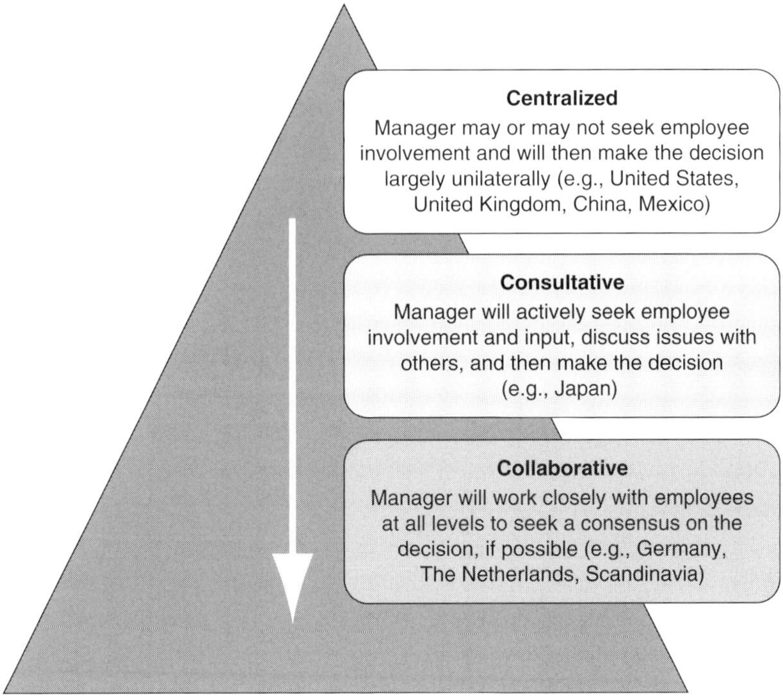

Meanwhile, the decision process described above is not dissimilar from that commonly found in Chinese *gong-si*, or family-based companies. Despite being a collectivistic country, China is still hierarchical, leading to centralized power in decision making. Problem identification is typically carried out either by supervisors or owner-managers using fairly rigid management and production control systems. The owner-managers then discuss and analyze the problem, often in consultation with extended family members or *guānxi* relationships. Because of the autocratic decision style, the rapid announcement of a decision to rank-and-file employees by management is possible (see Exhibit 4.11). Rapid acceptance and implementation of an owner-manager's decision by largely contingent employees is also possible, because of a combination of loyalty to the owner-manager and fear of the consequences of non-compliance. Employees' intrinsic motivation to implement decisions may be high, due to custom and loyalty to the firm, but extrinsic motivation may also be high, due to the importance of job security and income.

Exhibit 4.11 Decision analysis and implementation speed

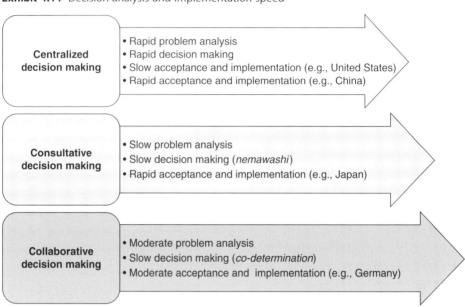

Consultative decision making

Managerial decision making in a typical Japanese *kaisha* (company) reflects Japanese culture and is seen by many observers as being quite distinct from that in the West. Not surprisingly, Japanese firms endorse the concept of problem solving on the basis of consensus up and down the hierarchy.[25] The system by which this is done is usually called *ringi-seido* (often shortened to simply *ringi-sei*), or circle of discussion.

When a particular problem or opportunity is identified, a group of workers or supervisors will discuss various parameters of the problem and try and identify possible solutions. At times, technical experts will be brought in for assistance. If the initial results are positive, employees will approach their supervisor for more advice and possible support. The whole process is generally referred to in Japan as *nemawashi*. The word *nemawashi* is derived from a description of the process of preparing the roots of a tree for planting.[26] The concept here is that, if the roots are properly prepared, the tree will survive and prosper. Similarly, if a proposal is properly prepared, it too should survive and prosper.

When a group has achieved informal consensus, a formal proposal is then drafted for submission up the chain of command. This formal document, known as a *ringi-sho*, is reviewed by successively higher levels of management. If a manager agrees with the proposal, he stamps his or her name on it; if not, he or she either refrains from stamping it or stamps it on the reverse side. By the time the document reaches upper management, it has become clear whether it has broad-based support or not. If it does enjoy support, in all likelihood top management will formally adopt the proposal. In this way, upper management frequently has little input into the decision-making process. If a proposal has universal support up the chain of command, top managers will be hard-pressed to oppose it.

While discussions concerning a particular decision or course of action are proceeding, two seemingly contradictory processes often occur that tend to confuse many Westerners. In Japan, doing or saying the right thing according to prevailing norms or social customs is referred to as *tatemae*, while doing or saying what one actually prefers to do (which may be difficult) is referred to as *honne*.[27] Thus, in a conversation or meeting, to some Westerners a Japanese manager may speak in contradictions, or, worse, speak insincerely. In reality, the manager may simply be saying what he or she believes he or she is obliged to say, while hoping that through subtle signals the recipient of the message will discover his or her true desire or intent. This can be confusing to many Westerners, and requires them to listen carefully and observe body language as well as formal speech (e.g., reading someone's face). After all, Japan is a high-context culture (see Chapter 6), while most Western nations are not.

A key point to remember here is that the *ringi-sei* process tends to result in slow decisions, which is often a disadvantage in a fast-paced and competitive global business environment. This process yields considerable support for and commitment to the emergent solution when it is achieved, however. By contrast, many Western decisions are typically made unilaterally much higher up in the management hierarchy, but, once they have been made, they frequently face considerable opposition or apathy as managers and workers attempt to implement them. As a result, strategic planning is frequently accomplished more quickly in the West, while strategic implementation is frequently accomplished more quickly in Japan.

Collaborative decision making

Finally, the decision-making process found in many German, Dutch, and Scandinavian firms tends to be more participative than any country in either the Anglo or the Asian clusters. This is due in large measure to the presence of co-determination laws and works councils.

Collaborative decision making can be highly complex, on account of the knowledge and power of the various stakeholders. In this process, problems are most frequently identified either by supervisors or workers through a combination of job experience and sophisticated production control processes. Lower-level employees in a section or department begin by working with supervisors to help identify the underlying causes of the problem, as well as possible solutions. Next, department heads, section chiefs, and supervisors meet to discuss and develop a proposal to remedy the situation. Technical experts and works council members are frequently consulted as needed to achieve the best possible solution. The problem and possible solutions are then passed up the management hierarchy. Management discusses the problem and possible solutions widely and then makes a formal decision, often in consultation and negotiation with works council members and the local industrial union leadership.

The resulting decisions are likely to be widely accepted by rank-and-file employees, because of the representative process through which they were made; workers at all levels have had a voice throughout the process. As a result, decision implementation typically proceeds at a moderate pace, although union resistance may still occur because of structural or contract issues. Employees' intrinsic motivation to implement the decision is typically reasonably high, since their representatives had a voice in determining it and the decision typically does not threaten job security.

In summary, as we have seen throughout this discussion on organizational decision making, a lot is heard about the role of employee participation and involvement. In some countries, employee participation is a preciously guarded right; it is assumed. In other countries, workers have no expectations of employee participation; indeed, they often see managers who seek their opinions as being weak. In still other countries (some include Canada and the United States in this category), participation is often honored more in rhetoric than in actual practice. In other words, although many companies may proclaim their interest in the opinions of subordinates, they are often more interested in results than in process. Consider: how does a manager determine how much participation to encourage or allow among his or her subordinates, and what should a manager do if the advice offered by subordinates is self-serving, excessively expensive, or simply unrealistic?

Organizational culture

The behavioral manifestations of organization design are typically brought to life through a firm's *organizational culture*. If management structures are the fingerprints of organizations, then organizational cultures are the personalities. Organizations provide managers with a set of rules, procedures and norms of behavior to guide action in the form of standard operational procedures and organizational cultural norms. The organizational culture reflects the norms, values, and approved (and proscribed) behaviors of particular companies, divisions, or departments within organizations. The concept of culture was discussed at length in the previous chapter. Here, we briefly consider culture as it relates to specific organizations and variations across organizations.

Organizational culture may either replicate or reject national culture values and norms, creating a microenvironment in which national norms are reinforced or do not apply. For example, even though a country may embrace a polychronic time orientation, an organization in that country may reject this cultural norm and enforce punctuality in its activities. Indeed, many global organizations deal with the challenges posed by multiple national cultures by creating clear behavioral guidelines across the organization. In intra-organizational interactions, organizational norms and rules may serve to decrease the impact of multiple institutional environments. In inter-organizational relationships, the organizational environment may exacerbate differences. Through the development and reinforcement of norms of behavior, organizations define what is expected of managers.

The fundamental challenge facing managers is how to identify – quickly – the type of culture they are dealing with. Organizational culture expert Edgar Schein[28] suggests three possible ways.

- *Artifacts and behaviors.* Observe the manifestations of culture through the presence of artifacts and patterns of behavior. Organizations look and feel different from one another. Upon arriving at a new organization, we can observe symbols or physical characteristics that can provide important information. For example: are there offices or is it one open floor? Are doors open or closed? Is the environment formal or informal? How are people dressed? We can also observe patterns of behavior. Are there particular ways in which a number of people behave and others seem to treat this behavior as normal (e.g., interrupting in meetings, arriving late, answering the phone)?

- *Power distribution.* Study the power structure of the organization and seek to understand how a person can obtain, maintain, or lose power. This will point to what is really valued in this organization. A third cue into the organizational culture is its reward and punishment system. In other words, who or what gets rewarded or punished, and why?

- *Problem-solving mechanisms.* Analyze how an organization confronts problems. How do they respond? Are they primarily proactive or reactive? Do they panic quickly or are they ready for almost any change or challenge?

To see how this works, take a look at how two US companies developed very different organizational cultures in several countries in western Europe. One was successful; one was not.

Application 4.4   Global cultures at GE and Wal-Mart

Several years ago General Electric (GE) acquired several companies in western Europe, including Spain, Germany, France, and Italy.[29] Instead of tailoring business practices to fit each of the cultures involved, GE's approach was to integrate these companies and impose a whole host of US-based management practices. Among other things, managers were told that titles didn't matter and employees would be valued on the basis of their knowledge and performance, not their positions. By any measure of financial performance, GE pulled off the integration very successfully. At the same time, when Walmart Stores entered the German market, its lack of sensitivity and adaptation to the local environment created numerous problems that quickly led to its leaving the German market, with a significant financial loss.

Think about it. . .

(1)   Why was GE successful in implementing US practices in Europe, while Wal-Mart was not?

(2)   How important is a global organizational culture for companies operating across borders?

(3)   What are the consequences when the norms reflected in a particular organizational culture collide with local values?

As discussed earlier in this chapter, hierarchy, collectivism, and other Confucian principles tend to characterize traditional Chinese companies. What many people do not realize, however, is that an ever-increasing number of new high-tech start-ups in China are beginning to create very different organizational cultures. It is not Western, it is not traditional Chinese; it is a third way. An instance of it can be seen in the example of Alibaba in Hangzhou.

Application 4.5   Core values at Alibaba

On the fourth floor of the headquarters of e-commerce titan Alibaba is a massive workspace filled with hundreds of salespeople. This is Alibaba's army of cold callers. They telephone clients who have storefronts on the Web, urging them to buy keyword advertising or to pay to boost their online rankings. Each salesperson inhabits a cubicle furnished with a desk, a plastic sunflower, and a mirror – the last a reminder to smile, because it's an article of faith at Alibaba that a customer can hear a smile over the phone. "*Liuqian!*" yells one woman, popping up from her cubicle: "Six thousand!" She has just persuaded a client to buy 6,000 yuan of keyword advertising. On cue, all her colleagues raises their assigned celebratory device: a long plastic stick with three plastic hands at the end of it. The sound of three hands clapping is *click-click-click-click* nonstop on a good day. This is also the odd noise of China's changing organizational cultures.

Since corporations began popping up in China during the economic liberalization of the 1980s, workplace culture has been defined by what one might call the "Great Wall" model – a divide between the haves (the executives) and the have-nots (the workers). Today the old ways are under attack. With the Communist authorities increasingly aware of the nation's social divisions and potential restiveness, China has opened up to influences from other cultures, and practices from abroad have crept into corporate life quickly, particularly in the internet sector.

Leaders such as Ma Yún (Jack Ma in the West), founder and CEO of Alibaba, have been inspired by the examples of Silicon Valley's tech titans.[30] Like Ma, a new cohort of Chinese executives – educated and professionally seasoned in other countries – is returning home with new thinking about management and work, including a more "in the trenches" ethos, a heightened appetite for risk, and a different understanding of innovation. These execs have earned a well-known nickname: *haigui*, or "sea turtle," which in Mandarin is homonymous with the word for a person who goes overseas and then returns home to China.

Ma studied at Hangzhou Teachers College. Although he is not a sea turtle himself, his ranks at Alibaba include numerous alumni from major universities outside China. He got the idea for Alibaba after a visit to the United States. After starting the company, he and other executives went on a world tour, meeting the chiefs of long-lasting, successful corporations including General Electric and HSBC. He concluded that they all had not just strong corporate values but also a unified sense of purpose, that what made the difference between short-term and long-term success was a distinct organizational culture. So he organized Alibaba around six core values: customers come first; the embrace of change; integrity; passion; commitment to your job; and teamwork and cooperation. What resulted was a "Silicon Valley company" refracted through his unique Chinese lens – much like the Chinese versions of Western goods that you might find for sale on Alibaba.

Signs of Ma's whimsical management style are all over Alibaba's Hangzhou campus, from the three-handed celebration devices to an enormous statue of a naked man in the central courtyard to the receptionists' daily costume changes during festivals and holiday seasons. Employees even get cake on their birthday.

There are also interest-free loans for qualified employees to buy their first homes – and build more loyalty to Alibaba. The cafeteria even features a special menu for pregnant women. In hiring and in promotions, cultural fit is as much a priority as technological expertise. In quarterly evaluations, staff members are judged on Alibaba's six-point value system. The goal is to cultivate a team spirit that will drive profits and, according to Ma, "keep the state-owned enterprises up at night." None of this, however, can explain why some job candidates have been asked to do headstands in interviews!

Think about it. . .

(1)   What is your assessment of Alibaba's six core values? Is there anything particularly Chinese about these values?

(2)   In general, are organizational cultures more closely associated with their industry (e.g., high-tech start-ups, automobiles, pharmaceuticals) or with their national cultures (e.g., Chinese, French)? Why?

(3)   The organizational culture at Alibaba is a combination of attractive employee benefits (e.g., housing assistance) and whimsy (e.g., three-handed celebration). If you returned to this company in five or so years, do you think it would have the same organizational culture or might it be different? Why or why not?

We began this chapter by exploring several aspects of the global environment that exist outside organizational boundaries, yet place considerable pressures and constraints of the organizations themselves. They can also provide significant opportunities for managers willing to look. These include constraints on economic activity, political-legal constraints, technological limitations and opportunities, and so forth. National and regional cultures also place considerable constraints on organizations and their employees. Based on this discussion, we examined four aspects of the organizational environment: global strategy, global organizations (both general models and specific regional models), organizational decision-making patterns, and organizational cultures.

The organizational environment

Organizations are complex entities, and frequently not easily understood. The challenge for managers is how to learn enough about how particular organizations operate to be able to work with them. In this endeavor, we can suggest three general management strategies (summarized in Exhibit 4.12).

1   Understand the relationships between stakeholders, strategies, and structures

It has been suggested throughout this book that looking for relationships represents an excellent learning tool. With regard to stakeholders, strategies, and structures, several lessons seem important.

Exhibit 4.12 Action plans for working with global organizations

(1) Understand the relationships between stakeholders, strategies, and structures	(2) Understand the characteristics of local work environments	(3) Learn about other organizations by better understanding your own
• Understand stakeholder power and influence in the strategy-making process. • Understand how your organization differs from others in terms of their strategic objectives and organizing frameworks. • Look for interactions between strategic decisions and structures. • Remember that strategies and structures can evolve over time. • Consider the role of cultural differences in strategy–structure relationships.	• Understand how decisions are made across organizations, including the role of employee involvement. • Understand constraints on organizational decision making. • Understand your own organizational culture. • Understand differences in organizational cultures across companies, including artifacts and behaviors, power distributions, and problem solving mechanisms. • Learn how you as an outsider can work with people from a different organizational culture.	• Learn more about the relationships between your own culture and local organizing frameworks. • Based on this, learn more about other cultures as they play out in organizational settings. • Continue to develop your multicultural skills to be prepared for differing environments. • Finally learn the rules of the, game regardless of where you are working.

- We have seen in this chapter how culture can influence the ways in which firms approach strategic decisions. In Germany, for example, social pressures and the legal environment both require corporations to look beyond the exclusive interests of investors and stockholders in determining policy. The principle of co-determination requires this. Employees and the local communities must also be considered, as well as environmental issues and high ethical standards. In Japan, we saw how close business–government relations also dictate how firms make strategic choices, and how government policies can support corporate strategies, especially in the area of exporting. At the same time, other countries (e.g., the United Kingdom, the United States) have more of an adversarial relationship between business and government, and – sometimes by law – companies are required to favor investors and stockholders over all other stakeholders as the principal beneficiaries of corporate actions. The point here is simple: it would be naïve for managers from any country to assume that organizations around the world approach basic strategic decision making in the same manner. Each company experiences unique, but nevertheless very real, constraints on how it approaches its strategy, both short- and long-term, and these constraints can vary widely from country to country.

- Strategy and structure frequently interact with one another; each influences the other. Clearly, part of the reason behind this is that cultural differences influence organization design and management practice alike. It goes beyond this, however. Regardless of local cultural variations, organizations and their managers comprise learning systems, which build on past experiences and future expectations in ways that can change both the structure of the organization and its management strategies and practices.

- Remember that both strategies and structures continually evolve to varying degrees in response to global and local changes. A major factor here can be found in the various globalization pressures discussed in Chapter 1. Another influence can be found in the rapid evolution of information and computer-mediated technologies, which have the power to change the ways in which fundamental communications occur through the firm and with its partners.

- When dealing with business partners or prospective partners in other organizations, it is critical to understand what their strategy is, how they are organized, and how decisions are made. For example, recognizing the location of your counterpart in his or her organization structure will provide important information as to how much power the person has and how much discretion he or she has in making a decision.

Understanding his or her decision-making style is equally critical, because, although you may be pressed to reach a quick agreement, your counterpart may not be able to do that given the organizational constraints he or she faces. Be patient when you can.

- The four organizing frameworks discussed here are highly correlated with the cultural traits of their home countries. Japan is a collectivistic society that fosters inclusion and group membership. Not surprisingly, major Japanese *keiretsu* (as well as smaller firms) make use of a group mentality and paternalism in structuring their firms and managing their people. Everyone "belongs" to the company – and the company belongs to them. By contrast, Germany is a more individualistic country, but is still largely egalitarian in nature. As such, German firms may be somewhat more bureaucratic, but they still provide a strong basis for employee participation and involvement at all levels. Thus, while both Japanese and German firms foster employee participation, the basis for such inclusion is very different: participation in Japanese firms is based on societal norms, while in Germany it is based on the prevailing legal system. Meanwhile, non-family employees in a Chinese *gong-si* seldom have expectations of participation. Finally, terms such as "employee participation" or "involvement" are frequently heard throughout the corridors and factories of American and Canadian enterprises, but such words often carry little real meaning beyond the rhetoric. The lesson here is simple: cultures do matter when attempting to understand or manage organizations around the world.

2 *Understand the characteristics of local work environments*

A second management strategy that follows from the above discussion relates to understanding the unique characteristics of local work environments. In this chapter, we have focused on two aspects of the work environment in which wide differences can often be found across borders: decision-making processes and organizational cultures.

- One of the most important things managers do is make decisions concerning the use and applications of their company's limited resources. As a result, understanding how decisions are made in different organizations and different countries is an important part of doing one's job. In particular, managers need to understand both the principal constraints on decision-making processes and the role of employee involvement. Who (e.g., particular people or units) is involved in making key decisions and how much discretion do they actually have? What level of information do people want from others to make a decision? Some people want to know everything, while others simply want to know if they trust the other party. What criteria do people use to judge whether a decision is good or bad?

- Whether managers are assigned to a new location within their own organization or are working with people from other companies, one key question stands out as a critical factor in success: understanding the local organizational culture. Organizational cultures often specify – sometimes overtly, but sometimes covertly – the rules of the road. They both limit and encourage behaviors, and in this sense influence success in no small way. As a result, regardless of the assignment, managers are advised to learn to recognize and understand local artifacts and behaviors, power distributions, and problem-solving mechanisms. Finally, managers would do well to learn how they as outsiders might fit in or whether this would be an impossible task. Throughout, the best advice is to know one's surrounding environment in ways that can work to your advantage.

3   Learn about other organizations by better understanding your own

Finally, although managers may have a familiarity with the operations of their own firm, understanding the general trends – and idiosyncrasies – of various local firms can be far more difficult than it may appear. To the extent that this is correct, what frames of reference can managers use when trying to understand the organizational models in other countries? From a managerial standpoint, three action recommendations emerge from this analysis that have to be resolved for managers to work successfully with organizations across cultures (see Exhibit 4.13):

- Managers must develop an understanding of cultural trends, organizational patterns, and management styles in their own country. This is often easier said than done. We often assume, incorrectly, that we already know this, but looking deeper might reveal that we have something to learn here.
- Based on this local understanding, and as discussed earlier in the book, managers must develop sufficient insight into and understanding of the other countries and cultures with which they or their companies do (or wish to do) business.

Exhibit 4.13 Learning from different organizational models

- Managers must continue to develop their management and multicultural skills so that they can successfully bridge these two cultures and help meet corporate objectives.

Throughout this endeavor, managers should strive to understand the subtle – and not so subtle – rules of behavior within organizations. Understanding the general behavioral patterns of a national culture is not enough; managers need also to understand the rules of behavior within the particular organization with which they are doing business. Developing the skills to quickly observe patterns of behaviors and gather information about expectations is critical for survival in such a multicultural business environment. This is particularly true with regard to understanding different organizational cultures. As illustrated above, organizations that can outwardly appear to be similar may conceal significant differences in what is acceptable and what is expected. To the extent that managers can gain insight into this by doing their homework prior to arrival, their ease in making the rules play to their advantage is enhanced.

In summary, it should again be noted that, although the organizing models discussed here represent central tendencies in various countries, wide variations can obviously be found everywhere. As a result, while these frameworks may be instructive for the purposes of general comparisons across cultures, they are not intended to represent universal patterns of organization.

Summary points

- Organizations are not just about how to put people into boxes or cubicles. Instead, they serve as a principal command and control system for focusing human, financial, and physical resources on the accomplishment of valued tasks. Organization designs live or die on the basis of their ability to assist managers with their responsibilities. Globalization requires a diversity of answers, not a one-size-fits-all approach to organization and management. This includes having a global vision and strategy, but it also means tailoring organizational designs to fit both local conditions and the available resources.
- The choice of an appropriate organization design typically evolves over time as companies increase their involvement in global activities. This evolutionary process often begins with some form of domestic organization design, in which international activities are largely an appendage to the more central domestic

activities, and evolves over time into a more integrated global organization design that places international business at the center of the organization's strategy.

■ An appropriate global organization design should help the firm integrate four types of strategic information in order to facilitate successful competition: (1) area knowledge, involving an understanding of the local area's culture, economics, and social conditions; (2) product knowledge, involving an understanding of local customer needs and possible markets for company products; (3) functional knowledge, involving local access to expertise in the various functional areas of business (e.g., finance, production, etc.); and (4) customer knowledge, involving an understanding of each customer's particular needs for sales and service.

■ Understanding the strategy and type of organizational structure is critical for managers, as it provides information as to what the priorities of the organization are (product standardization versus country adaptation), and accordingly influences the degree of managerial discretion.

■ It is possible to identify four of the more common organization and management models on the basis of the central question of who derives the greatest benefit from the organizations' operations. Obviously, all organizations have multiple stakeholders, and many major or minor groups benefit in various ways. The question here, however, is: who stands to gain the most, as a general trend?

■ Making timely, relevant, and wise decisions about the future directions of a firm is, clearly, a principal function of management. Critical to this process is where, when, and how information is sourced for optimum results. In other words, who has useful and important information or viewpoints that can lead to better decisions and who can be ignored, for reasons either of confidentiality or of efficiency? At the heart of this disagreement is the issue of employee involvement and participation in decision making.

■ Organizational culture reflects the norms, values, and approved behaviors of particular companies, divisions, or departments within organizations. It may either replicate or reject national culture values and norms, creating a microenvironment in which national norms are either reinforced or do not apply. In intra-organizational interactions, organizational norms and rules may serve to decrease the impact of multiple institutional environments. In inter-organizational relationships, the organizational environment may exacerbate differences through the development and reinforcement of norms of behavior; organizations define what is expected of managers.

Notes

1 Geert Hofstede, *Culture's Consequences: International Differences in Work-Related Values.* Thousand Oaks, CA: Sage, 2001, p. 373.

2 David Thomas, *Essentials of International Management: A Cross-Cultural Perspective.* Thousand Oaks, CA: Sage, 2002, p. 189.

3 Chester I. Barnard, *The Functions of the Executive.* Cambridge, MA: Harvard University Press, 1938.

4 Jonathan Browning, "Vodafone tears down its walled garden," *Bloomberg Business Week*, December 5, 2011, pp. 32–3.

5 Pankaj Ghemawat, "Managing differences: the central challenge of global strategy," *Harvard Business Review*, 2007, 85(3), pp. 59–68.

6 Kerry Capell, "The world's most influential companies," *Bloomberg Business Week*, August 12, 2011, p. 29.

7 Personal communication, Nancy J. Adler, McGill University, Montreal, 2008.

8 It should be remembered that the term "Anglo" came into widespread use by cultural anthropologies and social psychologists in the 1970s and 1980s to describe this cluster, and much has changed in the intervening years.

9 Ming-Jer Chen, *Inside Chinese Business: A Guide for Managers Worldwide.* Boston: Harvard Business School Press, 2001.

10 Confucius (551 BCE–479 CE) (*Kǒng Fūzǐ*), literally "Master Kong," was a Chinese thinker and social philosopher whose teachings and philosophy have deeply influenced Chinese, Korean, Japanese, Taiwanese, and Vietnamese thought and life. His philosophy emphasized personal and governmental morality, correctness in social relationships, justice, and sincerity. These values gained prominence in China over other doctrines, such as Legalism or Taoism, during the Han Dynasty (206 BCE–220 CE). Confucius' thoughts have been developed into a system of philosophy known as *Confucianism*. It was first introduced into Europe by the Jesuit Matteo Ricci, who was the first to Latinize the name as "Confucius." His teachings may be found in the *Analects of Confucius*, a collection of "brief aphoristic fragments," which was compiled many years after his death. Modern historians do not believe that any specific documents can be said to have been written by Confucius, but for nearly 2,000 years he was thought to be the editor or author.

11 Wenzhong Hu and Cornelius Grove, *Encountering the Chinese: A Guide for Americans*, 2nd edn. Yarmouth, ME: Intercultural Press, 1999.

12 *Guānxi* describes the basic dynamic in the complex nature of personalized networks of influence and social relationships, and it is a central concept in Chinese society. In Western media, the pinyin romanization of this Chinese word has tended to oversimplify the meaning of this term into "connections" or "relationships." Neither of these terms sufficiently reflects the wide cultural implications that *guānxi* describes. At its most basic, *guānxi* describes a personal connection between two people in which one is able to prevail upon another to perform a favor or service, or be prevailed upon. The two people need not to be of equal social status. *Guānxi* can also be used to describe a network of contacts, which an individual can

call upon when something needs to be done, and through which he or she can exert influence on behalf of another. In addition, *guānxi* can describe a state of general understanding between two people, in which both parties are aware of the other's needs and wants, and take these into account when making decisions or taking action. The term is not generally used to describe relationships within a family, although *guānxi* obligations can sometimes be described in terms of an extended family. The term is also not generally used to describe relationships that fall within other well-defined societal norms (e.g., boss–worker or teacher–student friendship). The relationships formed by *guānxi* are personal and not transferable. When a *guānxi* network violates bureaucratic norms, it can lead to corruption, and *guānxi* can also form the basis of patron–client relations.

13 Christopher Earley, *Face, Harmony, and Social Structure: An Analysis of Organizational Behavior across Cultures*. New York: Oxford University Press, 1997.

14 Sameena Ahmad, "Behind the mask: a survey of business in China," *The Economist*, March 20, 2004, pp. 3–19.

15 Chen, *Inside Chinese Business*.

16 S. Gordon Redding, *The Spirit of Chinese Capitalism*. Berlin: Walter de Gruyter, 1995.

17 Toyohiro Kono and Stewart Clegg, *Trends in Japanese Management: Continuing Strengths, Current Problems, and Changing Priorities*. London: Palgrave, 2001; Masahiko Aoki and Ronald Dore (eds.), *The Japanese Firm: Sources of Competitive Strength*. Oxford University Press, 1994.

18 James Abbeglen and George Stalk, *Kaisha: The Japanese Corporation*. New York: Harper & Row, 1985.

19 Hofstede, *Culture's Consequence*.

20 Edward T. Hall and Mildred Reed Hall, *Understanding Cultural Differences: Germans, French and Americans*. Yarmouth, ME: Intercultural Press, 2000.

21 Richard Hill, *We Europeans*. Brussels: Europublications, 1997.

22 Ingrid Brunstein (ed.), *Human Resource Management in Western Europe*. Berlin: Walter de Gruyter, 1995.

23 Victor Vroom and Philip Yetton, *Leadership and Decision-Making*. New York: Wiley, 1973.

24 We use the terms "centralized" and "collaborative" here instead of Vroom and Yetton's original "autocratic" and "group" in view of the nebulous meanings and normative ascriptions associated with the original terms.

25 Hiroki Kato and Joan Kato, *Understanding and Working with the Japanese Business World*. Englewood Cliffs, NJ: Prentice Hall, 1992.

26 *Nemawashi* is an informal process of quietly laying the foundation for some proposed change or project, by talking to the people concerned, gathering support and feedback, and so forth. It is considered an important element in any major change, before any formal steps are taken, and successful *nemawashi* enables changes to be carried out with the consent of all sides. *Nemawashi* literally translates as "going around the roots," from *ne* (root) and *mawasu* (to go around something). Its original meaning is literal: digging around the roots of a tree, to prepare it for a transplant.

27 *Honne* and *tatemae* are Japanese words used to describe recognized social phenomena. *Honne* refers to a person's true feelings and desires. These may be contrary to what is expected by society or what is required according to one's position and circumstances, and they are often kept hidden, except from one's closest friends. *Tatemae*, literally meaning "facade," is the behavior and opinions one displays in public. *Tatemae* is what is expected by society and required according to one's position and circumstances, and these may or may not match one's *honne*. This *honne/tatemae* divide is considered to be of paramount importance in Japanese culture. The very fact that the Japanese have single words for these concepts leads some Japanese experts to see this conceptualization as evidence of greater Japanese complexity and rigidity in etiquette and culture. *Honne* and *tatemae* are arguably a cultural necessity, resulting from a large number of people living in a relatively small island nation. Even with modern farming techniques, Japan today domestically produces only 39 percent of the food needed to feed its people, so close-knit cooperation and the avoidance of conflict remain of vital importance today, as they did in ancient times. For this reason, the Japanese tend to go to great lengths to avoid conflict, especially within the context of large groups. The conflict between *hone* and *giri* (social obligations) is one of the main topics of Japanese drama throughout the ages. In such dramas, the protagonist would typically have to choose between carrying out his obligations to his family or feudal lord and pursuing a forbidden love affair or other personal interest. In the end, death would often be the only way out of the dilemma.

28 Edgar H. Schein, *Organizational Culture and Leadership*. San Francisco: Jossey-Bass, 1988.

29 Vas Taras, Piers Steel, and Bradley L. Kirkman, "Three decades of research on national culture in the workplace: do the differences still make a difference?," *Organizational Dynamics*, 2011, 40(3), pp. 189–98.

30 April Rabkin, "What is the sound of three hands clapping?," *Fast Company*, February 2012, pp. 79–98.

CHAPTER 5

The situational environment

In Chapter 3 we discussed how the cultural environment exerts pressures on individuals and organizations. In Chapter 4 we discussed how the organizational environment can also influence managerial behavior. In this chapter we explore the third environment influencing managerial success or failure: the situation. This environment consists of a combination of individual differences and contextual factors that collectively define the situation in which managers find themselves. The challenge for managers is that they typically face different situations every time they go out into the field. These differences may be as simple as working with people with different personalities or as complicated as attempting to meet their responsibilities or goals in a highly competitive environment. In all cases, the challenge is to understand the particular situation in which managers are working and how the present situation may differ from the previous ones. Once this is understood, the challenge is to develop a model that integrates these three factors – cultures, organizations, and situations – in way that helps managers better understand their options and opportunities.

Chapter outline

Applications

> You get very different thinking if you sit in Shanghai or São Paulo or Dubai than if you
> sit in New York.
>
> Michael Cannon-Brookes[1]
> Vice president, business development – India and China, IBM Corporation

> There is nothing wrong with smiling and telling the lady with the pad and pen that
> you will have two burritos and a coke, unless she is a traffic cop. And when it is your
> job to play the organ, there is nothing wrong with whipping the crowd into an
> impassioned frenzy, unless you work in a funeral home.
>
> Terry O'Reilly[2]
> Broadcaster, CBC Radio, Canada

Juliana and Lucas both moved from Brazil to North America. She settled in the United States, he in Canada. In Brazil both were widely described as introverts, but in North America they were seen as extroverts. How is this possible? Did their personalities change as a result of their changed circumstances or did they find themselves in a culture with a very different frame of reference? Obviously, it is the situation that has changed.[3] Today Juliana works teaching Brazilian language and culture to future expatriates, while Lucas works for the Canadian government as a tax accountant. Juliana's cultural background is considered an asset and she is expected to behave as a typical Brazilian at work, while many of Lucas's colleagues do not even know that he is originally from Brazil. At work, he is expected to behave as a typical Canadian would. Thus, not only have their situations changed, but so too have people's expectations regarding their behavior.

Less experienced managers often tend to overlook the differences in their surroundings when they are in the field, and try instead to "focus on business." In many cases, this is an unwise strategy. In reality, the situation facing a manager at any given point in time is the stage on which action is determined. As the opening quotes suggest, many behaviors are not inherently good or bad, but must be interpreted within certain contexts. What may be seen as funny at a party may be considered rude in a business meeting, and so forth. Behaviors that feel natural with people of our own culture may feel uncomfortable with foreigners. Indeed, research has found that people often behave differently when they are in cross-cultural situations from when they are among people of their own culture. Often the norms of behavior towards people of our own culture are different from the ones guiding behavior towards foreigners. For example, research on women expatriates suggest that, even though local women in Asia may not have as many opportunities as their male counterparts, this difference seldom applies to foreign women, particularly those from the West. Each of them is, first and foremost, a *gaijin* ("foreigner" in Japanese), and, as such, they are treated differently from how local women are treated.[4] In other words, although national culture is a major force in influencing behavior, the impact of culture on behavior does not happen in a vacuum. Situations and contexts differ, and these differences are important for understanding behavior.

We refer to the workspace in which such interactions transpire as the *situational environment*. It can be seen most directly at the point of contact between people with different backgrounds, goals, and responsibilities when they come together to do business. It is largely represented by differences in goals and tasks, people, roles and responsibilities, and locations (see Exhibit 5.1). It is embedded within national and organizational cultures, but also carries with it its own unique characteristics and challenges. This is where "the rubber meets the road" in terms of managerial performance, and it is highly situation-specific.

As managers work to understand the critical dimensions that characterize the situation, as well as their managerial implications, several key *situation-specific questions* come to mind.

(1) Who is involved and what does each party want? What is the nature of our relationship?
(2) What are we trying to accomplish, individually or collectively?
(3) Who are the various parties responsible to? Who is in charge?
(4) What are the potential opportunities and constraints? Who has the technology? Who has the financial resources? Why do we need each other?
(5) How are we going to proceed? Who makes the first move? Where are we meeting?

The answers to questions such as these form the basis for this chapter in situational differences. We begin where most companies and organizations begin: with its people. We then consider three additional related situational factors: goals and plans; individual

Exhibit 5.1 The situational environment

roles and responsibilities; and location. Collectively, these four factors help illustrate how managerial actions on the ground can vary widely, and why it is important to avoid naïve generalizations about "appropriate" managerial behavior in the global environment.

People, cognition, and behavior

People in the global workplace obviously come in different shapes and sizes, abilities and skills, ages and genders, educational and income levels, and so forth. They may be colleagues, managers, subordinates, advisors, customers, clients, and personal friends. They may speak different languages, behave differently, approach problem solving in different ways, and sometimes seek different rewards and outcomes for doing the same job. These simple facts can make the job of a manager particularly challenging.

Consider Jes Allersted, who works for software giant Microsoft in the company's Danish headquarters near Copenhagen. As a Danish employee working for a US company, he understands the pressures imposed on him and his colleagues by the often conflicting American and Danish cultural and institutional environments. He also understands the Microsoft organizational environment, with its unique strategy, structure, norms, and procedures. At the end of the day, however, this is insufficient for him to succeed. In a very real sense, Allersted is not working entirely in Denmark. He is also in the office building – and organizational culture – of a large US multinational technology firm. While he may be Danish, some of his colleagues are from the United States and other countries (see Exhibit 5.2). His performance will be assessed largely on his results and those of his team, not on his overall mastery of the English language and the American culture, or on his understanding of Microsoft's structure and procedures. He is fortunate in that he was educated in both Denmark and the United States, speaks English fluently, and has traveled widely around the world. Even so, his success or failure will depend largely on how he is able to deal with the unique – and often highly diverse – job situations, tasks, and business challenges that face him in the job on a daily basis.

Think about this: most of our behavior is both intentional and conditional. In other words, people seldom act without having a direction or without being cognizant of the situation around them. They make choices about what they intend to do. Are they among friends or strangers? Do they have more or less power or status than their colleagues? Is their job secure or in jeopardy? And so forth. This variability alone creates uncertainty even in what appears to be simple or straightforward situations. For instance, in our above example with Microsoft, the fact that only one organization is involved simplifies things somewhat. Imagine how much more complicated it would become if two or more companies were involved, such as a partnership negotiation between British and Chinese companies. Even so, both situations can be challenging.

Our conclusion, therefore, is that people are the same, only different. This by itself is not very helpful. From a managerial standpoint, the important question is: why? When

Exhibit 5.2 Work environment for Jes Allersted and co-workers at Microsoft, Denmark

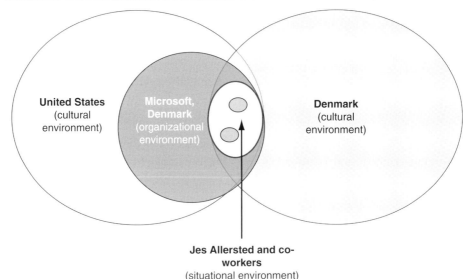

dealing with people, a fundamental question is why they do what they do. There are many factors that can influence behavior. Much of what we do is *learned behavior* (see Chapter 3). As a result of our upbringing, including normative beliefs and values, we are taught what is expected of us and what is prohibited. When we enter companies and other organizations, we continue learning. We also learn as a result of previous experiences. *Individual differences*, such as our personality, skills, and abilities, also influence our behavior, as discussed below. People who are introverted, for example, might be less likely to participate openly in team meetings, and might prefer to linger after the meeting so as to express their views privately. People also behave in certain ways because of their *motivation* (see Chapter 9). Pay-for-performance jobs are very popular among achievement-oriented individuals, but others prefer greater job security or opportunities for social interactions, even if the pay is somewhat lower.

Space does not permit a broad-based exploration of people, so instead we focus on two issues that pertain especially to working across cultures: (1) personality and individual differences; and (2) cognitive structures and behavior. Both topics relate to how people work with other people across and within borders.

Personality and individual differences

People don't have to cross borders to recognize the importance of personality and individual differences in influencing people's attitudes and behaviors. Indeed, the entire field of psychology is based on this assumption. As such, it is an easy conclusion to reach that personality and other individual differences exist both within and across national cultures. This fact alone yields two pieces of advice for managers. First, any manager who begins a sentence with "Italians (or Indians or Mexicans, etc.) do this or that…" is on shaky ground. The Italian people are indeed heterogeneous, like everyone else. Second, if managers recognize that individual differences occur in all cultures, it necessarily follows that on-the-job behaviors can be different – a factor that can require considerable attention. In this regard, we can identify two aspects of this issue that can make important differences in the workplace.

- *Individual differences between cultures*. Global travelers frequently point to general differences – trends, really – between one culture and another. Some might suggest, for example, that the average Japanese is more introverted than the average American. In reality, most of these travelers are talking in generalities, not specifics. All the same, such observations, however superficial, are difficult to ignore, and, indeed, can sometimes be useful. Take, for example, the concept of *locus of control*. This is a concept that has been used to investigate how much control people believe they have over their own destiny. (This concept is not substantively different from the mastery/harmony concept discussed in Chapter 3, except that it is more person-centered.) Researchers on this topic suggest that people can be divided into two groups. People with an "internal" locus of control believe that they largely create their own destiny; it is in their hands to succeed. By contrast, people with an "external" locus of control believe that the future, including their own personal level of success, is largely determined by fate or other external factors. It has been suggested, for example, that many people in both Latin America and the Middle East often believe their fate is externally determined, while many people from Europe and North America often believe that their future is in their hands. What, therefore, is the difference from a managerial standpoint? Simply put, if we are managing people in a Canadian or British company, we would likely use motivational techniques that include some recognition of individual performance. This should motivate people who believe they can succeed if they wish to. By the same token, if we are motivating employees in Mexico or Honduras, we might place less emphasis on pay for performance, since, according to research, they would have less faith in their control over their performance environment. Note that we are making huge generalizations here, as there are significant individual differences within cultures, as is discussed below.

- *Individual differences within cultures.* Looking within cultures can also provide useful lessons for global managers. Take, for example, our Canada/Mexico example above. In point of fact, many Mexicans have a strong internal locus of control. Witness, for example, Carlos Slim, owner of Telmex and many other companies, and one of the richest people in the world. These Mexicans are genuinely entrepreneurial. Likewise, many Canadians have an external locus of control; they don't want to accept responsibility for much that happens around them. Again, note that we are making huge generalizations here.

Application 5.1 Carlos Ghosn

To see how such differences can work, look at what can happen when an executive from one culture is sent to run a company in another. Ask yourself: what might happen when a Brazilian of Lebanese decent with a French passport and work experience in the United States is sent to Japan to turn around an ailing company? This is precisely what happened to Carlos Ghosn. When Nissan was looking for a strategic partner, it turned to France's Renault. Renault agreed to send out one of its top executives as Nissan's new CEO. Outsiders, and many within Nissan itself, predicted that he would be gone within a year; traditional Japanese business culture would force him out.

After spending several months reviewing Nissan's operations, Ghosn announced a draconian turnaround plan, including closing five Japanese factories and terminating 16,000 employees. The plan shaved operating costs by over $10 billion. Still in control after a year, Ghosn next addressed Nissan's traditional inward-looking corporate culture. He moved swiftly to redirect company managers' attention by refocusing their efforts on improving profits and enhancing customer satisfaction. He established a network of Western-style multinational cross-functional teams to reexamine and reinvigorate each of the firm's principal activities. He even began openly discussing a Western-style pay-for-performance compensation system for managerial and non-managerial employees alike to replace the existing seniority system, which was so deeply entrenched in Japanese work culture. Moreover, to drive the point home that Nissan would become a truly global firm, not just a Japanese firm operating internationally, Ghosn suggested that henceforth the company's official language should be English, not Japanese.

While all this was going on, and despite an incredibly busy work schedule, Ghosn began studying the Japanese language, never becoming proficient but learning enough to converse in simple ways and show employees his commitment to the firm and its Japanese culture. This also aided in his efforts to better understand local customs and practices. Looking back on his efforts, what Ghosn had done in short order was to challenge the traditional Japanese approach to organization and management and force employees at all levels not to Westernize but to globalize – to build a new management system that focused more on the global than the local. The result was a new way of managing that ultimately led the company to record profits and an enhanced reputation.

Think about it . . .

(1) What was it about Carlos Ghosn that made him a suitable candidate for this position?

(2) What actions did Ghosn initiate at Nissan that may be explained at least in part by his personality, and what actions are simply the results of his approach to management? Is there a relationship here?

(3)   What explains Ghosn's success in helping to transform Nissan into a global competitor?

(4)   Is it generally easier for outside (i.e., foreign) executives to implement major organizational and managerial changes in global companies such as Nissan than for local executives? If so, why? When might this not be the case?

(5)   In the realm of conjecture, when Ghosn leaves Nissan, do you think the company should appoint another foreigner or a Japanese CEO? Why?

The conclusion here is simple: from a managerial standpoint, both the generalizations and their exceptions can at times be important, up to a point. For example, thinking that all Japanese tend to be introverts may make us consider learning more about subtle nonverbal communication (see Chapter 6). It should also force us, however, to recognize that Japan has its share of extroverts too. As a result, we may be so busy looking for subtle cues in the environment that we ignore what is explicitly said to our face. We may ignore the obvious. The lesson: situations, including individual differences, matter.

Cognitive structures and behavior

If we ask psychology and management experts to identify the process by which people acquire, transform, and utilize information about the world in order to achieve their goals, psychologists will call it *cognition*, while managers will call it management. Both would be right. Management requires an understanding of what lies behind action. More specifically, it requires knowledge about how our minds function, how the minds of others function, and how we relate our mental patterns to the patterns of others within an organizational context. This is an important point. We cannot deal successfully with others if we do not understand them. As such, we begin here to see how and why the minds of managers and employees in different cultures work in ways that are simultaneously similar and dissimilar.

The existence of cultural variations in *cognitive processes* may sound a bit strange to people who have given the topic little thought. To put this topic into perspective, however, consider that the human brain at birth weighs only about one-fourth of what it does when people reach young adulthood, when the physical maturation of the brain is complete. As a result, three-quarters of human brain growth – including almost all its cognitive development – occurs outside the womb and in contact with its surrounding external environment, in culturally influenced and constrained settings.[5] As such, culture and cognition can be seen – and perhaps best understood – in terms of an interactive relationship between thought and action in which culturally determined thought processes influence our behaviors, which, in turn, often reinforce or challenge our thoughts and beliefs. Individuals cannot be fully understood in isolation from their environments, and culture and cognition go hand in hand in any effort to understand how people think and behave in organizational settings.

Basic cognitive processes: attention, interpretation, and action

In trying to understand how cognition works in social situations, including in the business world, we can identify a simple model of cognition that involves just three variables. Each of these variables, however, is influenced by our cultural background, context, and previous experiences (see Exhibit 5.3).

- *Attention.* When we first experience events in the external world, we choose what to see and what not to see. Sometimes we don't even notice these events, as when someone uses eye signals to express his or her disagreement but his or her partner is not watching. This is called perceptual selection, or, simply, attention. It represents what we focus on for future analysis and possible action.

Exhibit 5.3 Basic model of cognition

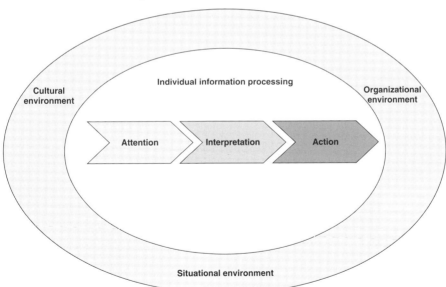

- *Interpretation*. Following this, we tend to categorize or classify what we have seen or experienced according to some relational comparative guideline; we consider what is important or unimportant, what is good or bad. This is referred to as cognitive evaluation, or interpretation.

- *Action*. Based on these interpretations, we decide whether or not we are going to take any action and, if so, what it will be.

Application 5.2 **Symbolism of chairs**

In a true story, consider what happened during an impromptu negotiation session between two managers, one from the United States and one from Austria. Facing a minor disagreement on some contractual details, the two managers decided to sit down in a nearby conference room to find a solution. The American manager entered the room and sat down in the first chair he came to. The Austrian manager noticed that her counterpart had sat in the higher chair in the room and interpreted this action as an attempt to assert power. She concluded that the American manager was not being sufficiently collaborative and decided to play tough. The American, oblivious of the difference in chair heights, noticed that his colleague was being difficult, maybe even unreasonable, and decided that she could not be trusted. They did not reach an agreement.

     Think about it...

(1)   What was each of the managers paying close attention to during this meeting?

(2)   How did their interpretations of the environment differ from one another? Explain.

(3)   What could each manager have done differently to avoid or at least minimize this conflict?

    The final thing to note here is that cultural, organizational, and situational environments can influence this process to no small degree. Factors such as one's particular socialization experiences (e.g., what's important), place in the organizational hierarchy (e.g., deference to seniors), stakeholders (owners, colleagues), relationships (e.g., trust levels), language (ours or theirs), location (again, ours or theirs), and incentives (what we are rewarded for) all influence what is noticed and what is not. Such factors can influence what we pay attention to, how we interpret what we pay attention to, and the repertoire of actions available to us to respond.

For example, if we discover at work that we are receiving a lower salary than our peers and this concerns us (attention), we will likely evaluate the situation from various perspectives (interpretation). This involves raising various questions, such as whether your peers are actually better performers than you or whether they are better connected. Perhaps seniority plays a role here, or perhaps your boss just doesn't appreciate your talents. Perhaps salary is not that important to you, since you enjoy the work itself. In any case, as a result of your cognitive evaluations, you will decide on what response is best for you (action). Perhaps you decide to ask for a rise or perhaps you look for a different job. Maybe you ignore the inequity out of fear of losing your job. Maybe you decide to get even and try in some way to retaliate against your employer, supervisor, or colleagues. Whatever you decide to do, it will likely be aimed at restoring your sense of equity or perceived fairness in this particular situation.

Application 5.3 Interpreting messages

A small Malaysian manufacturer located outside Kuala Lumpur recently contracted with a large Australian distributor to produce model trains for the Australian/New Zealand market. After receiving the first shipment, the distributor sent the manufacturer a short list of discrepancies between what was ordered and what was delivered, including some incorrect specifications and a minor quality control issue. The manufacturer in Malaysia interpreted the communication as an attempt to solicit a reduction in price. He therefore focused his efforts on cutting costs and did little to address the quality or specification discrepancies. The partnership ended soon thereafter. In both cases, it was what the people saw – what they paid attention to – that influenced their behavior.

Think about it...

(1)   What was the Australian distributor trying to say in her communication?

(2)   Why do you think the Malaysian manufacturer interpreted the communication in the manner he did?

(3)   What could each side have done to avoid this misunderstanding?

Cognitive schemas

People can learn a great deal about contemporary realities from their histories and traditions. Old accounts from settlers and explorers, immigrants and slaves, historians and public figures illustrate earlier incarnations of local cultures and inform current generations about what differentiates one culture from another. One such account from colonial Spain illustrates nicely the relationship between culture and cognition. The story goes that, in 1526, an Aztec scribe was told by a Spanish colonial official to keep a record of all the items collected in tribute for the king of Spain. The scribe carefully entered each item he inventoried into its appropriate category: gold quills, cotton and feathered robes, fine and coarse stones, cacao beans, and so forth. After several weeks the Spanish official visited the scribe to check his progress. He examined the long lists with increasing perplexity, commenting in anger that all the record keeping was worthless, since he could not find the amounts of gold, silver, or precious stones. The scribe answered that he had kept the records the way they always had, up to the smallest item, in clear categories: all the durable items were listed first, followed by round objects, flat objects, cylindrical objects, and hard objects. The official did not know how to react to such a curious (and, in his view, obviously useless) explanation. He personally knew the scribe to be an honest and intelligent man, but the result was completely out of line with the whole purpose of the assignment.[6]

Global managers often find themselves in situations similar to those of the Spanish official or the Aztec scribe when dealing with people from other cultures. There is something in the way many "foreigners" make sense of reality that can easily interfere with both our understanding of what is going on and any possible collaboration across cultures. Despite the oft-cited commonalities in mental capability and functioning among all humans, all too often our mental processes seem to work towards separating rather than uniting us. Experienced managers have learned that, unless they can make sense of the mental screens that separate people from different cultures, their work is likely going to be painful, ineffective, and time-consuming.

Research in social psychology has found that our cognitions (thought processes) and subsequent behaviors (e.g., working hard, quitting a job) are heavily influenced by what are called our *cognitive schemas*. Schemas are simply mental repositories of knowledge that store representations about what things are, their characteristics, and what they might be related to.[7] They include people's knowledge base, expectations, experiences, and biases – that is, how people make sense of the world. They do not need to be correct or accurate; they are based simply on what we believe to be accurate. For example, when we hear the word "entrepreneur," we frequently have in our mind our own idea of what entrepreneurs look like, what characteristics they have, and what activities they typically engage in. We might see entrepreneurs as being young, or male, or Asian. Again, none of this has to be true; it is only what we see in our mind. It is our cognitive schema. The contents of such schemas are highly cultural, as we typically learn about things and events within our own cultures. They are highly personal and individual experiences, however, and people can modify previous mindsets with new ones as a result of new experiences, changed expect-ations, or education. As we apply our cognitive schema in real life, we are likely to learn new things through trial and error, and modify our knowledge base accordingly.

Application 5.4   What is a supervisor?

A good example of how schemas and cognitions work can be seen in a single word: *supervisor*. What does this term mean? What does it conjure up in people's minds? In English, the word "supervisor" carries with it connotations of authority, control, and power; a supervisor is a boss (see Exhibit 5.4). In Japanese, by contrast, the word often assumes a more familial connotation; a supervisor is a senior role model and protector of subordinates, much like parents. Indeed, *kachou* in Japanese means "supervisor" (or, more accurately, "section chief"), but it also means "patriarch" or "family head." In German, the word "supervisor" carries strong connotations of technical competence and expertise. Indeed, a supervisor is sometimes referred to as *meister* (or master technician). German supervisors are generally chosen for their knowledge, technical competence (*technik* in German) and training abilities, and not necessarily for their ability to control others. In Mexico, a supervisor is considered to be a patron, looking after the interests of his or her employees in exchange for allegiance and obedience (*capataz* or *jefe*). Same word, basically, but very different meanings – and sometimes very different behavioral consequences.

Think about it . . .

(1)   What are the implications of these different schemas for the behavior of supervisors in the workplace and for those who report to them? Explain.

(2)   What is your personal schema for a "supervisor"? Where did your schema come from? How did it develop?

Constraints on information processing

Finally, we examine one additional aspect of cognition across culture; how people from various cultures and regions sometimes process available information in different ways, leading them to different conclusions and different actions. Specifically, we examine the research on the cognitive constraints that can influence how people access, organize, and transform information into patterns of meaning. Indeed, culturally influenced cognitive patterns can affect a wide variety of behaviors, from leadership and decision making to motivation and negotiation. This is effected through the ways in which information is acquired and retained, organized and categorized, and evaluated, learned, and utilized (see Exhibit 5.5).

Exhibit 5.4 Cognitive schemas for "supervisor"

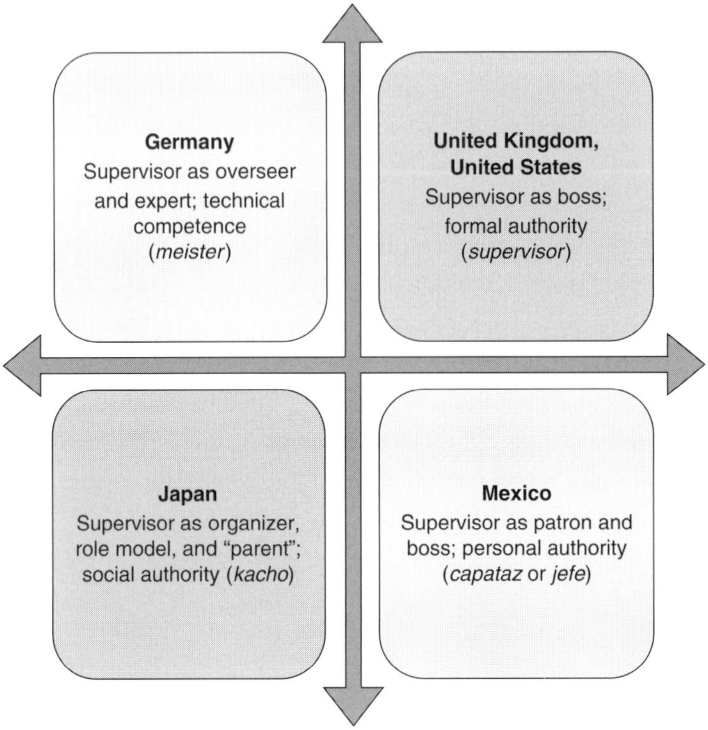

- *Information acquisition, retention, and recall.* The mental representations of time and space that are embedded in particular cultures affect attention processes and memory for temporal information, with direct implications for the encoding and retrieval of information, as well as memory and learning.[8] In a series of experiments in Mexico and Morocco, psychologist Daniel Wagner found substantive evidence that the structure of memory is universal across cultures, but that its associated control processes for information acquisition and retrieval are culturally influenced.[9] In other words, people memorize things in the same way regardless of where they live, but their cultural background can influence what information they choose to acquire and remember. Moreover, people tend to have better recall of information when it is consistent with their cultural knowledge and values.[10] For example, many managers from mastery-oriented cultures tend to recall the specific successes of their subordinates that involved sales or financial achievements, but not their interpersonal or team-building successes. Meanwhile, in more harmony-oriented cultures, managers tend to recall more about their subordinates'

Exhibit 5.5 Constraints on information processing

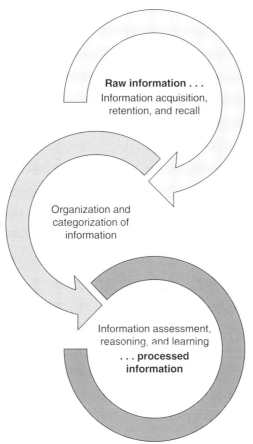

interpersonal or team-building successes, regardless of their sales or financial successes. In addition, when facing the possibility of alternative interpretations of specific events (such as a team success), managers will almost invariably choose the interpretation that is most consistent with their cultural outlook.[11] In other words, managers from highly individualistic cultures will typically ascribe team success to the team leader's skills and efforts, while managers from more collectivistic cultures will typically ascribe it to the skills and efforts of the entire team.

- *Categorization of information.* Societies define different traits in their environment as being disproportionately meaningful and worthy of attention for their assumed practical importance to their culture.[12] It is not surprising, therefore, that mechanical skills are highly prized in Germany and Scandinavia, where large economic sectors are based on engineering, while financial and legal skills are highly prized in the United Kingdom, the United States, and Canada, where so much of the economy is based on initial public offerings, stock transfers, and leveraged buyouts. At the same time, cultures vary in the manner in which people develop categories for purposes of classification. For example, many Chinese raised in a collectivist environment classify people on the basis of criteria that emphasize relationships and contexts. As a result, a woman and a child are often seen as belonging together (as opposed to a man and a woman), because the child needs the woman and the woman takes care of the child. By contrast, Americans raised in more individualistic contexts rely more on isolated properties of the objects in the classification. As a result, a woman and man belong together, rather than with the child, because they both are adults of similar ages.[13] This same pattern can be seen in managers who are likely to work and socialize with people of similar training (accountants with accountants, salespeople with salespeople, etc.), compared to Chinese managers, who more frequently work and socialize with people with highly diverse training. Researchers have also studied how different people describe themselves and categorize the idea of self. On the one hand, many managers from Australia, Canada, and the United States, for example, hold an independent concept of self, seeing it as bound, concrete, and comprising mostly fixed and enduring qualities. On the other hand, many managers from China, Japan, and South Korea, for example, maintain a concept of self that is more interdependent, socially diffused, relational, context-bound, changing, and malleable. American managers, for instance, describe themselves in abstract and fixed ways ("I am a good boss"), whereas Chinese, Japanese, and South Korean managers refer more often to their social roles and relationships ("I work for Samsung" or "I am a Hitachi salary-man").[14] Similar dynamics were found in a comparison of the concept of self of Americans (independent), southeast Asians (interdependent), and Hindu Indians (the self as religiously defined by invoking notions of reincarnation, karma, and the interconnectedness of all living beings, including multiple lifetimes and forms).[15]

- *Assessment, reasoning, and learning.* Before the idea of intelligence as being multi-dimensional in nature and scope gained currency, experts recognized that the concept of intelligent behavior varies widely across cultures and, accordingly, that cultures require different skills to cope with their unique environments.[16] As a result, cultural factors often influence what will be learned in a given environment and at what age, leading to different patterns of general ability among people.[17] For example, due to a particular (but not universal) interpretation of the Qur'an, Kuwaiti women were only recently educated about local politics and allowed to vote in regional elections. When inferring mental states of other people, research indicates that several cultures in North America and western Europe emphasize a norm of authenticity (i.e., external actions and emotional displays are seen as consistent with internal states), while east and southeast Asian societies often tend to consider such manifestations as immature, impolite, and sometimes bizarre. For example, "speaking one's mind" or "telling it like it is" often appears in a positive light among Australians and Americans, but not to the Japanese or Malaysians. Moreover, some South Koreans, Japanese, and Thais may give more importance in communication processes to what is left unsaid instead of what is said in open and direct ways, while the opposite applies in many Western societies.[18] Reasoning processes also play out differently across cultures. Attributions of causality (i.e., what caused something to occur) differentially focus on either the personal characteristics of the individual in more individualistic societies or the overall social circumstances surrounding the events among more collectivist peoples. In this sense, attributions in contexts as varied as the explanation for mass murders, success in sports, and managerial behavior in the workplace all follow a similar pattern that is largely culturally determined.[19]

Application 5.5 Customer service

Is customer service the same all over the world? Yes, in the sense that customers are served (some better than others, of course), but also no, in the sense of the mindsets and information processing of the customer service representatives. For example, foreign observers have long noted how naïve Western customers in their home countries can be in responding favorably to widespread promises of customer satisfaction.[20] By contrast, many Japanese sales clerks do not guarantee customer satisfaction; instead, they will aim at doing their best, and just hope that it happens.[21] For many Japanese managers, a guarantee of satisfaction sounds too pretentious, almost like an invasion of privacy. "Who are we to judge whether customers will really be satisfied?" the logic goes.

This behavior is related to differing images concerning the relationship between buyer and seller. In the West, this is seen as a horizontal exchange among equals. Japanese, however, tend to view the relationship with customers in more hierarchical terms, in which the buyer is more like a master and the seller like a servant. Expressions often heard in the West, such as "The customer is always right," make

Application 5.5 (cont.)

little sense within a hierarchical framework, because the very assessment of right and wrong implies a position of superiority by those making the assessment. If customers are always right in the West, they are beyond right and wrong in Japan. As a consequence, commercial relationships in the West focus on the transaction and its balance for both buyers and sellers, while caring for the relationship and a mixture of loyalty and interdependence is generally stressed in Japan.

Finally, sales clerks in Japan typically take buyers' complaints, remarks, and requests at face value, while trying to understand exactly what they want. This is done with a lack of personal involvement that Westerners often see as too cold or lacking in emotion. The Japanese salesperson presents product information without drawing conclusions for the customer, unlike Western tactics, whereby, in what often resembles a contest of wills, sellers try to persuade customers of the need to purchase the product – preferably immediately, because it is "on sale." In Japan, sales clerks who interject themselves into the sale too much lead to customer doubts about the quality of the product or service. Instead, they will frequently take themselves out of the buyer's equation and let the product speak for itself.

Think about it...

(1) What is your definition of good customer service? Explain.

(2) How can the schemas of both customers and sales clerks influence this definition in practice? What happens when these two sets of schemas are far apart?

(3) How might information processing among customer service clerks differ across cultures? Why?

Goals and plans

Quo vadis? is a Latin term meaning "Where are you going?," and it aptly describes strategic planners' first responsibility in the situational environment. Simply put, what is the organization trying to accomplish? What are its goals? This is a highly complex topic – university courses are often organized around it – but our focus here is simply on understanding how goals, plans, and specific tasks can represent a major influence on situations, as well as the implications for global managers. With this in mind, we can identify several key aspects of plans and planning that serve to guide managerial actions. When journalists attempt to write a story about a current event, they are told to focus on five things: who, what, when, where, and why. These same parameters can be useful in understanding why a company is working across borders in the first place. This is the essence of the *Quo vadis?* question, and includes the following.

- *Who*. Who are you dealing with? Who is evaluating your performance? Who are you accountable to?
- *What*. What are you trying to accomplish in this venture? Is this an expansion of the company overseas or is it a joint venture with other companies? In either case, what are your goals and how will you know when you have achieved them?
- *When*. What is the timeline for completing this task? Do you have the necessary resources to do what is expected?
- *Where*. Where will most of your interactions or tasks be accomplished? What is it about the specific locale that may help or hinder your success?
- *Why*. Why is this task taking place? Why are you involved?

To see how goals and plans can help define the situation in which managers and executives operate, take the example of Air France, one of the industry's premier airlines. The global airline industry has changed dramatically in recent years as a result of increased fuel costs, decreased regulations, and rising labor costs. Competition has challenged the so-called "legacy" (traditional) carriers, as new low-cost entrants, such as EasyJet and Ryanair, have entered the field. The situation has definitely changed. The question is whether the more traditional carriers will survive and, if so, how.

Application 5.6 Work rules at Air France

In an industry in which sparse service has become de rigueur, Air France has made much of its full-service operations.[22] There's a limit, however, to how much coddling the French carrier's in-flight staff are willing to provide to passengers. Recently Air France began asking passengers on new regional flights from French cities to carry their own trash with them when leaving the plane to recycling bins in the passenger boarding bridge. The reason: cabin crews refuse to do so. This is just one of the challenges Pierre-Henri Gourgeon, CEO of Air France–KLM, faces as he tries to update the airline's operations and fend off the advance of discounters EasyJet and Ryanair in his home market. Gourgeon's strategy involves shifting part of Air France's fleet of airplanes from Paris to airports in Marseille, Nice, and Toulouse. Then the airline can fly dozens of new routes from these hubs to north Africa, eastern Europe, and Scandinavia. Staffers stationed at the regional bases would work longer hours under more flexible work rules. Ground-based plane cleaning on short hauls would be cut to every fourth flight, from every one or two now. Such changes would pare costs and trim the turnaround time between flights to less than thirty-five minutes, boosting each plane's time in the air to about twelve hours a day from the current eight or nine.

Air France's share of domestic and international traffic from its homeland has fallen significantly in recent years. EasyJet more than quadrupled its share of this market in recent years. EasyJet declined to comment on the Air France plan, but Spain's no-frills Vueling Airlines noted, "Our cabin crew go through and do a cleanup because they're already onboard. But you won't get Air France staff to do that." Air France's pilots union accepted the regional strategy, but talks with its two cabin crew unions broke down over issues including reduced rest periods and lower hourly pay. Union wrangling has already forced Air France to abandon plans for a fourth large plane hub in Bordeaux. It has also delayed opening the Marseille base to allow for extra union consultation, says Gourgeon. "The delay is mainly because we want to do it in a win-win way with staff," he says. "We don't force anybody. We don't have to say, 'OK, you have to work more and make less money.'" Instead, the airline is seeking 300 volunteers to staff the Marseille operation.

Think about it . . .

(1) Describe the current situation facing Air France's CEO Pierre-Henri Gourgeon using the traditional journalism questions: who, what, when, where, and why?

(2) In your view, what are Gourgeon's principal goals and plans as he faces the challenge of making Air France more globally competitive? Do you agree with his goals and plans? Explain.

(3) Air France's pilot's union has agreed to Gourgeon's proposed changes in work rules, but the cabin crew's union has not. Why is this?

(4) If you were the CEO of Air France, how would you try and resolve this conflict?

Individual roles and responsibilities

The location of people in the organizational hierarchy, including their assigned individual roles and responsibilities, can also be a significant determinant of the situational context in which managers find themselves, and, as such, can be an important factor in their attention, interpretation, and subsequent behaviors (see Exhibit 5.6). Consider a few examples.

- *Formal job responsibilities.* Throughout the organization structure, managers are assigned specific roles and positions in a particular social group that carries certain normative expectations.[23] These roles help shape the interpretations that people make about their approach to work and other people. For example, while we may expect to see the kitchen staff serving food or clearing tables in the company cafeteria, the same behavior by the CEO would likely draw particular attention; it would be "out of context." Questions therefore arise. What are the role expectations for managers? What are the manager's formal responsibilities? What is his or her job title, and what weight does this carry (or not carry)? If he or she is in charge of finance, for example, he or she will likely focus on costs, return on investment, and

Exhibit 5.6 Examples of individual roles and responsibilities

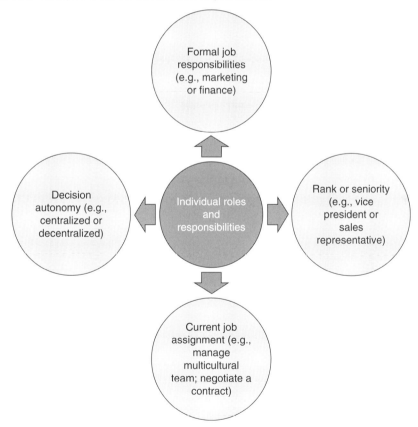

budgets. By contrast, if he or she is working in marketing, he or she will likely focus on sales or new product opportunities.

- *Rank or seniority.* One of the authors was recently at a lunch meeting with two managers (one junior, one senior) from an east Asian company. During the entire lunch the junior manager said nothing. He sat there in silence. Only later, over dinner and not in the presence of the senior manager, did he offer his opinions, observations, and suggestions to the author. Knowing who is "important" and when and where to speak is critical, whether you agree with it or not (see Chapter 6).

- *Current assignment.* What exactly is the manager's current assignment? Does it involve negotiating a new strategic alliance with a foreign company, resolving a conflict between partners, managing a global team, or what? The current assignment is closely tied with the goals and tasks discussed above. For example, the goal of a particular meeting may be to negotiate a joint venture partnership, in which multiple people are involved. Some may be tasked with the legal aspects of the venture, others with negotiating the financial arrangements, and still others with smoothing the relationship. The question here is: who is doing what?

- *Decision autonomy.* How centralized is decision making within the organization? Where, and by whom, are decisions made? How much autonomy will the manager in the field or at the negotiating table have to sign off on agreements? Must he or she report back to company headquarters before taking any actions or can he or she make decisions – or decisions within certain parameters – on the spot without referring back to anyone for prior approval (see Chapter 7)?

Application 5.7 Perils of being a junior manager

The story of Jeff Depew is a story of individual roles and responsibilities. It is also a caution to junior managers that, when something goes wrong in a large company, the people at the bottom are often likely to receive the blame. Depew worked for a major US electronics giant and was assigned the responsibility of laying the groundwork for a strategic alliance between his employer and its Japanese counterpart. He was fluent in the Japanese language and culture and was looking for an opportunity to impress his boss with his ability to build bridges across cultures. It was made clear to Depew that success in this assignment would position him well for continued career progression upon his return to the United States.

With this in mind, Depew set off for Tokyo and immediately began laying the groundwork. He worked diligently to nurture relationships with his counterparts in

Application 5.7   (cont.)

Japan and, over time, won their respect and trust. What he envisioned as a result of his hard work was a quantum leap in business relationships that would catch the attention of his employer, who had long valued managers who could take control and make deals happen. Finally, Depew secured the commitment of the Japanese firm to form the alliance. All that was needed was to set up an *aisatsu*, or formal ceremonial meeting, between the CEOs of the two companies that would formally establish the partnership.[24]

Shortly thereafter the American CEO arrived for the formal signing. Depew had emphasized to his boss that this was only a formal ceremony and that the details of the partnership would be negotiated at a later date. This meeting was all about relationship building. About halfway through the meeting, the visiting CEO brought up the fact that his company had tried to do deals with other big Japanese companies, but had always had troubles. Maybe this time would be different, he observed. He also noted that both firms had large bureaucracies, but that this should not get in the way. Then he surprised everyone by suggesting that the two companies should agree to a deal then and there. When his Japanese counterpart expressed surprise and reluctance to move with such haste, the American CEO left. Leaving for the airport, he was heard saying that he felt he had been sandbagged and insulted.

Several weeks later Depew received a call from his boss in New York telling him that his employer was no longer interested in the Japanese deal, and that the company was changing its overall Asia-Pacific strategy. As a result, it was eliminating Depew's position.

Think about it...

(1) What could Jeff Depew have done differently to achieve a more positive outcome in terms of a potential strategic alliance between the two companies?

(2) What could Depew have done differently to protect his own job?

(3) This case tells Jeff Depew's side of the story. Most stories have multiple sides, however, and there can be several versions of the "truth." What questions might you ask people if you were interested in discovering the "full story" of Depew's misadventures? Explain.

(4) Why is it important for managers in global contexts to seek out different sides of conflicts or events?

Location, location, location

When asked what people should look for when buying a house, the universal response from realtors is "location, location, location." As in real estate, the location where business is transacted can have a profound impact on outcomes. This is particular true for frequent flyers, who flit into one location only to jump to another the next day. In this process, missing local signals from differing environments or situations can often make the difference between success and failure.

Why is location so important? It is important because location is, in reality, a multi-faceted concept. The physical setting, including its geographic locale and the characteristics of this locale, is a key variable in guiding people's attention and interpretation (consider how different it is to study at the library or at the cafeteria of a university center). Whether a meeting takes place in the home or host country, face to face or virtually, in the office or off-site, all serve to guide the attention of managers and employees towards some aspects of the situation and away from others. So too does the language (or languages) in use at the relevant locations. We examine each of these two factors briefly.

- *Location of work or assignment.* The location of work, negotiations, or meetings can often influence the social dynamics – and even outcomes – by affecting frames of reference, stress levels, and topics of conversation. For example, a plant location is more likely to make manufacturing issues salient, while an off-site meeting may invoke new ideas. Likewise, an off-site meeting may call for more informal inter-action and relax some of the normative constraints around behavior expectations. Meetings at headquarters may make the home culture more salient, while a meeting at the host country may favor local cultural norms. Return to the example of Ghosn at Nissan (above). Would Ghosn have faced the same challenges or acted in the same manner if he had been managing in France instead of Japan? Would his patterns of communication or decision-making have been the same? Would his power and status as an executive have been the same? At the same time, consider the challenges of virtual managers who may work with global teams in Japan or else-where, but without being physically present (see Chapter 10). What special chal-lenges do they face? Finally, consider the same two managers from separate companies who are working to negotiate a partnership (see Chapter 8). Would their demeanor, dialog, and level of formality be the same if they were negotiating virtually instead of face to face? Would it be the same if they were in a restaurant or an executive conference room? There is a reason why meals and coffee or tea breaks are such a major part of global business.

- *Language-in-use*. Language is also an important part of location. The ability to speak the local language not only allows managers to converse more easily with local business people; it also enhances their cultural understanding (see Chapter 6). Think about this: more people speak Mandarin Chinese as their first language than any other runner-up language in the world, including (in descending order) Spanish, English, Bengali, and Hindi.[25] The average Dutch manager speaks four languages (typically, French, German, and English in addition to Dutch); the average Chinese or Mexican manager speaks between two and three languages (including English); and the average American speaks one.

Application 5.8 Tata's new factory

In 2008 India's Tata Motors was searching for a location in which to assemble its new micro-car, the Nano.[26] The Nano was designed to be the world's cheapest car, and was squarely aimed at developing nations. In searching for a suitable site, Tata was encouraged by local administrators in West Bengal to locate its new $300 million factory in Singur. The new facility would help stimulate economic development in a very impoverished region by ultimately creating 10,000 new jobs, plus perhaps another 10,000 jobs for local suppliers. As the factory neared completion, however, local farmers began demanding that the company go elsewhere. In particular, they objected to losing farmland that had traditionally supported the local economy. Moreover, many farmers claimed that the local government had forced them to sell their lands. Despite government backing and Tata's reputation for social and environmental consciousness, local farmers continued to protest. As a result, Tata decided to close its nearly completed factory and move everything to Sanand (near Ahmedabad), in Gujarat.

Looking back on the experience, company chairman Ratan Tata observed, "We lost a lot of time, unfortunately, but I think we can set out to do what we need to do on Gujarati soil." Although the company likely had the power, money, and influence to go ahead with its original plans, its concern for local environmental – and political – conditions led it to rethink its location decision. As a result, West Bengal remains a largely farming region (a local priority), while Gujarat is moving closer to its ambition to lead India in economic development (also a local priority). Also as a result, and despite the added cost and lost time, Tata will likely benefit from the move over the long term by having a more supportive local community in which to operate.

Application 5.8   (cont.)

Think about it...

(1)   How is it possible that Tata Motors nearly completed a very expensive factory in West Bengal before discovering that many local people objected to it?

(2)   Despite the creation of a possible 20,000 new jobs, local farmers in West Bengal publicly lobbied against building the new factory there because they said they would lose valuable farmland and felt coerced by the local government. Do you accept these reasons or do you think other issues were involved here? Explain.

(3)   Did Ratan Tata make the correct decision to move the factory from West Bengal to Gujarat? Why or why not?

Application 5.9   Rethinking the BP–Rosneft partnership

To see a very different example of challenges created by different locations, take a moment to examine a recent agreement between BP and the Russian energy company Rosneft. This joint venture aimed to exploit huge potential deposits of oil and gas on Russia's Arctic shelf.[27] As part of the agreement, Rosneft would take 5 percent of BP's shares in exchange for approximately 10 percent of Rosneft's shares. "BP executives see this as the first piece of good news since that disastrous oil spill in the Gulf of Mexico," said the BBC's business editor Robert Peston. The deal was controversial from the beginning, however, with disagreements among various stockholder groups and intermittent and unpredictable interventions against the joint venture from various parts of the Russian government. Concern was expressed in the United Kingdom that the Russian government owned 75 percent of Rosneft, suggesting to some that the Russian government was, in essence, taking a 5 percent stake in a British company with strategically important oil reserves all over the world. At one point, armed police commandos raided BP's Moscow office, but then quickly retreated for no apparent reason. Throughout, BP's executives remained optimistic. Its CEO said the "historic" deal would "create value, deliver growth, and meet the world's demand for energy." The agreement would meet the needs of consumers, shareholders, and governments. Several months after both sides initialed the agreement, however, the deal fell apart, as a result of continued disagreements and legal actions by various stockholders and intransigence by the Russian bureaucracy. Outside observers noted that Russia's prime minister had publicly supported the venture, adding a sense of mystery regarding what was needed to secure an investment in that country. Another observer suggested that the deal fell apart because the Russian government faction that had supported it fell from power. In any case, the joint venture failed, and shortly thereafter BP's arch-rival Exxon signed an agreement with Rosneft to do what BP had long planned.

Think about it . . .

(1)   In your view, what role did location play in the failure of this joint venture?

(2)   Could BP and/or Rosneft have done anything differently to enhance the likelihood of reaching an agreement on this venture? Explain.

(3)   Would the results have been different if the venture had involved oil companies from France and Algeria or China and Kazakhstan? Why or why not?

(4)   What lessons emerge from this case for companies in search of mutually beneficial joint ventures?

MANAGER'S NOTEBOOK
The situational environment

We have tried to make a simple point in this chapter: that, in addition to understanding differences in both cultures and organizations, managers are well advised to understand the unique situation that characterizes most episodes in international business. In other words, they need to understand how to manage local situations. In this endeavor, one size definitely does not fit all.

From a managerial standpoint, trying to understand situations may be more difficult than trying to understand either cultures or organizations, since each situation is both different and dynamic. Multiple and often hidden factors are frequently involved, and any misstep can have long-term negative consequences. Once broken, relationships are often difficult to rebuild, since trust, face, and sometimes money are involved. With this in mind, and based on the foregoing discussion, we close with three key lessons for global managers relating to contexts, cognitions, and learning (see Exhibit 5.7).

Exhibit 5.7 Action plans for understanding situational differences

(1) Manage contexts	(2) Manage cognitions	(3) Learn on the fly
• Clarify goals and tasks for upcoming meetings or projects. • When possible, select the context that best fits your goals. • Understand the people you are working with, including personal characteristics, qualifications, and formal roles. • Understand the implications of various locations for interpersonal relations and project success.	• Develop an understanding of how cognitive processes work across and within cultures. • Understand what gets attention and what actions might be misinterpreted. • Influence others' interpretations by highlighting the characteristics of the situation and explaining behaviors. • Work to understand how cognitive schemas can affect individual and group behavior.	• Recognize that a significant part of behavior must be learned "on the fly," so managers must become quick learners. • Recognize that managers need to rapidly understand the situations before them, as well as their role in helping shape both situations and outcomes.

1 *Manage contexts*

Once managers recognize the importance of the situation in shaping what behaviors are considered appropriate or inappropriate, it is easier to see that they can be more purposeful in manipulating and changing the characteristics of the context to their advantage. Clearly, not all aspects of a situation can be changed, and sometimes the individual manager may have influence over very few elements. Nevertheless, managers do have control over clarifying goals and tasks for upcoming meetings or projects. Clarifying goals for all the parties involved can save time and confusion and allow all sides to prepare for a productive discussion or effort.

In addition, managers often have discretion over who represents the company in meetings or on projects. Do these people have sufficient status or decision-making authority to represent the company suitably? Are they bilingual? Experienced travelers are aware of countless meetings or experiences with prospective partners when one company sent a junior manager to meet with his or her senior counterpart, thereby sending a signal about the lack of importance it attached to the meeting. Choosing people with appropriate formal roles and responsibilities represents an important factor in any such enterprise,

Finally, managers sometimes have discretion in selecting a meeting site, the physical arrangement of the space (e.g., moving a chair to sit side by side rather than across the table), and even who is involved in a particular interaction. For example, managers may choose to hold a particularly controversial discussion at an off-site location at which work norms may be relaxed and individuals may be more open to speak openly, rather than at the more formal meeting room. At a minimum, awareness of how these contextual forces shape cognitions and behaviors may prepare managers for possible challenges and suggest different strategies.

2 Manage cognitions

As discussed above, cognitions play a major role in our behaviors. As such, the more managers can understand about the people they are working with – including their cognitions – the more progress they can make. This includes working to recognize and understand the individual differences between people, as well as how others analyze and respond to events around them. Neither of these is easy, and, at times, little information may be forthcoming. Nevertheless, the effort is important, since it can yield useful information about the setting and about future possible behaviors by others. This is particularly true of understanding differences in the cognitive schemas that people have. Again, although they can be difficult to organize, informal conversations can often be useful in better understanding the other parties and their viewpoints.

Following this principle, success across borders depends not only on how adaptable the manager is but also upon the extent to which others embrace the manager's definition of the situation. In a cross-cultural situation, this may be explaining behaviors that usually do not require explanation and helping others to make sense of it. For example, a manager who tends to speak informally and disregard titles may explain that the behavior is meant to demonstrate that individuals are not valued on the basis of their position but their contributions. In other words, managers may move away from a preoccupation with "mimicking behaviors" of the foreign cultures to a focus on "explaining and framing behaviors" so that they are understood appropriately.

3 Learn on the fly

As discussed in this chapter, the situations facing managers are highly dynamic and variable. As a consequence, there is a huge amount that managers can learn in preparation for the difficulties of global work, and a significant part of the learning must happen "on the fly," as new situations emerge and evolve. Thus global managers must become, first and foremost, quick learners, adjusting to and negotiating each situation as it develops. Managers may compensate for a lack of knowledge about unique individuals, situations, or contexts by developing and drawing on their learning skills, as discussed in Chapter 2.

The success of any cross-cultural interaction (and monocultural interactions as well) is the result of some type of *interdependent learning*, in which the parties involved learn about each other's goals, preferences, styles, and limitations, and negotiate ways of working together. This learning is a continuous and ongoing activity that, over time, will shape the way a manager thinks and acts, but also will shape the situation itself. For example, as a multicultural team learns about each member and incorporates different work habits to accommodate the diversity of cultures and personalities among its members, it develops work procedures that are respectful of multiple cultures and make it easier for newcomers – who may not have participated in the learning – to adjust to the work environment.

Learning on the fly implies that the manager is able to understand the situation in front of him or her quickly and is cognizant of his or her role in shaping or influencing that situation. For example, a (unsuccessful) manager may complain that team members do not present any new ideas, but does not realize that he or she is the first one to criticize any new idea that is introduced. To prepare for learning on the fly, managers must learn about themselves. Self-learning may sound a little esoteric and disconnected from the business world, but self-awareness is probably one of the most critical tools for a successful global career. Being self-aware means knowing one's own values, beliefs, styles, and patterns of behavior, and being able to explain them to others or recognizing when they are not having the desired effect. For example, a manager who is typically very assertive and direct when communicating may need to adjust or explain his or her style in a cross-cultural setting in which individuals from other cultures expect more subtle and indirect ways of communicating. Given the innumerable situations facing a global manager on a day-to-day basis, it may not be feasible to learn about all individuals and situations a priori, but knowing about oneself is already half the work.

Choices for the manager: putting it all together

We have now come to the close of Part II, so what have we learned? Culture. Organization. Situation. This is the environment in which global managers find themselves and must work to succeed. Each part of this environment is important and each can exhibit considerable variability. The question now is how to put these three dimensions of the work environment together to better understand both the managerial challenge *and* what managers can actually do in the field. Although global managers obviously face a number of demands and constraints in the workplace, they also have a number of opportunities. The challenge is to understand how these can be realized.

Linking these environments together is a simple model of managerial choice and action originally introduced by Oxford University professor Rosemary Stewart.[28] Stewart makes a cogent argument for rethinking our approach to management, global or otherwise. She sets forth her aim in this model as

> trying to change how the reader thinks about managerial work. I believe this is necessary because the language commonly used for talking about managerial work takes too little account of what managers actually do. It is often too general, treating managing as primarily a common activity, and also too formal and idealistic, hence divorced from reality. The model provides a new way of thinking about the nature and the diversity of managerial jobs and about how individuals actually do them.[29]

This model is based on the central argument that all managerial work is confined in varying degrees by existing *demands* (what people must do) and *constraints* (what people must not do). Within these limitations, however, managers typically have *choices* about what is done and how it is done (see Exhibit 5.8). This is where managerial abilities and skills take center stage. The challenge for the manager is to understand the

Exhibit 5.8 Choices for the manager: a model

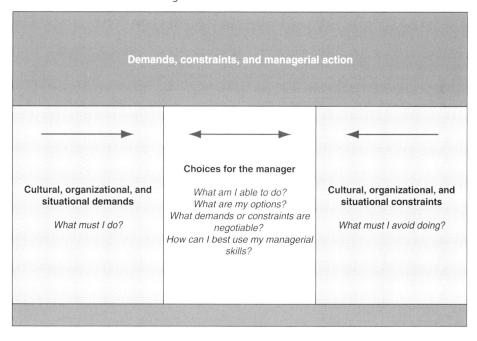

Demands, constraints, and managerial action

Choices for the manager

Cultural, organizational, and situational demands

What must I do?

What am I able to do?
What are my options?
What demands or constraints are negotiable?
How can I best use my managerial skills?

Cultural, organizational, and situational constraints

What must I avoid doing?

constraints – cultural, organizational, and situational – within his or her environment and then act within these limitations.

In this sense, the model provides a framework for thinking about the nature of managerial work and how managers do it. We can build upon this model to explore managerial work in a global context. In other words, this basic framework can be adapted such that global managers can visualize the environment in which they work, including constraints on what they can do and demands about what they must do. Within these two sets of parameters, global managers are free – or relatively free – to use their skills to achieve their goals and objectives. Stewart refers to this domain as *choices for the manager*. It is the area in which they can make decisions (choices) concerning their actions. Within this area, several logical questions for managers to ask here include the following.

- What am I able to do?
- What are my options?
- What demands or constraints are negotiable or changeable?
- How can I best use my managerial skills?

Both as a developmental tool and a managerial guide, this approach should prove useful, and we return to this model as we move through the topic of developing global management skills in Part III.

Summary points

- The situational environment is represented by differences in goals and tasks, people, roles and responsibilities, and locations. It is embedded within national and organizational cultures, but it also carries with it its own unique characteristics and challenges. It consists largely of individual differences, differences in cognitions, and differences in contexts at the point of contact between parties. Managers often ignore their surroundings, or situations, when in the field and try instead to focus on business, but this may be an unwise strategy.

- In trying to understand how cognition works in social situations, we can identify a simple model of cognition that involves just three variables. When we first experience events in the external world, we choose what to see and what not to see. This is called perceptual selection, or, simply, attention. It represents what we focus on for future analysis and possible action. Following this, we tend to categorize or classify what we have seen or experienced according to some relational comparative guideline; we consider what is important or unimportant, what is good or bad. This is referred to as cognitive evaluation, or interpretation. Based on these interpretations, we decide whether or not we are going to take any action and, if so, what it will be. Finally, as discussed below, culture influences what we pay attention to, how we interpret what we pay attention to, and the repertoire of actions available to us to respond.

- Our cognitions and ultimate behaviors are largely the result of interactions between our schemas (our knowledge base) and contexts (the uniqueness of our current situation). Schemas are simply mental repositories of knowledge that store representations about what things are, their characteristics, and what they might be related to. They include people's knowledge base, expectations, experiences, and biases – that is, how people make sense of the world.

- Schemas are not separate from contexts in their effects on cognitions, however. People tend to link their knowledge of objects and events with the contexts in which they belong. The resulting cognitions influence actual behaviors as moderated by personal characteristics and preferences, such as personality, individual skills, and so forth. We can summarize some of the more important contextual differences into four categories: organizational roles and responsibilities; physical settings; relationships; and goals and tasks.

- Managers work in a complex environment that consists at a minimum of three intersecting environments. We refer to these as the cultural, organizational, and situational environments. This is the environment in which global managers must work and succeed. Each is important and each can exhibit considerable variability. The question now is how to put these three dimensions of the work environment together to better understand both the managerial challenge and what managers can actually do in the field. While global managers clearly face a number of demands and constraints in the workplace, they also have a range of opportunities. The challenge is to understand how these can be met. A model comprised of demands, constraints, and choices for the manager is presented suggesting how this can be accomplished in the field.

Notes

1 Michael Cannon-Brookes, "The empire strikes back," *The Economist*, September 20, 2008, p. 12.
2 Terry O'Reilly, CBC Radio, 2010.
3 True story; personal communication.

4 Nancy J. Adler, *International Dimensions of Organizational Behavior*. Mason, OH: Thompson, 1987.

5 Bradd Shore, *Culture in Mind: Cognition, Culture and the Problem of Meaning*. New York: Oxford University Press, 1996, p. 1.

6 Richard A. Thompson, *Psychology and Culture*. Dubuque, IA: W C Brown, 1975, p. 10.

7 Paul DiMaggio, "Culture and cognition," *Annual Review of Sociology*, 1997, 23, pp. 263–87, p. 269.

8 Adesh Agarwal, "Time, memory, and knowledge representation: the Indian perspective," in Jeanette Altarriba (ed.), *Cognition and Culture: A Cross-Cultural Approach to Psychology*. Amsterdam: North-Holland, 1993, pp. 44–55.

9 Daniel Wagner, cited in Marshall Segall, Pierre Dasen, John Berry, and Ype Poortinga, *Human Behavior in Global Perspective: An Introduction to Cross-Cultural Psychology*. New York: Pergamon, 1990, p. 171.

10 Richard Harris, Lawrence Schoen, and Deana Hensley, "A cross-cultural story of story memory," *Journal of Cross-Cultural Psychology*, 1992, 23(2), pp. 133–47.

11 Ralph Reynold, Marsha Taylor, Margaret Steffensen, Larry Shirley, and Richard Anderson, "Cultural schemata and reading comprehension," *Reading Research Quarterly*, 1982, 17(3), pp. 353–66.

12 Ben Blount and Paula Schwanenflugel, "Cultural bases, for folk classification systems," in Altarriba, *Cognition and Culture*, pp. 3–22; Pei-Jung Lin and Paula Schwanenflugel, "Cultural familiarity and language factors in the structure of category knowledge," *Journal of Cross-Cultural Psychology*, 1995, 26(2), pp. 153–68; Barbara Malt, "Category coherence in cross-cultural perspective," *Cognitive Psychology*, 1995, 29(2), pp. 85–148.

13 Chi-Yue Chiu, "A cross-cultural comparison of cognitive styles in Chinese and American children," *International Journal of Psychology*, 1972, 7(4), pp. 235–42; Alejandro López, Scott Atran, John D. Coley, Douglas L. Medinn, and Edward E. Smith, "The tree of life: universal and cultural features of folkbiological taxonomies and inductions," *Cognitive Psychology*, 1997, 32(3), pp. 251–95.

14 Chi-Yue Chiu, Ting-Yi Hong, and Carol Dweck, "Lay dispositionism and implicit theories of personality," *Journal of Personality and Social Psychology*, 1997, 73(1), pp. 19–30; Alan P. Fiske, Shinobu Kitayama, Hazel R. Markus, and Richard E. Nisbett, "The cultural matrix of social psychology," in Daniel T. Gilbert, Susan T. Fiske, and Gardner Lindzey (eds.), *Handbook of Social Psychology*. New York: McGraw-Hill, 1998, pp. 915–81.

15 Richard Shweder, "Cultural psychology: what is it?," in Nancy R. Goldberger and Jody B. Veroff (eds.), *The Culture and Psychology Reader*. New York University Press, 1995, pp. 41–86.

16 Howard Gardner, *Frames of Mind: The Theory of Multiple Intelligences*. New York: Basic Books, 1983; Daniel Coleman, *Emotional Intelligence: Why It Can Matter More than IQ*. New York: Bantam Books, 1995; John Berry, "On cross-cultural comparability," *International Journal of Psychology*, 1969, 4(2), pp. 119–28; Philip E. Vernon, *Intelligence and Cultural Environment*. London: Methuen, 1969.

17 George A. Ferguson, "On transfer and the abilities of man," *Canadian Journal of Psychology*, 1956, 10(3), pp. 121–31.

18 Kaiping Peng, Daniel Ames, and Eric Knowles, "Culture and human inference: perspectives from three traditions," in David Matsumoto (ed.), *Handbook of Culture and Psychology*. Oxford University Press, 2001, pp. 245–64.

19 Inchoel Choi, Richard E. Nisbett, and Ara Norenzayan, "Causal attribution across cultures," *Psychological Bulletin*, 1999, 125(1), pp. 47–63; Fiona Lee, Mark Hallahan, and Thaddeus Herzog, "Explaining real life events: how culture and domains shape attributions," *Personality and Social Psychology Bulletin*, 1996, 22(7), pp. 732–41; Michael Morris and Kaiping Peng, "Culture and cause: American and Chinese attributions for social and physical events," *Journal of Personality and Social Psychology*, 1994, 67(6), pp. 949–71.

20 It is easy to attribute manipulative motivations to slogans of the "satisfaction guaranteed" type, and some of that will likely be at play in at least some instances. Note, however, that when marketing is seen as a *science* based on the *laws* of human behavior, which, as we have mentioned, is typical in Western countries, customer satisfaction is something that can be reasonably promised on the premise that the relevant variables (regarding what customers need and the characteristics of the products offered) have been scientifically pondered. The problem lies more with the premise than with the promise.

21 Johnny K. Johanson and Ikujiro Nonaka, *Relentless: The Japanese Way of Marketing*. New York: Basic Books, 1996.

22 Lawrence Frost, "Attention passengers: take out the trash," *Bloomberg Business Week*, July 18, 2011, pp. 22–4.

23 Nanette Fondas and Rosemary Stewart, "Enactment in managerial jobs: a role analysis," *Journal of Management Studies*, 1994, 31(1), 83–103.

24 *Aisatsu* is the Japanese word for greetings or giving a brief speech. It is formed from two *kanji*, both of which have the same literal meaning: to come up close to someone. Greetings in Japan are, like anywhere else, considered polite and preferable to not greeting, but, like most social interactions in Japan, they are more ritualized than in the West.

25 *Language Magazine*, April 2000, 10(3), pp. 3–4.

26 Eric Bellman, "Tata to shift production of minicar after protests," *Wall Street Journal*, October 8, 2008, p. A-14.

27 "BP and Russia in Arctic oil deal," BBC News, January 14, 2011.

28 Rosemary Stewart, *Choices for the Manager*. Englewood Cliffs, NJ: Prentice Hall, 1982.

29 Stewart, *Choices for the Manager*, p. vii.

PART III

DEVELOPING GLOBAL MANAGEMENT SKILLS

CHAPTER 6

Communicating across cultures

People have often observed that communication is the essence of good management. It lies at the heart of effective organizations. In view of this, it is surprising how difficult it can be communicating with others, especially across cultures. We may unintentionally come across as impatient, condescending, and sometimes just rude. From a managerial standpoint, such behavior serves only to erect barriers to organizational success. To communicate effectively across cultures, managers need to understand the fundamental influences on both effective and ineffective communication, as well as strategies for reaching a higher level of mutual understanding between people.

Chapter outline

Applications

> *A different language is not just a dictionary of words, sounds, and syntax. It is a different way of interpreting reality, refined by the generations that developed the language.*
>
> Federico Fellini[1]
> Filmmaker and director, Italy

> *Whatever the culture, there's a tongue in our head. Some use it, some hold it, and some bite it. For the French it is a rapier, thrusting in attack; the English, using it defensively, mumble a vague and confusing reply; for Italians and Spaniards it is an instrument of eloquence; Finns and East Asians throw you with their constructive silence. Silence is a form of speech, so don't interrupt it.*
>
> Richard D. Lewis[2]
> Communication consultant, United Kingdom

With this chapter, we begin the third and final section of the book. This part focuses on developing global management skills. In other words, based on an understanding of both the challenges facing managers and the environment in which they work, we are now in a position to consider several of the more important skills that are required of managers in the field (see Exhibit 6.1). These include communication, negotiation,

Exhibit 6.1 Developing global management skills

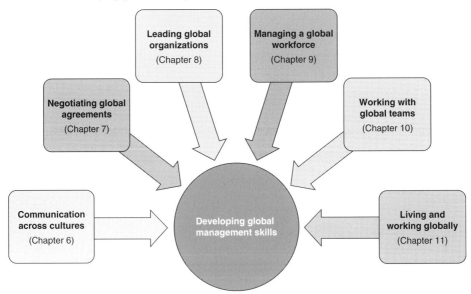

leadership, managing people, working with teams, and living and working in unfamiliar environments – all from a global perspective. We begin with the topic of communicating across cultures.

Interpersonal communication

Namasté is a common greeting used on the Indian subcontinent. It literally means "I bow to you," and it is used as an expression of deep respect in India and Nepal by Hindus, Jains, and Buddhists. In these cultures, the word (from the ancient Sanskrit) is spoken at the beginning of a conversation, accompanied by a slight bow made with the hands pressed together, palms touching and fingers pointed upwards, in front of the chest. This silent gesture can also be performed wordlessly and carry the same meaning, as is often done at the close of a conversation. As such, *namasté* is a form of both verbal and nonverbal communication. When used appropriately, it signals to the parties to a conversation that the people involved likely understand something about prevailing social norms and values. They are one of "us," and a bond is easily formed. It may be only one word, but it carries significant symbolism.

Communication is all about conveying meaning to others. It is the principal way we reach out to others to exchange ideas and commodities, develop and dissolve relationships, and conduct business. Within one culture or language group, communication can often be problematic – particularly across age groups, geographic regions, and gender. These problems pale into insignificance, however, in comparison to the challenges of communicating across cultures. Not only do the principal communicators have different cultural backgrounds, they must also work with other team members of employers who also have different backgrounds and expectations. Third parties to conversations (e.g., interpreters) can also add confusion as they attempt to provide clarity (see Exhibit 6.2).

Application 6.1   Dinner in Prague

Signs, symbols, and colors can often carry deep meanings that can vary across cultures. During a dinner meeting in Prague between Japanese marketing representative Hiroko Numata and her Czech host, Irena Novák, confusion quickly emerged when the Japanese guest went off to find the bathroom. She began to open the door to the men's room when her host stopped her. "Don't you see the sign?" Novák asked. "Of course I do," Numata responded, "but it is red. In our country, a

Exhibit 6.2 Key relationships in multicultural communication (example)

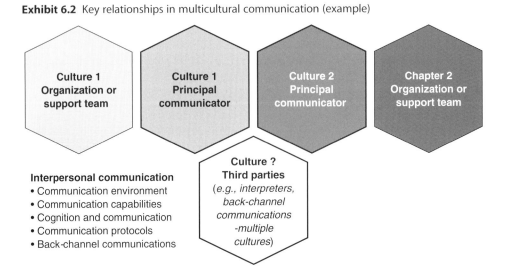

Interpersonal communication
- Communication environment
- Communication capabilities
- Cognition and communication
- Communication protocols
- Back-channel communications

Culture ?
Third parties
(*e.g., interpreters,*
back-channel
communications
-multiple
cultures)

Application 6.1   (cont.)

red-colored sign means it's the ladies' room. For men, it should be blue or black."
Novák returned to her table, remembering that she too had looked at the sign but
had focused on what was written, not its color. She wondered how many other
things she and her Japanese colleague had seen but interpreted very differently.[3]

Think about it...

(1) What is the fundamental basis for the misunderstanding between these two
     women?

(2) If you were in this situation, what would you have done to prepare more
     thoroughly for the dinner meeting?

(3) Can you identify signs, symbols, or colors that carry different meanings in
     your own culture compared to others?

Examples such as this – and there are many – highlight how simple and often
unintended words, behaviors, signs, and symbols can lead to misunderstandings, embarrassment, conflict, and even lost business opportunities. Global managers understand this.
When managers are asked to identify their most serious challenge in the field, the response
is almost universal: communicating effectively across cultures. Why? Because communication is the principal vehicle through which people reach out to others to exchange ideas
and commodities, develop and dissolve relationships, and conduct business.

We often hear what we want to hear, however. Our frames of reference and personal experiences – and even our world views – can all work to filter message transmission and reception by screening in or out what we will likely attend to and by attaching meanings to how messages are interpreted and dealt with. Financial analysts tend to pick up threads of conversation involving money, while sales managers pick up on market opportunities. Consider, though, that, while communication can often be problematic within one culture – particularly across occupations, age groups, geographic regions, and gender – these problems pale in comparison with the challenges of communicating across cultures. In any cross-cultural exchange between managers from different regions, the principal purpose of communication is to seek common ground – to seek out ideas, information, customers, and sometimes even partnerships between the parties. Business in general and management in particular both rely on people's willingness and ability to convey meaning between managers, employees, partners, suppliers, investors, and customers. Indeed, it can be argued that most efforts to build or to understand organizations begin with an understanding of basic communication and exchange processes.

Recognizing the importance and difficulty of multicultural communication, academics, consultants, and fellow managers have long sought to provide advice to those setting off for global assignments and foreign locations. Much of this advice focuses on learning the rules of the road when dealing with people from other cultures. Managers are told that communication is an interactive process between senders and receivers in which senders encode their messages into a medium and then transmit them through often noise-infested airways to receivers, who, in turn, decode the messages, interpret them, and respond appropriately. Throughout this process, cultural differences and potential cross-cultural misunderstandings are typically subsumed under a broad category of *noise*. The more a manager can reduce this noise, the greater the message clarity.

Although this advice is useful as far as it goes, it neglects what we consider to be two major impediments to effective communication: *attention* and *interpretation*. In other words, messages are effective only to the extent that recipients are both paying attention to them and capable of processing the information in ways that facilitate common meaning. While some may lump these challenges into the general category of "noise," we suggest that in the realm of multicultural communication such a catch-all category can easily lead managers to overlook two of the more critical influences on effective message construction, transmission, understanding, and response.

We suggest here that, in order to significantly enhance communication effectiveness across borders, simple encode–noise–decode models must be augmented with a deeper understanding of the processes underlying them. We further argue that many of these

Exhibit 6.3 AIM model of interpersonal communication

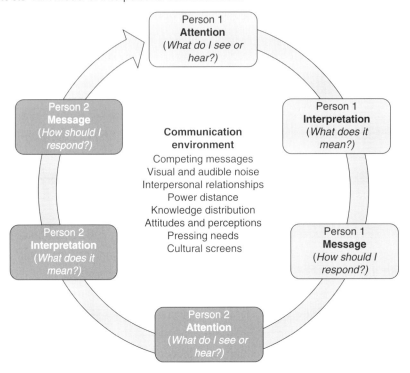

processes do not occur within culturally complex black boxes; in fact, they are often relatively easy for managers to identify and understand if they know what they are looking for.

To this end, we begin with a look at how culture and cultural differences often screen the ways in which people create, send, receive, and interpret messages. As a starting point, we suggest an *attention–interpretation–message* (or *AIM*) *model* that can usefully serve the needs of managers engaged in cross-cultural communication (see Exhibit 6.3).[4] (This model is based on the attention–interpretation–action model of cognition discussed in the previous chapter.) As discussed in greater detail below, this model highlights three key ingredients in effective interpersonal communication.

- *Attention*. First, when messages are sent, recipients must notice them – that is, they must select out the intended messages from a barrage of other often simultaneous messages for particular attention. The basic question here is: "What do I see or hear?" Hence the challenge for the global manager is how first to capture the attention of the other party.

- *Interpretation.* Second, once a message is selected out for attention, the recipients must interpret or decode it. Here the questions are: "What does this message mean to me? How do I make sense out of it?" Again, cultural differences can play a crucial role.
- *Message, or response.* Finally, the recipient must decide whether or not to reply and, if so, how to construct and transmit a response. The question in this stage is: "What is an appropriate response?"

Throughout this process, numerous factors in the *communication environment* can serve to reinforce, attract, or distract attention towards or away from some messages at the expense of others. These factors include other competing messages, the particular languages in use, visual and audible noise, the nature of interpersonal relationships, the power distance between speakers, the degree of shared knowledge among the speakers, attitudes and perceptions, and pressing needs as experienced by both parties. In addition to attracting or deflecting attention, these factors can often serve to influence message interpretation and analysis, as well as message construction and delivery mechanisms.

Thus, while the traditional encode–noise–decode model can be helpful, we prefer an AIM approach as a means of better identifying the challenges facing managers working across cultures. In our view, this approach gives weight not just to what people are doing but also to what they are thinking. It also lays the groundwork for looking more deeply into why, from a manager's viewpoint, it is easier to communicate with some "foreign" counterparts than others. Much of this difference resides in the ways that cultural differences influence the communication process from start to finish.

Cultural screens on interpersonal communication

At its core, communication is all about conveying meaning to others – not just words. Business in general and management in particular both rely on people's willingness and ability to convey meaning between managers, employees, partners, suppliers, investors, and customers. Language and culture not only provide a guide as to what is acceptable behavior and what is unacceptable, they focus attention on different parts of the exchange and provide parameters for interpreting information. Understanding the ways in which culture guides attention and meaning creation is a key component in creating understanding across cultures. Clearly, moreover, the greater this understanding, the greater is the opportunity for the effective exchange of ideas and subsequent business success.

We focus here on the two critical influences mentioned above: two interrelated *cultural screens*, or lenses, that can affect both interpersonal interactions in general

Exhibit 6.4 Cultural screens on interpersonal communication

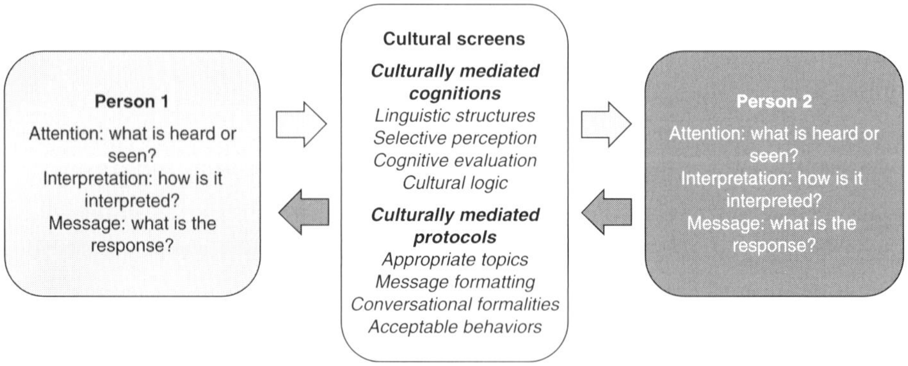

and multicultural communications in particular.[5] These two screens often emerge as a result of cultural differences between senders and receivers, and they can have important implications for how various parties to a conversation receive, interpret, and respond to messages (Exhibit 6.4). Cultural screens can perhaps be best understood as part of the communication environment; they represent potential impediments or barriers in the basic AIM model discussed above.

- *Culturally mediated cognitions in communication.* The first screen involves cultural influences on individual cognitions surrounding communication episodes – that is, how people and messages are often evaluated and processed in the minds of senders and receivers alike.
- *Culturally mediated communication protocols.* The second screen involves cultural influences on communication protocols, or required behaviors, such as how we construct or shape our messages in ways that may be culturally consistent for us but, we hope, not problematic for our intended receivers.

In other words, culture routinely influences both how we think and how we behave, and nowhere is this influence more evident than with respect to communication processes. As a result, we suggest that managers committed to improving multicultural communication need to dig deeper and work harder to understand the underlying cultural forces at play in interpersonal communication.

Cognition and communication

As noted earlier, when people receive messages from others they routinely screen and interpret what they hear and see so as to determine how to respond. Sometimes they will categorize messages based on their sources ("Is the source believable?"). At other times

Exhibit 6.5 Culturally mediated cognitions in communication

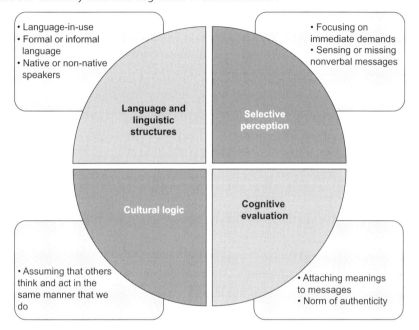

they will prioritize messages based on the degree to which they think the messages are important ("Do I need to respond immediately or can this wait?"). Such processes require both senders and receivers to pay attention to intended messages; they require cognition. At least four commonly used culturally mediated cognitions can be identified: language and linguistic structures, selective perception, cognitive evaluation, and cultural logic (see Exhibit 6.5).

Language and linguistic structures: choose your words

Consider the challenges posed by language differences, or, more specifically, language competencies. When two American tourists were traveling on a bus in Stuttgart recently and one of them sneezed, a German passenger turned around and said, "*Gesundheit*." One visitor looked at the other and noted, "How nice that they speak English here."[6]

Whether it is correctly or poorly used, language is central to human communication. It plays an important role in initiating conversations and conducting most aspects of human affairs. It facilitates socialization, organization, and management. It also allows us to express our feelings and facilitate problem solving by thinking, both silently and vocally. Moreover, it is due to language that we are able to retain our histories, passing knowledge from one generation to the next. In this regard, *language and linguistic structures* (i.e., the manner in which words, grammar, syntax, and the meaning of words are organized and used) are closely linked to cultures, because, while culture provides the meanings and meaning-making mechanisms underlying existence, language provides the symbols to facilitate the expression of such meanings.

Language is always a potential impediment to effective cross-cultural communication. In this regard, there are two issues that are worthy of note. First, which language should be used in a conversation? Some argue that English is increasingly becoming the lingua franca of global business; as such, everyone should speak English.[7] As a Texas preacher once observed, "If English was good enough for Jesus, it's good enough for me."[8] Not everyone agrees with this, obviously. Indeed, both Mandarin Chinese and Spanish have more native speakers around the world than English. Why shouldn't everyone speak Chinese or Spanish? Others have suggested that the language to be spoken should be determined by who has the money – consistent with the oft-cited phrase "Serve the customer." If the French are buying, it is logical for both parties to speak French. This debate may never be resolved, since, among other things, mass conversions to a foreign language can threaten the cultural integrity of a country or region.

For managers living largely in the English-speaking parts of the world, there is a second challenge. Which English are we speaking? For example, Norman Schur has compiled a British-English/American-English dictionary that contains nearly 5,000 entries that are translated from one version of English to the other.[9] We are told that "to pass out" means "to lose consciousness" in British-English but "to graduate" in American-English. "Lifts" are "elevators," "companies" are "corporations," "corporations" are "municipalities," "sheltered trades" are "domestic monopolies," and "to hire" means "to lease." We are further told that, in the United Kingdom, "shares" are "stocks" and "stocks" are "government bonds." We are told that a clerk in the United States is pronounced "clark" in the United Kingdom, and that schedule is pronounced "shed-ule." Spellings can also differ ("behavior" or "behaviour"). Furthermore, this is all before we recognize that many sectors of British culture often speak differently and use very different words to communicate. If this were not enough, we must remember that people in Canada, New Zealand, Singapore, and other locales are different still in their choice and use of "English" words.

Languages and their associated linguistic structures are also intricately intertwined with the cognitive processes that affect managerial and employee behaviors, however. As noted above, Italian film director Federico Fellini observed, "A different language is not just a dictionary of words, sounds, and syntax. It is a different way of interpreting reality."

Languages can also vary considerably in their precision. Take English and Chinese, for example. Like other European languages, English consists of over 1 million words, each of which has a relatively constant and precise (though certainly not universal) meaning. By contrast, Chinese is an ideographic language that consists of only about a fourth as many words – or, more accurately, characters. As a result, each character must "work harder" – that is, Chinese characters create meaning through the images and concepts they stimulate, not through dictionary-type definitions. Everything that is written is open to multiple interpretations. Often one Chinese symbol will contain eight or ten different meanings. As a result, using nonverbal signals to support your verbal messages takes on added significance in creating shared meanings compared to the West.

Application 6.2 The fourth floor

Consider how even direct and clear translations of words can still carry different meanings and hence lead to confusion. When a group of Americans attend a meeting scheduled on the "fourth" floor of a New York office complex, they in fact go to the fourth floor (or level in the building), since Americans typically use the terms "ground" and "first" floors interchangeably. Not so the British and most Europeans, who distinguish between the ground and first floors and would thus likely go to the fifth level of the building in London, Paris, or Berlin. When foreign travelers attend a meeting on the "fourth" floor of a Seoul office building, even the more experienced travelers can become puzzled. While the number four (pronounced *sa* in Korean using traditional Chinese characters) is not in itself unlucky, as many believe, its oral pronunciation sounds very similar to the word for "death" – something that is seldom, if ever, discussed in local society. As a result, many South Korean buildings either use the English letter "F" ("fourth") for this floor or they simply don't have one. (Note that many older high-rise buildings in the United States don't have a thirteenth floor, for similar reasons.)

Think about it. . .
(1) What does something as simple as the location of the fourth floor in a building tell us about cross-cultural communication processes?
(2) Can you identify a similar example from your own culture in which a particular word carries an entirely different meaning elsewhere?
(3) What can managers do to avoid similar, but potentially more serious, mis-understandings in interpersonal communication?

Languages also provide subtle yet powerful cues about what to account for in our dealings with other people (respect, social distance, and so forth). For example, languages vary in the number and type of forms of address available to people when meeting others. In English, for example, there is typically only one word for "you." Native speakers use this same word when speaking to almost any person, regardless of age, gender, seniority, or position. On the other hand, Romance languages, such as Spanish and French, distinguish between a formal and an informal mode of address (*usted/tú* in Spanish, *vous/tu* in French). In Japanese, there are many equivalent words for "you," depending on someone's age, seniority, gender, family affiliation, and position. The implication of these linguistic differences is that, depending on the language being spoken, managers must attend to different cues and focus on different aspects of their context and message.

Those who are not conscious of these differences risk missing key information about situations facing them, leading to further communication errors. Needless to say, knowledge of the other party's language helps develop understanding that goes beyond the content of the messages exchanged. Indeed, learning the language of the host country is one of the most common recommendations offered by expatriates to young managers for understanding a different culture.

Finally, the choice of language in cross-cultural conversations can serve as a major impediment to successful job completion, as, for example, when everyone in a team or organization is required to speak in the dominant language.

Exhibit 6.6 Communicating with non-native speakers (English-language example)

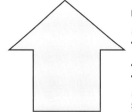

Native English speaker speaking English

Cognitions
• Thinks in English; no ongoing translations or interpretations required.
• Speaks in English, with extensive vocabulary.
• Understands subtleties of English-language conversations.

Communication behaviors
Since messages are usually clearly understood, responses and action implications are typically clear.

Non-native English speaker speaking English

Cognitions
• Thinks in language other than English; often must interpret incoming and outgoing messages.
• Speaks in English as a second language, often with limited vocabulary.
• Often lacks sensitivity to subtleties of English language conversations.

Communication behaviors
Since messages are not always clearly understood, responses and action implications can often be unclear.

Application 6.3 **Native speakers**

For instance, consider what happens when a native English-speaking supervisor meets with a global team or work group consisting largely of non-native English speakers. More specifically, consider what happens when an Anglo-American supervisor from California meets with her eastern European product development team, consisting of members from Romania, Slovakia, and Croatia. (We use English as an example here, but any other language would yield similar results.) As illustrated in Exhibit 6.6, our native English-speaking supervisor will likely have an easier time in the exchange than her eastern European counterparts. This, in turn, might lead the supervisor to conclude that the non-native speakers are less educated, less bright, less committed, more obstinate, and so forth. At the same time, the European non-English speakers may face numerous frustrations trying to make themselves heard and understood, with potentially serious, if unintended, consequences. Their lack of a broad vocabulary can often lead to the use of simple sentences to discuss complex issues, with predictable results. Moreover, when two non-native speakers talk together in a third language (e.g., English), the possibilities for confusion multiply even further.

   Think about it. . .

(1)   When a native speaker meets with a non-native speaker to negotiate a contract, what can each side do to ensure an open and accurate exchange of ideas? Explain.

(2)   If English is increasingly becoming the international language of business, why bother to learn a second language, such as German, Chinese, or Spanish?

Selective perception: the eye of the beholder

Since people cannot simultaneously focus on all the events surrounding them at a given time, they use *selective perception* to choose what to focus on and what to ignore. In other words, they make mental choices about what is important, useful, or threatening, and focus their mental powers on these particular issues. As such, the information that becomes important is in the eye of the beholder – the information he or she is expecting or looking for – while other potentially useful information is often left by the wayside.

Throughout this process, cultural differences can play a key role. We saw this in the opening example of the meeting in Prague, when each woman saw what she wanted to see, or, perhaps more accurately, what she expected to see. The result was confusion.

Consider another example dealing with *nonverbal communication*. While non-verbal communication is commonly used throughout much of Asia as a way to convey information with subtlety (e.g., rejecting a request without anyone losing face), many in the West simply fail to notice it. They are not looking for it. In fact, many managers in the West much prefer to hear and speak plainly and publicly – "Say what you mean, and mean what you say." As a result, Asians often believe they have communicated a message (nonverbally) when in reality it was not received, while Westerners believe no communication was forthcoming since they did not hear any words. Both sides can experience frustration. To overcome such problems, communications expert Richard Lewis reminds us: "Silence is a form of speech, so don't interrupt it."

Application 6.4   Offensive behavior at Ain Shams

Selective perception and nonverbal communication can be seen in many different ways. What may be comfortable to one person may be offensive to another. Consider the plight of a visiting British professor who was reading to his poetry class at the prestigious Ain Shams University in Cairo.[10] Reflecting on what he was reading, the professor became so relaxed that he inadvertently leaned back in his chair and crossed his legs, thereby revealing the sole of one of his shoes to his students. Obviously, in much of the Muslim world, this is the worst insult anyone can inflict on another. The following morning the Cairo newspapers carried banner headlines about the student demonstrations that resulted. They denounced what they saw as British arrogance and demanded that the professor be sent home immediately.

Think about it. . .

(1) In this example from Egypt, is anyone at fault here or is this just one of those misunderstandings that often occurs across cultures?

(2) What could both sides (the British professor and the Egyptian students) have done to avoid an escalation of this conflict?

Cognitive evaluation: interpreting words and actions

When people see or hear something, they have a tendency to categorize the information so they can make judgments about its authenticity, accuracy, and utility. They try to relate it to other events and actions so they can make sense out of it and know how to respond. This process is called *cognitive evaluation*, and culture can play a major role (see Chapter 5). For example, research has shown that Americans, raised in an individualistic society, often rely on the isolated properties of people or objects they are examining in order to attach meaning or enhance understanding. As a result, when they see an individual they tend to mentally classify him or her as a man or woman, black or white, professional or blue-collar, and so forth. By contrast, Chinese, raised in a more collectivist environment, tend to classify people on the basis of criteria that emphasize relationships and contexts. As a result, they are more likely to see someone first as a member of a particular group, clan, or organization, instead of focusing on his or her individual characteristics.

At the same time, people tend to have better recall of information when it is consistent with their cultural knowledge and values. For example, many managers from mastery-oriented cultures tend to recall the specific successes of their subordinates that involved sales or financial achievements, but not their interpersonal or team-building successes. In more harmony-oriented cultures, managers tend to recall more about their subordinates' interpersonal or team-building successes, regardless of their sales or financial successes.

When inferring the mental states of other people, research indicates that several cultures in North America and western Europe emphasize a *norm of authenticity* (i.e., a belief that external actions and emotional displays are, or should be, generally consistent with internal states), while east and southeast Asian societies often tend to consider such beliefs as immature, impolite, and sometimes bizarre. For example, "speaking one's mind" or "telling it like it is" frequently appears in a positive light to many Westerners, but not to many Asians. Many in Asia give more importance in communication processes to what is left unsaid instead of what is said in open and direct ways, while the opposite tends to apply in many Western societies. In this regard, note that many wedding ceremonies in the West contain the admonition to the audience "Speak now or forever hold your peace." In other words, speak up if you have something to say. No such statement is heard in most Asian ceremonies.

Finally, reasoning processes also play out differently in communication across cultures. In other words, when people face the possibility of alternative interpretations of specific events (e.g., the success of a work team), they will almost invariably choose the interpretation that is most consistent with their own cultural outlook. For example, managers from highly individualistic cultures will typically attribute team success to the team leader's skills and efforts, while managers from more collectivistic cultures will typically attribute it to the skills and efforts of the entire team. Likewise, managers in individualistic cultures will often attribute team failure to the team members, while managers from more collectivistic cultures will accept blame for such failures. These examples illustrate the power of cognitive evaluations in terms of what is said and what remains unsaid, and how both are interpreted.

Cultural logic: assumptions about shared meanings

Interpersonal communication is an interactive process, requiring two or more people to exchange thoughts, ideas, emotions, questions, proposals, and so forth in an effort to find common ground. It is at the heart of how we do business, negotiate contracts, lead groups, work with team members, and motivate employees. In this regard, one of the least understood aspects of communicating with people from different countries is the *cultural logic* that underlies any message. (Some refer to this as "cultural logics," to emphasize the fact that this process consists of a series of logical assumptions that do not necessarily represent a unified whole – that is, cultures have a variety of logics relating to different aspects of social interaction.) When people converse with one another, they often rely on these culture-based logical assumptions to facilitate the conversation.

Cultural logic is the process of using one's own assumptions about normative behavior to interpret the messages and actions of others, thereby hypothesizing about their motives and intentions. It is the process by which people attribute meaning to the words and actions of others on the basis of the local meanings embedded within their own culture. Cultural logic provides people with a system of assumptions about what is mutually known and understood among individuals (i.e., a common ground). People often rely on this logic to facilitate communication and reduce what needs to be said to a manageable level, since it is often too difficult and time-consuming for people to express all the thoughts and assumptions behind everything they say. A shared cultural logic helps people fill the gaps left by what is unsaid, thereby facilitating the process of creating a shared meaning. It also allows for simplified and rapid communication. When moving across cultures, however, there is often an assumption of a common knowledge that, in fact, is not common.

Application 6.5 **Scheduling appointments**

To illustrate how cultural logic works, consider a recent interchange between a Canadian sales representative and her potential Brazilian customer. In order to schedule an appointment with Sergio, Sarah contacted him to propose a meeting in her office the following Monday at 9:00 in the morning. In doing so, she created a mental image of the message she was trying to convey, using her own cultural logic (in this case, relying on her Canadian emphasis on punctuality). To do so, however, she required some form of verbal shorthand – that is, she needed to make some assumptions about what was in Sergio's mind, or else her message might become excessively long and risk being ignored. To this end, she assumed that Sergio would make the same assumptions about the use of words that she was making. For example, she would have assumed that "9:00" meant 9:00, not later in the morning, when she had other appointments. She also assumed that Sergio would understand her message, and his agreement to the meeting indicated that he would arrive at 9:00 a.m. sharp.

While Sarah was making her assumptions, however, so too was Sergio, and his assumptions about the message differed considerably. Following his own cultural logic (particularly the Brazilian perception of time), Sergio assumed that "9:00" was only a targeted or approximate time, and that slippage in the time schedule was perfectly acceptable, since he had other commitments around the same time. He further assumed that Sarah was also flexible and that she would agree with his loose interpretation of when the meeting would begin. After all, since she had invited him, she must have understood his culture.

The end result of this episode is predictable. Using their own very different cultural logics, both Sarah and Sergio ran the risk of being disappointed or frustrated when they met. Had both parties – or even one party – understood their variability in cultural logic, perhaps the results would have turned out differently. Instead, due to a miscommunication regarding what time the meeting should actually take place, Sarah risked coming away from the meeting thinking that Sergio was unreliable; while Sergio risked concluding that Sarah was too rigid to base a partnership on. The result could easily have been a lost business opportunity.

Think about it. . .

(1) Is either Sarah or Sergio correct in this situation? Why or why not?

(2) How could this misunderstanding with respect to time have been handled differently?

(3) Have you personally experienced a similar event in which differences in cultural logic led to conflict or confusion?

Together, these four cultural screens on cognition – language and linguistic structures, selective perception, cognitive evaluation, and cultural logic – are likely to influence the communication process. Referring back to the AIM model discussed above, languages help determine the structures and meanings underlying intended messages; selective perceptions guide people's attention to particular parts of intended messages; cognitive evaluations guide the process of attaching meaning to received messages; and cultural logic guides senders' choices of what needs to be communicated and receivers' interpretation of the message. Managers who understand how these cultural screens can mediate the process of attention–interpretation–message creation can thus improve their chances of finding the common ground necessary for effective communication and productive exchanges.

Communication protocols

All cultures and subcultures foster socio-normative beliefs and values that guide members' thoughts and actions. These beliefs include what members can and can't do as well as what they should and shouldn't do. This is a world of obligations, responsibilities, and privileges, which together form the interpersonal foundations of a culture. Not surprisingly, these norms and values influence how we choose to converse not just with members of our own culture but with members of others as well. Included here are a variety of expected *communication protocols*, or behaviors, such as appropriate topics for discussion, message formatting, conversational formalities, and acceptable behaviors (see Exhibit 6.7).[11] Each of these is likely to influence what people attend to in a message, how they interpret it, and how they respond.

Appropriate topics for discussion: hold your tongue

What people can and cannot talk about varies by culture. Consider just one example that happened to one of the authors recently. When asked by a South Korean friend how the family was doing, an American visitor replied that his younger brother had

Exhibit 6.7 Culturally mediated communication protocols

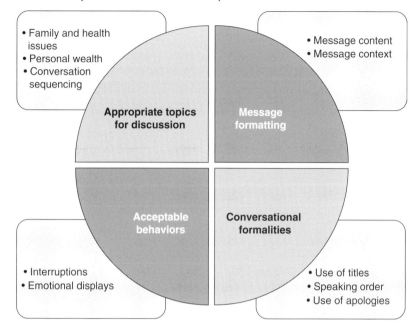

recently died. The Korean friend looked puzzled, and there was an awkward moment of silence. Then he responded, "Did you see the baseball game last night?" This was obviously not a subject he wished to discuss.

In some cultures, it is perfectly acceptable to ask about one's family; indeed, it is often considered impolite not to ask. In other cultures, however, this topic is off limits. Likewise, some cultures prefer not to talk about illness or bad fortune, perhaps in the belief that not talking about something will make it less likely to happen. Other cultures do talk about healthcare issues, sometimes including the topic of serious illness or even death; others resist doing so, as just noted. People in some cultures may also brag to anyone who will listen about how much money they've made or how they used questionable tactics to make a sale; others prefer not to discuss this, even if true. It is typically inappropriate to discuss money in France or personal matters in England. Moreover, people are expected to talk about themselves in south Asia and Latin America, but not in Germany or the Netherlands.

Equally important here is the ordering or sequencing of conversational topics. While many Western managers believe in avoiding "small talk" and getting right down to business ("Time is money!"), managers in South America and east and southeast Asia typically believe that conversations must first be warmed up with broad or general discussions on topics other than business. Only then should serious conversations about business commence.

Application 6.6   Privacy and taxes

Why is it that no one wants to talk openly about either their incomes or their income taxes? While some societies believe that failure to pay one's share of corporate or personal taxes represents a theft from society and is morally reprehensible, other societies (and other people in the same society) merely pay lip service to their tax obligations and acknowledge – and, indeed, sometimes encourage – people's efforts to minimize or eliminate such a financial imposition. Recently, for example, a major Italian city accidentally posted the tax rolls for all its citizens on a website, allowing everyone to see what everyone else paid in taxes. A moral eruption of outrage resulted, but with a curious twist: half the city was outraged because so many of their fellow citizens flagrantly avoided their tax obligations, while the other half was equally outraged because the city's error in publicizing the information caused embarrassment to its non-taxpaying citizens.

Think about it...

(1) Who is morally correct here? Why?

(2) Other than personal information, are there topics on which organizations (both public and private) and their managers should keep silent? Why?

(3) How might cultural differences influence which topics should be made public and which should not?

Message formatting: content and context

Communication is so pervasive in our everyday lives and so intertwined with culture that some researchers argue that it is impossible to separate communication from culture. For them, culture *is* communication.[12] For instance, noted anthropologist Edward Hall points out that people communicate with each other through behaviors, not just words, suggesting that cultural assumptions in general are often part of a *silent language* used to convey meaning without words. Silent communication is the use of nonverbal or visual communication (e.g., facial expressions, gestures, the use of personal space, opulent surroundings, etc.) to convey messages to senders or receivers alike. Such messages are typically subtle in nature and can be difficult to notice unless one is looking for them. Senders usually intend such messages to be received or discovered by others, however. In fact, to someone who can "read" these silent messages, they can sometimes scream very loudly.

The importance of silent, or nonverbal, communication can be found in a recent finding that verbal communication typically carries less than 35 percent of the meaning in two-way communication. In some cultures, this percentage is even lower. This suggests that nonverbal characteristics become extremely important when communicating across cultures. To make matters worse, research also suggests that, when verbal and nonverbal messages contradict each other, we are more likely to believe the latter.[13] The meaning of the message is not explicit in the content of the message, and has to be sought.[14]

As was discussed in Chapter 3, Hall suggests that this difference lies in how much *message context* surrounds the *message content*.[15] Hall distinguishes between high- and low-context cultures, as shown in Exhibit 6.8. In *low-context cultures*, such as those in Germany, Scandinavia, and the United States, the context surrounding the message is far less important than the message itself. The context provides the listener with little information relating to the intended message. As a result, speakers must rely more heavily on providing greater message clarity, as well as other guarantees such as written documents and information-rich advertising. Language precision is critical, while assumed understandings, innuendos, and body language frequently count for little.

Exhibit 6.8 Communication in low- and high-context cultures

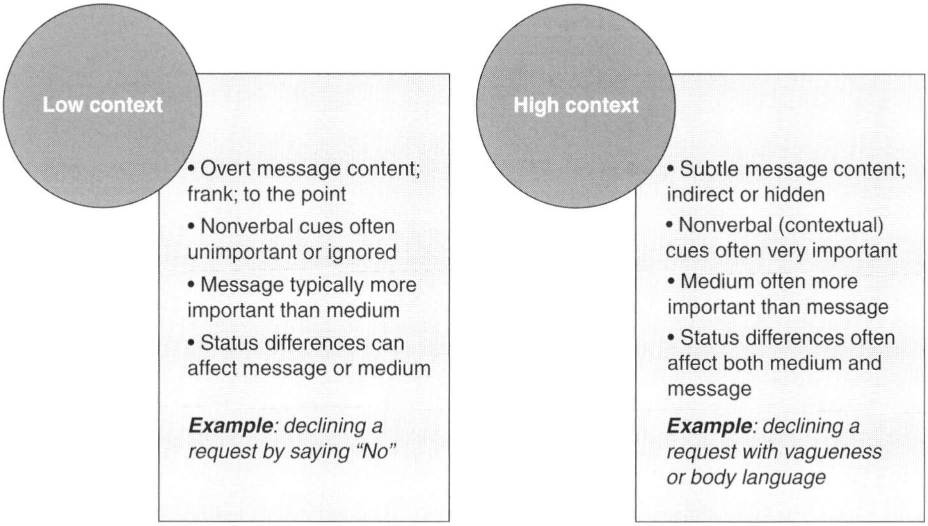

By contrast, in *high-context cultures*, such as those found in many parts of Asia and the Middle East, the context in which the message is conveyed – that is, the social cues surrounding the message – is often as important as the message itself. Indeed, the way something is said can even be more important in communicating a message than the actual words that are used. Here, communication is based on long-term interpersonal relationships, mutual trust, and personal reputations. People know the people they are talking with, and reading someone's face becomes an important – and necessary – art. As a result, less needs to be said or written down. These subtleties in communication patterns often go unnoticed by many outsiders, who listen very carefully to every word that is spoken – only to miss the real message.

Application 6.7 Nigerian communities

In ethnically diverse Nigeria, communication styles vary considerably across regions. In the southwest, where the people are largely from the Yoruba tribe, people's communication employs proverbs, sayings, and songs to enrich the meaning of what they say. This is especially true when speaking their native language, although many of the same characteristics have been carried into their English-language usage. The Yoruba often use humor to prevent boredom during long meetings or serious discussions. They believe that embedding humor in their message guarantees that what they say is not readily forgotten. By contrast, Nigerians who live in other regions of the country, including the Igbo and Hausa, tend to speak more directly. Nigerians also make extensive use of nonverbal behavior (e.g., facial expressions) to communicate their views. In discussions, Nigerians frequently begin with a general idea and then slowly move to the specific, often using a somewhat circuitous route. Their logic is often contextual – that is, they tend to look for the rationale behind behavior and attempt to understand the context. Thus, behavior is viewed in terms of its surrounding context, and not simply in terms of what has been observed. As a result, what is not said is often more important than what is.

Think about it. . .

(1) Is your home culture characterized by high or low context? How does this influence how you personally speak with others?

(2) Can you find any differences in the communication styles common to various regions of Nigeria and those of your home country?

(3) As a manager working in Nigeria, how might you approach talking to employees differently from how you would in your home country? How easy is this to do?

Experienced managers understand that how a message is constructed can have a profound impact on how it is received. Should a message be explicit and direct, or subtle and perhaps even obtuse? To what degree should messages be communicated through verbal or nonverbal mechanisms? To what extent is message content more – or less – important than message context? Some cultures emphasize rigid written communication, while others prefer the more flexible spoken communication. Some cultures prefer that messages from outsiders come through "proper" channels (e.g., up the formal chain of command), while others prefer the use of informal channels (e.g., close associates or friends).

The principal challenge for managers here is sending clear and meaningful messages that are understood by other parties without offending them. An equally important challenge, however, is conveying these messages in culturally appropriate ways that may be unfamiliar to the message senders. For example, a typical Western manager with little experience using nonverbal communication techniques runs the risk of doing more harm than good when trying to be culturally sensitive. Nonverbal communication means much more than being silent or making awkward facial expressions. It is an art form to be studied and practiced, again suggesting the importance of ongoing learning and reflective experience.

Conversational formalities: "When in Rome..."

Conversational formalities encompass formal or implicit guidelines and rules governing what constitutes acceptable or preferred formal conversational etiquette. Every culture places constraints on how, when, and where we speak to others, and the knowledgeable manager can benefit from such understanding. Such formalities include the use of titles, the manner in which ideas or proposals are presented, and the role of apologies.

It is easy to say that some cultures are more formal than others, but it is necessary to ask what this means. There is typically an underlying purpose in the use of formalities. The use of titles, for example, can represent a sign of respect or a sign of power – not necessarily the same thing. Similarly, an absence of titles can indicate an egalitarian culture that eschews artificial status-based boundaries or a close relationship between parties. Clearly, the informed manager needs to understand these differences.

Conversational formalities also include knowing when and where apologies are required. Formal apologies are used throughout much of east and southeast Asia to restore harmony after an unpleasant incident or crisis. They demonstrate empathy and acceptance of responsibility. By contrast, apologies in many Western countries are often used to admit guilt, and, as a result, are used sporadically.

Application 6.8 Making apologies

To understand how this works, consider the public apology by Toyota CEO Akio Toyoda before a US congressional investigation over a series of safety problems involving the company's cars. Toyoda drew widespread attention, because few people could remember when a Western CEO had done such a thing. Toyoda apologized not only to his customers but also to stockholders for the company's declining profits and to employees for recent layoffs. He observed, "In the past few months, our customers have started to feel uncertain about the safety of Toyota's vehicles, and I take full responsibility for that. Today, I would like to explain to the American people, as well as our customers in the US and around the world, how seriously Toyota takes the quality and safety of its vehicles." Japan's *Asahi Shimbun*, one of Japan's largest newspapers, wrote in an editorial that Toyoda's testimony "not only determines Toyota's fate, but may affect all Japanese companies and consumer confidence in their products. President Toyoda has a heavy load on his shoulders."

In the West, such behavior by a CEO is often interpreted as a sign of weakness or lack of confidence – or, worse still, acceptance of legal responsibility. Witness the recent actions by BP CEO Tony Hayward, also before a US congressional investigation, following an oil spill in the Gulf of Mexico. Hayward offered a tepid apology and downplayed the long-term environmental implications. Some of his statements were: "I think the environmental impact of this disaster is likely to have been very, very modest"; "There is no one who wants this over more than I do. I would like my life back"; and "What the hell did we do to deserve this?" He also stressed that many other companies were also involved in the oil leak, not just BP. Two crises, and two very different public responses.

Application 6.8 (cont.)

Think about it...

(1) Why is the symbolism underlying the apologies from these two companies so different?

(2) Should either Toyota or BP have handled this situation differently? Why or why not?

(3) In working across cultures, what is your opinion of the proper role of apologies? When are they appropriate and when are they inappropriate? Why?

Acceptable behaviors: behave yourself

Finally, cultures often place constraints and expectations on what are considered to be acceptable behaviors that accompany interpersonal interactions. For example, research has shown that managers in North America are often expected or encouraged to be assertive and take the initiative in conversations; in much of Asia, by contrast, managers are often expected to remain silent and wait for an invitation to speak. Managers in North America are often allowed to leave a conversation once the main topic is finished; managers in Spain are generally expected to linger awhile and talk about other things before departing. Many North American managers tend to communicate linearly, with explicit links between topics and ideas, favoring a planned approach to communication; many Asian managers prefer a more nonlinear approach, following a circular pattern of communication; and many managers from the Mediterranean region tend to favor a zigzag approach, in which tangential ideas may be explored and elaborated before returning to the main point.

Moreover, it is not uncommon for more than one manager to speak at the same time throughout much of Latin Europe, while managers in northern Europe are more likely to wait until another speaker finishes. Conversations in much of Latin America tend to have very few lapses of silence – indeed, silence or "dead air" often makes such people uncomfortable, forcing them to speak again. By contrast, silent periods are very common in east and southeast Asia, and few feel uncomfortable.

Application 6.9 Emotional displays

Differences can also be seen in what are considered to be acceptable displays of emotions. Consider a recent example of a Spanish manager assigned to work in Germany. The day after she arrived in Germany, she received news that a close relative had suddenly died. The woman was emotionally upset and burst into tears. She was appalled by the lack of sensitivity of her German colleagues, who did not inquire about what had happened or provide emotional support. On the other hand, her German colleagues were surprised by her reaction and thought she was immature and unprofessional. Thus, while outward displays of emotions are often acceptable and even expected at times in Spain, these same behaviors are often considered inappropriate, and taking interest in a colleague's personal affairs can be deemed rude and unprofessional in Germany.

Think about it...

(1)   Who is right here? Should the Germans have been more sensitive and understanding of the Spanish woman's misfortune, or should she have been more respectful of the local culture? Why?

(2)   Can you identify a particular emotional display that is inappropriate in your own culture? Why is it inappropriate?

Finally, disagreements throughout much of Asia are often communicated with silence; disagreements in Spain are often communicated through emotional outbursts; and disagreements in northern Europe tend to be clearly, calmly, and directly stated and discussed. Similarly, praise is a common motivational strategy for many supervisors in North America, but is typically reserved for extraordinary accomplishments in Russia. In France and Indonesia, by contrast, praise is sometimes considered offensive to employees, because it suggests that the supervisor was surprised that the employees had done so well.

Cultural protocols therefore serve as a very useful tool in facilitating communication both within and between cultures. It is through these protocols that people signal what parts of the message are important and how they should be interpreted. They also guide message senders by providing a repertoire of acceptable responses depending upon the situation. Ignorance of these simple mechanisms is often blamed for much of the noise and miscommunication across cultures. In this regard, managers who understand these required behaviors are better able to focus attention on salient comments and events, make more sense out of the messages they receive, and craft more effective replies and responses in their global endeavors.

Communicating across cultures

Consider the following dilemma. You are a partner in a small, but global, electronics firm that does business primarily in western Europe and east Asia. You are trying to sell your IT services to two small companies, one in Spain and one in South Korea. When you try to telephone each of the presidents of the two small firms, however, no one answers. Question: should you leave a message informing them that you will call back at a particular time? The correct answer is "Yes and no." Why? In Spain it is perfectly acceptable to leave a message for others (including more senior people) saying that you will call back at a given time. Of course, the person you are calling has no obligation to be there when you call back, but at least you can record your intent. In doing so, you are being polite in saying that you will take the responsibility to link up at a future time. By contrast, leaving such a message on the phone of someone in South Korea (particularly if he or she is older) is often considered rude and inconsiderate, because it obligates the other person to sit by the phone at a specific time waiting for your call. Many Koreans consider constraining the behavior of superiors an offense against social norms. Instead, etiquette requires that you either leave no message or leave a simple message saying that you called but without reference to a possible callback time.

Routine behaviors such as these can have major ramifications for success or failure in social situations around the globe, and, while a lack of understanding here can be appreciated or even forgiven, it nevertheless seldom leads to positive outcomes. Once again, we return to the inescapable conclusion that global managers must be well prepared for new situations and new contacts if they wish to succeed. Center stage in these preparations is knowing how and when to talk – and what to say.

Multicultural communication: assessing demands and constraints

With increasing globalization and the associated need to communicate on an almost daily basis with people from different cultures, developing the abilities and skills to communicate effectively across cultural boundaries is fundamental to all managers. To a manager (or anyone else, for that matter), the realization that, despite his or her best efforts, the message was met with a blank stare, a grimace, inaction, or actions that demonstrated a lack of understanding can be distressing. When this same manager fails to understand either why the message was unsuccessful or how to improve future communication, however, frustration can turn into despair.

Following the *demands, constraints, and choices model* outlined in Chapter 5, perhaps the best place to begin any efforts to improve communication across borders is to identify factors in the external environment that can serve to inhibit or open opportunities for effective interpersonal communication. Each interaction is likely to be unique, based on the situation facing the parties involved, so this seems like a logical starting point. This cautions against a generalized approach to cross-cultural communication. Much energy can be wasted in such efforts.

As illustrated in Exhibit 6.9, a number of cultural, organizational, and situational factors can emerge to limit managerial options and choices. For example, communication in high-context cultures will likely focus as much on what is not said (e.g., nonverbal communication) as on what is. Likewise, company formalities or status systems may provide hints about appropriate behaviors during meetings. Finally, the location of a meeting (on-site or off-site) or the language-in-use can also serve to constrain what is said

Exhibit 6.9 Assessing the multicultural communication environment (examples)

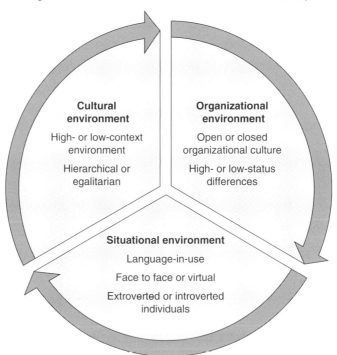

or how it is said. This exhibit illustrates only some of the possible impediments to effective communication. The point here is very simple: the more managers understand about the limitations surrounding their communication endeavors, the greater the possibility that they will select communication channels that will be appropriate – and effective.

Multicultural communication: developing action plans

As the above discussion suggests, a lot can go wrong when communicating across cultures if environmental factors are ignored. This is not a new conclusion. Over two thousand years ago Roman poet Horace observed, "A word, once sent abroad, flies irrevocably."[16] Differences in language, cultural logic, expectations and interpretations regarding message content, context and communication protocols may all distort meanings and jeopardize communications. With this in mind, we now come to the issue of what global managers can do to reduce or minimize such impediments to clear communication. As noted above, although cultural processes are multifaceted, complex, and at times secretive, there are nonetheless concrete strategies that managers can initiate to adapt to such differences in their interactions with others. In this regard, managers have at least three choices or options to pursue in order to improve the likelihood of finding common ground with other parties (see Exhibit 6.10). They are all "doable" for managers committed to learning and skills building.

Exhibit 6.10 Action plans for multicultural communication

(1) Expand knowledge and understanding of cultural dynamics	(2) Recalibrate perceptual and critical analysis skills	(3) Enhance behavioral repertoire of applied communication skills
• Develop a greater understanding of your own culture and its common communication patterns. • Develop in-depth knowledge of the beliefs, values, and behavioral expectations of other key cultures. • Expand relevant foreign-language skills for both increased understanding and improved communication. • Seek advice from local cultural experts, when appropriate	• Examine your own reasoning, as well as the reasoning of others. • Explore the assumptions you make about others. • Use your expanded cultural knowledge to view situations through the eyes of others. • Look for subtleties and nuances in interpersonal interactions that explain what others are thinking. • Seek to understand the "whys?," not just the "whats?," in the comments and behaviors of others.	• Broaden your message-formatting skills, including nonverbal communication skills. • Develop country-specific knowledge of appropriate topics, formalities, and behaviors. • Develop your active listening skills, with particular attention to common communication failures across cultures and possible resolution strategies.

1 Expand knowledge and understanding of cultural dynamics

Simply put, global managers can and should invest the time and energy required to learn more about how the world of work often differs across cultures, as well as the implications of such differences for management. In practice, this is not as difficult as it may at first appear. Exploring other cultures is not unlike learning computer games; at some point it becomes intuitive, allowing the manager to work almost seamlessly in settings that previously seemed alien. Of particular importance here is knowledge of how local beliefs, values, and behavioral expectations can differ across cultures and how managers can prepare themselves for such differences. Much of this learning can be accomplished though independent reading and study, sponsored programs on cross-cultural issues, discussions with foreign nationals, and focused observations of what others are doing. None of this is difficult to accomplish.

Multicultural learning can also be facilitated by language study. Understanding the language of one's counterparts can go a long way towards capturing the essence of cultural differences – an important factor in working successfully across borders. Although it is often noted that "everyone" speaks English, there is ample room for misunderstandings and missed cues when people are forced into an unfamiliar language, as we have seen above.

Finally, in expanding cultural knowledge, it is also important not to forget one's own culture. Frequently managers take their own culture for granted and fail to realize that their own social environment creates its own screens that affect communication. Self-awareness about one's culture can serve as a useful point of departure for better understanding others. It can also serve to enhance one's understanding of how one is viewed by others.

2 Recalibrate perceptual and critical analysis skills

Based on this expanded knowledge and understanding of cultural differences, a second communication strategy emerges that involves seeking a better understanding of the cognitive processes underlying the comments and actions of others. This is not as extreme as it may sound. We are not suggesting altering basic cognitive processes; rather, we suggest recalibrating them. In other words, on the basis of their newly acquired multicultural awareness and understanding, managers should be in a position to use somewhat modified cognitive templates or frames of reference when trying to understand why people with different cultural backgrounds do or say what they do. Recent research has shown that experienced global managers often exhibit an ability to look behind external appearances or behaviors and try to understand the "Whys?," not just the "Whats?" They work to understand interpersonal interactions through the eyes and ears of others. They look for subtleties and nuances in social interactions that may help explain what others are thinking. They observe more than they judge. To a large extent, these are learned behaviors that motivated managers can develop with practice.

It will be remembers from Chapter 2 that Google has developed a training program for new managers in which participants are sent abroad in small groups to India, China, and Japan to learn first-hand how business works. Participants live in the local economy and meet with local managers, shopkeepers, and farmers to explore divergent world views. The assumption underlying Google's endeavor is that these first-hand experiences will enhance their employees' critical thinking skills in cross-cultural interactions.

At the same time, successful global managers seek to understand their own beliefs and values, assumptions, biases, and perceptions. Stepping outside one's comfort zone allows managers to take a fresh look at situations that confront them. Are their assumptions about certain situations correct, or are there alternative assumptions that are equally valid? Developing shared meanings requires letting go of previous judgments and understandings, and tolerating uncertainty until a new understanding can be created. The point for managers to understand is that they may be "right" with respect to something, but in a cross-cultural environment what is right is relative. Arriving at a common meaning requires an ability to tolerate uncertainty and ambiguity in order to seek a deeper understanding of what one's counterparts are trying to say or do.

3   Enhance applied communication skills

Finally, on a very practical level, managers can improve their knowledge of various communication protocols, which can vary from culture to culture. In addition to knowing where or when certain languages are preferred or required (discussed above), developing message-formatting skills can be critical to successful communication, especially as it relates to the use of nonverbal communication techniques, such as reading facial expressions and other forms of body language. Numerous cultures use such techniques as a core communication strategy, and misreading these – or ignoring them completely – can lead both to missed signals and missed opportunities.

Related to this is the need for managers to broaden their knowledge of what topics may be required or forbidden in certain conversations or messages (e.g., talking about money, illness, or families), what formalities are required or preferred in various communication arenas (the use of titles, bowing, dress codes, seating arrangements), and what behaviors are acceptable or unacceptable (e.g., raising one's voice, interrupting, verbal rejections, touching someone).

In this regard, many companies (e.g., Hewlett-Packard, Intel, GE, and Ford in the United States, Wipro and Tata in India, Sony and Mitsubishi in Japan, LG and Samsung in South Korea, and so forth) offer their employees extensive training programs in local business practices and social etiquette prior to sending them on overseas assignments. Some companies sponsor entire corporate "universities" (e.g., Motorola University) aimed at developing an extensive managerial and cultural skills set for global managers.

Finally, developing active listening skills has long been recommended for managers facing ambiguous situations. This is particularly important in cross-cultural settings, when communication failures can be commonplace. Recognizing such failures – not always an easy task – and finding a remedy can be key to saving a conversation and possible business deal. Again, corporate training programs can be of great assistance here.

In closing, as we have noted before, no one ever said that the manager's job was easy. Because of this, managers look logically for tools and techniques that can help them achieve their goals and objectives. In this pursuit, improved multicultural communication skills rank – or should rank – at the top of any manager's list of desired attributes. None of the three communication strategies discussed here is necessarily easily attained, but all are required if enhanced multicultural communication is to be achieved. Enhancing these skills requires both effort and commitment. It requires a mindset that sees the managerial role as a continual developmental process characterized by experience, reflection, analysis, and, most importantly, learning.

We began this chapter by pointing out that multicultural communication is frequently cited as one of the most serious challenges facing global managers. We close by observing that cross-cultural communication is also one of the most important sources of business opportunity. It is through communication that relationships are formed, conflicts are resolved, and innovative ideas are created and shared. While the perils of poor cross-cultural communication may appear daunting at first glance, we believe that increased awareness of the ways in which cultural differences can affect how meaning is constructed in interpersonal interactions is an important first step towards improved communication. We further believe that, in order to succeed, managers must be willing to make the effort and risk some initial missteps and perhaps embarrassment. In the end, effective multicultural communication is a matter of personal commitment and a willingness to learn. Above all, however, it is a willingness to listen. As the Venetian explorer Marco Polo reportedly observed long ago, "It is not the voice that commands the story; it is the ear."[17]

Summary points

- Communication is the principal way we reach out to others to exchange ideas and commodities, develop and dissolve relationships, and conduct business. Within one culture or language group, communication can often be problematic – particularly across age groups, geographic regions, and gender. These problems pale into insignificance, however, in comparison to the challenges of communicating across cultures.

- In any cross-cultural exchange between managers from different regions, the principal purpose of communication is to seek common ground – to seek out ideas, information, customers, and sometimes even partnerships between the parties.

- Communications are effective only to the extent that recipients are both paying attention to the message and capable of processing the information in ways that facilitate common meaning.

- The attention–interpretation–message model highlights three key ingredients in effective interpersonal communication: attention, interpretation, and message (or response).

- Cultural screens are potential impediments or barriers in the basic AIM process. Two cultural screens that affect both interpersonal interactions in general and multicultural communications in particular were discussed. These screens often emerge as a result of cultural differences between senders and receivers, and can have important implications for how various parties to a conversation receive, interpret, and respond to messages. The first screen involves cultural influences on individual cognitions surrounding communication episodes – that is, how people and messages are often evaluated and processed in the minds of senders and receivers alike. The second involves cultural influences on communication protocols, or required behaviors, such as how we construct or shape our messages in ways that may be culturally consistent for us but, hopefully, not problematic for our intended receivers.

- Improving communication across cultures involves three main strategies: expanding one's knowledge and understanding of cultural dynamics; recalibrating one's perceptual and critical analysis skills; and enhancing one's behavioral repertoire of applied communication skills.

Notes

1 Cited in Richard Hill, *We Europeans*. Brussels: Europublications, 1997, p. 345.

2 Richard D. Lewis, *When Cultures Collide*. London: Nicholas Brealey, 1999, p. 94.

3 Xiaohong He, Mohammad Elahee, Robert Engle, Chadwick Nehrt, and Farid Sadrieh, *Globalization and International Business: Living Ever Closer Together*. Garfield Heights, OH: NCP, 2007, p. 54.

4 Luciara Nardon, Richard M. Steers, and Carlos Sanchez-Runde, "Seeking common ground: strategies for enhancing multicultural communication," *Organizational Dynamics*, 2011, 40(2), 85–95.

5 Nardon, Steers, and Sanchez-Runde, "Seeking common ground," p. 86.

6 Larry A. Samovar, Richard E. Porter, and Edwin R. McDaniel, *Communication between Cultures*. Belmont, CA: Thomson/Wadsworth, 2007, pp. 165–7.

7 *Lingua franca* (from Italian, literally meaning "the Frankish language") is a language that is systematically used to communicate between persons not sharing a mother tongue, in particular when it is a third language, distinct from both persons' mother tongues. "Lingua franca" is a functionally defined term, independent of the linguistic history or structure of the language. It may also refer to the de facto language within a more or less specialized field. A synonym for "lingua franca" is "vehicular language." Whereas a *vernacular* language is used as a native language in a single speaker community, a *vehicular* language goes beyond the boundaries of its original community, and is used as a second language for communication between communities. For example, English is a vernacular in England, but is used as a vehicular language (that is, a lingua franca) in the Philippines.

8 Private communication, 2007.

9 Norman Schur, *British English: A to Zed*. New York: HarperCollins, 1991.

10 Nardon, Steers, and Sanchez-Runde, "Seeking common ground."

11 Nardon, Steers, and Sanchez-Runde, "Seeking common ground."

12 Edward T. Hall and Mildred Reed Hall, *Understanding Cultural Differences: Germans, French and Americans*. Yarmouth, ME: Intercultural Press, 1990.

13 Samovar, Porter, and McDaniel, *Communication between Cultures*.

14 Gary P. Ferraro, *The Cultural Dimension of International Business*, 5th edn. Upper Saddle River, NJ: Pearson/Prentice Hall, 2005, p. 80.

15 Edward T. Hall, *The Silent Language*. New York: Anchor Books, 1981.

16 Horace, *The Satires, Epistles, and Art of Poetry* (trans. John Conington). Oxford University Press, 2010.

17 Marco Polo, cited in Laurence Bergreen, *Marco Polo: From Venice to Xanadu*. New York: Vintage Books, 2007, p. 1.

CHAPTER 7

Negotiating global agreements

MANAGEMENT CHALLENGE

If building global partnerships is important to competitiveness, as most agree, how do managers and their companies negotiate such alliances? What special skills are required? Can these skills be developed or are some people just naturally born negotiators? It has been said that negotiation is an art, not a science. If so, the question before us is how to develop this art. Understanding basic negotiation processes is a good beginning. Developing specific bargaining strategies and tactics is another. Once agreements have been signed, knowing how to implement them is also important. Throughout, an understanding – and willingness – to build mutually beneficial long-term relationships is perhaps most important of all.

Exhibit 7.2 Preparing for global negotiations

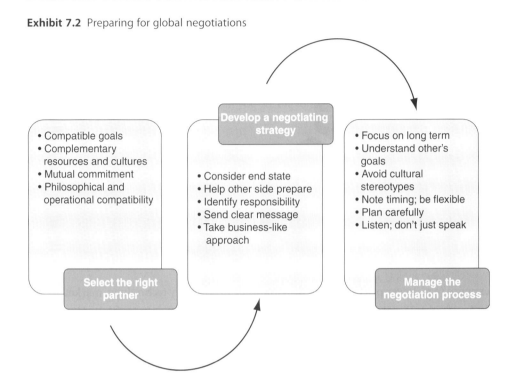

Criteria for selecting global partners

In view of the high "divorce rate" among global partnerships (e.g., joint ventures, strategic alliances, suppliers, distributors), a key question emerges concerning how and where to find the right partners and then negotiate a workable partnership. This challenge faces many, if not most, global partnerships today. In this regard, consider what it is that a company most requires in its partners in order to expand its business in ways that are both efficient and effective and support its overall mission. Five key success factors can be identified.

- *Compatibility of strategic goals and tactics.* First and foremost among these factors is the need to ensure that prospective partners have goals and objectives that mutually reinforce each other's long-term objectives and short-term tactics. Without this congruence, organizational and managerial efforts are likely to dissipate while each partner expends time and resources trying to go its own separate way.

- *Complementary value-creating resources.* In addition, partners' approaches to methods, systems, inputs, and distribution channels should be similar, and therefore understandable and comfortable to each partner. Ideally, moreover, each partner would contribute assets to the partnership that the other partner may not have in abundance. The long-standing alliance between Samsung Electronics and Corning Glass is a case in point. When Samsung decided to enter the television market, it had little understanding of critical glass technologies that were essential to manufacturing success. At the same time, Corning was looking to expand its overseas ventures in east Asia based on its previous success in Japan. Both needed partners. As a result of the partnership, Samsung provided a highly educated workforce and capital to match Corning's highly sophisticated glass technology. Both learned from each other and complemented one another through their particular resource contributions to the joint enterprise.

- *Complementary organizational cultures.* Successful partners typically have complementary organizational cultures (see Chapter 4). Partnering with a firm that has a secretive culture is likely to be unsustainable for a company that thrives on openness. This is not to say that successful partners must have open and cooperative cultures, although this certainly makes partnerships more likely to succeed. Rather, it is to suggest that, at the very least, whatever the cultures are, they should be compatible in their characteristics.

- *Strong commitment to the partnership.* A major factor in selecting successful partners is the degree to which both partners have a strong interest in and commitment to creating and managing a successful partnership. In the case of General Electric and Siemens, discussed above, we saw that both partners had only a tepid interest in making the venture succeed, with predictable results.

- *Strong philosophical and operational compatibility.* Finally, successful partnerships tend to share a common philosophical outlook, as well as strong operational capabilities. They share things in common and, as organizations, often look alike in many ways. At the same time, they frequently share basic philosophies of operational and human resource management (HRM). For example, when US-based Davidson–Marley was looking for a British partner, it sought (and found) a viable partner that shared many common characteristics that the US company felt would be required in order for the venture to succeed.[5] Both used consensus-style management. Both were part of a larger organization that was highly decentralized. Both desired to move onto the Continent with a manufacturing presence. Both had similar views on how to grow the business. Both had similar philosophies about running the business and managing human resources. Both sought an open and fair relationship. As a result, the two partners got off to a good start and began business well along the learning curve.

Application 7.1 GM and SAIC

A good example of matchmaking – finding the right partners – can be illustrated by the strategic partnership between General Motors (GM) and Shanghai Automotive Industrial Corporation (SAIC) to design and build cars.[6] This venture has been growing in both size and importance since its inception more than a decade ago. The goals of each partner are very clear, as are the required tasks to succeed. When asked to explain GM's Asian expansion, GM executive Steve Girsky observes, "It's simple: do the math." GM's joint ventures sold more than 2 million vehicles in China in 2011 – more than it sold in the United States – and it expects to double that number in five years. SAIC is now the largest automaker in China and is eager to expand its technological capabilities, product lineup, and penetration of foreign markets, and it relies on GM for expertise and know-how. The partners already cooperate in a dozen ventures covering almost every aspect of automotive engineering, manufacturing, and distribution, and any disputes are kept far from public view. The explosion of Chinese auto sales opens up some interesting possibilities. Over the coming ten years, GM believes China will grow by another 12.7 million units – in effect adding another market the size of the United States – and that GM's share will rise along with it. These two companies have worked to understand each other and build a working partnership. SAIC received automotive technology and manufacturing skills; GM received new markets and competitively priced cars.

Think about it...

(1) What are GM's long-term strategic objectives in this venture? What are SAIC's long-term strategic objectives?

(2) How much overlap is there between these two sets of goals? In particular, in what areas do these two firms differ in their long-term objectives?

(3) What specific talents or skills must the managers on both sides of this venture have in order to continue with this successful partnership? Explain.

Developing a negotiating strategy

Finding suitable partners may not be as easy as first thought, therefore. Again, the marriage metaphor can be useful in understanding this mating game. Once a potential partner has been identified, however, companies turn their attention to the negotiation process with the aim of building a useful partnership. The negotiation process is the first step in relationship building, and represents an opportunity for both parties to determine the nature, scope, and ground rules for the partnership. As discussed above, despite the many benefits of a global partnership, there are several drawbacks, and partners must obviously work hard to make it work. During the negotiation process, partners have an opportunity to learn about each party's organizational and national cultures, their interests, commitments, and potential synergistic opportunities to create value.

Unfortunately, when negotiating such a partnership, negotiators frequently commit the mistake of focusing exclusively on signing the deal, assuming that, once the contract has been signed, everything else will follow smoothly. In reality, however, signing a contract is just the beginning of most partnerships. Given the high rate of failure in global partnerships, the real challenge is not signing the contract but putting the deal into practice. Companies that are able to use the negotiation process to get to know their future partners can often foresee and prevent future problems and avoid undue hardships. For these situations, negotiations expert Danny Ertel suggests that negotiators need a new mindset focused on implementation. He notes that the product of a negotiation isn't a document; it's the value produced once the parties have done what they agreed to do. Negotiators who understand that prepare differently from how dealmakers do. They don't ask "What might they be willing to accept?" but, rather, "How do we create value together?" They also negotiate differently, recognizing that value comes not from a signature but from real work performed long after the ink has dried.[7]

To this end, he suggests five approaches towards an implementation mindset.

- *Start with the end in mind.* Think about how the deal will work twelve months after it has been signed. How will you know when it is successful? What can go wrong? These questions focus negotiations on the implementation phase, making the partnership work after the deal has been signed.
- *Help the other side to prepare.* Surprising the other party in order to win concessions is likely to backfire, as the other party will not be able to deliver on its promises and both sides will lose.
- *Treat alignment as a shared responsibility.* If your interests are not properly aligned, problems will likely emerge at some time in the future. It is worthwhile investing in time to gain acceptance by all those involved in the deal, who will have to make the deal work later on.
- *Send one clear message.* Share information with everyone involved in the deal. Withholding information may create early wins, but it will cause problems in the implementation phase if one of the parties feels deceived.

- *Manage negotiations like a business process.* Signing a contract is just the first step; the implementation of the deal brings with it important associated costs. To ensure that the implementation is smooth, negotiators use careful preparation and post-negotiation reviews.

Curiously, Nancy Adler and John Graham investigated negotiation behaviors in both domestic and cross-cultural bargaining, and found that people behaved differently when they were negotiating with people from the same culture from how they did when they were negotiating across cultures. They also found that Japanese negotiators adapted their behavior more often than their American counterparts.[8]

Managing the negotiation process

Successful international negotiators are comfortable in multicultural environments and are skilled in building and maintaining interpersonal relationships. A career in this arena is not for the faint of heart, however; this is a difficult job that requires a number of very specific skills, as well as an ability to handle significant amounts of conflict and stress. Successes come slowly and failures are commonplace. Even so, it is possible to identify a number of personal factors that often differentiate between successful and unsuccessful negotiators: a tolerance of ambiguity; patience, patience, patience; flexibility and creativity; a good sense of humor; solid physical and mental stamina; cultural empathy; curiosity and a willingness to learn new things; and a knowledge of foreign languages.

Among these recommendations, the one suggesting knowledge of a foreign language is perhaps the most controversial. Specifically, how important is it to speak two or more languages? Moreover, when negotiating with a foreign partner, which language should be used? When should it be used?

Application 7.2 Language and negotiation

Consider the perils when someone speaks only one language and uses an interpreter for negotiations. A British manager was recently on a business trip to Mexico City and her local host took her to visit the famous Teotihuacán pyramids outside the city. Near the great Pyramid of the Sun, they ran across a Mexican peasant who was selling trinkets. The manager found something she liked, and her Mexican host offered to help her negotiate. The peasant made an initial offer, and the visitor's host translated and then suggested a low counter-offer. "If we counter with this, he will then counter with that," said the host. Not surprisingly, the peasant rejected the counter-offer and offered only a slightly lower price. The host then suggested a higher counter-offer, again explaining that, if she offered X, the peasant would likely come back with Y. Bidding and counter-bidding went on like this for several minutes. Finally, the frustrated visitor, who had made little headway in gaining an advantageous price, gave in and agreed to pay almost full price for the item. At that, the poor Mexican peasant looked at the British manager and asked, in near-perfect English, "Would you like to charge this on your Visa card?" The lesson here is very simple: if you do not understand the local language, at least know who you are bargaining with – and who is doing your translation.

Think about it. . .

(1)   What are some of the potential problems of using a translator to conduct business across languages? How might these problems be minimized?

(2)   Have you ever been in a similar situation, in which you were talking with someone not realizing others were listening? Why did this happen?

One last question here about language: has English replaced all other languages as the required language for global trade today? If so, why should anyone study another language? Or is there still a competitive advantage in having an ability to negotiate in a partner's home language?

Beyond these personal qualities, experts suggest several general strategies that have been found to facilitate successful negotiations, including the following.[9]

- *Concentrate on building long-term relationships with your partner, not short-term contracts.* Long-term partners usually yield greater long-term results for both parties.
- *Focus on understanding the organizational and personal interests and goals behind the stated bargaining positions.* The Latin *Cui bono?* ("Who benefits?") is certainly appropriate here (see Chapter 4).[10] What do the various parties to the negotiation hope to gain from an agreement?
- *Avoid over-reliance on cultural generalizations.* Although there may be cultural trends within specific countries, no nation is monolithic, and people can vary widely in their personal characteristics.
- *Be sensitive to timing.* Some cultures – and some negotiators – require considerable patience in working towards an agreement, while others demand prompt resolution of all issues or they will go elsewhere.

- *Remain flexible throughout the negotiations.* Circumstances, available information, and opportunities often change, and success sometimes hinges on being both prepared and alert.
- *Plan carefully.* Nowhere is the old adage "Knowledge is power" more apt than in understanding international negotiations. Solid preparations can make all the difference.
- *Learn to listen, not just to speak.* Develop good listening skills to understand both the content and the context of the message. Use body language and facial expressions to identify informal or subtle cues as to intentions.

The negotiation process

In many cultures, business is built on long-standing personal relationships. This is as true in France and Mexico as it is in China and India. People do business with partners they know, people they can trust. As such, many international negotiations begin with both sides trying to establish a personal bond. This does not necessarily mean they plan to become lifelong friends; rather, each side needs to determine if the other party is sufficiently trustworthy to conclude an agreement and stick with it. In many countries, it is insulting (as well as unproductive) to begin a business discussion until after such relationships have been firmly established. In these cultures, it is often said that business relationships must be "warmed up" before getting down to serious negotiations. This is a good principle to remember.

Ironically, the one place where such relationships, while important, are not necessarily critical to a successful negotiation is the United States, where legal contracts are frequently seen as a substitute for personal relationships (see below). As a result, US negotiators are notorious for wanting to get down to business immediately – a practice that frequently leads to frustration and failure. More successful US negotiators understand the critical importance of subtleties and patience, not brashness and drive. Accordingly, most successful international managers – regardless of their home country – invest considerable time and effort in getting to know their prospective partners. This frequently includes a variety of social activities (dinners, golf, etc.), at which it is often inappropriate to discuss any business whatsoever. The stage is being set.

Competitive versus problem-solving strategies

Generally speaking, there are two basic strategies for negotiation: competitive negotiation and problem-solving negotiation. The competitive approach views negotiations as

Exhibit 7.3 Competitive and problem-solving negotiation strategies

Stages in negotiation	Competitive bargaining	Problem-solving bargaining
(1) Preparation	Identify current economic and other benefits your firm seeks from the deal. Prepare to defend your firm's position.	Define the long-term strategic interests of your firm. Prepare to overcome cross-cultural barriers to defining mutual interests.
(2) Relationship building	Look for weaknesses in your opponent's position. Learn about your opponent, but reveal as little as possible.	Adapt to the other side's culture. Separate the people involved in negotiation from the problems and goals that need to be solved.
(3) Information exchange and first offer	Provide as little information as possible to your opponent. Make your position explicit. Make a hard offer that is more favorable to your side than you realistically expect to achieve.	Give and demand to receive objective information that clarifies each party's interests. Accept cultural differences in speed of response and type of information needs. Make firm but reasonable first offer.
(4) Persuasion	Use dirty tricks and pressure tactics when appropriate to win.	Search for new creative options that benefit the interests of both parties.
(5) Concessions	Begin with high initial demands. Make concessions slowly and grudgingly.	Search for mutually acceptable criteria for reaching accord. Accept cultural differences in starting position and in how and when concessions are made.
(6) Agreement	Sign only if you win and then ensure that you sign an ironclad contract.	Sign when the interests of your firm are met. Adapt to cultural differences in contracts when necessary.

a win-lose game, while the problem-solving approach seeks to discover a win-win solution from which both sides can benefit, if at all possible. Exhibit 7.3 illustrates how these two different strategies are played out during negotiation.

In *competitive negotiation*, each side tries to give as little as possible. They frequently begin with unrealistically high demands and make concessions only grudgingly. Competitive negotiators will, at times, use dirty tricks or other tactics that allow them to win. Little thought is given to building a long-term relationship between the parties. Since starting from inflexible positions often leads to outcomes that satisfy neither side, each side often develops negative attitudes towards the other. As a result, losers in the agreement often seek revenge, such as reneging on parts of the contract at a later date or substituting inferior-quality materials in production orders.

By contrast, *problem-solving negotiation* begins with the basic tenet that negotiators must separate positions from interests. Instead of defending a company's position as a major goal in the negotiation process, problem-solving negotiators begin by seeking a mutually satisfactory ground that is beneficial to the interests of both sides (see Exhibit 7.4). Dirty tricks are avoided because they poison the development of long-term mutually advantageous relationships. Objective information is preferred whenever possible as a basis for discussion and problem-solving efforts, instead of unrealistic sales pitches or hyperbole. Often problem-solving negotiation facilitates the identification of creative new ways to provide both parties with what they want to achieve. Furthermore, even

Exhibit 7.4 Competitive and problem-solving negotiation strategies (example)

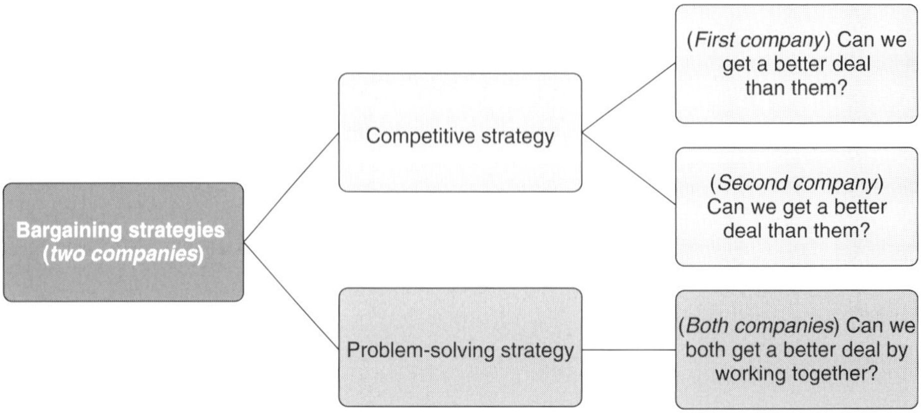

when mutually advantageous solutions are not found, both sides leave the table believing that sincere efforts were made on both sides. This leaves open the possibility of returning to the bargaining table in the future when another opportunity presents itself.

Three important points emerge from this case regarding the choice between using either competitive or problem-solving bargaining strategies. First, it is very easy in cross-cultural negotiation to misread the intentions of the other party. Hence a detailed understanding of the cultural backgrounds of one's opponent becomes critical in determining whether he or she is stating a highly inflexible position or offering a genuine opportunity to strike a deal. This is why many successful international negotiators always have advisors at their side who are intimately familiar with the culture and traditions of the other party. Second, culture sometimes predisposes negotiators to select one approach over the other. For example, observers note that some US managers believe there has to be a winner and a loser, while many Japanese managers prefer a problem-solving approach. The smart bargainer understands this and adjusts his or her strategy accordingly. Finally, when possible, most experts on international negotiation recommend a problem-solving approach, because it tends to lead to better long-term solutions and relationships. This is particularly true in negotiating global partnerships. Winning now may mean big losses later. It is important to remember that the failure of the partnership may be more expensive than small concessions given during the negotiation process.

Information exchange and initial offers

Exhibit 7.5 illustrates how culture can influence the specific issue of information sharing and making first offers. In other words, managers in some cultures seek

Exhibit 7.5 Information exchange and initial offers by culture

Cultures	Information exchanged	First offer
East Asians	Extensive requests for proposal details and technical information. Assumption that all details of the proposal must be discussed before agreement can be reached.	10–20% below their desired end result.
Latin Americans	Focus more on information about the relationship and less on technical details of the proposal. Preliminary discussions focus on why we should do business together, not how we should do it.	20–40% below their desired end result.
Middle Easterners	Focus more on information about the relationship and less on technical details of the proposal. Preliminary discussions focus on why we should do business together, not how we should do it.	20–50% below their desired end result.
North Americans	Information is provided directly and briefly, often through multimedia presentations. Assumption that, if an agreement can be reached in principle, details can be resolved later.	5–10% below their desired end result.
Russians	Extensive requests for proposal details and technical information. Assumption that all details of the proposal must be discussed before agreement can be reached.	50–60% below their desired end result.

Source: Based on Lillian H. Chaney and Jeannette S. Martin, *Intercultural Business Communication*. Englewood Cliffs, NJ: Prentice Hall, 1995, pp. 183–4.

seemingly inexhaustible technical details about a product or service being discussed, while managers in other cultures often ignore most of the product details and continue to focus on relationship building. In any event, at some point in the process each side will make its first offer, its initial bargaining position. In some cultures (e.g., those in Russia, Saudi Arabia) first offers are often totally unrealistic, whereas in other cultures (e.g., those in Japan, South Korea) they are often close to the final bargaining position. This first offer initiates the negotiating process that, it is hoped, will culminate in a final agreement.

Bargaining and concessions

Clearly, the ultimate goal of a negotiation is to arrive at a mutually agreed contract that is legally binding in both countries. To achieve this, concessions must be made. What is interesting here is that culture can, at times, influence how these concessions are determined. In North America, for example, companies frequently use what is called a *sequential approach* to concession making (see Exhibit 7.6). In other words, they prefer to go through a proposed contract item by item and get agreement on each item as they proceed sequentially through the proposals.

By contrast, and popular throughout much of Asia, there is the *holistic approach* to concession making. In this the two parties work their way through the entire proposed agreement, but do not agree to anything until they have completed their review. They then discuss the contract in its entirety and make final proposals and counter-proposals

Exhibit 7.6 Sequential and holistic bargaining strategies

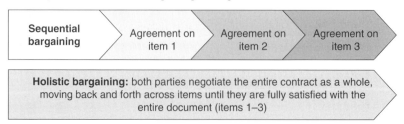

Exhibit 7.7 Bargaining tactics (Brazil, Japan, United States)

Bargaining tactics	Brazil	Japan	United States
Giving orders	14	1	6
Interrupting	29	13	10
Saying "No"	83	6	9
Silent periods	0	6	4
Touching others	5	0	0

aimed at reaching a complete agreement. The holistic approach frequently perplexes novice North American negotiators when they learn that a point they thought was already agreed upon resurfaces to be discussed later by their Asian counterparts.

Bargaining tactics

To better understand how this process works, it is useful to review an interesting and well-crafted study of bargaining tactics among Japanese, Brazilian, and US managers.[11] In this study, managers from the three countries were put in twenty-minute negotiation sessions, and the investigators simply counted the number of times managers from each country used either a verbal or nonverbal negotiating tactic. Significant differences in both verbal and nonverbal bargaining or negotiating tactics were found during bargaining sessions between managers (see Exhibit 7.7). Notice, for example, how often negotiators from each country said "No" during just twenty minutes (6, 9, and 83 for Japan, the United States, and Brazil, respectively), touched their opponents (0, 0, 5), or had silent periods during which they said nothing (6, 4, 0). What does this say about cultural variations in negotiations?

Going a step further, consider what cultural anthropologists and management researchers have discovered when analyzing some of the cultural drivers underlying the negotiating strategies of the three groups (see Exhibit 7.8). These findings illustrate clearly some of the principal challenges of negotiating and building successful global partnerships across cultures. One key factor in determining whether to do business with

Exhibit 7.8 Foundations of bargaining tactics (Brazil, Japan, United States)

Negotiating strategies	Japanese firms	Brazilian firms	US firms
Ultimate goal	Long-term profitability, usually without personal benefit.	Long-term mutually beneficial relationships.	Short-term profitability, often with personal benefit for negotiator.
Ideal negotiating climate	Oblique and at times personal.	Impromptu; difficult to generalize.	Straightforward and impersonal.
Risk orientation	Risk-averse.	Risk-averse.	Risk-oriented.
Communication style	High context; talks indirectly; seldom blunt; extensive use of technical language.	High context; talks indirectly; frequently emotional; frequently exaggerates.	Low context; talks directly; frequently blunt; sometimes exaggerates.
Emotional sensitivity	Emotional sensitivity avoided; strong personal relationships critical for success.	Emotional sensitivity highly valued; strong personal relationships critical for success.	Emotional sensitivity avoided; negotiators often avoid close personal relationships.
Basis of decisions	Decisions usually made on cost–benefit basis for the long term.	Decisions often tied to emotional or family considerations.	Decisions usually made on a cost–benefit basis for the short term.
Importance of face saving	Face saving critical; embarrassing either party to the negotiation should be avoided at all costs.	Face saving critical; embarrassing either party to the negotiation should be avoided, if possible.	Face saving not critical; embarrassing opponent may lead to an advantage in negotiations.
Dispute resolution	Preference for conciliation and contract renegotiation over litigation.	Preference for conciliation and contract renegotiation over litigation.	Preference for contract language and litigation over conciliation.
Conflict	Seldom argumentative; uncomfortable with serious conflict.	Argumentative, but uncomfortable with serious conflict.	At times argumentative, especially when put on the defensive.

someone in Japan is *shinyo. Shinyo* refers to the mutual confidence, trust, and honor that are required on both sides for a business relationship to succeed. Unless you trust your partner implicitly, it is not wise to pursue a business relationship. When the Japanese have dealings with individuals or businesses, choosing someone they can trust is extremely important. Of course, everyone wants to deal with people and companies they believe will do right by them, but in Japanese society the idea of working only with trustworthy entities is elevated to a much higher cultural level. One way to make sure you're working with people you can trust is the concept of *shokai*, a type of introduction whereby someone who is already trusted by a third party will formally introduce you to them, in effect sharing the goodwill they've already established with both you and the third party. Because both parties have a trust relationship involved, they have an obligation to make sure everything goes smoothly to avoid "stepping on the face" (to use the Japanese phrase) of the person who brought you together. There is no single aspect of Japan that isn't improved by this trust-based relationship system, and time and time again managers have found themselves depending on people who have been formally introduced to them by someone else they trusted.

This concept, while easy to understand, is nonetheless difficult for some foreigners to implement. This is in part because of many Westerners' fervent belief in the power of the legal contract over the importance of a personal relationship. In addition to *shinyo*, other differences can be identified between Japanese negotiators and their Brazilian and American counterparts.

Not surprisingly, Brazil's culture – and its approach to negotiation – differs from that of Japan. In contrast to Japan's position as a long-established industrial power, Brazil is often described as one of the world's most attractive emerging markets. Multinationals from various countries are increasingly establishing subsidiaries or doing business in Brazil in one way or another. In this environment, knowing how to negotiate with Brazilians is crucial for any serious global manager. In other words, international negotiators dealing with Brazil are more likely to succeed if they know a little about the country and understand its culture, its way of doing business, and its negotiation style.

The typical negotiating style of Brazilian managers reflects the country's cultural characteristics and business environment. This is summarized in Exhibit 7.7 above, as it compares to typical Japanese and US approaches. At the heart of Brazilian negotiating style is its emphasis on building, maintaining, and capitalizing on one's personal relationships. Brazilians are often seen as being highly engaged with their opponents or prospective partners during negotiation. They tend to believe that, regardless of what happens during and after the negotiation, making friends and enjoying life is important. This focus on relationships leads Brazilians to avoid conflict and attempt to please the other party to the extent possible. There is also a tendency to use indirect language, hide unpleasant information, make false promises, and at times embellish the truth.[12]

The Brazilians' focus on personal relationships has been attributed to a need to deal with what some observers describe as a national inferiority complex.[13] Brazilians tend to be sensitive about their identity. They do not like to be compared with their neighbors and prefer to call themselves South Americans rather than Latin Americans. Brazilians need to feel accepted and become impatient when there is a conflict. When dealing with conflicts, aggressiveness is not a good alternative. Rather, a solution is most likely to emerge through active but friendly engagement.

The Brazilian tendency towards improvisation and flexibility is clear in their negotiation style as well. Many Brazilians do not follow logical steps in a negotiation, and instead may jump back and forth between topics. At times, they may not have a clear goal in mind. Risk-averse, Brazilians are likely to focus on seemingly irrelevant details, bargaining and negotiating for long periods of time. They enjoy the process of negotiating and are not in a hurry to make a deal. They seldom make decisions solely on the basis of analysis. Most likely, they consider emotions as well. In a recent article, a prominent Brazilian magazine interviewed successful Brazilian managers about their views on negotiation.[14] Among other things, the managers agreed that successful negotiations are typically conducted informally and with spontaneity. They are guided by intuition, and not by reason alone. Finally, real negotiations seldom happen at the negotiation table. Instead, they take place in parallel informal meetings, at which the relationship is developed. To be successful in negotiating with Brazilians, foreigners need to be both friendly and patient.

It is interesting to consider differences between Brazilian and Japanese negotiating styles. The above review suggests that both cultures would have few problems negotiating with each other. Both emphasize building strong personal relationships, emotional sensitivity, trust, pride, confidence, and a personal sense of honor. In addition, both communicate indirectly, using context as much as content, and both are uncomfortable with high degrees of conflict.

These characteristics are very general, however, and allow for important variations. Brazilians develop relationships by clearly expressing emotions, hugging, and touching the other party, often using exaggerations and euphemisms, and behaving in informal and open ways. By contrast, the Japanese are often hesitant to display emotions, remain silent and physically distant from others, and stress respect and formality when dealing with others. Thus, while both cultures' values are similar (e.g., strong personal relationships), they are expressed in very different ways. Moreover, although Brazilians and Japanese both communicate indirectly and expect the other party to understand innuendos and subtleties, this does not guarantee that the two sides will understand each other. Indirect communication relies on culturally established codes that communicate difficult information without causing embarrassment. Since these codes are culturally embedded, however, two indirect communicators from different cultures may have a hard time understanding each other.

Application 7.3 Bargaining tactics

This study of negotiating tactics in Brazil, Japan, and the United States raises some interesting questions. First and foremost, how are global managers supposed to learn about these differences before sitting down at the negotiation table? How are they expected to know what to do? Should they try to adapt their own negotiation style to fit local circumstances or simply follow their own cultural lead and be

Application 7.3   (cont.)

themselves? With so much often riding on negotiations, these questions deserve some consideration.

Think about it. . .

(1)   In your view, do the Brazilian, Japanese, and American negotiators all wish to reach the same objective? If so, why are they using such markedly different bargaining tactics?

(2)   If you were from a fourth country (e.g., Australia, Singapore, Slovakia), how might you approach a bargaining session differently with Brazilians, Japanese, or Americans? Why?

(3)   In bargaining with people from other countries, how do you know when you have reached the best deal you can get? Explain.

Successful (and unsuccessful) negotiators can be found in all countries and cultures. In this section we have focused on typical bargaining behavior in Brazil, Japan, and the United States. Similarities and differences were noted as an illustration of how culture may influence negotiating behavior. It is important to remember, however, that not all Japanese or Brazilians necessarily fit this pattern. People are complex and do not necessarily follow the rules of their culture all the time. Besides, cultural norms are cued more strongly in some situations than others. For instance, a US negotiator is more likely to behave according to American negotiation norms when working in the United States with other Americans than when negotiating in Japan with Japanese counterparts. People adjust their behavior – with varying degrees of success – depending on the context in which they find themselves.

Ethics in global negotiations

In a perfect world, everyone would follow the same rules on a level playing field. Few companies actually get to play on such a field, though. For many companies, the challenge is managing in a very imperfect world. As we saw in the opening example, corruption and bribery can obviously make it much more difficult to negotiate contracts or otherwise conduct business in a foreign country, not just because of the unethical nature of such activity and the unjustified increases in operating costs incurred but because of the resulting uncertainty surrounding future government actions or the actions of competitors.

Exhibit 7.9 Global corruption index

Country	Corruption index	Country	Corruption index	Country	Corruption index
Argentina	2.8	Hungary	4.9	Portugal	6.3
Australia	8.6	India	2.7	Russia	2.7
Austria	7.8	Indonesia	3.1	Singapore	9.3
Azerbaijan	1.4	Ireland	7.1	Slovakia	3.7
Belgium	7.1	Israel	7.3	South Africa	4.8
Brazil	4.0	Italy	5.2	South Korea	4.5
Canada	9.0	Japan	7.1	Spain	7.1
Chile	7.5	Luxembourg	9.0	Sweden	9.3
China	3.5	Malaysia	4.9	Switzerland	8.5
Colombia	3.6	Mexico	3.6	Taiwan	5.6
Czech Republic	3.7	Netherlands	9.0	Thailand	3.2
Denmark	9.5	New Zealand	9.5	Turkey	3.2
Finland	9.7	Nigeria	1.2	United Kingdom	8.7
France	6.3	Norway	8.5	United States	7.7
Germany	7.3	Philippines	2.6	Venezuela	2.5
Greece	4.2	Poland	4.0		

Note: This scale runs from 1.0 to 10.0, with 10.0 representing high incorruptibility and highly ethical behavior.
Source: Data compiled from *The Economist*, *The Economist Pocket World in Figures*. London: Profile Books, 2011.

Several organizations have tried in recent years to classify countries on the degree to which political corruption represents a major problem in international business. One such effort is *The Economist*'s corruption index, shown in Exhibit 7.9. Using this index, corruption is more likely to be found in Nigeria, Azerbaijan, and Venezuela (with scores of less than 2.5 on a scale going from 1.0 to 10.0) than in Finland, Denmark, and New Zealand (with scores of around 9.5). As with any index, however, rankings of corruption can be imprecise, and they are meant only to highlight the need for further investigation before making investment decisions. Moreover, such ratings can sometimes be surprising. For example, while many people repeatedly point to commonalities between Canada and the United States, note that their ratings on corruption are significantly different.

The Organisation for Economic Co-operation and Development (OECD), discussed in more detail in the Appendix, promotes ethical managerial behavior through the promulgation of ethical standards on which it seeks multinational government agreements. Just because governments agree to such standards, however, there is no guarantee that they will be followed. All the same, having government backing does carry some weight, as does public pressure. One area in which the OECD has been particularly active is with respect to ethical behavior in negotiations and contracting. Here, OECD guidelines place considerable emphasis on fighting corruption and bribery both in the negotiation process and in subsequent multinational partnerships. In this regard, these guidelines proscribe the following.

- *Bribes*. Managers are not allowed to offer, nor give in to demands, to pay any portion of a contract payment to public officials or the employees of business partners. Nor should they use subcontracts, purchase orders, or consulting agreements as means of channeling payments to public officials, to employees of business partners, or to their relatives or business associates.
- *Remuneration*. Managers should ensure that the remuneration of agents is appropriate and for legitimate services only. When relevant, a list of agents employed in connection with transactions with public bodies and state-owned enterprises should be kept and made available to competent authorities.
- *Transparency*. Managers should enhance the transparency of their activities in the fight against bribery and extortion. Measures could include making public commitments against bribery and extortion and disclosing the management systems the company has adopted in order to honor these commitments. The manager should also foster openness and dialogue with the public so as to promote its awareness of and cooperation with the fight against bribery and extortion.
- *Advocacy*. Managers should promote employee awareness of and compliance with company policies against bribery and extortion through appropriate dissemination of these policies and through training programs and disciplinary procedures.
- *Controls*. Managers should adopt management control systems that discourage bribery and corrupt practices, and adopt financial and tax accounting and auditing practices that prevent the establishment of off-the-book or secret accounts or the creation of documents that do not properly and fairly record the transactions to which they relate.
- *Contributions*. Managers should not make illegal contributions to candidates for public office or to political parties or to other political organizations. Contributions should fully comply with public disclosure requirements and should be reported to senior management.

Application 7.4 What is a bribe?

Although the OECD has its stated principles, the implementation of these principles on a global level can be problematic. Management ethicist Eileen Morgan points out that one of the principal problems when discussing ethics and corruption is that such terms sometimes have different meanings – and different means of

Application 7.4 (cont.)

implementation – across borders.[15] Think about it: what is the difference between a bribe, a gratuity, and a commission? Are there fundamental ethical differences or is everything in the eye of the beholder? In Russia, for example, "business" is not a concept that comes naturally in the Russian language. There is no original Russian word for it. *Biznez*, as it is incorporated into the language, carries with it strong cultural baggage dating from communist times, and it is still associated with ideas such as exploitation and corruption. Unlike some Westerners, Russians differentiate between ethics and corruption. "Corruption" is seen as institutionalized, hierarchical behavior that falls out of the control of individuals. "Ethics," on the other hand, is seen as the set of principles that should guide one-on-one relationships between individuals. Corruption, then, refers more to the institutional environment in which individuals, like it or not, must operate. It is neither good nor bad; it is just necessary, and individual behavior is not commensurate with the presence or absence of corruption. If one partner steals from another partner, there is a breach in ethical behavior, but not an incidence of corruption.

Think about it. . .

(1)   Does the Russian concept of "ethics" and "corruption" differ from the prevailing view in your own country? If so, in which ways is it different?

(2)   In your view, is there a morally correct position on ethical behavior, or is it situationally determined? Explain.

(3)   If you were negotiating a new contract with a prospective Russian partner, would you follow your own conception of ethics or would you follow common practice in Russia? Why?

Conflict resolution strategies

Despite well-intended efforts to develop a common culture and eliminate sources of conflict, the chances are that conflicts are still likely to emerge at various points throughout the negotiation process. Not only are such conflicts often inevitable, they can at times be helpful in forcing both parties to look deeply into what each side is actually trying to accomplish. The important issue is this: when conflicts between partners or prospective partners emerge, what are managers supposed to do? A long tradition of studies on conflict management points to several common strategies for dealing with conflict.[16]

Exhibit 7.10 Conflict resolution strategies

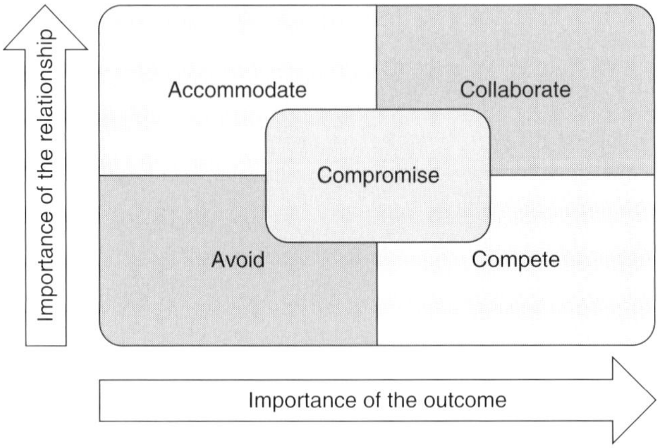

Process strategies for resolving conflicts

To begin with, consider five common *process strategies* for resolving conflicts, along with some factors that may help managers decide which one fits best the specifics of their unique situation (see Exhibit 7.10). These strategies are accommodation, collaboration, competition, avoidance, and compromise. From a negotiation standpoint, determining which of these strategies may be most suitable is influenced – though not exclusively – by two factors. First, how important is the *relationship*? Is it highly valued (perhaps essential) or just convenient? What would happen if this relationship were broken? Second, how important is the *outcome*? Is this contract or partnership essential for your organization's goals and objectives or are there alternative ways to accomplish them?

Think about the options. First, in some situations, developing and nurturing a relationship may be more important than the specific outcome of a particular issue of conflict. In these cases, strong assertive strategies may be counterproductive, and *accommodating* the other party may be the best strategy. Small losses may represent big wins later on, as they will strengthen a relationship that is critical for success. Second, at other times the relationship is important, but so too is the outcome of the particular issue on the table. In such cases, perhaps the most successful strategy is to look for ways of *collaborating*; jointly looking for a solution to the problem that represents a win-win for all involved. Third, there are times when the relationship is not that important, yet the outcome may be critical. These are occasions when *competition* is most appropriate. Fourth, there are times when a conflict is just not worth bringing forward. The issue itself may not be that important and the relationship may not be not critical. At such times the advice is "Don't sweat the small stuff," and *avoid* the conflict altogether. Finally, in situations in which both the relationship and the outcome are reasonably important, but time does not allow negotiators to engage in a collaborative problem-solving exercise, parties may decide to *compromise*, or split the difference in a solution that is acceptable all round.

Obviously, these five strategies are not always as clear-cut as they might at first appear, and other approaches may combine a variety of strategies to work more effectively. Moreover, several contingency factors can also enter into decisions concerning the most appropriate conflict resolution strategy. These include the following.

(1) How crucial is a particular solution to one or more team members? If this is the case, a short-term imposition of a solution or long-term educational efforts are likely to make more sense than avoidance, negotiation, and accommodation. Of course, experienced global managers also need to understand that taking actions such as the unilateral imposition of a solution can have adverse consequences. For example, causing someone to lose face in many Asian countries presents very real risks for the long-tcrm viability of the team.

(2) How much power does each party have vis-à-vis the others? Stronger team members, for instance, can afford competitive strategies to which weaker members may have to acquiesce and be accommodating, while similarly powerful members may need to engage in collaborative forms of negotiation.

(3) The viability of a given strategy is also dependent on the timing with which a solution needs to happen. Urgent action may be easily compatible with avoidance and accommodation strategies, but less so with collaboration or compromise, which can be more time-consuming.

(4) It is also important to think about any precedents that may be created by negotiators looking for expediency. For example, accommodation by a negotiator in order to secure a contract or partnership quickly may limit approaches that managers wish to take in the future. Expectations would have been created that may be difficult to modify.

People strategies for resolving conflicts

Taking a somewhat more applied viewpoint, conflict resolution expert Nike Carstarphen suggests several *people strategies* to consider when dealing with conflicts during the negotiation process.[17]

- *Prepare people.* Preparing successful negotiators includes fostering a positive and open attitude towards dialogue, focusing on commonalities, not differences. People are central to any conflict, and in order to find common ground the attitude of "us versus them" must be replaced by "we."

- *Assess the situation.* Preparing the negotiation process means fully assessing the situation, identifying the parties that should be present and the appropriate interventions to deal with the conflict. For instance, is it necessary to ask for outside help or can the conflict be solved with the people at the table? Is the conflict widespread or concentrated on a particular person?

- *Explore past and present.* Exploring the past and the present, the origins of the conflict and its current dynamic, helps uncover cultural assumptions and meanings that may be obstructing collaboration. Giving negotiators an opportunity to explore how things were in previous meetings and what frustrates them now may make it possible to identify the real issues causing the conflict.

- *Envision the future.* By asking negotiators to imagine a common future, creativity and imagination may help to find solutions to the conflict. By envisioning a future together, common values and needs are likely to become salient, and a common solution may emerge.

- *Create solutions.* Resolving conflicts is not just about envisioning possibilities; it is also about taking action. Here, negotiators must identify concrete actions to be taken to ease the conflict, and then take those actions, evaluating their effectiveness along the way and adjusting them if necessary.

- *Rejuvenate and reflect.* Dealing with conflicts is an intensive, energy-consuming endeavor. It is important to pause from time to time, to reflect, regroup, and recover energies before the process can continue. It is also important to take time to celebrate successes and give a boost to morale.

- *Don't forget relationships.* Finally, conflicts are often about relationships between individuals or groups. It is the very interdependence among people that can create conflict, and no solution will be found if this interdependence is not acknowledged and fostered.

Application 7.5 Conflicting strategies at Secoinsa

When Japan's Fujitsu joined forces with Spain's Telefónica to create Sociedad Espanola de Comunicaciones e Informatica SA (or simply Secoinsa), everyone knew that it would be a challenging alliance. Few realized just how challenging, however.[18] The Japanese managers who arrived to help run the new partnership seemed totally unprepared for Spanish culture and ways of doing business. At the same time, their Spanish partners were equally perplexed about how to work with the Japanese. Problems began almost immediately.

The first notable problem in the partnership involved language. Both partners had to rely on English, since few Japanese partners could speak Spanish and none of the Spaniards could speak Japanese. The Japanese soon became frustrated because they could not express their true feelings in English, while the Spaniards were equally frustrated with what they considered to be the Japanese "all business all the time" approach to interpersonal relations. The Spaniards concluded early on that their Japanese counterparts were not well rounded, because all they talked about was business. They also felt that the Japanese were looking down on their local Spanish traditions and customs. The Japanese, in turn, questioned the work ethic of their Spanish counterparts because of their excessively long meals and time away from work. Neither side had an easy time building rapport, and numerous misunderstandings emerged. Stress levels increased on both sides.

Differences in decision-making styles also created problems. Substantial disagreements arose over the ways in which decisions were made at the new company. The Japanese side tried to use a consensual decision process that required considerable time but led to broad-based support for final decisions. The Spaniards preferred to have senior managers make decisions more autocratically and lost patience with the endless rounds of discussions requested by their partners. Compounding the problem was a significant difference in manufacturing quality control strategies. Fujitsu managers insisted on maintaining strict controls over production processes so as to ensure quality control and prevent imitation by their competitors. They wanted all components used in the manufacturing process to be manufactured in Japan. If this proved to be unfeasible, they at least wanted all the parts to be tested in Japan at Fujitsu's testing facilities. Their Spanish partners preferred using components manufactured in Spain (or at least the European Union), and saw no reason to ship them to Japan for testing. Fujitsu finally agreed to this so long as the components were manufactured by Secoinsa and not by any outside vendor.

Both sides came to see the other as difficult, narrow-minded, inflexible, and overly nationalistic, but the venture continued because Fujitsu wanted access to the

Application 7.5   (cont.)

Spanish (and European) market and the Spanish wanted access to Japan's cutting-edge technology. Neither side was happy, though, and problems continued to mount. After several years of conflicts and tense relationships the partnership was dissolved, and Fujitsu assumed ownership and control over the entire enterprise.

Think about it. . .

(1)   Despite having compatible goals, this partnership failed. Why?

(2)   What role did culture and other contextual factors play in this failure?

(3)   What might have been done to save this partnership? Why wasn't this done?

Agreements, contracts, and mutual trust

If countries often approach negotiating strategies so differently, it is not surprising that other aspects of building and managing partnerships can also be quite different. Consider contracts. In most Western countries, a contract – especially a written contract – represents a company's most effective tool against uncertainty and risk. This is not surprising in view of the largely monochromic orientation of these countries, where message content is often far more important than message context. Every dictionary in the world gives roughly the same definition of a contract: an agreement between two or more parties that establishes rules governing their business transactions.[19] Contracts typically spell out levels of investment, areas of responsibility and accountability, cost data when appropriate, control over proprietary technology, and procedures for sharing the benefits (and losses) of the enterprise. As such, most managers from most countries believe that written contracts are far superior to the proverbial handshake among honorable people. Or, as legendary MGM co-founder Louis B. Mayer observed long ago about negotiating with screen actors, "A handshake is only as good as the paper it's written on."

Mutual trust and contract interpretation

Even so, in many regions of the world, much of the business is conducted on the basis of personal relationships and mutual trust, as in the case of *guānxi* in China (see Chapter 4). In these regions, prospective partners often see written contracts as a sign of distrust; contracts are unnecessary among trusted friends. It is very easy for this divergence across cultures to create a dilemma for global managers. What do they do when trying to develop a secure business relationship in countries where written securities are not commonplace? Again, how much can you trust a handshake?

In theory, a contract is a legally binding instrument that guarantees for all parties to the contract what will happen and when (e.g., what each item or product will cost, when materials will be delivered, the costs of technology transfer, etc.). Also, in theory, certain penalties are stipulated for noncompliance with the contract (e.g., financial penalties for late payments, criminal penalties for fraud or theft, etc.). Good negotiators are adept at capturing the essence, as well as the details, of contracts in clearly understandable wording. Moreover, experienced negotiators typically use specialized attorneys to ensure that contracts are internally consistent (i.e., there are no vague or conflicting clauses within the contract) and comply with local and international laws. They will also often have contracts translated into all the languages of the parties to it, so that the details and provisions are clear to everyone.

Unfortunately, most experienced managers also know that there can be a sharp difference between what a contract says and what it actually means. At times local governments will refuse to implement a contract for various reasons or will support the local partner to an agreement. As a result, there is a critical need for all parties to a contract to trust each other's personal integrity and corporate intentions. This is when culturally based practices such as *guānxi* come into play. A written contract between strangers represents a conflict waiting to happen in much of the world. This is why successful global negotiators invest so much time in getting to know their partners and nurturing this relationship after the contract is signed and implemented. As a result, the importance of doing business with long-term and trusted partners should not be underestimated.

Doctrine of changed circumstances

One of the principal reasons for contract disputes around the world is the cultural variation in the meaning of a contract. To many Westerners (e.g., people in the United Kingdom, Australia, Germany, Canada, the United States), a contract is a legal document that spells out the obligations of all the parties. It is the culmination of a successful negotiation process. In the West, where people tend to have an internal locus of control (i.e., they believe that they largely control their own fate), a contract is a contract. It can be renegotiated upon expiration, but not until then unless otherwise specified in advance. As a result, Western negotiators have to anticipate and prepare for every conceivable future problem, leading to rather lengthy business contracts.

Exhibit 7.11 Contracts and the doctrine of changed circumstances

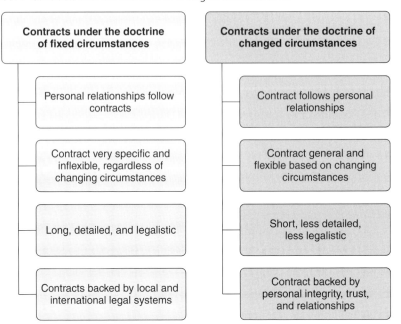

Elsewhere in the world, where people tend to have a more external locus of control (i.e., they believe that the future is largely influenced by fate or karma), many businesses accept something called the *doctrine of changed circumstances* (see Exhibit 7.11). This doctrine holds that, when circumstances beyond the control of a business partner change (e.g., hurricane damage, changes in government policies, price increases for raw materials), both partners are obliged to renegotiate the original contract so that neither party loses materially. Under this doctrine, which can be found throughout much of Asia, Africa, and Latin America, a contract is thought of as a written recognition of a personal relationship between the two parties. As such, it is the beginning, not the end, of the process of mutual benefit as a result of working together.

Application 7.6 Changed circumstances at Cosco

It is not unusual for companies that charter ships to fail to pay their owners, and for the owners to have these vessels and their cargoes impounded. Normally, though, this is either because the company is in financial trouble or because of disputes over

Application 7.6   (cont.)

delays. It is rare for a charter company to insist that it could pay but won't, simply because shipping rates have gone down since it signed the contract. That is what Cosco did, however.[20] Cosco, China's largest shipping firm, is a major owner as well as a charterer of the huge dry-bulk vessels that feed China's appetite for raw materials. In recent years it has signed numerous long-term contracts to carry goods around the world. When contract rates dropped, however, the company sent word to its partners that it needed to renegotiate their contracts. When partners balked, Cosco began withholding payments on the contracts, describing this as a normal "market-based" approach for the company. The company, owned by the Chinese government, clearly had an ability to pay. Instead, however, it used its market position and refusal to meet its financial obligations to exact revised contracts that were more favorable to the company. In the West, such behavior borders on the illegal or unethical; in this case, apparently, it represents sound business practices. The logic is simple: conditions have changed, so we must renegotiate the contract.

Think about it . . .

(1)   Are Cosco's actions illegal or unethical or simply the way business is done today?

(2)   What recourse do Cosco's partners have in this dispute?

(3)   What are the long-term consequences of Cosco's actions?

A former US Secretary of State once observed about his negotiating experiences in China, "The Chinese think in terms of a process that has no culmination. Westerners think in terms of concrete solutions to specific problems."[21] Indeed, many Asian, African, and Latin American companies prefer to have only very brief general contracts (perhaps two or three pages in length), in the belief that it is impossible to anticipate all future circumstances that may affect the contract. As circumstances change, it is often expected that the contract will be modified to fit the new situation. After all, an honorable person would not take advantage of his or her partner if changes occur that were not caused by the two partners. Honorable people look after the interests of each other.

In the East, the doctrine of changed circumstances is supposedly designed to maintain harmony among partners; in the West, it violates the pursuit of mastery over one's environment. This fundamental difference underlying both contract negotiations and contract implementations between global partners often represents a major threat to the long-term prospects of global partnerships. Consider: if written (or even unwritten) contracts in one part of the world frequently mean something very different in another part, and two parties are negotiating an international joint venture, how can either side have confidence, predictability, and trust in their agreements? What happens to the rookie manager who fails to understand this?

MANAGER'S NOTEBOOK
Negotiating global agreements

This chapter has focused less on theory and more on application. Management guidelines have been suggested throughout the chapter, and there is little need to repeat them here. Rather, we focus, albeit briefly, on how these various negotiation processes and strategies fit together from a managerial standpoint. As before, we begin with an understanding of the particular environment in which managers find themselves.

Global negotiation: assessing demands and constraints

Exhibit 7.12 suggests several types of environmental constraints that help determine the choices or options that managers have available to themselves. Remember, these are only examples. Even so, it can be seen that factors found in the cultural, organizational, and situational environments can all influence managerial choices. For example, a culture based on harmony or rules will likely require different managerial behavior from one based on mastery or relationships. Similarly, managerial behavior in the field can be influenced by the degree of centralization in one or more organizations (e.g., who makes the decisions?), as well as whether the organizations in question – and their managers – are risk-averse or risk oriented. Finally, managerial action can be constrained by such situational factors as the degree to which the negotiating partners have mutual or competing goals, where the negotiations are taking place, and the time pressures involved (i.e., do negotiators have sufficient time to build a personal relationship or not?).

Global negotiation: developing action plans

With these demands and constraints in mind, managers face three key issues as they approach bargaining and negotiations with other parties: preparations, negotiations,

Exhibit 7.12 Assessing the global negotiation environment (examples)

Exhibit 7.13 Action plans for global negotiation

(1) Manage preparations	(2) Manage negotiations	(3) Manage agreements
• Select a suitable partner with complementary goals and objectives • Develop a negotiation strategy • Prepare to manage the negotiation process	• Build initial relationships • Exchange information (competitive or problem-solving) • Bargain in good faith • Make concessions (sequential or holistic) • Finalize agreement	• Build mutual trust • Interpret the contract • Determine contract flexibility (e.g., changed circumstances) • Manage the partnership

and agreements (see Exhibit 7.13). These may be considered three strategies for action. Once again, the interplay between understanding the environment in which these negotiations take place and taking well-considered actions at the table should serve to clarify both what managers attempt to do and how well they accomplish their task.

1   Manage preparations

First, we have already discussed several preparation issues, including selecting a partner, developing a negotiation strategy, and preparing to the extent possible to manage the negotiation process. This last requirement suggests that managers should consider multiple options or negotiation scenarios prior to actual negotiation, so that they can move quickly as circumstances or positions change. Since negotiations are dynamic by nature, experienced managers typically view them much like a chess game. It is usually advantageous to have several moves identified in advance. It is also wise to look for subtle or even silent moves that may help explain future actions (see Chapter 6).

2   Manage negotiations

The second issue involves the negotiation process itself. Various aspects of this process have been discussed in detail in the chapter, including management strategies and tactics. Two key points should be made here. The first involves the importance of building relationships prior to serious negotiation. Getting to know one's prospective partners can avoid considerable problems either later in the negotiation process or after an agreement has been signed. The second involves ethical behavior. Definitions of acceptable ethical behavior often vary by culture. The problem is that many managers don't realize this, and insist on applying their own standards to situations around the globe. One could suggest that this is naïve. Worse, one could suggest that this is dangerous, in that such managers may be impervious to subtle suggestions or actions that can become problematic later. This reality suggests that managers would be well advised to avoid anyone who talks or acts in ways that give rise to questions about his or her ethical standards. Working with such individuals – or companies – is much like the proverbial "playing with fire." It is simply not worth the risk, either to your reputation or the reputation of your company.

3   Manage agreements

A third and final issue also emerges that people tend to ignore. Once a formal contract or agreement has been signed, it is not the end of the process; it is actually only the beginning. Contracts are living documents. As noted earlier, while some cultures believe a written and signed contract represents a permanent document, others believe it remains flexible. Understanding this in advance is crucial. Beyond this, research discussed above has demonstrated that relationships are ever-changing, and global agreements are no exception. They must be nurtured and managed through time if they are to succeed. Indeed, one of the principal responsibilities of many frequent flyers is to visit partners on a regular basis to renew the relationship and resolve disagreements before they get out of hand and cause genuine harm.

All this clearly requires considerable time, and suggests a straightforward conclusion: global partnerships should be pursued only when and if all parties to the agreement see genuine mutual advantage. If corporate goals are compatible and trust can be developed, partnerships can be fruitful for all parties. Lacking this, they become risky propositions that should, more often than not, be avoided.

Summary points

- Some experts have suggested that the most important skills that will be needed in the organizations of the future will be an ability to win friends and influence people on a personal level, to structure partnerships, and to negotiate and find compromises when possible. Business will be much more about finding the right people in the right places and negotiating the right deals. To the extent that this is correct, negotiating skills and skills in building long-term and mutually beneficial relationships will certainly be placed highly in the set of the most important management skills.

- People do business with partners they know and trust. As such, many international negotiations begin with both sides trying to establish a personal bond. This does not necessarily mean that they plan to become lifelong friends but, rather, that each side needs to determine if the other party is sufficiently trustworthy to conclude an agreement and stick with it.

- In many countries it is insulting to begin a business discussion until after such relationships have been firmly established. In these cultures, it is often said that business relationships need to be "warmed up" before the parties get down to serious negotiations.

- Successful negotiators are comfortable in multicultural environments and are skilled in building and maintaining interpersonal relationships. Successes come slowly and failures are common. Nonetheless, it is possible to identify a number of personal factors that can differentiate between successful and unsuccessful negotiators: a tolerance for ambiguity; patience, patience, patience; flexibility and creativity; a good sense of humor; solid physical and mental stamina; cultural empathy; curiosity and a willingness to learn new things; and a knowledge of foreign languages.

- There are two basic strategies for negotiation: competitive and problem solving. A competitive approach views negotiations as a win-lose game, while the problem-solving approach seeks to discover a win-win solution from which both sides can benefit, if at all possible. The choice between using either competitive or problem-solving bargaining strategies is often influenced by three factors. First, it is very easy in cross-cultural negotiation to misread the intentions of the other party. Second, culture sometimes predisposes negotiators to select one approach over the other. Third, when possible, most experts on international negotiation recommend a problem-solving approach, because it tends to lead to better long-term solutions and relationships. This is particularly true in negotiating global partnerships.

- The ultimate goal of a negotiation is to arrive at a mutually agreed-upon contract that is legally binding in both countries. To achieve this, concessions have to be made. Cultural differences can influence how these concessions are determined. In North America, for example, companies frequently use what is called a sequential approach to concession making, in which the parties go through a proposed contract item by item and gain agreement on each item as they go sequentially through the proposals. Throughout much of Asia, a holistic approach is often preferred, in which the two parties work their way through the entire proposed agreement but do not agree to anything until they have completed their review. They then discuss the contract in its entirety and make final proposals and counter-proposals aimed at reaching a complete agreement.

- Corruption and bribery can obviously make it much more difficult to negotiate contracts or otherwise conduct business in a foreign country, not just because of the unethical nature of such activity and the unjustified increases in operating costs incurred but also because of the resulting uncertainty surrounding future government actions or the actions of competitors.

- In most Western countries, a contract – especially a written contract – represents a company's most effective tool against uncertainty and risk. This is not surprising, in view of the largely monochromic orientation of these countries, where message content is often far more important than message context. Even so, in many regions of the world, much of the business is conducted on the basis of personal relationships and mutual trust, as in the case of *guānxi* in China. In these regions, prospective partners often see written contracts as a sign of distrust; the view is that contracts are unnecessary among trusted friends.

▓ To many Westerners, a contract is a legal document that spells out the obligations of all parties. It is the culmination of a successful negotiation process. In the West, where people tend to have an internal locus of control, a contract is a contract. It can be renegotiated upon expiration, but not until then unless otherwise specified in advance. As a result, Western negotiators must anticipate and prepare for every conceivable future problem, leading to rather lengthy business contracts. Elsewhere in the world, where people tend to have a more external locus of control, many businesses accept something called the doctrine of changed circumstances. This doctrine holds that, when circumstances beyond the control of a business partner change, both partners are obliged to renegotiate the original contract so that neither party loses materially. Under this doctrine, a written contract is thought of as a written recognition of a personal relationship between the two parties. As such, it is the beginning, not the end, of the process of mutual benefit as a consequence of working together.

Notes

1 Two old Russian proverbs, cited by Yale Richmond, *From Nyet to Da: Understanding the Russians*. Yarmouth, ME: Intercultural Press, 1992, pp. 39, 139.
2 Margaret Omar Nydell, *The Acquisition of Egyptian Arabic as a Native Language*. Washington, DC: Georgetown University Press, 2007.
3 *The Economist, The Economist Pocket World in Figures*. London: Profile Books, 2008.
4 Charles Handy, *Business: The Ultimate Resource*. London: Bloomsbury, 2002, p. 75.
5 Randall S. Schuler, *Managing Human Resources*, 6th edn. Boston: South-Western College Publishing, p. 44.
6 "Will China displace North America as the key to GM's future?," *Fortune*, September 5, 2011, pp. 42–3.
7 Danny Ertel, "Getting past yes: negotiating as if implementation mattered," *Harvard Business Review*, 2004, 82(11), pp. 60–8.
8 Nancy J. Adler and John L. Graham, "Cross-cultural interaction: the international comparison fallacy?," *Journal of International Business Studies*, 1989, 20(3), pp. 515–37.
9 Gary Ferraro, *Cultural Dimensions of International Business*, 4th edn. Upper Saddle River, NJ: Prentice Hall, 2002.
10 *Cui bono?* ("To whose benefit?" or "As a benefit to whom?") is a Latin adage from Roman times that is used today either to suggest a hidden motive or to indicate that the party responsible for something may not be who it at first appears to be. With respect to motive, a public works project that is purported to benefit the city may have been initiated rather to benefit a favored campaign contributor with a lucrative contract. Commonly, the phrase is

used to suggest that the person or people guilty of committing a crime may be found among those who have something to gain, chiefly with an eye towards financial gain. The party that benefits may not always be obvious or may have successfully diverted attention to a scapegoat, for example.

11 John L. Graham "The influence of culture on the process of business negotiations," *Journal of International Business Studies*, 1985, 16(1), pp. 84–8.

12 Luis A. C. Junqueira, "The Brazilian way to deal with the crisis and recovery," Instituto MVC, São Paulo, available at www.institutomvc.com.br/english/articles.htm.

13 Leila R. Magalhaes, "Negociando no mercosul," R H Portal, São Paulo, available at www.rhportal.com.br/artigos/wmview.php?idc_cad=t2yf2_h_2.

14 Cynthia A. Rosenburg, "A arte do aperto de maos," *Revista Exame*, 2003, 37(8), pp. 106–18.

15 Eileen Morgan, *Navigating Cross-Cultural Ethics: What Global Managers Do Right to Keep from Going Wrong*. Woburn, MA: Butterworth-Heinemann, 1998.

16 We rely here on the work of Paul F. Buller, John J. Kohls, and Kenneth S. Anderson, "When ethics collide: managing conflict across cultures," *Organizational Dynamics*, 2000, 28(4), pp. 52–66.

17 Nick Carstarphen, "A map through rough terrain: a guide for intercultural conflict resolution," in Michelle LeBaron and Venashri Pillay (eds.), *Conflict Across Cultures: A Unique Experience of Bridging Differences*. Yarmouth, ME: Intercultural Press, 2006, pp. 137–201.

18 Schuler, *Managing Human Resources*; Oded Shenkar and Yadong Luo, *International Business*. New York: Wiley, 2004.

19 Helen Deresky, *International Management: Managing across Borders and Cultures*, 2nd edn. Upper Saddle River, NJ: Pearson/Prentice Hall, 2008.

20 *The Economist*, "Can pay, won't," *The Economist*, August 27, 2011, p. 57.

21 *Newsweek*, May 7, 2001.

CHAPTER 8

Leading global organizations

More books have been written about leadership than any other topic in management, yet we still know very little about how or why leadership efforts succeed or fail. In addition, we know even less about how to train leaders, global or otherwise, despite the innumerable proffered training programs available. One thing is clear, however. Leadership is not a quality or skill that can be replicated around the world. In other words, leadership in India or China is based on fundamentally different traditions and assumptions from those in England or France, and these differences cannot be ignored. As a result, the challenge for global managers is to develop a sensitivity and understanding of how leadership efforts play out across countries and cultures, as well as how to behave when placed in or near such responsibilities. We explore this topic in this chapter, looking at the topic from different angles. We also discuss what is probably the most comprehensive study of global leadership (called GLOBE). Throughout, examples are used to illustrate the different "faces" of leadership in organizations.

Chapter outline

Applications

> *Leadership is like beauty; it's hard to define, but you know it when you see it.*
>
> Warren Bennis[1]
> Leadership expert, United States

> *A leader is best when people barely know he exists, who talks little, and when the work is done and the aim fulfilled, people will say, "We did this ourselves."*
>
> Lao Tzu[2]
> Ancient Chinese philosopher (6th century BCE)

More books have been written about leadership than any other topic in the field of management. Many of these books examine various theories of leadership, comparing the relative advantages and disadvantages of each. Other books represent serious empirical studies of actual leader behavior. Still others are popular books that seem to offer a secret elixir designed to transform ordinary managers into extraordinary leaders. What most of these books fail to do, however, is to recognize that leadership processes can vary significantly across geographic regions. In other words, much of what is written discusses or proposes a particular leadership model that has been constructed based on Western (mostly American) beliefs, values, and cultures, and then offers this model to the world as a precursor to managerial and organizational effectiveness.

Consider the two quotations above, both interesting and each diametrically opposed to the other. What does this tell you? Research has consistently demonstrated that some cultures (e.g., those in France, Russia, and the United States) prefer leaders who take charge and are visible and assertive, while others (e.g., those in China and Japan) prefer leaders who are much less visible and move behind the scenes to accomplish things. Some cultures (e.g., those in Mexico and Spain) prefer leaders who stand above the crowd and command respect, while others (e.g., those in Malaysia and Laos) prefer leaders who are humble and remain part of the crowd. Some cultures aren't sure what they want.

Management and leadership

An age-old debate in the management community involves the difference between management and leadership as concepts that are central to determining organizational effectiveness. To some, there are very stark differences between the two constructs of leadership and management; to others, these differences are negligible. Why? Some people see management as focusing on operational issues involved in getting things done through people (e.g., planning, decision making, controlling, coordinating, etc.), while leadership involves the influence processes through which managers accomplish this (i.e., "lead"). One is mundane; the other is sexy. Others see management and leadership as being so closely intertwined that it becomes almost impossible to separate the two: good managers are good leaders, and vice versa.

There are two ways to view this ongoing debate. The first view (the academic approach) involves attempts to tease out structural and behavioral differences between these two constructs – that is, what do leaders do compared to what managers do? How does each contribute to organizational success or failure? How do we train leaders? The second view (the managerial approach) involves recognizing that, for global managers, the integration of these two issues is probably more important than differentiation. In other words, on the street and in the workplace, managers must, in fact, do both if they are to succeed (one requires the other), and if they fail all this becomes moot. Hence the critical question becomes: how do we train managers, including their leadership capabilities?

Our approach here assumes the latter view – that is, we view leadership as an integral and inseparable part of good management. Some managers may be charismatic; others may not. Some situations or locations may suggest participative managers; others may not. Some cultures may value team-oriented managers; others may not. In the end, what matters most is how individual managers can see and understand the on-the-ground situational and cultural realities and then capitalize on their own unique personal skills and abilities (including their approaches to leadership) to get the job done by working through people from different cultural backgrounds (see Exhibit 8.1).

Herein lies the challenge for global leaders. Whether in Japan or the United States, China, India, or Mexico, global leaders up and down the hierarchy face the same problem: how to adapt their leadership style to fit local circumstances in order to achieve corporate objectives? When managers turn to the myriad materials written on the topic of leadership, however, they are often hard-pressed to find meaningful support. As managers around the globe increasingly face the challenges of leading employees from

Exhibit 8.1 Key relationships in global leadership (example)

Leader–member exchange
- Work values
- Basis of relationships
- Psychological contract
- Expectations, incentives, and rewards

Application 8.1   Howard Stringer, Sony

Consider the challenge of one such manager caught in a cultural crosscurrent. When British-born Howard Stringer took over as CEO of Tokyo-based Sony Corporation, his charge was to revolutionize the company and return it to its former competitiveness.[3] The company required new leadership, and Stringer had proved himself beforehand in other assignments. Upon arriving in Japan, however, the new change agent learned early on that his leadership had limits. "I don't want to change Sony's culture to the point that it's unrecognizable from the founder's vision," he observed. "That's the balancing act." He thought for a moment and then concluded, "You can't go through a Japanese company with a sledgehammer." The irony of his observation is that, in his previous assignment as a CEO in the United States, he could.

Think about it. . .

(1)   Given the very different cultures between Japan and the United States, where he was a former CEO, what factors might help Howard Stringer succeed in leading Sony? What factors might cause him to fail?

(2)   If you were Stringer, what are the first steps you would take to gain acceptance as you assume your new role as Sony CEO?

different cultural backgrounds with divergent expectations about hierarchy, power, and interpersonal relations, it becomes all the more important for them to understand how cultural dynamics can influence effective leadership. With this in mind, in this chapter we explore global leadership processes, as well as what managers can do to prepare for such organizational and managerial realities.

Leadership in a global context

We begin with a simple question: what is leadership? As we will see, however, the answer to this question can be very complex. Much of the confusion limiting our understanding of leadership processes in different countries can be traced to the initial assumptions we make about the topic. These assumptions guide what we choose to focus on. As we know from research on selective perception, people typically discover things on the basis of what they are looking for. Perhaps the best place to begin, therefore, is with the assumptions that typically inform a search for the essence of global leadership. In our experience, managers generally approach this issue in one of three different ways (see Exhibit 8.2).[4]

Exhibit 8.2 Contemporary approaches to global leadership

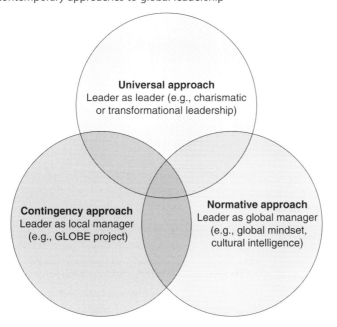

Universal approach
Leader as leader (e.g., charismatic
or transformational leadership)

Contingency approach
Leader as local manager
(e.g., GLOBE project)

Normative approach
Leader as global manager
(e.g., global mindset,
cultural intelligence)

Universal approach: leader as leader

Some managers – and some organizational researchers – consider leadership to be a generalizable, or universal, behavior regardless of where it is exercised. In other words, leadership is leadership is leadership. We refer to this as the *universal approach*. Underlying this approach is the belief that leadership traits and processes are relatively constant across cultures. To the extent that this is correct, the goal of managers is to adopt a leadership model, such as charismatic leadership, under the assumption that its applicability is universal regardless of location. Most Western theories of leadership are built on this premise.

A good example of this can be seen in the ongoing debate in the West over the relative merits of transformational and transactional leadership. Advocates of *transformational leadership*, whereby managers work to create a universally accepted vision of where the group or organization should go and then use moral persuasion (and often *charismatic leadership*) to reinforce this mission, argue that such an approach is superior to the *transactional leadership* model, in which it is concrete exchange relationships with employees that largely determine results. The problem here is that recent research in Japan found that neither of these approaches is very effective in that country. Transformational leaders are often seen as being too abstract, while transactional leaders are sometimes seen as being too mercenary – and both are criticized for being too manipulative. Instead, successful Japanese managers tend to prefer something called "gate-keeping leadership," in which they work to reduce the barriers to successful performance among their subordinates. Here is the problem: if these Western theories fail to work in Japan, one wonders where else they might also fail (e.g., Brazil, Russia, Egypt, India, etc.).

In this regard, it is unfortunate that, despite decades of research supporting situational approaches to leadership effectiveness, companies still routinely sponsor leadership training programs that stress a few "keys" to successful leadership and ignore critical variations in local environments. One might suggest that many of these programs are doomed to failure from the outset.

Normative approach: leader as global manager

A second approach to thinking about leadership in a global context is to focus on enduring personal skills and abilities that are thought to characterize effective "global" managers. These models are prescriptive in nature, and suggest how managers should approach leadership in global settings. We refer to this as the *normative approach*.

The focus is on the leader as a global manager. It is assumed that a common set of leader traits and abilities apply to all managers regardless of where they are working.

Recent work on the global mindset, cultural intelligence, and global leadership illustrate this approach. There are many definitions for this general phenomenon, but most of them center on a common theme. A *global mindset* can be defined formally as "a highly complex cognitive structure characterized by an openness to and articulation of multiple cultural and strategic realities on both global and local levels, and the cognitive ability to mediate and integrate across this multiplicity."[5] Simplified, this definition incorporates three skills: (1) an openness and attentiveness to multiple realms of action and meaning; (2) a complex representation and articulation of cultural and strategic dynamics; and (3) a mediation and integration of ideals and actions oriented towards global and local levels alike.

For example, successful global leaders are thought by some to exhibit cosmopolitanism, cognitive complexity, mental inquisitiveness, honesty, humility, and personal resiliency (see Exhibit 8.3 for details). Leaders who possess this cluster of skills and abilities are thought to be prepared to manage effectively throughout much of the world. As a result, the management development question is how to instill these traits and abilities into people who have to work successfully around the world in highly diverse cultural settings. Whether these traits are indeed commonplace among successful managers in different parts of the world has yet to be demonstrated, however. This raises questions about the normative assumptions underlying the model.

Contingency approach: leader as local manager

The third approach, which we refer to as the *contingency approach*, begins with the assumption that there are no universals in describing effective leadership. In other

Exhibit 8.3 Global mindset of effective leaders

Dimensions of a global mindset	Global mindset characteristics
Personal work style	High "cultural quotient" (CQ) Flexibility and open-mindedness Effective global communicator and collaborator Skills in being a global team player Ability to balance global and local goals, behaviors, and management practices
General perspectives	Ability to take broad, long-term systems perspective Emotional resilience and personal autonomy Ability to embrace and support change Ability to work across organizational boundaries Ability to operate seamlessly in cross-cultural and cross-functional environments Thirst for global learning as a path for career development

Source: Based on Gary P. Ferraro, *The Cultural Dimension of International Business*, 5th edn. Upper Saddle River, NJ: Pearson/Prentice-Hall, 2005.

Application 8.2   *Mary Barra, General Motors*

If we are looking for an example of a senior executive with a global mindset, we need look no further than Mary Barra, vice president for global product development at General Motors.[6] As the executive responsible for the design and engineering of every GM vehicle around the globe, as well as the highest-ranking woman executive, she oversees everything relating to car design. Barra has about 36,000 people reporting to her from around the world. When she's not at the company's proving ground in Milford, Michigan, she's working from her office on the thirty-ninth floor of the GM headquarters, in downtown Detroit, or at GM's sprawling technical center in Warren, Michigan. Alternatively, she may be traveling to Brazil, or to China, or to an assembly line somewhere in the United States, so that she can get a first-hand look at production and discuss problems and ideas with line workers. "I used to say I've been to every GM plant in the world," Barra says, "but there's a new one in China now that I haven't yet visited."

Friday is Barra's favorite day of the week, when she heads out to GM's proving ground northwest of Detroit to spend the day test-driving vehicles that are making their way through GM's product pipeline. Increasingly, GM's new cars are built on what are called "global platforms." This means that all the design and engineering work for a new model is done in one place (e.g., South Korea or Germany) and is then swiftly adapted to plants and markets around the globe. To Barra, it's the simplest way to get more vehicles to the marketplace more quickly. If more cars worldwide share common components, including engines and frames, the efficiencies of scale become obvious. A new model that has already been introduced in, say, Asia can be quickly tweaked and built for consumers in the United States or Brazil.

So far, about 30 percent of GM's products rely on global core architectures, but by 2018 Barra intends that number to reach 90 percent. There is a danger of leaning too heavily on a one-vehicle-fits-all strategy, however. "You don't want to say, 'Here's our global midsize car. Hope it works for you,' " she says. "What India might want is very different from what Canada might want." Nor is it only a matter of different tastes; it is designing an automobile that can span an emerging market such as India, where roads can be primitive and may create serious durability issues, to a developed market such as Germany, where the road system is among the best in the world. A car's global architecture, in other words, has to be flexible enough, both stylistically and mechanically, to be modified for any country in the world. For this to happen, GM needs people such as Barra who can listen across cultures.

To accomplish this, Barra has to be a leader for all audiences. She must understand how leaders influence behaviors in different locales around the world, from India to China to Brazil, not just the United States. To achieve this, she needs – and has – a clear global mindset aimed at understanding different cultures and how they influence attitudes and behaviors around the globe. She is flexible and open-minded, and a global team player. She thinks before she speaks and works to be sensitive to nonverbal signs and signals, not just the spoken word. Above all, though, Barra is committed to continual learning, about people as well as cars. The burden of solving this problem – which, Barra says, requires an interrelated solution of design, engineering, manufacturing, and marketing – falls "not just on her, but on her team," she notes. When that team is global, global solutions and multicultural competencies must come into play.

Think about it. . .

(1)   What qualities does Mary Barra have as a leader that should help her succeed in global assignments?

(2)   Why is Barra the first woman to reach the senior executive level at GM? Do you think it is discrimination, corporate culture, or something else?

(3)   Do you believe there are systematic differences between successful men and women as global leaders? If so, in what ways do they tend to be different? In what ways are they similar?

words, successful leaders in New York may fail in Tokyo or Paris if they are unable to modify their behaviors to suit the unique local environments. This approach looks at leadership as a culturally embedded process, not a series of personal traits of the manager or followers. Here the focus is on the leader as a local manager, not a global one, and it is assumed that the characteristics for success will vary with the situation.

A good example of this approach can be found in the recent *GLOBE project*, a multinational study of culture and leadership in sixty-two countries. The principal finding of this study is that, to a large degree, leadership is culturally contingent – that is, the qualities of effective leaders often vary across cultures. For example, successful US managers tend to score higher than their Chinese counterparts on such characteristics as assertiveness, performance orientation, and individualism, while Chinese managers tend to score higher than Americans on power distance and uncertainty avoidance.

The important point here is that GLOBE was able to track systematic trends in leadership characteristics across cultures. The GLOBE project is discussed in more detail below.

Another good example of how culture can influence leadership is *symbolic leadership*. Symbolic leadership occurs when people – usually senior executives or CEOs – accept full responsibility for setbacks or crises on behalf of the entire organization. This is commonplace in Japan, for example, and sometimes offered even when the executives are not at fault. The belief here is that, through voluntary resignation, harmony is restored and the organization can move forward. Not surprisingly, symbolic leadership is seldom seen in the West when things go wrong. Indeed, it can be seen as a sign of weakness.

Application 8.3   Masataka Shimizu, TEPCO

When companies succeed, it is commonplace to reward managers – and, hopefully, other employees. What happens when companies fail, though? What is management's responsibility? In some countries, the decline in stock prices or other setbacks can signal the demise of CEOs by disgruntled stockholders. In others, CEOs are seldom held accountable, even if they were directly responsible for the failure. What happens, however, if a company experiences a natural disaster for which it is not responsible. Should company CEOs be held accountable?

This is exactly what happed at Tokyo Electric Power Company (TEPCO) in 2011 in the wake of Japan's worst natural disaster in memory.[7] Some 20,000 people died and over 1 million were left homeless as a result of an earthquake, followed by a tsunami, followed by a nuclear meltdown in Fukushima. Many people were angry that TEPCO did not do more to prevent or resolve the crisis. Anger mounted as people watched helplessly as their fortunes and futures vanished. In an effort to ameliorate the situation and restore harmony, TEPCO executives publicly accepted responsibility for the problems and announced that their executives would take a 50 percent pay cut and that this money would go to help recent victims of the natural disaster. Company employees also agreed to a 25 percent pay cut. All told, the power company expects to save about $660 million annually, which it will use to compensate victims of the natural disaster. A short time later, in an act of symbolic leadership, TEPCO president Masataka Shimizu resigned in disgrace following the largest financial loss in the company's history. The key word here is "resignation," not "termination," as might have happened in the West. One wonders how many executives in other countries would have taken a similar course of action.

Think about it. . .

(1)   Should Masataka Shimizu have resigned his post as president over this crisis? Why or why not?

(2)   Why is symbolic leadership such as that illustrated in this example common in some countries, but not others?

(3)   Should more executives and CEOs in Western companies be held more accountable for the failures of their companies, even if they were not directly responsible for the setbacks? Why or why not?

Limitations on contemporary leadership models

While all three of the contemporary leadership models discussed above add value to our efforts to understand leadership in a global context, it is our opinion that they all miss the mark in sufficiently explicating the leadership construct as it relates to global diversity. As a result, our ability to help global managers prepare for overseas assignments remains somewhat limited. In particular, we suggest that focusing more squarely on two issues could advance our understanding of leadership processes: (1) the meaning of leadership as a cultural construct; and (2) the variations in local expectations regarding leader behavior. In short, in our view we must move beyond traditional Western models of leadership and take a more cosmopolitan approach to the subject.

Leadership as a cultural phenomenon

First and foremost, it is important to recognize that leadership is a cultural construct. Its meaning is embedded in the diverse cultures in which it is exercised, and changes accordingly. Most important here, it is not a Western construct that is easily expanded to global dimensions.

To understand this, consider our opening question once again: what is leadership? The difficulty in answering this question lies in the differing meaning of the construct itself in different cultures. In other words, leadership means different things to different people. In most Anglo-Saxon countries (e.g., the United Kingdom, the United States, Australia), leadership generally has positive connotations. Leaders tend to be respected, admired, and, indeed, sometimes revered, whether they are in the political or business arena. Clearly, this is not a universal truth. The opposite view of leaders can also be found in many countries (e.g., Mexico, Egypt, Romania), where widespread distrust and fear of power or the dislike of privilege prevail.

Moreover, a direct translation of the word "leader" into different languages can invoke a variety of images, including dictator, parent, expert, and first among equals. Some of these terms have strong connotations of highly directive or authoritarian styles of leadership that many people reject. Leaders are not necessarily to be trusted. We wonder about their motives and true goals, or about other potentially undesirable behaviors and characteristics. At the same time, in many egalitarian societies, terms such as "followers" or "subordinates" are also seen as being inappropriate. For instance, subordinates in the Netherlands are frequently referred to as co-workers (*medewerkers*) instead of subordinates, and leaders are careful to avoid appearing condescending.

With such a diversity of opinions concerning the characteristics of effective leaders, how is it possible to reach agreement on even a simple definition of leadership? Moreover, what does this diversity of views suggest about our ability to apply largely Western-based leadership theories across borders? What does this say about our ability to build or implement leadership development programs that can be used effectively in various regions of the world? What does this say about so-called leadership "gurus" who travel the world with their packaged leadership programs?

To make matters even more complex, not only does the term "leader" translate differently across various cultural groups, but also the meanings that are construed from these translations can also differ, sometimes significantly. For example, in individualistic societies (e.g., the United States, Canada, the United Kingdom) leadership typically refers to a single person who guides and directs the actions of others, often in a very visible way. In more collectivistic societies (e.g., South Korea, Japan, and China), however, leadership is often less associated with individuals and more closely aligned with group endeavors. In hierarchical societies (e.g., Saudi Arabia, Mexico, Indonesia) leaders are often seen as being separate and apart from their followers, while in more egalitarian societies (e.g., Sweden, Denmark) they are often seen as more approachable and less intimidating. Indeed, the rather common Anglo-American celebration of the accomplishments of various leaders stands in stark contrast to Lao Tzu's ancient observation cited above, that effective leaders work quietly and let workers (or employees) take the credit.

Culture and leader expectations

The second concern with existing approaches to leadership focuses on the expectations surrounding the behavior of successful leaders, including the cultural underpinnings of such expectations. These expectations arise from society at large, local circumstances, subordinates, co-workers, and the leaders themselves. The GLOBE study (discussed below) clearly contributes to this understanding, but more is required concerning the fundamental normative beliefs and processes underlying a leader's behavior. In other words, we need to have a better understanding of the "Whys?" and "Hows?" underlying the process, not just the "Whats?" or "Whos?"

If there is any doubt about the systematic variability in what constitutes effective leader behavior, we need look no further than the observations by various managers and employees from different countries. In the West, the French expect their leaders to be cultivated – highly educated in the arts and mathematics. The Dutch stress egalitarianism and are skeptical about the value and status of leaders. Terms such as "leader" and "manager" can even carry a stigma in some organizations. Americans are often schizophrenic in their choice of leaders; some like leaders who empower and encourage their subordinates, while others prefer leaders who are bold, forceful, confident, and risk-oriented.

By contrast, in the East, Chinese leaders are expected to establish and nurture personal relationships, practice benevolence towards subordinates, be dignified and aloof but sympathetic, and treat the interests of employees like their own. Malaysians expect their leaders to behave in a manner that is humble, modest, and dignified. Japanese leaders are expected to focus on developing a healthy relationship with their employees as employees and managers share the same fate. In short, expectations concerning appropriate leader behaviors can vary considerably across cultures. This is a point not lost on experienced expatriates and frequent flyers.

Application 8.4 Howard Stringer revisited

To see how this can work, let's return to Sony CEO Harold Stringer. Since being promoted from president of Sony's US operations to become Sony Corporation's first foreign chief executive, he has been slammed by Japanese financial analysts and Sony employees for being disconnected from the company's daily operations, especially during two big crises. Investors in the United States, meanwhile, have put him under constant pressure to fix Sony's financial and technological problems more quickly. In addition, he has consistently received conflicting advice from both sides. "Look, in America, I was told to cut costs, but in Japan, I was told not to cut costs. Two different worlds. In this country [Japan], you can't lay people off very easily. In America, you can," observed a frustrated Stringer. He bristles at criticism – mostly from Japan – that he lives in a hotel when in Tokyo and spends too much

Application 8.4   (cont.)

time in New York and London to run the company effectively. "If I'm not running the company, who the hell is?"[8]

Fixing this iconic Japanese company represents a major challenge, regardless of who is in charge. Stringer's dilemma is that he is caught between different management styles and cultures. He says he recognizes the risk of falling behind amid breakneck changes in electronics. As already noted above, though, he also says that there's an equal risk in moving too aggressively. "I don't want to change Sony's culture to the point where it's unrecognizable from the founder's vision," he says. "That's the balancing act I'm doing." Whether he can pull off a successful turnaround is still an open question. For the Welsh-born executive, the task is complicated by having to navigate a sea of obstacles, from uncommunicative top executives to poor public relations advice. The risk to Sony from his "management through persuasion" style is that the company could fall further behind nimbler and more aggressive rivals. He has already shifted gears once, adopting a more assertive stance after his softly softly approach faltered.

When he became CEO, Stringer started cautiously. He knew that, despite its global brand name, Sony remained a traditional Japanese company, full of employees with lifetime tenure who were suspicious of change. Japan had opened up to the idea of having foreign managers run Japanese companies, notably Carlos Ghosn at Nissan, but it hadn't necessarily embraced the Western style of management. Stringer, sixty-five years old, was stuck with the executive team he inherited. He tried gently persuading managers to cooperate with one another and urged them to think about developing products in a new way. The risks inherent in this approach quickly became clear. Two initial missteps – a delayed launch of the PlayStation 3 video game console and an embarrassing battery recall – tarnished his first few years in charge. In both cases, managers tried handling problems in the traditional Sony way: quietly and without informing top executives. Stringer counseled patience to his critics, noting that his turnaround of Sony's US operations had taken five years to complete. "You can't go through a Japanese company with a sledgehammer." Even so, his forbearance seems to be wearing thin. "I'm going to do what I want to do now. I'm not going to be following everybody's suggestions. I've got to be true to myself in some ways."

Stringer says nothing has changed in his management style since his arrival in Tokyo. The perception of him as a hands-off manager was fueled by his decision to

Application 8.4   (cont.)

live in a Tokyo hotel. The CEO says he now regrets that decision, but also rejects as "insane" the notion that he wasn't firmly in control. He says his response to the crises wasn't a change of heart but a quickening of his long-term plans. He adds that his record has been obscured by the battery crisis, "which took too long for bizarre Japanese reasons that I don't want to spend the rest of my life discussing."

Think about it. . .

(1) How have differences between Japanese and American (or perhaps British) culture influenced both Howard Stringer's actions and his Sony cohorts' reactions?

(2) Do you agree with Stringer's approach to leading change at Sony? Why or why not?

(3) What could Stringer do better than, or differently from, what he is currently doing as CEO? Explain.

GLOBE leadership study

What can we conclude from all this about the meaning and application of leadership across cultures? To start, we learn to be cautious about a one-size-fits-all portrait of successful leaders. A leader is not always a leader. Moreover, recent research seems to back this up. One of the more intriguing modern studies of leadership behavior across borders was conducted by a multicultural team of researchers who led the Global Leadership and Organizational Behavior Effectiveness project, or GLOBE for short. This project examined the relationship between culture and successful leadership and management patterns in sixty-two countries around the world. For the purposes of the study, *leadership* was defined as the ability of an individual manager to influence, motivate, and enable others within the organization to contribute towards the effectiveness and success of the enterprise.[9] Leadership is seen as an integral part of a manager's responsibilities. The project members' initial research led them to propose the nine GLOBE cultural dimensions: power distance, uncertainty avoidance, humane orientation, institutional collectivism, in-group collectivism, assertiveness, gender egalitarianism, future orientation, and performance orientation. These dimensions are discussed in greater detail in the Appendix.

Based on this, the researchers then identified twenty-two leadership attributes that were widely seen as being, in their view, universally applicable across cultures

Exhibit 8.4 Cultural perspectives on leadership effectiveness

Behaviors and traits universally considered facilitators of leadership effectiveness	Behaviors and traits universally considered impediments to leadership effectiveness	Culturally contingent beliefs about facilitators of leadership effectiveness
Trustworthiness, integrity	Antisocial, self-protective, loner	Individualistic, autonomous
Visionary, charismatic	Non-cooperative, malevolent	Status-conscious
Inspirational and motivational	Autocratic, dictatorial	Risk taking
Communicative, team builder		

Source: Based on Mansour Javidan, Peter W. Dorfman, Mary Sully de Luque, and Robert J. House, "In the eye of the beholder: cross-cultural lessons in leadership from Project GLOBE," *Academy of Management Perspectives*, 2006, 20(1), pp. 67–90, pp. 73–6.

(e.g., encouraging, motivational, dynamic, decisive, having foresight) and eight leadership dimensions that were seen to be universally undesirable (e.g., uncooperative, ruthless, dictatorial, irritable). Several other attributes were found to be culturally contingent, however – that is, their desirability or undesirability was tied to cultural differences (see Exhibit 8.4 for details). These included characteristics such as being ambitious and elitist.[10] Here it was found that people in some cultures favored traits in leaders that people in other cultures rejected. For example, some cultures (e.g., those in the United Kingdom, Germany, France, and the United States) often romanticize their leaders and give them exceptional privileges and prestige; they are held in high esteem. At the same time, however, other cultures (e.g., those in the Netherlands and Switzerland) denigrate the very concept of leadership and are often suspicious of people in authority. They worry about abuse of power and rising inequality.

Application 8.5   Women leaders in India

India is a land of strong tradition, but also of dynamic change.[11] One of the more notable changes is the increasing number of women who hold leadership positions in local companies or who have begun their own entrepreneurial firms. In past decades a small number of women have risen to the top and quietly broken through the barriers of social conformity, both at home and in the workplace, to become successful entrepreneurs and professionals. In recent years, however, this stream has become a flood. Some, such as Indu Jain of the privately held Bennett Coleman, is CEO of India's biggest media house. She has reached billionaire status, according to *Forbes* magazine. Kiran Mazumdar-Shaw started one of India's first biotech companies, Biocon, while Lalita Gupte and Kalpana Morparia run India's second largest bank, ICICI Bank. There are more. Simone Tata built one of the first indigenous cosmetic brands, Lakme, now a unit of Hindustan Lever. Anu Aga turned around an ailing company, the engineering firm Thermax Group, to become a highly profitable venture. Priya Paul became the president of Apeejay Surrendra Group at the age of twenty-four when her father was assassinated. Sulajja Firodia Motwani, managing director of Kinetic Motor, collaborated with firms in South Korea, Italy, and Taiwan to grow her company from a niche moped maker to a manufacturer of a full range of two-wheelers and auto components. Finally, Neelam Dhawan, as managing director for Microsoft India, has led a 35 percent growth spurt in the past five years.

Why are women doing so well in India? One reason is the country's long tradition of valuing education, so women who achieve academically are seen as smart and savvy. Another reason is this: "What really made them successful is their sheer determination to break through," says Indira Parikh, president of the Foundation for Management Education in Pune, outside Mumbai. Their formula for success is identical to those of their male counterparts: skills, drive, and opportunity. Finally, there is little evidence that these women leaders in India behave differently from their male counterparts. Consistent with the GLOBE findings, their behaviors are more Indian than female or male, although this finding may not be true around the world. In working with subordinates, they are described as encouraging, motivating, dynamic, and decisive – which, again, is consistent with GLOBE's overall view of effective leaders.

Think about it. . .

(1)   In general, do you believe that gender or national culture represents a more significant influence on leadership style and effectiveness around the world? Why?

(2)   Some countries and cultures provide fewer leadership opportunities for women than others. Is this an issue that should be addressed locally or globally? Why?

Leadership dimensions

The GLOBE researchers distilled their findings into six relatively distinct leadership dimensions: autonomous, charismatic/value-based, humane, participative, self-protective, and team-oriented (see Exhibit 8.5). Two of these leadership styles

Exhibit 8.5 GLOBE leadership dimensions

GLOBE leadership dimensions	Characteristics of dimensions	Regions where leadership dimensions are widely endorsed
Autonomous leadership	Individualistic, independent, unique.	Endorsed in eastern European and Germanic clusters; weaker endorsement in Latin American cluster.
Charismatic/ value-based leadership	Visionary, inspirational, self-sacrificing, decisive, performance-oriented.	Endorsed in all regions, but particularly in Anglo, Asian, and Latin American clusters; weaker endorsement in Arab cluster.
Humane leadership	Modest, tolerant, sensitive, concerned about humanity.	Endorsed particularly in Anglo, Asian, and sub-Saharan African clusters; less so elsewhere.
Participative leadership	Active listening, non-autocratic, flexible.	Wide variations in endorsements across all regions, but less so in Arab and Latin American clusters.
Self-protective leadership	Self-centered, procedural, status-conscious, face-saving.	Wide variations in endorsements across all regional clusters.
Team-oriented leadership	Collaborative, integrating, diplomatic.	Endorsed in all regions, but particularly in Anglo, Asian, and Latin American clusters; less so in Arab cluster.

Source: Adapted from Robert J. House, Paul J. Hanges, Mansour Javidan, Peter W. Dorfman, and Vipin Gupta, *Culture, Leadership, and Organizations: The GLOBE Study of 62 Societies.* Thousand Oaks, CA: Sage, 2004.

(charismatic/value-based leadership and team-oriented leadership) were strongly endorsed in all regional country clusters used in the study. Even so, the magnitude of this endorsement varied across regional country clusters. For example, both charismatic/value-based and team-oriented leadership styles were most widely accepted in the Anglo, Asian, and Latin American clusters. They were still accepted in other regions of the world, but with less intensity.

Meanwhile, the other leadership styles were found to be more culturally contingent. Humane leadership was strongly endorsed in the Asian, Anglo, and sub-Saharan African clusters, and less strongly endorsed in the Latin American and Nordic clusters. Autonomous leadership was generally seen as neither facilitating nor inhibiting a leader from being effective. Within the eastern European and Germanic clusters, however, this leadership style was considered to be more positively related to outstanding leadership than in other culture clusters. Finally, for self-protective leadership and participative leadership, there was substantial variability in the degree to which these styles were endorsed within the different country clusters. For more details and country breakdowns using the GLOBE methodology, see Exhibit 8.6.

In this exhibit, scales range from 1.0 to 7.0, depending on how important each society on average sees the six dimensions for leadership effectiveness, with 1.0 being very unimportant and 7.0 being very important. Two things should be remembered here. First, these are mean scores, and considerable variations can be found within them. Second, it is probably more useful to look at these numbers as relative differences, not numeric ones. In any case, these results and the GLOBE study in general provide some

Exhibit 8.6 Cultural beliefs about leadership styles

Country	Autonomous leadership	Charismatic leadership	Humane leadership	Participative leadership	Self-protective leadership	Team leadership
Australia	3.95	6.09	5.09	5.71	3.05	5.81
Brazil	2.27	6.01	4.84	6.06	3.50	6.17
Canada*	3.65	6.16	5.20	6.09	2.96	5.84
China	4.07	5.57	5.18	5.05	3.80	5.57
Denmark	3.79	6.01	4.23	5.80	2.82	5.70
Egypt	4.49	5.57	5.14	4.69	4.21	5.55
Greece	3.98	6.02	5.16	5.81	3.49	6.12
India	3.85	5.85	5.26	4.99	3.78	5.72
Ireland	3.95	6.08	5.06	5.64	3.01	5.82
Israel	4.26	6.23	4.68	4.96	3.64	5.91
Japan	3.67	5.49	4.68	5.08	3.61	5.56
Mexico	3.86	5.66	4.71	4.64	3.86	5.75
Nigeria	3.62	5.77	5.48	5.19	3.90	5.65
Philippines	3.75	6.33	5.53	5.40	3.33	6.06
Poland	4.34	5.67	4.56	5.05	3.53	5.98
Russia	4.63	5.66	4.08	4.67	3.69	5.63
Singapore	3.87	5.95	5.24	5.30	3.32	5.77
South Korea	4.21	5.53	4.87	4.93	3.68	5.53
Spain	3.54	5.90	4.66	5.11	3.39	5.93
Sweden	3.97	5.84	4.73	5.54	2.82	5.57
Thailand	4.28	5.78	5.09	5.30	3.91	5.76
Turkey	3.83	5.96	4.90	5.09	3.58	6.01
United Kingdom	3.92	6.01	4.90	5.57	3.04	5.71
United States	3.75	6.12	5.21	5.93	3.16	5.80

*English-speaking population.
Source: Robert J. House, Paul J. Hanges, Mansour Javidan, Peter W. Dorfman, and Vipin Gupta, *Culture, Leadership, and Organizations: The GLOBE Study of 62 Societies*. Thousand Oaks, CA: Sage, 2004.

evidence that acceptable managerial behaviors – including leader behaviors – are to some degree culturally contingent. To see how this works in actual practice, consider two examples.

Ethical leader behavior

Researchers in the GLOBE project also examined the endorsement of ethical leadership across cultures by surveying the ethics and leadership literatures to find several key attributes that characterize ethical leadership.[13] These attributes included: character and integrity; ethical awareness; community and people orientation; motivating, encouraging, and empowering people; and managing ethical accountability. Using the

Application 8.6   Richard Branson, Virgin Group

A good example of charismatic or value-based leadership can be seen in British entrepreneur Richard Branson, best known for his Virgin brand. Branson's first successful business venture came at the age of fifteen, when he published a magazine called *Student*. He later set up a mail-order record business, followed shortly thereafter with a chain of record stores, Virgin Records. With his flamboyant and competitive style, Branson's Virgin brand rapidly grew to include 360 different companies. Ever the opportunist, Branson recently registered the business name "Virgin Interplanetary" in case space travel becomes commercially viable. Today he is estimated to be worth close to $8 billion. Branson is passionate about life and living every minute to its fullest. He continues to get adrenaline rushes through his world-record-breaking attempts by boat and hot air balloon. Several distance and speed records have been attempted and achieved, but his attempt to be the first person to circumnavigate the world in a hot air balloon failed. Branson makes each record attempt a media event, with his Virgin logo prominently displayed during every launch, which has been an excellent source of free advertising and brand placement for the Virgin Group. He was awarded a knighthood for his contribution to entrepreneurship.

Why is Virgin one of the world's most recognized brands around the world? The answer is simple: Branson strives to be the best rather than the biggest, working towards making profits in small pieces of large markets. Now able to use the success of his brand to attract investors and negotiate controlling shares and the management of the company, Branson leaves his partners to supply the majority of the capital. A flamboyant, charismatic character, Branson believes in self-promotion, having fun, and risking it all to achieve his goals. This has meant that he has also experienced failure, however, as his ventures in vodka, computers, and magazines demonstrate. Even so, his positive attitude and ability to apply large amounts of enthusiasm to each project allow him to attract both investors and followers who seek to be part of his exciting – and Anglo-centric – world. For Branson, charisma works.

Think about it...

(1)   What personal characteristics or actions suggest to you that Virgin's Richard Branson is a charismatic leader?

(2)   In your view, would Branson have been as successful had he been a humanistic leader instead of a charismatic one? Why?

Application 8.7   Konosuke Matsushita, Panasonic

By contrast, a good example of humane leadership can be seen in the management and leadership style of Konosuke Matsushita, founder of the Matsushita Business Group (now Panasonic Corporation).[12] True to his culture, Matsushita encouraged his employees at all levels to think long term and to visualize the results of any projects, not just to ask how to build something. Indeed, he once challenged his employees to develop a business plan for the company "that would last a thousand years." Obviously, he had no intention of the plan lasting so long; rather, he wanted to encourage his employees to focus on competing for the future. Matsushita's management style was just as unusual as his approach to strategic planning. He stressed what he called the seven spiritual values of his company: national service through industry; fairness in all things; harmony and cooperation in social relations; struggle for betterment; courtesy and humility; adjustment and assimilation; and gratitude to those who participate. To develop these spiritual values, Matsushita established a management training school for his employees based on Buddhist principles – something not seen in the West. In doing so, he placed his personal reputation behind his company's determination to achieve greatness on behalf of both company and country.

Think about it . . .

(1)   What personal characteristics or actions suggest to you that Panasonic's Konosuke Matsushita was a humanistic leader?

(2)   In your view, would Matsushita have been as successful had he been a charismatic leader instead of a humanistic one? Why or why not?

(3)   Must leaders such as Branson or Matsushita be either charismatic or humanistic? In other words, is it possible for great leaders to be both? Why or why not?

GLOBE data, they derived four factors that matched closely four of the six attributes from the literature review, which they named "character and integrity," "altruism," "collective motivation," and "encouragement."

The results showed that the endorsement of each of the four dimensions of ethical leadership differed significantly across the country clusters used in their study.[14] Because the average endorsement of the attributes was beyond the midpoint average for all dimensions, however, the authors concluded that some degree of common agreement existed in the endorsement of the components of ethical leadership. This research suggests that the four dimensions of ethical leadership represent a fairly universal principle, according to which, while all cultures appreciate and value some common ethical leadership dimensions, they also allow for significant differences in their enactment.

To illustrate this situation, take, for instance, the "character and integrity" factor in the GLOBE study. This dimension received the highest endorsement by societies in the Nordic European cluster, and the lowest among the Middle Eastern cluster. Nordic and Middle Eastern countries, the authors pointed out, both value character and integrity in their leaders, but consistently rank very differently in international indexes of corruption (see below). The same Nordic European countries show the lowest endorsement of the "altruism" dimension, however, which societies in south-east Asia rank the highest. One could argue that this relates to the fact that southeast Asians also rank higher than Nordic Europeans on in-group pride, loyalty, and a humane orientation. Whatever the reason, however, a logical conclusion here would be that ethical values and acceptable or desired leadership roles vary across country clusters (see Chapter 3).

Application 8.8   What would you do?

Leadership is all around us. We have all had experiences in which we either led or followed the directives of some sort of leader to get a job done. Perhaps this was at work or in a college project or club. Some of these experiences were probably positive; others were probably not. In some cases, the leader worked hard for the good of the group; in others, he or she may have put his or her own interests ahead of the group's. Throughout at least some of these experiences, moreover, ethical issues may have arisen that forced group members to choose between their perceptions of right and wrong. The problem during such choices is that there are seldom any clear-cut boundaries between the two. As a manager, choices must be made, but options can often be cloudy.

Think about it. . .

(1) Consider Control Data chairman William Norris's predicament: "The computer is on the dock, it's raining, and you have to pay a bribe to get it picked up and delivered." Would you pay the bribe? Why or why not?

(2) A former CEO of Citigroup has observed, "We must never lose sight of the fact that we are guests in foreign countries and must conduct ourselves

Application 8.8   (cont.)

accordingly. Local governments can pass any kind of legislation and, whether we like it or not, we must conform to it." Should global managers follow local laws if they believe they are unethical or socially or environmentally irresponsible? Why or why not?

(3)   Recent history has witnessed several major environmental crises caused by oil spills, air and water pollution, and radiation hazards. Realistically, what is a company's responsibility when such a crisis occurs?

Patterns of global leadership

Moving from the conceptual to the practical, it is interesting to explore examples of how leadership processes can differ across cultures. In this section, we examine two very different approaches to leadership. The first comes from China and illustrates how traditional Chinese philosophy can influence such behavior, even in today's manufacturing facilities. The second comes from France and Belgium and illustrates how even comic book leaders can differ. Thus, while the first example compares West with East, the second example compares West with West.

Leadership in China: an example

When Westerners interact with Chinese managers and leaders, they often come away from the experience confused and frustrated. Common Western responses include perceptions that Chinese leaders refuse to act decisively, fail to respond candidly, are ambiguous about their goals and objectives, and generally don't act like "leaders." To many Western executives, this appears to be ineffectual or even deceitful, making it difficult to build good working relationships. If we examine leadership through a cross-cultural lens, however, the picture can look quite different.

To understand how local cultures can influence the definition and application of successful leadership, consider the example of leadership as it emerged – and, many believe, continues – in China compared to Western traditions. (Similar comparisons are in order with respect to the traditions and their modern-day implications in other regions of the globe, such as Africa, Latin/South America, and south and southeast Asia.) Although such comparisons can gloss over important variations within regions (e.g., it is obviously problematic to generalize about the entire "West"), on

Exhibit 8.7 Cultural foundations of leadership in China and the West

Leadership characteristics	Western traditions	Chinese traditions
Beliefs	Seek to achieve ideal end state (*eîdos* and *télos*).	Seek to balance countervailing forces (*yin* and *yang*).
Goals	Establish and pursue aspirational goals; manage the results.	Create conditions conducive to success; manage the process.
Logic	Logic of application; articulate objectives and determine reasonable means to desired ends.	Logic of exploitation; place oneself in a position to exploit opportunities as they emerge.
Preferences	Preference for action; capture the initiative.	Preference for patience; let events come to you.

a general plane they can serve to highlight some of the more salient contradictions underlying leadership processes. Moreover, such generalizations can serve to raise legitimate questions concerning what constitutes appropriate behavior.

According to the French philosopher François Jullien, the different foundations of leadership in Eastern and Western traditions can be traced to ancient Chinese and Greek thought. These foundations are based on the separate paths these two civilizations followed in their efforts to make sense out of human behavior (see Exhibit 8.7). What is generally referred to as Western civilization traces its origins to the culture, beliefs, and traditions of ancient Greece. The Greeks developed the concept of *eîdos* (ideal) as an ideal form that humans should aspire to and achieve as *télos* (goal). In this scheme, the work of a leader consists of bridging the gap between *télos* as an ideal state and reality (or actual practice) with a goal of achieving perfection.

By contrast, the concept of an ideal or archetype that could serve as a model for action and a desirable final state of affairs never developed in ancient China. Instead, reality in China was seen as a process emanating from the interaction between opposing and complementary forces, or *yin* and *yang*. Order did not result from an ideal to be accomplished but from a natural propensity of processes already in motion. Because the emphasis was on current processes evolving here and now, Chinese thinking focused on very concrete and specific situations of everyday life, rather than abstractions of the essence of an ideal form. Because Chinese thinking did not abstract and generalize in the search for the ultimate *eîdos*, traditional Chinese language did not include words for essence, God, being, ethics, and the like. Indeed, even today's modern Chinese language incorporates these concepts only out of a need to translate such concepts from Western languages.

Local traditions and logic

Understanding this difference helps explain the separate paths of social thought and practice in these two divergent regions of the world. In many cases, Western thinking is difficult to understand or interpret without reference to concepts such as "the ideal." In many ways, current management thought as taught in many parts of the world is based on the original Greek concept of the ideal and purposeful action. Strategy appears as the art of arranging means towards desired end states. Corporate vision and mission make for a concrete definition of organizational ideals. Executives manage by objectives, and leaders strive actively to move the firm closer to achieving business goals and ideals that are carefully and publicly defined and implemented.

Chinese tradition, on the other hand, emphasizes positioning oneself in the flow of reality in a more passive way, so that we can discover its coherence and benefit from its natural evolution. Rather than establishing a set of objectives for action, one has to flow within the potential of each situation and the dynamics that the situation affords. A common metaphor that can be found in traditional Chinese texts tells of a general and his soldiers benefiting from a given evolution of events, rather than behaving with particular heroism or bravery. As such, leaders must locate themselves in such a position that the desired path of events becomes the only viable alternative, the same way that they do not force the enemy (militarily or commercially) into a situation in which their only alternative is to behave bravely against them.

The leader in Chinese tradition does not begin by delineating an action plan on the basis of a particular set of agreed-upon objectives (*logic of application*). Instead, he or she assesses the favorable and unfavorable elements in the surrounding situation so that the favorable elements can be appropriated as the situation evolves (*logic of exploitation*). There is no sense of goal or finality, but a constant benefiting from the natural evolution of events. The result is assumed to be somehow preordained in the situation that contains it. We see the metaphor of battles already won or lost before actually being fought, for the winner benefits from the internal propensity of the situation rather than from some particular course of action that was wisely planned and implemented. As a result, while leaders in the West often follow a *logic of means and ends* hierarchically arranged through an action plan, leaders in China tend to follow a *logic of process* whereby the evolution of the situation leads naturally to the desired end state, practically without the need for action.

Performance in the Western tradition results from minimizing the gap between the goal and the achievement, the planned and the attained. Action in the West is seen as a separate entity, an external disruption to the natural order of things. In China, by contrast, performance results from a minimization of action itself, leaving the situation to achieve its full potential in terms that benefit the organization. Chinese leaders thus focus on continual processes following their own internal dynamics, uninterrupted. Western action is seen from the Chinese perspective as being extemporaneous, quick, direct, and costly, while the Chinese "effortless action" is slow, indirect, progressive, and natural. Western leaders act, while Chinese leaders transform. Transformation – as opposed to action – extends itself through time, as if without beginning and end, imposing itself albeit in natural ways. Because it comes from the inside of the situation, it imposes itself softly, without resistance. Changes emanate by themselves and do not require heroic efforts and determination as they are part of a continuous progression that is barely noticed.

This does not mean that the concept of action is not present in traditional Chinese thought. It is a subdued type of action, though: slow, subtle, anticipatory, naturally inserted in the natural flow of events. Rather than sudden action, occasions are anticipated, providing for the outcome of what will naturally appear. As a result, Chinese leaders pursue objectives in modest ways, silent and almost anonymous, vis-à-vis the grandiloquent apparatus and appearance of the heroic decision maker often seen or imagined in the West. Action is freed from activism and becomes discrete and subtle, confounded in the course of events, ignorant of particular protagonists. In this regard, Mencius talks of the need to clean and water around a plant and then let it grow on its own, while Confucius points to the ideal sovereign as he or she who lets order reign by itself, without the need for action.

As a result of these differences and traditions, Jullien and others suggest that leadership in parts of the East (east Asia in particular) and the West (notably western Europe, as envisioned by Jullien, but perhaps also including North America) follow different patterns of behavior. We see, for instance, a differential appreciation for action that is modest rather than grandiloquent, for leaders that prefer the natural-ness of process and evolution to the abruptness of radical change. Of course, the naturalness and modesty are also expected to translate into specific personal behav-iors on the part of those at the top of the organization. This view on action and performance also tells us about the origins of particularly Chinese modes of attribu-tion, accentuating the force of situations and circumstances over the behavior of isolated individuals.

Application 8.9   Emerson Electric – Suzhou

Consider the experience of Emerson Electric when it opened a new manufacturing facility in Suzhou, near Shanghai. According to China Europe International Business School (CEIBS) professor Juan Antonio Fernandez, the initial aim of the facility was to be the company's showcase operation throughout east and southeast Asia. When the facility opened, a US-educated Taiwanese manager, supported by a small group of Anglo-American expatriates, led the initial management team. Although the operation became an early success in meeting its production quotas, cross-cultural conflicts and leadership issues began to emerge from the very beginning. These issues were centered in three principal areas: the nature of team dynamics, the focus on leadership initiatives, and divergent views of time. The American view of team dynamics favored team diversity, encouraging multiple viewpoints in team meetings to tease out alternative solutions to complex problems. Along with this diversity of opinions came the predictable interpersonal conflicts. Members were encouraged to confront such conflicts head-on in the hopes of leading to more creative innovative solutions. Better results, rather than the quality of personal interactions, signaled the success of the operation. For the Chinese, however, this created an uncomfortable work environment that they were not used to. To many Chinese, teams should have a single, clear, and unified vision, transmitted through a single voice established by the leader. Conflict indicated poor understanding and leadership of the situation. It was something to be avoided, for it signaled a lack of direction, and might cause someone to lose face.

In addition, these prevailing team dynamics rested on a particular approach to leadership that was more Western than Eastern. The Americans followed a largely functionalist approach to management and interpersonal relations, in which leader competence was viewed in terms of task accomplishment, which was seen as instrumental for success. By contrast, the Chinese approach to leadership was largely "personalist" in nature. In other words, it was the personal integrity of each manager that was deemed instrumental for the success of the new plant. The Chinese valued personal integrity in an effort to win the trust and respect of their followers, while the Americans valued job competence and expected their followers to perform well on the tasks at hand. Chinese management rested on individual commitment, often of a personal nature, whereas the Americans valued professional competence. These different approaches to team leadership also influenced the way managers dealt with confrontation and mis-understandings. In line with the more personal Chinese approach, interpersonal exchanges among participants provided a basis for developing mutual relation-ships (*guānxi*). This, in turn, facilitated problem resolution. By contrast, the Americans often preferred the more confrontational "trial-style" alternatives. They emphasized company policies and rules, rather than personal interactions. They saw formal behavior as a sign of professionalism. The Chinese saw this approach as being childish, since, in their view, norms and regulations seldom allowed for the complexity that was required to actually resolve complex issues and problems.

Finally, time perspectives also affected the quality of the interactions between the Chinese and the Americans. In particular, American managers usually favored relatively short time horizons, since they were expatriates who saw their positions as stepping stones to further career advancement. To advance, they needed short-term recognition of results. By contrast, their Chinese coun-terparts, who had no goals of leaving either China or Emerson, preferred a longer-term perspective. They largely believed that results would follow from setting the proper course of events in motion. Results would then happen naturally; they did not need to be forced.

As a result of these differences, conflicts and misunderstandings continued, until Emerson stepped in and largely replaced the American management team with Chinese leaders who were more attuned to local conditions. Today the Suzhou facility is a star player in the Emerson Electric network of companies. This is in no small part attributable to the wisdom of the firm in developing leadership and management practices that were compatible with, and supportive of, the local operating environment. If there is a lesson to be drawn from this example, it is that leadership style is not universal. Local cultures and conditions can have a profound influence on the success of global ventures.

Think about it. . .

(1) What are the primary lessons of this example?

(2) How did the Chinese and Americans each view leadership effectiveness?

(3) Was the resolution of this conflict appropriate or was there a better way for Emerson Electric to move forward?

Leading global organizations

What, therefore, are the leadership implications of these findings for global managers – and local managers who find themselves working increasingly with global firms? Business success in the global arena is predicated on achieving and maintaining a competitive edge. In this endeavor, managers are charged with the responsibility of outperforming their opponents using the toolkit that is available to them. Simply put, the better the toolkit, the greater the probability of success. In particular, the more that managers can understand the environment in which they work, as well as themselves as potential leaders, the greater their odds of success. Exhibit 8.8 illustrates some examples of the types of demands and constraints faced by leaders working across borders.

Global leadership: assessing demands and constraints

As illustrated in Exhibit 8.8, leadership effectiveness can be influenced in no small way by what local cultures mean by leadership. Do they want leaders who are subtle or overt? Do they base leadership on rules or relationships? How are leaders chosen? Similarly, the ownership patterns of an organization can determine who becomes a leader, as well as what is expected of him or her. For example, owner-managers some-times become leaders by definition, while leaders in investor firms may have to fight their way into leadership positions or use charisma to gain attention and support (see Chapter 4). Leadership patterns are also often influenced by whether the group or team are on-site (face to face) or virtual. Each location here can require very different behaviors. Finally, trust levels between leaders and followers are often important, and are often earned in different ways. The lesson for leaders here is to consider the environment as a source of multiple contingencies that must be met with the leadership style that is used or allowed.

Global leadership: developing action plans

Within these constraints, which can differ from event to event, managers usually have multiple choices in their leadership endeavors. At least three factors come into play here: the personal traits of both leaders and followers; the expectations of both leaders and followers, including the extent to which these expectations are in agreement; and

Exhibit 8.8 Assessing the global leadership environment (examples)

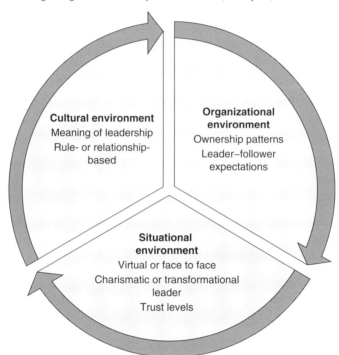

the actual leader behaviors on the ground (see Exhibit 8.9). These factors suggest that managers placed in leadership roles might profitably begin by making sure that they understand themselves as potential leaders (which is easier said than done), as well as the characteristics of the followers and the situations in which they will find themselves.

1   Understand yourself as a leader

First, it can be highly instructive for managers facing global assignments to think about how they conceptualize leadership and managing people. What does the concept of leadership mean to them as managers? Do they believe in a one-size-fits-all approach to leadership or a more tailored approach that recognizes local differences? Do they take a universal, or normative, or contingency approach? What are the limitations of their approach in the field in which it matters? Finally, is there a better – perhaps broader – way to do this? Spending some time considering just what leadership means can go a long way towards preparing managers for success in upcoming global assignments. We saw a good example of this when comparing Chinese traditions and leadership patterns

Exhibit 8.9 Action plans for global leadership

(1) Understand yourself as a leader	(2) Clarify leadership expectations	(3) Manage leader behaviors
• Understand how you get things done working with others. • Understand your own particular leadership style. • Understand what additional skills you should learn to be a more effective leader.	• Clarify the expectations you have about yourself as a leader. • Clarify the expectations you have about others as followers. • Clarify the expectations others have about you as a leader.	• Be authentic, but mindful of local constraints. • Tie available rewards to followership. • Be honest and transparent in your leadership efforts. • Continually listen for feedback about your leader behavior.

with those of the West in the example of Emerson Electric, but there are many more examples that come to the same conclusion.

A related part of this consideration is the particular leadership skills that individual managers need to develop as part of their overall approach to management. How complete are their communication or negotiation skills? How much do they under- stand – or can they learn – about the environment in which they work? It goes without saying that the more managers can understand how they approach leadership, as well as the skills they possess to do the job, the greater the likelihood of success.

2   Clarify leadership expectations

With this understanding – and with their antennae out – managers on global assign- ments can and should go the extra mile to understand the uniqueness of the local environment and work to accommodate cultural differences when they exist. This general topic was considered in Chapters 3 through 5 earlier in the book. Understanding environments – cultural, organizational, and situational – represents a necessary first step in preparing to lead multicultural groups or organizations. In fact, there are many ways to accomplish this, including reading books about particular cultures, talking with people who are familiar with various cultures, and keeping one's eyes open when travelling to new locations. However it is accomplished, the global manager either learns to learn quickly about how leadership processes work or runs the risk of suffering the consequences.

A major part of this challenge deals with expectations. Specifically, what are managers' expectations about their own leadership capabilities? What do they expect from others and, equally, important, what do others expect of them? Expectations clarify rules and roles and can support efforts to reduce employee anxieties about how their boss (their leader) will operate. As such, the power of these expectations – as well as efforts to clarify them all round – should not be ignored or downplayed.

3   Manage leader behaviors

Global managers are advised to be authentic – that is, be themselves to the extent that local conditions will allow. "Going native" often risks losing authenticity as a manager, leading to confusion and even distrust among subordinates. Indeed, there are many examples of foreign leaders who were chosen largely because they would approach their jobs in radically different ways, not local ones. The challenge for global managers is not to capriciously try to imitate local behaviors – a task fraught with risk and often doomed to failure. Rather, it is to try to understand local conditions and then act in authentic ways that are compatible, but not necessarily synonymous, with local expectations. Being unique can often prove to be a successful behavioral strategy, so long as such behavior is clearly understood by others to be supportive of local goals and objectives and not contradictory to cultural values and expectations. In this regard, global managers who are well prepared in advance of their assignments may have greater leeway in the exercise of leadership than they might imagine. For this to occur, however, a solid understanding of local conditions must come first.

Finally, it is important to remember the simple fact that working with people from different cultural backgrounds can be very challenging, but it can also potentially be very rewarding. For many managers, though, it doesn't happen easily. To the extent that this is correct, the onus is on managers to prepare themselves for success in the future. Leading people from different cultures – and, in fact, being led by people from different cultures – opens up considerable opportunities to learn more about ourselves, discover new ways of doing things, and find creative solutions to problems both old and new. It is clearly part of the developmental process for managers. In this pursuit, continual learning plays a significant – and often underappreciated – role.

Summary points

- Leadership can be viewed as an integral part of good management. Some managers may be charismatic; others may not. Some situations or locations may suggest participative managers; others may not. Some cultures may value team-oriented managers; others may not. In the end, what matters is how individual managers see and understand the situational and cultural realities, and then capitalize on their own unique personal skills and abilities, including their approaches to leadership, to get the job done.

- Much of the confusion limiting our understanding of leadership in different countries can be traced to the initial assumptions we make about the topic. These assumptions guide what we choose to focus on. People typically discover things on the basis of what they are looking for. Perhaps the best place to begin, therefore, is with the assumptions we typically have as we go into a search for the essence of global leadership. In this regard, managers generally approach this issue in one of three different ways: the leader as leader; the leader as global manager; and the leader as local manager. Each has advantages and limitations for understanding and developing leadership skills.

- It is important to recognize that leadership is a cultural construct. Its meaning is embedded in the diverse cultures in which it is exercised, and changes accordingly. Most important here, it is not a Western construct that is easily expanded to global dimensions.

- GLOBE researchers identified twenty-two leadership attributes that were widely seen as being universally applicable across cultures (e.g., encouraging, motivational, dynamic, decisive, having foresight) and eight leadership dimensions that were seen to be universally undesirable (e.g., uncooperative, ruthless, dictatorial, irritable). Several other attributes were found to be culturally contingent, however. In other words, their desirability or undesirability was tied to cultural differences (see Exhibit 8.3 for details). These included characteristics such as being ambitious and elitist.

- Researchers in the GLOBE project also examined the endorsement of ethical leadership across cultures by surveying the ethics and leadership literatures, and found several key attributes that characterize ethical leadership. These attributes included: character and integrity; ethical awareness; community and people orientation; motivating, encouraging, and empowering people; and managing ethical accountability. Using the GLOBE data, they derived four factors that matched closely four of the six attributes from the literature review, which they named "character and integrity," "altruism," "collective motivation," and "encouragement." The results showed that the endorsement of each of the four dimensions of ethical leadership differed significantly across the country clusters used in their study. Because the average endorsement of the attributes was beyond the midpoint average for all dimensions, however, the authors concluded that some degree of common agreement existed in the endorsement of the components of ethical leadership. This research suggests that the four dimensions of ethical leadership represent a relatively universal principle, which, while all cultures appreciate and value some common ethical leadership dimensions, allows for significant differences in their enactment.

■ The different foundations of leadership in Eastern and Western traditions can be traced to ancient Chinese and Greek thought. These foundations are based on the separate paths these two civilizations followed in their efforts to make sense out of human behavior. What is generally referred to as Western civilization traces its origins to the culture, beliefs, and traditions of ancient Greece. The Greeks developed the concept of *eîdos* (ideal) as an ideal form that humans should aspire to and achieve as *télos* (goal). In this scheme, the work of a leader consists of bridging the gap between *télos* as an ideal state and reality (or actual practice) with a goal of achieving perfection. By contrast, the concept of an ideal or archetype that would serve as a model for action and a desirable final state of affairs never developed in ancient China. Instead, reality in China was seen as a process emanating from the interaction between opposing and complementary forces, or *yin* and *yang*. Order did not result from an ideal to be accomplished but from a natural propensity of processes already in motion. Because the emphasis was on current processes evolving here and now, Chinese thinking focused on very concrete and specific situations of everyday life, rather than abstractions of the essence of an ideal form.

■ Business success in the global arena is predicated on achieving and maintaining a competitive edge. In this endeavor, managers are charged with the responsibility of outperforming their opponents using the toolkit that is available to them. Simply put, the better the toolkit, the greater the probability of success. In particular, the more that managers can understand the environment in which they work, the greater their odds of success. Clearly, an understanding of cultural differences and how these differences play out in interpersonal and group relationships represent critical tools.

Notes

1 Warren G. Bennis, *On Becoming a Leader*, Reading, MA: Addison-Wesley, 1989, p. 1.
2 William G. Boltz, *Lao Tzu Tao Te Ching*, in Michael Loewe (ed.), *Early Chinese Texts: A Bibliographical Guide*. Berkeley, CA: Institute of East Asian Studies, 1993, pp. 269–92.
3 Yukari Kane and Phred Dvorak, "Howard Stringer, Japanese CEO," *Wall Street Journal*, March 3, 2007, p. A1.

4 Richard M. Steers, Carlos Sanchez-Runde, and Luciara Nardon, "Leadership across cultures: new directions in research and theory development," *Journal of World Business*, forthcoming.

5 Orly Levy, Sully Taylor, Nakiye Boyacigiller, and Schon Beechler, "Global mindset: a review and proposed extensions," in Mansour Javidan, Richard M. Steers, and Michael A. Hitt (eds.), *The Global Mindset*, Amsterdam: Elsevier, 2007, pp. 11–48, p. 29.

6 Jon Gertner, "How do you solve a problem like GM, Mary?," *Fast Company*, October 2011, pp. 104–8.

7 *Bloomberg Business Week*, "Tokyo Electric Power pay cuts all around," *Bloomberg Business Week*, May 2, 2011, p. 20.

8 Kane and Dvorak, "Howard Stringer, Japanese CEO."

9 Dorfman and House, "Cultural influences on organizational leadership," p. 15.

10 Robert J. House, Paul J. Hanges, Mansour Javidan, Peter W. Dorfman, and Vipin Gupta, *Culture, Leadership, and Organizations: The GLOBE Study of 62 Societies*. Thousand Oaks, CA: Sage, 2004, p. 5.

11 Megha Bahree, "India's most powerful businesswomen," *Forbes*, September 1, 2006.

12 John Kotter, *Matsushita Leadership: Lessons from the 20th Century's Most Remarkable Entrepreneur*. New York: Free Press, 1997.

13 Christian J. Resick, Paul J. Hanges, Marcus W. Dickson, and Jacqueline K. Mitchelson, "A cross-cultural examination of the endorsement of ethical leadership," *Journal of Business Ethics*, 2006, 63(4), pp. 345–59.

14 Empirically derived from the database, cultures were grouped along the following clusters: Anglo, Confucian Asian, eastern European, Germanic European, Latin American, Latin European, Middle Eastern, Nordic European, and southeast Asian.

CHAPTER 9

Managing a global workforce

MANAGEMENT CHALLENGE

It has been said that supervising others – taking responsibility for their work and welfare – is one of the most stressful jobs in the world. It is something like being a parent to other adults. In a very real sense, managing and motivating employees is the supreme test of managerial effectiveness. If a manager can't manage others successfully, his or her value to the organization as a whole diminishes significantly. Here is the problem, though. If managing and motivating employees is problematic in one culture, imagine the challenge when trying to supervise employees across cultures: different customs, different languages, and different expectations. How are managers expected to succeed here? In this chapter we explore this challenge. We examine the role of work values in employee behavior, as well as the psychological contracts that exist but are often unseen – particularly by new managers on the ground. We further examine how rewards or incentives that are effective in one culture may fail in another. We also consider the relative benefits and drawbacks of using local or expatriate managers in local situations. Throughout, the focus is on how managers can learn to improve their effectiveness in unique, and sometimes even hostile, environments.

Chapter outline

Applications

> *To motivate employees, you must bring them into the family and treat them like respected members of it.*
>
> Akio Morita[1]
> Founder and former CEO, Sony Corporation, Japan

> *Constantly refine your gene pool by promoting your best performers and weeding out your worst.*
>
> Jack Welch[2]
> Former CEO, General Electric, United States

Management is about working with and through people, and, as noted throughout this book, when these people have different cultural backgrounds, this challenge is multiplied considerably. Conflicts between managers and employees can easily result from different belief systems and work values, different cognitions and perceptions, different levels of self-esteem or uncertainty avoidance, and so forth. The above two quotations from Japan and Russia illustrate this challenge nicely. The quotation from Japan emphasizes building families of employees, while the quotation from Russia suggests the need for more direct and unambiguous control.

We can illustrate how these differing value systems play out through the example of Samsung Electronics' experience running an offshore manufacturing facility in northern Mexico. In this *maquiladora* facility, South Korean managers supervised Mexican assembly workers.[3] Value conflicts began almost as soon as the plant opened, and grew more intense over time. The Korean managers tended to believe that Mexicans viewed work not as a sacred duty, as in South Korea, but as a means to an end, or even a necessary evil. In their view, their Mexican subordinates routinely made commitments they had little intention of keeping. They also failed to distinguish between work and play. They played loud music and talked excessively during work, wasting time. The Korean managers were dumbfounded by such a lack of commitment.

Needless to say, the Mexican workers had a different point of view.[4] To many of them, the South Korean managers evaluated all people and work situations using their own "Confucian" values and standards. The workers often felt that the managers should not use Korean cultural values as a criterion when comparing work ethics between countries. To the Mexicans, their managers established unrealistic goals and then blamed the workers for being lazy when these goals were not achieved. Moreover, although the Korean managers might have been willing to work fifteen hours a day, this was Mexico, not South Korea. Finally, first-line Mexican supervisors in these plants suggested that the reason for poor plant performance had less to do with work ethics and more to do to with unwillingness on the part of the Korean managers to allow Mexican participation in the production-planning process. Who is right in this conflict may depend more on where you live than what you believe.

This example illustrates well the central theme of this chapter – and one of global managers' major concerns: how should we manage and motivate local employees when working in different cultures? In point of fact, the motivational basis of employee compliance with supervisory directions can vary considerably, both across individuals and cultures. Compliance can be based on allegiance to rules, interpersonal or group relationships, available incentives and rewards, or simple fear. Exhibit 9.1 illustrates an example in which a relationship-based manager is supervising a rule-based workforce (see Chapter 3). Generally speaking, people in these two cultures view the basis of compliance in different ways. For example, the relationship-based manager may emphasize network-ing and group relationships as a means to task accomplishment, while the rule-based

Exhibit 9.1 Key relationships in global management and motivation (example)

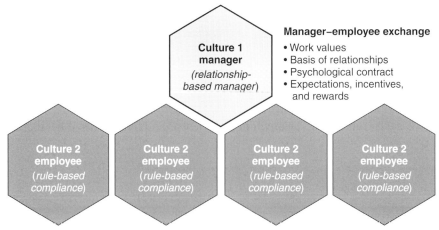

employees may expect the supervisor to take charge and simply issue directions. The challenge for managers is to understand these differences and respond accordingly.

Unfortunately, although there are many general models of employee motivation, few incorporate serious consideration of differences across borders. What, therefore, should managers do? To start with, they can prepare themselves by expanding their understanding of the local work environment. This includes understanding local work values and goals, as well as the prevailing psychological contract as seen by the local community. Moreover, managers must understand variations in the managerial role – the expectations people have about what managers should or shouldn't do – across cultures, including incentive and reward systems. In this way, they enhance their chances of succeeding in global operations, despite being an "outsider." Such managers may never become insiders, but the simple knowledge of how local systems work will likely make their jobs both easier and more productive. We begin this exploration by looking at personal work values and goals.

The world of work

Regardless of who constitutes the global workforce, understanding people at work remains a huge topic. It becomes a bit easier to tackle, though, if we can break it down into smaller units. Perhaps the best place to begin here is with an understanding of local prevailing values and beliefs. Developing such an understanding may be one of the most effective ways for outsiders to work towards becoming insiders. As a result, in this section, we ask two basic questions: first, what are some of the key differences between people in the global workplace in terms of their work values, and, second, how central is work in the lives of these people? While people within given cultures can obviously differ in many respects, most cultures exhibit core cultural traits that can provide conceptual entry into the work lives of local employees. We begin with the fundamental concept of personal work values and the meaning of work.

Work values and goals

Why do people work? This question lies at the heart of the topic of personal work values. What is it about work, if anything, that people genuinely value? What motivates people to go to work? *Work values* reflect individual beliefs about desirable end states or modes of conduct for pursuing desirable end states. As such, they serve a useful function by providing individuals with guidelines and standards for determining their own behavior and evaluating the behavior of others. Personal work values are important because they signal what individuals and groups of employees see as being most

Exhibit 9.2 Culture, work values, and behavior

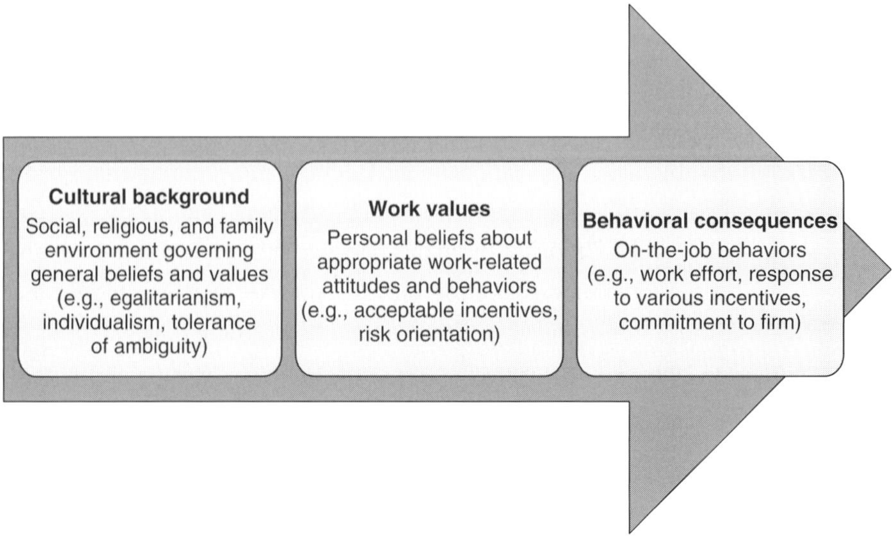

Cultural background	Work values	Behavioral consequences
Social, religious, and family environment governing general beliefs and values (e.g., egalitarianism, individualism, tolerance of ambiguity)	Personal beliefs about appropriate work-related attitudes and behaviors (e.g., acceptable incentives, risk orientation)	On-the-job behaviors (e.g., work effort, response to various incentives, commitment to firm)

important about their work efforts. They also influence the actual quality and focus of employee endeavors and the ways in which various employees may respond to work motivation strategies and tactics (see Exhibit 9.2). Throughout, the focus here is on understanding how personal values influence employee willingness and preparedness to contribute towards the attainment of organizational goals.

Personal work values have been studied systematically from a cross-cultural perspective for many years. One of the earliest studies was conducted by George England.[5] He and his colleagues focused on the impact of such values on employee behavior and found significant differences across managers in the five countries they studied. US managers tended to be high in pragmatism and achievement orientation and demanded competence. They placed a high value on profit maximization, organizational efficiency, and productivity. Japanese and South Korean managers also valued pragmatism, competence, and achievement, but emphasized organizational growth instead of profit maximization. Indian managers stressed a moralistic orientation, a desire for stability instead of change, and the importance of status, dignity, prestige, and compliance with organizational directives. Finally, Australian managers tended to emphasize a moralistic and humanistic orientation, an emphasis on both growth and profit maximization, a high value on loyalty and trust, and a low emphasis on individual achievement, success, competition, and risk.

This initial work by England and his colleagues formed the basis for a subsequent international study of managerial values called the Meaning of Work project.[6]

This study sought to identify the underlying meanings that individuals and groups attach to work in six industrialized nations: Belgium, Germany, Israel, Japan, the United Kingdom, and the United States. In this study, Japan was found to have a higher number of workers for whom work was their central life interest compared to both Americans and Germans, who placed a higher value on leisure and social interaction. A high proportion of Americans saw work as a duty, an obligation that had to be met. Japanese workers showed less interest in individual economic outcomes from work than their European and American counterparts.

As part of this survey, employees were asked to rank a list of common work goals in order of importance in their lives. These rankings illustrate that, while differences can obviously be found across cultures, such differences may not be as diverse as is commonly believed. In fact, some perhaps surprising commonalities can be found. Interestingly, work and pay consistently ranked at or near the top of the list for all countries. By the same token, promotion opportunities and convenient working hours ranked near the bottom of all lists. Japan ranked job–person fit first while Belgium ranked it eighth, and job security was ranked high in every country except Israel. It is important to note, however, that all the countries included in this study represented highly industrialized and technology-rich nations and all are essentially from the Northern Hemisphere. One wonders if these rankings would have been different if developing or underdeveloped nations had been included.

Although personal work values are often discussed in terms of being reasonably stable attributes, they are not set in concrete and can evolve over time. We can witness this in recent allegations that younger workers in many countries (e.g., Canada, Japan, France, the United States, etc.) are losing their historical work ethics. Instead, they seek more balance between work and family or work and leisure. At times, moreover, they seek simply less work. Their commitment and dedication to their employers have decreased, while their job expectations in terms of compensation and responsibility have increased. Whether these trends are accurate, universal, or reversible is open to debate. The point to be made here is that managers have a dual responsibility both to avoid stereotypes (e.g., 'South Koreans are all hard workers') and to learn to adapt when necessary to changing conditions. Flexibility and awareness are the keys here.

At the same time, work environments and managerial expectations are also changing, however slowly. For example, employees in some countries are increasingly demanding greater participation in major organizational decisions that affect them and their colleagues. New labor legislation in some countries (e.g., South Korea) tends to reinforce this trend. At the same time, however, other governments are seen to be moving in the opposite direction by attempting to reduce employee benefits, work rules, and security (e.g., France and the United States).

Work and leisure

A second question we must ask here is how central work is in the lives of employees. Put more bluntly, do people live to work or work to live? We saw one example of this with South Korean and Mexican employees (see above). Another example comes from Europe. A Danish colleague of one of the authors often points out that the fundamental difference between Danish and German managers is that the Germans live to work while the Danes work to live. (One wonders what the response of German managers might be.) Moreover, we sometimes hear that Americans work harder than Europeans – a comment more likely to be heard in New York than in London or Berlin. We hear, too, that Japanese and South Koreans work harder than anyone else – a comment heard in many places, East and West. Indeed, everyone seems to have an opinion about who works the hardest.

Consider some "facts" as far as they will take us: According to one study, American and Japanese employees work an average of 1,800 hours annually.[7] These data ignore the fact that many employees in both countries often work considerable overtime, however. In Japan this is called "free overtime" (it is required but not compensated). Indeed, it is estimated that almost one-half of Japanese employees between the ages of thirty and forty work over sixty hours per week but are compensated for just forty hours. Meanwhile, according to this same study, the average German employee works 1,440 hours annually, significantly less than either their Japanese or American counterparts. While many factors play into decisions about workloads, work hours, and vacation policies, culture is certainly one of these.

Several EU countries now have a standard thirty-five-hour working week, while the norm in the United States is closer to fifty. Many Europeans can retire at the age of sixty, while most Americans have to work until they are sixty-five or older. We see wide variations in official vacation policies across countries, ranging from one or two weeks in much of Asia to four or five weeks in much of Europe (see Exhibit 9.3 for examples). The unanswered question throughout this debate, however, is whether working harder than someone else is a badge of honor or a sign of necessity, or, worse still, some deep psychological malfunction. Perhaps the question on the table should not be who works the hardest but who is most productive and efficient.

Exhibit 9.3 Vacation policies in selected countries

Country	Typical annual vacation policy
France	Two and a half days' paid leave for each full month of service during the year.
Germany	Eighteen working days' paid leave following six months of service.
Hong Kong (China)	Seven days' paid leave following twelve months of continuous service with same employer.
Indonesia	Twelve days' paid leave after twelve months of full service.
Italy	Varies according to length of service, but usually between four and six weeks' paid leave.
Japan	Ten days' paid leave following twelve months of continuous service, provided employee has worked at least 80 percent of this time.
Malaysia	Varies according to length of service but usually between eight and sixteen days' paid leave.
Mexico	Six days' paid leave.
Philippines	Five days' paid leave.
Saudi Arabia	Fifteen days' paid leave upon completion of twelve months of continuous service with same employer.
Singapore	Seven days' paid leave following twelve months of continuous employment.
United Kingdom	No statutory requirement. Most salaried staff receive about five weeks' paid leave; paid leave for workers based on individual labor contracts.
United States	No statutory requirement. Typically varies based on length of service and job function; usually between five and fifteen days' paid leave annually.

Source: Based on Arvind Phatak, Rabi S. Bhagat, and Roger Kashlak, *International Management: Managing in a Diverse and Dynamic Global Environment*. New York: McGraw-Hill/Irwin, 2010, p. 125.

Application 9.1   **Work, leisure, and productivity**

When looking at the potential balance between work, leisure, and productivity, the findings of a *Business Week* study are informative. This survey looked at the number of vacation days actually taken (instead of official vacation policies), and found that Americans now take less vacation time than even the Japanese or South Koreans.[8] Specifically, the study found that, on average, employees took the following vacation times (including public holidays): forty-two days in Italy; thirty-seven days in France; thirty-five days in Germany; thirty-four days in Brazil; twenty-eight days in the United Kingdom; twenty-six days in Canada; twenty-five days in South Korea; twenty-five days in Japan; and thirteen days in the United States. Obviously, these are averages, and considerable variations can be found across the workforce. Even so, consider the effects of such long hours on home life, personal relationships, and even health. In the United States, the average employee gives back almost two unused vacations days annually, worth $20 billion to employers. Question: are such long hours necessary to get or stay ahead – either as an individual or a corporation – or are they a sign of something else?

Application 9.1   (cont.)

At least in theory, since labor costs are such a large portion of a company's overall cost structure, time away from the job detracts from productivity and the inevitable bottom line. Is this always the case, however? For example, a study by the OECD has found that the average European worker produced only two-thirds of the goods and services of his or her American counterpart on an annual basis.[9] Add to this the somewhat higher labor costs and it can be concluded that European companies are at a significant competitive disadvantage in the global marketplace. Among other things, their goods and services will likely cost more due to operational inefficiencies.

There is a second *Business Week* study, however, that discovered something very different. The vacation-loving French and Belgians outproduce Americans on an hourly basis.[10] In other words, while they typically work fewer hours than their US counterparts, they seem to make each hour count more. Searching for an explanation of these findings, the authors of the study suggested that, at some point across the course of a working day, there appears to be a declining rate of return as employees become increasingly inefficient or inattentive from working too long.

Think about it. . .

(1)   How should we calculate productivity: annually or hourly? Americans work longer hours on average and are more productive on an annual basis, while many of their European counterparts take more time off from work but are more productive on an hourly basis. Which is better for companies? Which is better for employees? Which is better for national economic development?

(2)   Some claim that the younger generation is more interested in the life–work balance than their predecessors. If that is true, what are the possible effects on work productivity – and for national economic development?

A recent poll of US workers found that, given a choice between two weeks of extra pay and two weeks of vacation, employees preferred the extra vacation by a margin of two to one. Moreover, consider the effects of work on employee well-being. It might be suggested that, while many Europeans load up on vacation time, many Americans load up on consumer products charged to their credit cards. As the work pace quickens, health-related problems are rising, most notably heart problems among both men and women resulting from increasing job-related stress. The pressure to succeed and concern about the economy and job security frequently lead American workers in the opposite direction, however: towards more work and less play.

Although it is perhaps overly simplistic, the work versus leisure conundrum provides an easy conceptual entry into cultural differences, especially as they relate to the world of work. It indicates how central work is in some people's lives. This debate is only part of a larger debate, however, over the social and economic consequences of increasing globalization. As noted earlier, many people believe – correctly or incorrectly – that the quickening pace of globalization and the competitive intensity of the new global economy are changing how people live in ways not imagined earlier. The open question is whether these changes are for the better or for the worse.

Culture and the psychology of work

Going one step deeper, it is possible to explore how social psychological processes found both within individuals and within their particular cultural backgrounds can influence attitudes and work behaviors. This can become a highly complex topic, so we focus here on just four such processes as they influence work behavior across cultures: psychological contracts, cognitions and expectations, causal attributions, and risk and uncertainty.

Psychological contracts

A *psychological contract* is an implicit – that is, unwritten – understanding between people concerning exchange relationships (see Exhibit 9.4). In the workplace, this is most commonly seen in perceived agreements between supervisors and employees over the wage–effort bargain – that is, what benefits are offered to employees in the form of salaries, benefits, job security, and so forth, in exchange for their talents, efforts, commitment, and performance? Such contracts can also be seen in mutual agreements between colleagues, co-workers, and team members, however. Psychological contracts can be tenuous, in the sense that they are mutual understandings between individuals or groups, yet nothing is written down. Perceptions and trust (and sometimes history) play a major role in their mutual acceptance.

Imagine the challenge facing expatriates who sign on as sales or marketing representatives for foreign companies. What does the organization expect of them? What do their fellow sales representatives expect of them? Are they expected to work nights and weekends to secure business, even if they are paid only for working weekdays? Are they expected to meet their sales quota or exceed it? Are they supposed to wait their turn for

Exhibit 9.4 Culture and the psychological contract

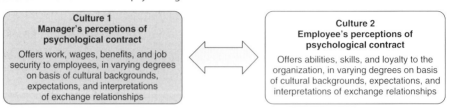

promotion or overtake senior colleagues if they can? In short, what are the unwritten rules governing their employment and performance?

The reason psychological contracts become important here, again, is that they contain information that the new manager typically won't have yet will affect his or her job success. Once more, the admonition remains true to gain as much inside knowledge as possible before beginning new assignments. Although a complete understanding of such contracts may be impossible, a simple awareness of their fundamentals can go along way towards making an outsider an insider.

Expectations, equality, and equity

Cultural influences on individuals' cognitions and expectations were discussed in Chapter 5. We return to this subject now because such processes play a critical role in motivational decisions and subsequent actions. Indeed, cognitive approaches to behavior remain a dominant force in the study of organizational behavior today.[11] These theories are based largely on the assumption that people tend to make reasoned choices about their behaviors on the basis of their expectations and culturally based world views. These choices, in turn, influence job-related outcomes and work attitudes. While the majority of cognitive theories, as well as much of the empirical work relating to them, derive from North American efforts, a number of studies have also been conducted to test the external validity of these models in other regions of the world.

Research has long demonstrated that people's cultural surroundings can frequently influence their hopes and *expectations*.[12] Likewise, what people expect or prefer as reward for hard work is also culturally based to some degree. Research has identified an *equity principle* in many Western countries, through which people are motivated to achieve or restore equity (i.e., fairness) between themselves and others they compare themselves to. Some international researchers have suggested that the equity principle may be somewhat culture-bound, however.[13] In Asia and the Middle East, notably, examples abound concerning individuals who apparently readily accept a clearly recognizable state of inequity in order to preserve their view of societal harmony.

For instance, men and women frequently receive different pay for doing precisely the same work in countries such as Japan and South Korea.[14] One might think that equity theory would predict that a state of inequity would result for female employees, leading to inequity resolution strategies such as those mentioned above. In many cases, however, no such perceived inequitable state has been found, thereby calling the theory into question. A plausible explanation here may be that women workers view other women as their referent other, not men. As a result, so long as all women are treated the same, a state of perceived equity could exist. This is not to say that such women feel "equal"; rather, compared to their female reference group, they are receiving what the others receive. A state of equity – if not equality – exists.[15]

These cultural idiosyncrasies create at least two cultural limitations on the acceptable actions of managers and employees alike. The first limitation focuses on problem analysis. In other words, cultural drivers can at times affect in no small way how problems are identified and understood by both managers and employees. Indeed, they can even sometimes help determine whether something is seen as a problem at all. For example, while managers in one culture (e.g., that in Singapore) may focus very seriously on problems of employee absenteeism, managers elsewhere (e.g., in Sweden) may see such behavior as more of a personal employee issue and acceptable within broader limits. The issue in these two cultures is not whether absenteeism is good or bad; rather, it is the magnitude or severity of the problem compared to other behaviors and actions.

In addition, cultural drivers can influence the variety of possible solutions or preferred outcomes that are acceptable on the part of organizations, managers, and employees. Using the employee absenteeism example again, managers in some cultures (e.g., that in Singapore again) may see strict punitive actions (e.g., financial penalties or termination) as either acceptable or even desirable when employees fail to come to work. In other cultures (e.g., that in Sweden again), this may seem overly harsh and lacking in understanding of the underlying causes of the absences; such cultures may accept counseling but not termination. In still other cultures (e.g., that in Saudi Arabia), no action may be taken at all, in the belief that absences are largely beyond the control of individuals and, as such, should not be a legitimate issue for managers.

Application 9.2   Lincoln Electric in Germany

Consider the example of Lincoln Electric as it attempted to expand its operations from the United States to Germany. Lincoln Electric is a medium-sized company based in Cleveland, Ohio, that manufactures arc-welding equipment. By any measure, it is a success story.[16] The company's business strategy is simple: sell high-value, high-quality products at competitive prices and provide outstanding customer service. The key to Lincoln Electric's success is its stable, hard-working, and highly skilled workforce. In a country that lavishes sizable executive bonuses on CEOs and other senior managers who can squeeze maximum productivity out of workers, Lincoln was founded – and continues to operate – on the twin principles of self-determination and equal treatment of all employees. Above all, it stresses pay for performance.

Lincoln Electric has an abiding respect for the ability of the individual and believes that, properly motivated, ordinary people can achieve extraordinary results. It also believes firmly that gains in productivity should be shared with consumers in the form of lower prices, with employees in the form of higher pay, and with shareholders in the form of higher dividends. This philosophy has been reinforced by the creation of an incentive system that continues unchanged to this day, more than seventy years after its introduction. All workers at Lincoln are paid on a piece rate system; they are paid for each unit they produce and do not receive either a salary or an hourly wage. There is no paid vacation, no paid sick leave, and no bonuses or job security for seniority. This principle applies to all employees up to and including the company president, with minor adjustments for the nature of managerial work. In addition to receiving piece rate wages, however, workers can earn substantial bonuses on the basis of their individual job performance and company profits. Bonuses are paid twice each year based on performance. Under this system, employee bonuses have been paid each year since 1934, and the company claims that its workers are the highest-paid blue-collar workers in the world.[17] Indeed, employee bonuses often exceed annual wages, thereby more than doubling their income. There have been no layoffs in the company's long history, and absenteeism and turnover rates are the lowest in the industry. Indeed, it is said that, when a severe snowstorm shuts Cleveland down, Lincoln employees make it to work. Moreover, despite its high employee compensation, Lincoln Electric's workers are so productive that the company has a lower cost structure than any of its competitors.

In recent years Lincoln Electric decided to expand its operations internationally and become a bigger player in the emerging global economy.[18] It set its sights on Germany, buying a small German arc-welding equipment manufacturer. None of the US executives involved in the acquisition decision had any international experience, but they believed that, because they had been so successful in the United States, success would likewise follow elsewhere. One of their first decisions was to retain the local German managers, on the grounds that they best understood local customs and work practices. It was assumed that the Lincoln Electric compensation system would be adapted to fit local conditions, leading to increased productivity through heightened individual motivation. It quickly became apparent, however, that the local German managers were either unable or unwilling to introduce Lincoln Electric's individualistic incentive plan among workers used to a somewhat more collectivistic work culture. Finally, out of exasperation, US headquarters ordered it to be implemented. The response of the employees was quick and decisive. Employee grievances and even lawsuits arose challenging the newly imposed system, which was seen by many as being exploitative and even inhumane. Workers were being asked to work ever harder with little consideration for their quality of living. Many workers rejected the piece rate concept on principle, while others preferred extra leisure time over higher wages and were not prepared to work as hard as their US counterparts.

After a visit to the German facility, Lincoln Electric's president observed, "Even though German factory workers are highly skilled and, in general, solid workers, they do not work nearly as hard or as long as the people in our Cleveland factory. In Germany, the average factory workweek is thirty-five hours. In contrast, the average workweek in Lincoln's US plants is between forty-three and fifty-eight hours, and the company can ask people to work longer hours on short notice – a flexibility that is essential for our system to work. The lack of such flexibility was one of the reasons why our approach would not work in Europe."[19] Looking back over their German misadventure, Lincoln Electric executives drew what for them was a surprising conclusion: "We had long boasted that our unique culture and incentive system – along with the dedicated, skilled workforce that the company had built over the decades – were the main sources of Lincoln's competitive advantage. We had assumed that the incentive system and culture could be transferred abroad and that the workforce could be quickly replicated."[20]

Think about it...

(1)   How would you describe the psychological contract in this example?

Application 9.2   (cont.)

(2)   How did the job and reward expectations, and perceptions of equity, differ between the US company and its German employees?

(3)   What could the US (and German) managers have done to improve the motivational environment in their German operation? How successful do you think such attempts might be?

Managing employee performance

Think about this: managers in both Russia and Japan make use of a variety of motivational strategies and techniques to facilitate employee performance, but, in terms of central tendencies, they could not be more different. As noted above, one stresses a top-down autocratic approach to control subordinates, while the other stresses a cooperative and supportive approach to empower them. Both can be highly successful at times, but not so at others. Both have the power to enhance employee commitment to the organization and both have the power to drive employees away. The unanswered question here is why two fundamentally different approaches to work motivation can both be successful.

Observations on work motivation

Observations by experts on employee motivation around the world echo this dilemma. Consider the following comments on the psychology of work motivation from different countries.

- In Thailand, "the introduction of an individual merit bonus plan, which runs counter to the societal norm of group cooperation, can result in a decline rather than an increase in productivity from employees who refuse to openly compete with each other."[21]

- In the Netherlands, "you can't get the Dutch to compete with one another publicly."[22]

- In the United States, "to get the best people, you have to continually refine the gene pool; you must grade on a curve."[23]

- In Mexico, "everything is a personal matter; but a lot of [foreign] managers don't get it. To get anything done, the manager has to be more of an instructor, teacher, or father figure than a boss."[24]

- "Efforts to improve managerial performance in the UK should focus more on job content than on job context. Job enrichment programs are more likely to improve performance in an intrinsically oriented society such as Britain, where satisfaction tends to be derived from the job itself, than in France, where job context factors, such as security and fringe benefits, are more highly valued."[25]

- British and Canadian companies motivate their employees primarily through financial incentives, while German and Dutch companies focus on providing employment stability and employee benefits.

- Indonesian and South Korean companies prefer rigid and often autocratic organizational hierarchies in which everyone knows his or her place, while Swedish and Norwegian companies stress informality, power sharing, and mutual benefit in the workplace. Some countries, such as Germany, even combine formality and rigid hierarchies with power sharing and an emphasis on securing mutual gain for all employees.

The conclusion here is inescapable: different countries often use different motivational and managerial strategies to get work done. The organizational goals may be similar, but the psychology and concomitant behaviors can be very different. This leads us to a fundamental question facing all managers, global and domestic: how can we best motivate employees through the use of locally valid incentive and reward systems?

Clearly, working with a global workforce is no easy task. Even so, the task can be made somewhat easier if managers have a frame of reference or toolbox that can provide some structure for observation, understanding, and action. We suggest that work motivation theory can provide this structure. As such, we examine here the challenges of working with employees from different countries and cultures through the lens of work motivation. In doing so, we intend to raise three questions. First, on a general level, what is it that motivates (or fails to motivate) employees on the job? Second, on a more specific level, do these motivational drivers differ across cultures? Third, what is the role played by managerial efforts to involve employees in work-related decisions in securing employee motivation and performance? Throughout this analysis, the underlying question here relates to the utilization of human capital – that is, how can organizations maximize their return on their human resources, and is this goal best accomplished through direction or participation?

Even so, managers involved in international business must recognize that, if employee behavior is critical for the success of an organization, and if culture influences such behavior, it represents a major influence on the ultimate competitiveness of the firm. Knowledge of this fact and an understanding of how culture influences employee behavior and performance represent critical strategic assets for global managers in a highly competitive world. Without a highly motivated workforce that uses its brains, not just its backs, competitive advantage becomes highly problematic. This is particularly true as we move further into an era in which technology and knowledge often determine winners and losers. Simply put, competitive organizations need to have all their employees striving on behalf of their goals and objectives, not just the people at the top. The challenge for the global manager is to accomplish this within a work context in which behavior is often determined by cultural variations beyond their control. The question for managers, then, is how to use this knowledge to further their organization's competitive edge. This was the challenge faced by Lincoln Electric in its foray into Germany, and it is the challenge faced by most managers in their overseas assignments.

Motivational strategies and employee responses

To understand how and why motivation affects work behavior, it may be useful to review an example of how people from two different cultures see the motivational or performance environment (see Exhibit 9.5). This particular example is from India and

Exhibit 9.5 Culture, motivational strategies, and employee responses (examples from the United Kingdom and India)

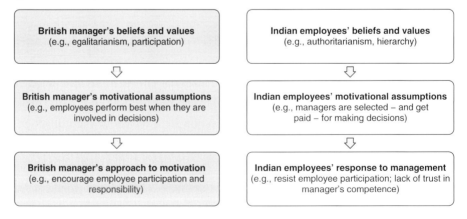

Exhibit 9.6 Culture and work motivation strategies

Core cultural dimensions	Motivational strategies
Hierarchical	Emphasize extrinsic rewards and large salary differentials. Provide clear directives to subordinates. Support decisive and powerful leaders. Reward subordinate compliance with management directives.
Egalitarian	Emphasize intrinsic rewards and minimal salary differentials. Encourage participative or consultative decision making. Support flexible and collaborative leaders. Reward constructive feedback and creativity.
Individualistic	Emphasize extrinsic rewards (e.g., pay, promotion) tied to personal achievement. Emphasize individually based incentives. Stress personal responsibility for accomplishment. View employees as performers. Provide employees with autonomy and opportunities for advancement.
Collectivistic	Emphasize intrinsic rewards (e.g., meaningful work) tied to commitment and loyalty. Emphasize group-based incentives. Stress group norms and moral persuasion. View employees as family members. Build teams and networks focused on task performance.
Mastery-oriented	Create a competitive environment within the organization to stimulate best efforts. Emphasize performance-based incentives using monetary rewards. Showcase high performers. Encourage thinking big, conquering the environment. Provide assertiveness training programs.
Harmony-oriented	Emphasize harmony and team effort for collective results. Emphasize seniority- or membership-based incentives. Showcase team efforts and organization-wide accomplishments. Encourage respect for traditions and the environment. Encourage continued membership for entire workforce.
Monochronic	Provide simple and straightforward directions, one task at a time. Provide strict time limits for each project; require intermittent written progress reports. Focus on the job; keep personal relations to a minimum.
Polychronic	Identify task requirements, but let employees choose how best to accomplish them. Provide flexible time limits for various tasks; check progress through personal discussions. Focus on personal relations as a means of succeeding on the job.
Rule-based or universalistic	State rules, regulations, and policies clearly and publicly. Enforce rules and regulations uniformly. Tie rewards to rule compliance. Where possible, provide employees with security and certainty. When possible, make decisions on basis of objective criteria.
Relationship-based or particularistic	Create opportunities for employees to develop social relationships at work. Invest time meeting with employees individually and in groups; build relationships and informal networks. Use influential people to help motivate. Account for extenuating circumstances in rule enforcement. When possible, show patience with first-time rule breakers. Keep your word; build trust with employees.

Source: Adapted from Richard M. Steers and Luciara Nardon, *Managing in the global economy*. Armonk, NY: M. E. Sharpe, 2006, pp. 310–13.

the United Kingdom, and illustrates why motivating local employees can be so challenging. In this example, we have a local group of employees who see the supervisor's
role as making decisions, giving orders, and taking responsibility for task completion,
while the manager believes employee involvement and participation in decisions

Application 9.3   Work motivation across cultures

Exhibit 9.6 summarizes some trends in work motivation strategies across cultures. Experience tells us that these are only trends, however, and that variations clearly exist. The question for managers, then, is how useful such information is when working in different field situations.

Think about it. . .

(1)   Identify some of the more common factors that might cause variations in these general motivational trends within single cultures. How widespread do you think these variations might be? Why?

(2)   From the list of motivational strategies listed in the exhibit, identify the five that you think would be most effective in motivating yourself on the job. Why did you select these five?

(3)   What are the potential problems or challenges of making use of general motivational strategies such as those listed in the exhibit?

affecting their jobs are the key to high job performance. The motivational assumptions of each group would be expected to be different. Hence, when all players get to the actual work environment, we might expect – even predict – that managerial efforts to achieve certain performance levels may fail. Quite simply, there is a disconnect between what each side deems to be fair and appropriate.

Going a step further, we can examine some general tendencies in motivational strategies as they relate to cultural differences around the globe. This is illustrated in Exhibit 9.6. Remember, however, that these are only general trends and that every culture and country has its own variations and differences. Perhaps the most important lesson from this exhibit is how different motivational strategies can be in different parts of the world, requiring managers to adjust accordingly.

Managing incentives and rewards

What do people expect to happen – and, indeed, what do they wish to happen – as a result of their work efforts? Performance consequences can vary widely, as can reward structures. In general, when people are offered incentives to perform or rewards for good performance (or even punishment for poor performance), such actions are viewed and evaluated by employees as being appropriate or inappropriate, acceptable or unacceptable, with corresponding attitudinal and behavioral consequences. If these positive or negative consequences are important to managers, then, clearly, care must be taken in developing incentives and reward systems.

Consider the variety of outcomes and rewards offered to employees in exchange for their efforts on behalf of the organization. Generally, we refer to two types of incentives and rewards.

- *Extrinsic rewards* are rewards (or punishments) that are provided to employees as a result of good (or poor) performance, and usually include such items as salaries, bonuses, benefits, and job security. They are largely "administered" by the firm, not the employee, as a consequence of his or her performance.
- *Intrinsic rewards* are rewards that arise from doing one's job in a satisfactory way. They are largely "self-administered"; in other words, employees may feel pride or satisfaction from a job well done or they may enjoy the holiday time they receive as a consequence of hard work.

Looking across cultures, it readily becomes apparent that reward preferences are, to a degree, culture-bound. Some cultures emphasize security, while others emphasize harmony and congenial interpersonal relationships, and still others emphasize individual status and respect. For example, a study examined the employees of a large multinational electrical equipment manufacturer operating in forty countries around the world and found important similarities, as well as differences, in what rewards employees wanted in exchange for good performance.[26] Interestingly, in all countries, the most important rewards that were sought involved recognition and achievement. Second in importance were improvements in the immediate work environment and employment conditions such as pay and work hours. Beyond this, however, a number of differences emerged in terms of preferred rewards. Some countries, such as the United Kingdom and the United States, placed a low value on job security compared to workers in many nations, while French and Italian workers placed a high value on security and good fringe benefits and a low value on challenging work. Scandinavian workers de-emphasized "getting ahead" and instead stressed greater concern for others on the job and for personal freedom and autonomy. Germans placed high on security, fringe benefits, and "getting ahead," while Japanese ranked low on personal advancement and high on having good working conditions and a congenial work environment.

In this section, we examine three such rewards: financial incentives, gender and pay, and employee benefits.

Financial incentives and distributive justice

Many merit-based, or pay-for-performance, incentive systems that are in use around the world (particularly in the West) attempt to link financial compensation and promotional opportunities directly to individual, group, or even corporate performance. Managers employing such systems view them as a statement of equity, if not equality. On other words, the higher one's performance, the greater the rewards – a simple performance-reward contingency. Other cultures believe compensation should be based on group membership or group effort, thereby emphasizing equality. Everyone is deserving of more or less the same rewards. To understand the logic underlying such differences, it is helpful to understand the concept of *distributive justice* across cultures, especially as it relates to individualism or collectivism. One example of this can be seen in an effort by a US multinational corporation to institute an individually based bonus system for its sales representatives in a Danish subsidiary. The sales force rejected the proposal because it favored one group over another. The Danish employees felt that all employees should receive the same amount of bonus instead of being given a percentage of their salary, reflecting a strong sense of egalitarianism.[27]

Similar results were found for Indonesian oil workers; individually based incentive systems created more controversy than results. As one manager commented: "Indonesians manage their culture by a group process, and everybody is linked together as a team. Distributing money differently amongst the team did not go over that well; so, we've come to the conclusion that pay for performance is not suitable for Indonesia."[28] Similar results were reported in studies comparing Americans with Chinese, Russians, and Indians. In all three cases, Americans expressed greater preference than their counterparts for rewards to be based on performance instead of equality or need.[29]

It is interesting to note that the basis for some incentive systems has evolved over time in response to political and economic changes. China is frequently cited as an example of a country that is attempting to blend quasi-capitalistic economic reforms with a reasonably static socialist political state. China's economy has demonstrated considerable growth, as entrepreneurs are increasingly allowed to initiate their own enterprises largely free from government control. Within existing and former state-owned enterprises, moreover, some movement can be seen towards what is called a reform model of incentives and motivation. In this regard, a distinction can be made between the traditional Chinese incentive model, in which egalitarianism is stressed and rewards tend to be based on age, loyalty, and gender, and the new reform model, in which merit and achievement receive greater emphasis and rewards tend to be based on qualifications, training, level of responsibility, and performance. Some researchers have suggested, however, that the rhetoric in support of the reform model far surpasses actual implementation to date.

In Japan, meanwhile, efforts to introduce Western-style merit pay systems have often led to an increase in overall labor costs. Since the companies that adopted the merit-based reward system could not simultaneously reduce the pay of less productive workers for fear of causing them to lose face and disturb group harmony (*wa*), everyone's salary tended to increase.

Similar results concerning the manner in which culture can influence reward systems as well as other personnel practices emerged from a study among banking employees in South Korea.[30] The two South Korean banks studied were owned and operated as joint ventures with banks in other countries, one from Japan and one from the United States. In the American joint venture, US personnel policies dominated management practice in the South Korean bank, while, in the Japanese joint venture, a blend of Japanese and South Korean HRM policies prevailed. Employees in the joint venture with the Japanese bank were significantly more committed to the organization than employees in the US joint venture. Moreover, the Japanese-affiliated bank also demonstrated significantly higher financial performance. However you look at it, employees do not always seek the same rewards and outcomes for job performance.

Application 9.4   Lincoln Electric revisited

Let's return to our example of Lincoln Electric. Lincoln Electric's disappointment in Germany was soon replaced with optimism following its experience with a Mexican subsidiary that occurred about the same time. The company had purchased a unionized manufacturing plant in Mexico City. Despite the fact that piece rate systems are generally rejected by Mexican workers (like their German counterparts), Lincoln introduced its system gradually and only following discussions with workers in the plant. Initially, when employees expressed reservations about the Lincoln plan, executives asked for two Mexican volunteers to test-drive the system. They were guaranteed that they would not lose money under the system during the trial period, but could keep any additional income they earned. Two employees reluctantly agreed to try the system. Soon, as the two workers began making more than their colleagues, other employees asked to join the plan. Over the next two years everyone in the plant gradually asked to join. Today, the Mexican facility continues to prosper under the Lincoln incentive system.

From its experience in Germany and Mexico, Lincoln Electric concluded that moving across borders must be done slowly and only after a thorough understanding of local cultures. Moreover, they learned that transplanting ideas – whether they relate to incentive systems, management practices, or anything else – would succeed only after a thorough dialog with the workers who are directly involved. As we look back on this example, one wonders why the Lincoln Electric incentive program that had worked so well for decades in the United States was so soundly rejected in these two other countries. Could this rejection be attributed exclusively to cultural differences, or were there other factors in play here? If so, what are these other factors?

Subsequent to these experiences, Lincoln Electric opened a welding company in Shanghai, China.[31] Using what they had learned about cross-cultural challenges, this time managers were more sensitive to local differences and demands. They spent considerable time getting to know not just the employees but also their families. They held open discussions with employees and sought their input into developing a culturally sensitive compensation system. In the end, management decided to move slowly towards some form of merit-based compensation system, but perhaps with a Chinese flavor. At the same time, Lincoln management discovered that many younger Chinese workers were moving towards a more general acceptance of such systems.

Think about it. . .

(1)   Why was Lincoln Electric more successful in both Mexico and China than in Germany? Explain.

(2)   What are the lessons here for other companies and managers who are faced with the challenge of motivating employees in their overseas facilities?

Gender, rewards, and opportunities

In many countries, significant differences can be found in pay levels between men and women. This can be a difficult topic to explore, because it can very quickly turn into disagreement over beliefs and values irrespective of cultural differences. Put another way, should this discussion focus on what companies across borders do in their compensation policies or on what they should do? In addition, who gets to determine the definition of "should"? Moreover, in making pay comparisons between genders, are we discussing

Exhibit 9.7 Wage gaps between men and women across nations

Country	Wage gap (%)	Country	Wage gap (%)	Country	Wage gap (%)
New Zealand	6	Sweden	15	Finland	20
Belgium	9	Spain	17	United States	21
Poland	11	OECD average	18	Canada	22
Greece	12	Czech Republic	19	Switzerland	22
France	12	Portugal	19	Germany	24
Hungary	12	Ireland	20	Japan	32
Denmark	14	United Kingdom	20	South Korea	40
Australia	15				

Note: Numbers indicate the percentage difference between the average wage of men and women by country, expressed in terms of men's wages.

Source: Date derived from OECD, *Women and Men in OECD Countries*. Paris: OECD, 2007, pp. 15–18.

disparities between the pay of men and women in similar jobs (e.g., assembly line workers, marketing representatives, healthcare providers, etc.) or in different jobs that someone has determined to be on a par with each other in terms of the skills or qualifications required (e.g., a teacher and a manager – the issue of comparable worth)?

Our focus here is on basic statistical differences between what men and women make by job category in different countries. To accomplish this, we turned to a recent OECD study of gender wage gaps, as summarized in Exhibit 9.7. As can be seen, gender-based wage gaps can be found in all the countries studied, ranging from a low of 6 percent wage disparity in New Zealand to a high of 40 percent disparity in South Korea. Some of these disparities can be explained by the fact that women are more likely to be found in contingent labor categories, which typically pay less than permanent job status. Other disparities can be explained by differing sex role expectations and norms in some countries. Some can be explained by simple job discrimination. In this regard, it is interesting to note that in no country do men on average make less than women, disputing the notion that such wage differences are random in nature.

From both a managerial and a motivational standpoint, this issue can become intractable for the following reason. When global managers are assigned abroad, what is (or should be) their philosophy on compensation policies? Should they abide by prevailing local wage patterns (e.g., paying women lower salaries than men doing similar work) or should they apply the equal-pay-for-equal-work policies that may prevail in their home countries? Simply put, should global managers strive to play by local rules as defined by local cultures (particularism) or be agents of change as defined by their home-country beliefs and values (universalism)? This value conflict illustrates another challenge facing managers who work in foreign assignments.

Application 9.5   Women managers in China

Women make up 46 percent of China's labor force, a higher proportion than in most Western countries. In large part, this can be traced back to Mao Zedong's efforts to get more women into the workforce with his famous dictum "Women hold up half the sky." In recent years China has been generally recognized as being more open to women than other east Asian countries. Its women expect to be taken seriously; as one Chinese female investment banker in Beijing puts it, "We do not come across as deferential."[32] Young Chinese women have been moving away from the countryside in droves and piling into the electronics factories in the booming coastal belt, leading dreary lives but earning more money than their parents ever dreamed of. Others have been pouring into universities, at home and abroad, and graduating in almost the same numbers as men. Once they have negotiated China's highly competitive education system, they want to get on a career ladder and start climbing. Here are just two examples.

Pully Chau spent eight years working for the Chinese office of a big international advertising agency and never got a pay rise; there was always some excuse. "It was stupid of me not to ask," she says. "If I had been a Caucasian man, I would have done better." She stuck around because she liked the idea of working for an outfit that was well known in China and hoped to learn something. Eventually she got fed up and took a job with another Western agency, Draftfcb, for which she is now chairman and CEO for Greater China, based in Shanghai. Highly confident and with boundless energy, today she could pick and choose from any number of jobs. There are lots of opportunities for women in China, she says – but, in business, life is still easier for men.

A second example is Iris Kang, who heads the business unit for emerging markets at Pfizer. Kang was trained to be a doctor in a state-owned hospital, but soon changed careers for the global pharmaceutical industry. She says there is less sex discrimination in multinationals than in Chinese companies, and the number of women in senior posts in her firm is rising rapidly. Hers is another tale of relentless self-improvement. Soon after she joined the private sector she took an executive MBA at one of China's leading business schools, the CEIBS in Shanghai. Last year she added a masters degree in pharmaceutical medicine, all the while heading a team of 120 people in her job with Pfizer.

Think about it. . .

(1)   Statistics suggest that women in China have greater opportunities on the executive ladder than their counterparts in other east Asian countries. What might explain this difference?

Application 9.5   (cont.)

(2)   The examples of Pully Chau and Iris Kang illustrate highly successful women executives. In the realm of speculation, why do you think these two women succeeded whereas other have not?

(3)   In general, do you think women in various countries are largely motivated by the same factors as their male counterparts? Explain.

Employee benefits

Finally, as HRM executives know all too well, employee benefits and prerequisites represent a sizable portion of overall labor costs for any operation. These costs typically range from 33 to 50 percent of salaries. These same executives also understand that such benefits can vary significantly across cultures, not just in their magnitude but also in their nature. As expatriate packages decline and global growth increasingly seeks to attract local talent from around the world, employers who ignore local quirks and customs do so at their own risk.[33] Companies that extend their stock options plans abroad often discover that the local tax systems substantially reduce any income – or motivational – advantages. The trick for managers here is to study local customs and work to match corporate benefits to local conditions. To understand the extent to which these customs can vary, consider several examples.

- In many parts of the world, past financial crises mean that employees aren't very interested in deferred compensation plans such as 401(k) plans, which are commonly used in the United States as one way to save for retirement. Why be rewarded in stocks and bonds that could collapse?
- Indian firms frequently pay the expenses for the aging parents of employees.
- Companies in China are often required to chip into housing funds, usually on a matching basis, so that employees can buy their own houses.
- Likewise, companies in India and Russia often arrange for home mortgages for their employees and sometimes even pay part of the monthly mortgage expenses.
- Employers in both Japan and the Philippines traditionally receive a monthly family allowance (called a *rice allowance* in the Philippines and *kazoku teiate* in Japan) in addition to their wages.
- Many Mexican firms offer *pollution escape trips* to allow employees to escape from polluted Mexico City and other cities to holidays in either the Pacific or Gulf of

Mexico coasts. In Mexico as well, Mother's Day is on a weekday, and employees often receive the entire day off to take their mothers to lunch.

- Executives in both Brazil and Mexico are often given chauffeur-driven cars with bulletproof windows to protect them against kidnapping.

- As if the high number of days off were not enough, some French employers offer the use of company-owned ski chalets and beach houses to employees for a nominal fee. Such perks are also occasionally seen in Germany.

- In recognition of the litigious nature of American society, many US companies pay for employee legal services insurance just as they do employee healthcare insurance. In the United States as well, most company healthcare insurance policies pay for Viagra (considered to be medication for a "medical condition"), but not birth control pills (not considered to be a "medical condition").

These are significant – and at times very expensive – benefit differences. Not receiving them can anger local employees and even lead to more drastic behavior. It is more a question of local, rather than global, equity.

Application 9.6   Company cars

A small Dutch high-tech firm was recently acquired by US electronics giant Intel. Consistent with Dutch tradition, the small company had long provided many of its middle managers with company cars to offset the country's high tax rate on personal incomes. In the eyes of its employees, this was part of their compensation package. To many outsiders, however, the proliferation of new BMWs among the managers of the small start-up seemed a bit excessive. After the acquisition of the company by Intel Corporation, Intel's HRM executives sought to rescind the Dutch company's car policy, since it was far more generous than that of the parent company back in the United States. Following a number of complaints and several key resignations, however, the parent company policy change was dropped. This example illustrates the conflicts and challenges faced by many of today's global managers. From their standpoint, the Intel executives were seeking equality in their employee personnel policies across the two countries, but from the Dutch standpoint the company cars were part of this equality, since their income tax rate on salaries is substantially higher than that for their US counterparts.

Think about it. . .

(1) Should reward systems within one company be the same across the globe or tailored to each country? What problems may each of these approaches create?

(2) Faced with a disparity of benefit and reward systems across borders, as in the case of Intel, what can global organizations and their managers do?

(3) Sitting in the corporate headquarters of a multinational firm, how can a manager discover what level of compensation and benefits is both fair and functional in other regions of the world? What would you do?

Finally, it is important for managers to remember that no culture or country has an absolute preference for one incentive system over the other. In other words, almost all cultures make use of a combination of extrinsic and intrinsic incentives. What does differ, however, is the relative balance between the two. Some cultures place greater emphasis on concrete, typically financially based, incentives, in the belief that, at the end of the day, money matters. Others obviously recognize the importance of money as a motivator but prefer to emphasize and support improvements in such areas as work design and employee involvement, in the belief that challenging and interesting work will maximize individual and collective contributions to organizational goal attainment. In any case, managers must discover, understand, and respond to work environments as they are influenced by cultural differences.

Expatriate and local managers

The final issue we should address here concerns the type of managers a company typically uses in its overseas operations. We are referring here to the choice between using expatriates or local managers to manage local people.

Consider the following problem: as an HRM executive for a large multinational mining company, you have been asked to hire the best manager you can find to run your company's operations in Bolivia. The job will require considerable technical expertise as well as managerial competence. Operational success is important, and your reputation (and career) as an executive is riding on your decision. What do you do? Perhaps your first challenge is to decide whether you want to hire a "local" (i.e., Bolivian) manager to run the facility or someone from another country. There are obvious advantages to hiring local managers, in terms of their understanding both the language and local customs. The Bolivian government would probably also be pleased. Your choice of qualified candidates may be limited, however. Besides, sending someone from corporate headquarters, perhaps a European or North American, might bring a more international perspective to the Bolivian operations, as well as providing valuable training for one of your company's up-and-coming junior managers. How do you weigh these advantages and disadvantages in a way that will help you make an optimal decision?

As you make your decision, the first thing to understand is that you have two possible options for hiring: expatriates or local managers. Many multinationals prefer to hire local employees to operate overseas branches and subsidiaries. These managers frequently have greater local acceptance and can provide for the training of local employees for future organizational needs. At other times, however, companies find it preferable to send in expatriate managers, to provide at least three advantages for the multinational firm.[34] Global assignments can help companies coordinate and control operations that are widely dispersed geographically or culturally. With managers traveling back and forth between headquarters and local operations, information flow is increased as expatriate managers come to understand local conditions and challenges and relate these issues back to senior management. In addition, global assignments can provide important strategic information for managers and their companies alike, especially when the managers spend two or three years in one location and genuinely begin to understand the local culture and customs. Last, global assignments can help managers develop new skills for working with both colleagues and customers around the world. Indeed, many companies use global assignments as a central part of their management training efforts, especially for potential higher-echelon executives.

Although such advantages are fairly obvious, finding suitable expatriates who can actually succeed in global assignments can be problematic. Indeed, the first lesson to be learned in global staffing is that, while all people may be created equal, their travel skills are not. While traveling abroad (perhaps on a vacation or business trip) is often seen by people as an enjoyable experience, actually *living* abroad can be frustrating and stressful, and sometimes very unpleasant (see Chapter 11). For many, staying in a four-star hotel, eating in fine restaurants, seeing new sights, and knowing that soon you will be back in your own bed is far preferable to setting up a household in a strange neighborhood where few people speak your language, finding schools for the kids, shopping in local markets stocked with foods you can't identify, and using public transportation. For others, these same experiences provide a sense of adventure and learning. The challenge

Exhibit 9.8 Benefits of hiring local and expatriate managers

Local managers	Expatriate managers
Critical skills can be developed locally to help improve operational efficiency and effectiveness.	Critical skills can be transferred overseas to help improve local efficiency and effectiveness.
Using host-country nationals is typically (although not always) less expensive than transferring in expatriates.	Providing expatriates with interesting overseas assignments helps retain their services for future assignments.
Host-country nationals have fewer local adjustment problems.	Opportunities to develop internationally experienced senior management team.
Better ties to local government and local business community.	Better ties to parent company and global business community.

Exhibit 9.9 Problems with local and expatriate managers

	Percentage of firms reporting problems		
Problems reported by firms	Japan	Europe	United States
Local managers			
Difficulty in attracting high-quality locals to work for the company	44	26	21
High turnover of locals	32	9	4
Friction between locals and home-country nationals	32	9	13
Complaints about lack of promotional opportunities by locals	21	4	8
Legal challenges to company HRM policies by locals	0%	10%	0%
Expatriate managers			
Lack of expatriates who have sufficient global management skills	68	39	29
Lack of expatriates who want to work abroad	26	26	13
Reentry problems experienced by returning expatriates	24	39	42

Source: Data from Helen Deresky, *International Management: Managing across Borders and Cultures,* Upper Saddle River, NJ: Prentice-Hall, 2010, pp. 395–7.

for managers – and their companies – is to discover which type of person you are *before* getting on the airplane.

By way of summary, Exhibits 9.8 and 9.9 identify several of the potential benefits and possible drawbacks of using either host-country nationals or expatriates. (Note that American, Japanese, and European companies report different problems with their overseas operations.) Selecting the right employees for overseas assignments continues to be a difficult decision for most multinational firms throughout the world. So much depends on the quality of employees a firm can attract. Perhaps the best advice here is first to understand a firm's global strategic objectives, as well as its prevailing corporate culture. With this information in mind, managers should be in a better position to determine the appropriate mix of personnel to staff their global operations.

Managing a global workforce

While many of the theories and recommendations surrounding employee motivation appear to be straightforward, in actual practice this is a difficult challenge – even before considering cross-cultural settings. People's expectations and demands – and their perceptions of fairness – vary widely both within and across organizations, and it is the manager's job to coordinate these disparate needs, expectations, and behaviors into a cohesive force for goal accomplishment.

Global management and motivation: assessing demands and constraints

Once again, following our model from Chapter 5, effective motivational efforts begin with an analysis of the unique circumstances in which managers must work. As illustrated in Exhibit 9.10, the first step is to consider how the cultural, organizational, and situational environments come into play to constrain managerial options and practices. For example, societal norms regarding individualism or collectivism can represent a major factor in using individual and group, or merit-based or seniority-based, incentive systems.

Likewise, organizational design and organizational cultures can also influence global management and motivational practices. For example, investor organizations tend to have more centralized management than mutual benefit organizations (see Chapter 4). The issue here is who must agree – or "sign off" on – the performance evaluation incentive systems in use. Moreover, we would expect the use of either local or expatriate managers to influence both employee response and behavior.

Finally, circumstances unique to the particular situation can also have an influence on management and motivation. For instance, local customs and government regulations often place constraints on compensation practices. Moreover, the practices of local competitors can also play a role. The point here is simple: know the local environment and working conditions before considering the shape of incentives and rewards or performance management systems. In this regard, the lesson of Lincoln Electric should be a clear wake-up call for managers.

Exhibit 9.10 Assessing the global management and motivation environment (examples)

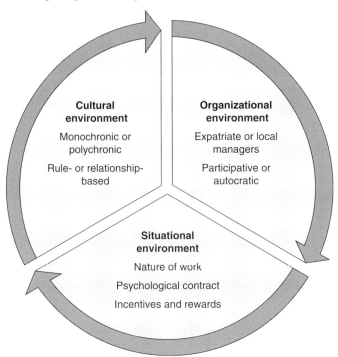

Global management and motivation: developing action plans

Based on this assessment, a number of motivational tools exist that managers can draw upon to help shape their local incentive and reward systems. These include the following.

1   Understand the local work environment

As discussed in this chapter, work values, incentives, and rewards often vary widely across cultures. Individuals assigned to work or manage in foreign cultures need to understand the local work environment in order to succeed (see Exhibit 9.11). This entails advance preparation, when possible, including readings and discussions with people from the local culture. It also requires clear observations and a willingness to learn and adapt upon arrival. Simply put, the more that managers know and understand about a new place of work prior to their arrival, the greater the chances of success. This topic was explored in some detail in Chapter 2, and the reader might wish to review this material.

Exhibit 9.11 Action plans for global management and motivation

(1) Understand local work environments	(2) Understand corporate constraints on rewards	(3) Manage employee expectations and rewards
• Understand local work environment, including personal work values and psychological contracts. • Understand local work–life balance. • Build productive working relationships with subordinates and others	• Understand company expectations and resources regarding performance expectations and rewards. • Develop long-range incentive and compensation program. • Develop managerial flexibility to fit local situations.	• Create realistic employee expectations regarding wage–effort bargain. • Develop and reinforce a psychological contract that is mutually understood and accepted. • Manage fair and equitable distribution of rewards as seen locally, not just organizationally.

2   Understand corporate constraints on rewards

Organizations face equity pressures from two fronts. On the one hand, employees frequently compare themselves with others in similar positions in the country where they operate. On the other hand, individuals in the same position in different countries may be paid very differently but work side by side in on-site or virtual environments. For example, many international air carriers pay flight attendants according to their local wage environments (that is, the country in which they were hired and officially posted), even though they are working side by side in the cabin. What is fair here? The adage "When in Rome, do as the Romans" is not as simple to implement as it may appear when dealing with global organizations. Consider the example of company cars discussed above. Is it fair to offer employees the same rewards that their colleagues in similar companies in the same country receive or the same rewards they would receive in the same position within their firm but in different countries? What happens to expatriates moving from one country to another?

To get around these issues, organizations often come up with corporate policies that leave some leeway to accommodate local conditions – such as the availability and quality of a health program – but at the same time establish a set of parameters to guide incentives and rewards across locations. In many cases, individual managers have limited discretion in how much they can offer in terms of rewards. As such, they need to understand what the home- and host-country constraints are that they have to deal with as they work to motivate the workforce.

3   Manage expectations and rewards

Finally, managers can work hard to create realistic job expectations. This includes being candid about what jobs entail and what is expected of local employees. This seems obvious, but people are frequently surprised how often managers are ambiguous (and sometimes less than truthful) about specific job requirements. In addition, managers can also be transparent concerning what specific rewards are realistically available in exchange for employee work effort. It also includes being candid with employees concerning the available rewards for superior performance, as well as the potential consequences of poor performance.

A famous illustration of this from several years ago involves an auto company that asked its employees to work doubly hard during the coming year to improve the company's productivity and balance sheet. One year later company executives announced that, due to productivity increases, it was laying off many of its employees because they were no longer needed. Once again, trust issues become salient when managers pursue such shortsighted strategies.

In summary, managers have a responsibility to balance – and manage – long-term expectations with outcomes and rewards. While gamesmanship or ambiguity may be a common strategy in the world of compensation, it is not usually a successful one.

Summary points

- Whether a manager's assignment is to supervise local employees in an overseas operation, build or manage a global partnership, or simply fly in to check on the progress of a team project, the challenge basically remains the same: he or she is immersed in a foreign environment with unfamiliar or uncomfortable norms and then expected to perform. In most cases, moreover, it is the responsibility of the singular outsider – the global manager – and not the multitude of insiders to make adjustments.
- Work values reflect individual beliefs about desirable end states or modes of conduct for pursuing desirable end states. They provide individuals with guidelines and standards for determining their own behavior and evaluating the behavior of others. They are important because they signal what individuals and groups of employees see as being most important about their work efforts. They also influence the actual quality and focus of employee endeavors and the ways in which various employees may respond to work motivation strategies and tactics.

- A psychological contract represents an implicit understanding between people concerning exchange relationships. In the workplace, this is most commonly seen in perceived agreements between supervisors and employees over the wage–effort bargain. What benefits are offered to employees in the form of salaries, benefits, and job security in exchange for their talents, efforts, commitment, and performance? These contracts can also be seen in mutual agreements between colleagues, co-workers, and team members. They can be tenuous, in the sense that they are mutual understandings between individuals or groups, yet nothing is written down. Perceptions and trust play a major role in their mutual acceptance. The reason psychological contracts become important for new managers is that they contain information that they typically won't have, but will affect their job success.

- People's cultural surroundings often influence their hopes and expectations. Likewise, people's expectations or preferences as rewards for work are also culturally based to some degree.

- Research has identified an equity principle in many Western countries whereby people are motivated to achieve or restore equity (i.e., fairness) between themselves and others they compare themselves to. Some international researchers have suggested that the equity principle may be somewhat culture-bound, however. Notably in Asia and the Middle East, examples abound concerning individuals who on the face of it readily accept a clearly recognizable state of inequity in order to preserve their view of societal harmony.

- Without a highly motivated workforce that uses its brains, not just its backs, competitive advantage becomes highly problematic. This is particularly true as we move further into an era in which technology and knowledge often determine winners and losers. Simply put, competitive organizations need all their employees striving on behalf of the organization's goals and objectives, not just the people at the top. The challenge for global managers is to accomplish this within a work context in which behavior is often determined by cultural variations beyond their control.

- Different countries often use different motivational and managerial strategies to get work done. The organizational goals may be similar, but the psychology and concomitant behaviors can be very different. If employee behavior is critical for the success of an organization, and if culture influences such behavior, then it represents a major influence on the ultimate competitiveness of the firm. Knowledge of this fact, as well as an understanding of how culture influences employee behavior and performance, represents a critical strategic asset for global managers in a highly competitive world.

Notes

1　Akio Morita, Edwin M. Reingold, and Mitsuko Shimomura, *Made in Japan: Akio Morita and Sony*. New York: Morrow, 1988.

2　Carol Hymowitz and Matt Murray, "GE's Welch discusses his ideas on motivating employees," *Wall Street Journal,* June 21, 1999, p. A1.

3　Yongsun Paik and Yong Suhk Pak, "The changing face of Korean management of overseas affiliates," in Chris Rowley and Yongsun Paik (eds.), *The Changing Face of Korean Management*. London: Routledge, 2009, pp. 165–88; Yongsun Paik, Praveen Parboteeach, and Won Shul Shim, "The relationship between perceived compensation, organizational commitment, and job satisfaction: the case of Mexican workers in the Korean maquiladoras," *Journal of Human Resources Management*, 2007, 18(10), pp. 1768–81.

4　Paik and Pak, "The changing face of Korean management," p. 168.

5　George England, *The Manager and His Values: An International Perspective from the United States, Japan, Korea, India, and Australia*. Cambridge, MA: Ballinger, 1975.

6　George England, *National Work Meanings and Patterns: Constraints on Management Action*. Norman, OK: Center for Economic and Management Research, 1986; David Thomas, *International Management: A Cross-Cultural Perspective*. Thousand Oaks, CA: Sage, 2002, pp. 210–12.

7　*The Economist*, "Jobs for life," *The Economist*, December 22, 2007, pp. 68–9.

8　Diane Brady, "Rethinking the rat race," *Business Week*, August 26, 2002, p. 143.

9　Gregory Viscusi, "US production still tops Europe's," *Register Guard*, August 27, 2002, p. B-1.

10　Diane Brady, "Rethinking the rat race," *Business Week*, August 26, 2002, p. 143.

11　Terrence R. Mitchell and Denise Daniels, "Motivation," in Walter C. Borman, Daniel R. Ilgen, and Richard J. Klimoski (eds.), *Comprehensive Handbook of Psychology,* vol. XII, *Industrial and Organizational Psychology*, 5th edn. New York: Wiley, 2002, pp. 225–54; Wendelien Van Eerde and Henk Thierry, "VIE functions, self-set goals, and performance: an experiment," in Miriam Erez, Uwe Kleinbeck, and Henk Thierry (eds.), *Work Motivation in the Context of a Globalizing Economy*. Mahwah, NJ: Lawrence Erlbaum, 2001, pp. 131–47; Lyman W. Porter, Gregory A. Bigley, and Richard M. Steers, *Motivation and Work Behavior*. New York: McGraw-Hill, 2003.

12　Porter, Bigley, and Steers, *Motivation and Work Behavior*.

13　Geert Hofstede, *Culture's Consequence: International Differences in Work-Related Values*. Beverly Hills, CA: Sage, 2001; Carl F. Fey, "Opening the black box of motivation: a cross-cultural comparison of Sweden and Russia," *International Business Journal*, 2005, 14(3), pp. 345–67.

14　James Abegglen and George Stalk, *Kaisha: The Japanese Corporation*. New York: Basic Books, 1985; Kae H. Chung, Hak Chong Lee, and Ku Hyun Jung, *Korean Management: Global Strategy and Cultural Transformation*. Berlin: Walter de Gruyter, 1997.

15 Ken I. Kim, Hun-Joon Park, and Nori Suzuki, "Reward allocations in the United States, Japan, and Korea: a comparison of individualistic and collectivistic cultures," *Academy of Management Journal*, 1990, 33(1), pp. 188–98.

16 Frank Koller, *Spark: How Old-Fashioned Values Drive a Twenty-First-Century Corporation*. New York: Public Affairs, 2010.

17 Donald F. Hastings, "Lincoln Electric's harsh lessons from international expansion," *Harvard Business Review*, 1999, 77(3), pp. 163–78, p. 164.

18 Jamie O'Connell, *Lincoln Electric: Venturing Abroad*. Boston: Harvard Business School Press; Hastings, "Lincoln Electric's harsh lessons."

19 Hastings, "Lincoln Electric's harsh lessons," p. 174.

20 Hastings, "Lincoln Electric's harsh lessons," p. 178.

21 Fritz Rieger and Durhane Wong-Rieger, "A configuration model of national influence applied to southeast Asian organizations," in *Research Conference on Business in Southeast Asia: The Proceedings of a Conference, May 12–13*, 1990. Ann Arbor: University of Michigan Press, pp. 87–106.

22 Paul Thorne, quoted in Richard D. Hill, *EuroManagers*. Brussels: Europublications, p. 160.

23 Carol Hymowitz and Matt Murray, "General Electric's Welch discusses his ideas on motivating employees," *Wall Street Journal*, June 21, 1999, p. A-1.

24 *Business Week*, "Detroit south," *Business Week*, March 16, 1992, p. 64.

25 Rabindra Kanungo and Robert Wright, "A cross-cultural study of managerial job attitudes," *Journal of International Business Studies*, 1983, 14(2), pp. 115–29, p. 115.

26 Richard M. Steers and Carlos Sanchez-Runde, "Culture, motivation, and work behavior," in Martin J. Gannon and Karen L. Newman (eds.), *The Blackwell Handbook of Cross-Cultural Management*. Oxford: Blackwell, pp. 190–215.

27 Steers and Sanchez-Runde, "Culture, motivation, and work behavior."

28 Steers and Sanchez-Runde, "Culture, motivation, and work behavior," p. 205.

29 Steers and Sanchez-Runde, "Culture, motivation, and work behavior."

30 Sang Nam, "Culture, control, and commitment in an international joint venture," *International Journal of Human Resource Management*, 1995, 6(3), pp. 553–67.

31 Ingmar Bjorkman and Charles Galunic, "Lincoln Electric in China," in Dennis Briscoe and Randall Schuler (eds.), *International Human Resource Management*. London: Routledge, 2004, pp. 420–36.

32 *The Economist*, "Women in China: the sky's the limit," *The Economist*, November 28, 2011, pp. 14–16.

33 Jena McGregor, "The right perks," *Business Week*, January 28, 2008, pp. 42–4.

34 McGregor, "The right perks."

CHAPTER 10

Working with global teams

MANAGEMENT CHALLENGE

So far we have considered four multicultural competencies designed to improve global management techniques: communication, negotiation, leadership, and managing a global workforce. We now come to the fifth competence: working with global teams. If one-on-one relationships can be complicated, imagine how much more difficult it can be to create or work in a cohesive, collaborative work team consisting of multiple individuals from around the world. The challenges here include understanding the strengths and weaknesses of various types of work teams, knowing how to build and then lead a global team, and understanding how to build trust among team members. Clearly, this is no easy task, but in today's highly competitive environment managers have little choice but to learn how to get the best out of the people around them.

Chapter outline

Applications

Getting Americans and Japanese to work together is like mixing hamburger with sushi.

Atsushi Kagayama[1]

Former vice president, Panasonic Corporation, Japan

When we sit together as Germans, Swiss, Americans, and Swedes, with many of us living, working, and traveling in different places, the insights can be remarkable. But you have to force people into these situations.

Percy Barnevik[2]

Former CEO, ABB, Switzerland

Willy Chiu was parked outside a Palo Alto, California, Seven-Eleven store early one evening when he heard the ping of an instant message arriving.[3] It was the Tokyo-based head of IBM's Asia operations, with urgent news: a major competitor was homing in on a pivotal project IBM had been chasing. The job, to develop a new IT system for a South Korean bank, could be worth up to $100 million. Chiu, who runs IBM's worldwide network of elite labs, was needed to help develop a pilot product. The plea ignited a flurry of online, BlackBerry, and iPhone conversations across four continents. Within minutes Chiu had eighteen chat windows open simultaneously on his laptop. "How do we mobilize resources worldwide?" he typed in one message to the head of worldwide operations in San Jose. "I'll take the lead," responded IBM's country manager in Seoul. Chiu dashed off a note asking a team in Beijing to free up staff and quickly received confirmation that they were on the case. Then a banking specialist from England chimed in: "Our team can provide reference cases from Spain." Chiu to his administrative assistant: "Stella, please change my flight to a later time tonight. Also, looks like I may go to Korea again in a few weeks." Chiu to his wife: "Will be working late."

IBM aims to set itself apart, with a spate of Web-based services that make it easier for its 360,000-member staff to "work as one virtual team," says Chiu. The company has launched what it calls an *innovation portal*, whereby any employee with a product idea can use online chat boxes to organize a team, line up resources, and gain access to market research. Developers in IBM labs around the world can then collaborate on prototypes and testing. This way, enterprising staff can build a global team in as little as half an hour and cut the time to start a business from at least six months to around thirty days. To see how this works, IBM organized a twenty-member group including staff from Japan, Brazil, and the United Kingdom for a major US telecom client that needed a Web-based tool to launch new services, such as video streaming for cellphones (see Exhibit 10.1). IBM staff experts built a working prototype in two weeks and delivered a finished product in two months.

Exhibit 10.1 Key relationships in global teams (example: IBM)

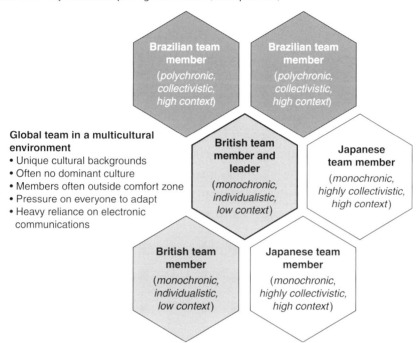

Global team in a multicultural environment
- Unique cultural backgrounds
- Often no dominant culture
- Members often outside comfort zone
- Pressure on everyone to adapt
- Heavy reliance on electronic communications

Brazilian team member
(*polychronic, collectivistic, high context*)

Brazilian team member
(*polychronic, collectivistic, high context*)

British team member and leader
(*monochronic, individualistic, low context*)

Japanese team member
(*monochronic, highly collectivistic, high context*)

British team member
(*monochronic, individualistic, low context*)

Japanese team member
(*monochronic, highly collectivistic, high context*)

For global corporations, the borderless world of Willy Chiu offers a glimpse of what is to come. International success once meant having employees and factories on the ground from São Paulo to Silicon Valley to Shanghai. Coordinating their activities was a deliberately planned effort managed from corporate headquarters. Today the challenge is very different, and includes building sizable and globally dispersed workforces into superfast, efficient organizations. Given the conflicting needs of multinational staff and the swiftly shifting nature of competition brought about by the internet, some think that this has become an almost impossible task. Meanwhile, getting global employees to collaborate instantly – not tomorrow or next week, but now – requires nothing less than a management revolution. Complicating matters even further is the fact that the very idea of a company is evolving from a single outfit with full-time employees and a recognizable hierarchy to something much more fluid, with a classic corporation at the center of an ever-shifting network of suppliers and outsourcers, some of which join the team only for the duration of a single project.

In order to adapt, global firms are hiring sociologists to unlock the secrets of teamwork among colleagues who have never met one another. They are arming staff with an arsenal of new-tech tools to keep them perpetually connected. They include software that helps engineers co-develop 3D prototypes in virtual worlds and services that promote social networking and that track employees and outsiders who have the skills needed to nail a job. Using Global Positioning System locators has become commonplace. Corporations are investing lavishly in posh campuses, crafting leadership training centers, and offering thousands of online courses to develop pipelines of talent.

While IBM may be ahead of the curve here, most firms now make some use of on-site or virtual teams to manage and operate various aspects of their global operations. They have to in order to compete. Sometimes these teams consist of groups of employees from one country or culture who join forces to work on an issue of local or global nature (e.g., developing a business strategy for the Baltic region, launching a new product or service in southeast Asia, etc.). At other times teams are made up of individuals from different parts of the world who work together to achieve a common goal. In this chapter we focus on the latter – that is, teams consisting of sometimes highly diverse members from different countries or cultures working together either on-site or virtually.

Global teams

A *global team* is a group of employees selected from two or more cultural contexts, and sometimes two or more companies, who work together to coordinate, develop, or manage some aspect of a firm's global operations.[4] Companies usually turn to such teams either when they need specific cross-cultural expertise on some aspect of the business (e.g., developing a new product marketing strategy for a particular geographic region) or when they partner with a foreign firm (e.g., form a strategic alliance or international joint venture). Many firms prefer using such teams because they can often do a better job than homogeneous teams consisting exclusively of either home- or host-country nationals. Multicultural global teams can provide an opportunity to incorporate widely differing social, cultural, and business perspectives into key decisions affecting the success of international operations.

Types of global teams

Not only do teams vary in their degree of heterogeneity and tasks, but they also vary regarding the location of their team members. At one extreme, team

Exhibit 10.2 Types of teams

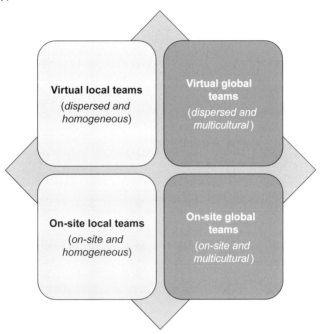

members are all located in the same place and meet face to face to accomplish most of the tasks. (This is sometimes referred to as a traditional, or on-site, team.) At the other extreme, teams are dispersed around the global and seldom – or never – meet face to face. Instead, tasks are accomplished virtually, with the help of information and communication technology, such as videoconferencing, Skype, and even e-mails (see Exhibit 10.2). Each approach has its own unique advantages and challenges.

In real life, however, teams may not always fit neatly into these boxes. Both virtuality and heterogeneity are a matter of degree. For instance, on-site teams may meet face to face periodically but accomplish a significant amount of tasks independently and communicate primarily through e-mail and telephone, even though they are working in the same building. Likewise, so-called local teams may include members from different cultural backgrounds even though they may live in the same town. Our principal focus here, however, is the right-hand side of this exhibit, dealing with both forms of global teams: *on-site teams* and *virtual teams* (see Exhibit 10.3).

Exhibit 10.3 Characteristics of on-site and virtual global teams

Global team characteristics	On-site global teams	Virtual global teams
Team location and working patterns	Team members work regularly in close proximity; strong reliance on face-to-face interactions.	Team members work separately from various locations; strong reliance on virtual communications technology.
Team composition	Heterogeneous; multicultural.	Heterogeneous; multicultural.
Required skills for interaction	Emphasis on interpersonal and intercultural skills.	Emphasis on interpersonal, intercultural, and technical skills.
Principal uses	When face-to-face discussions are important and possible, building trust and relationships are important, and decision time horizons can vary.	When key players are unable to co-locate, when contextual information from different locations is important, when tasks are well defined and can be accomplished independently, when ambiguity is low.
Principal team challenges	Communicating, making decisions, and taking actions in a largely face-to-face environment, in which interpersonal styles can differ significantly (e.g., nonverbal communication; language subtleties, preserving or losing face).	Communicating, making decisions, and taking actions in a largely distributed and often computer-mediated environment, in which interpersonal style, communication, and body language are largely unseen. Developing cross-cultural understanding and sensitivity from a distance. Developing productive working relationships from a distance. Understanding communications and reaching decisions in a largely computer-mediated environment.
Principal leadership challenges	Sensitivity to cross-cultural differences. Accommodate divergent viewpoints. Coordinate interpersonal group dynamics and keep members on-task. Master intercultural communications by listening for contextual messages behind content messages. Lead group efforts to achieve targeted objectives.	Sensitivity to cross-cultural differences. Accommodate divergent viewpoints. Coordinate computer-mediated group dynamics and keep members on-task. Master intercultural communications by reading between the lines on written messages and videoconferencing. Lead group efforts to achieve targeted objectives.

Application 10.1   Working together, working apart

Sometimes, global project teams evolve from on-site to virtual, depending on the situation. One example of this concerns the three authors of this book, an American, a Spaniard, and a Brazilian now living in Canada. This "global team" began as an on-site project team and grew out of necessity into a virtual project team. At the beginning of the project, two members of the team each knew the third author, but did not know each other. Electronic communications were used to bring the three team members together. Soon all three members were living in separate countries, increasing the reliance on electronics. This dispersion, in our view, led to a better outcome, not unlike project teams in the business world. It

Application 10.1   (cont.)

opened numerous opportunities for taking multiple, and not necessarily congruent, perspectives on various topics.

The lessons were many. First and foremost, we learned that facts and realities often have transient meanings, and can change both across time and borders. We learned that neither individualism nor collectivism is inherently good; that mastery and harmony can at times work in tandem; and that time has many different definitions and applications. Calendars and stopwatches do not necessarily lead to meaningful progress. Goal-directed behavior is often complemented, not displaced, by the more jumbled intersections of multiple simultaneous activities. We learned that rules and relationships can both create a vibrant and committed multicultural team that works closely together in a spirit of flexibility and goal orientation. We learned that nonlinear systems can often trump linearity in both quality and completeness. We learned that cultural friction between partners is often a desirable quality, not something to be avoided. In our case, it led to greater creativity and a more realistic view of the world of work. We learned that assuming a leadership role can be both loud and assertive or quiet and subtle, but both approaches involve disagreements and debates. Finally, we learned that working in a global team can be a great deal of fun, and can create an environment in which much can be learned and shared.

Think about it . . .

(1) This project team involved people from three countries writing a book (this book). How might an academic team like this differ from a business project team? Are these differences significant for purposes of team management or team success? Explain.

(2) If you were assigned the responsibility of recruiting a multinational team in your company, how would you go about finding and securing the services of the best team members possible?

(3) If you were assigned the responsibility of managing a multinational team, what kind of introduction would you give at the beginning of your first meeting?

(4) What do you think your own personal strengths are in managing a global team? What would you be good at? At the same time, what possible weaknesses might you have in such an assignment?

Advantages and drawbacks of global teams

Despite their name, most multinational corporations probably have more national (or single-nation) teams than they do multinational teams. This is not surprising, since, in many ways, multinationals are collections of multiple companies with multiple local operations. For example, if we look at marketing teams within Velux America, a division of the Danish manufacturer of skylights and solar water heaters, it is not surprising that most of these teams are comprised exclusively of Americans. The same can be said for Velux Company Ltd., the division covering the United Kingdom and Ireland. Team members are almost exclusively English, Irish, Scottish, or Welsh. Indeed, within this sphere, all the local marketing teams in Ireland are specifically Irish. This practice makes sense in terms of understanding and serving local markets. Within the larger Velux operations, however, headquartered in Denmark, *global* marketing strategies and coordination across various local divisions requires teams composed of people from across the company's marketing regions.

Global teams come in a variety of shapes, forms, and sizes. Some companies use multicultural or transnational development teams or product launch teams to help develop or refine products that are aimed at multiple international markets. Other firms use multicultural functional business teams in such areas as international marketing or core R&D technology development. Multicultural teams bring cultural diversity to help solve specific challenges, and exist naturally in both the regional and the global head-quarters of many multinational firms, and in various international strategic alliances and joint ventures.[5] Multicultural teams also bring international expertise to decision making and managerial actions that can otherwise be missing in less diverse teams. These benefits – and some disadvantages – are summarized in Exhibit 10.4.

Exhibit 10.4 Advantages and drawbacks of global teams

Team functions	Advantages and drawbacks of global teams
Creativity and problem solving	Frequently more creative in developing ideas and solutions.
Group cohesiveness	Often more difficult to develop close-knit groups.
Understanding foreign markets	Often increases understanding of global markets.
International marketing	Often more effective in working with international customers.
Decision-making effectiveness	Frequently takes longer to make decisions or reach consensus, but resulting decisions are often more comprehensive, realistic, and acceptable to all.
Time to implementation	Action plans can take longer to implement.
Work habits	Different work habits can lead to conflicts and misunderstandings.
Managing employees	Often better understanding of multinational employees.

Virtual global teams

An increasingly popular approach to global teams today is the *virtual global team*. The virtual global team takes advantage of technology to draw knowledge and resources from different parts of the organization and different geographical locations without relocating workers. Virtual global teams are characterized by a collaborative network of people dispersed across spatial, temporal, cultural, and organizational boundaries, and working together to achieve common goals. In other words, while on-site teams emphasize time, virtual teams emphasize space.

Although culture does play a role in the acceptance and use of technologies and work arrangements, technology also influences culture and norms of behavior in a reciprocal fashion. As people incorporate technologies into their lives, they develop new ways of dealing and relating to tasks and people. For example, a few years ago, when people needed information, they went to the nearest library. Today most people go first to Google or some other internet search engine. The way – and frequency – we get information has changed. Similarly, the persistent use of technology may very well shape the way individuals work and relate, changing the way cultures interact.

Special challenges of virtual global teams

For managers, this means great opportunities, but also challenges. As technology changes the way work is organized, managers need to help members to make sense of new ways of working and relating to the organization.[6] Not only is our relationship with technology likely to change, but our relationship with work and with each other will also have to be adjusted. Managers will be in charge of keeping it together, preventing dispersed forces from pulling organizations apart, and holding the organization together through effective communication and the enunciation of clear goals and shared meaning.

Successful global managers understand that technology alone will not do the trick. It does not matter how good the technology is, and how effectively the task may get done; it is important to remember that individuals are behind the computer. As such, human dynamics and relational issues are just as important as – or more so than – the technology and the task-related issues at hand.[7] In other words, the leader in a virtual team is a social problem solver and needs to create the conditions for workers to succeed in a virtual environment.

Perhaps the biggest challenge of working with virtual teams is that the members, spread as they are across different boundaries, have to learn a completely different way of interacting, overriding age-old human preferences for social interaction. Many of these changes can be beneficial for communication and team performance, but some negative consequences also exist. Three such limitations can be identified that lead to a lack of shared understanding. Shared understanding requires more than information exchange; it requires people to learn together, relate to one another, and develop mutual expectations about the nature of the goal, the task, and the processes necessary to accomplish it.[8]

Lack of mutual knowledge and context

First, consider the lack of mutual knowledge. When team members are dispersed across a distance, they typically work in different contexts, live in different time zones, and have access to different information.[9] Geographically dispersed teams are able to take advantage of these differences to obtain and use knowledge from multiple contexts. Whereas on-site teams must search for and may miss important market, cultural, and contextual information, teams with greater geographic reach have access to diverse knowledge. While greater geographic reach provides access to more diverse information, dispersed team members lack mutual knowledge, which can lead to an obstruction of information flow. Also known as "common ground," mutual knowledge is the knowledge that individuals have in common and are aware that they share.[10] In other words, mutual knowledge refers to the common basis of information that does not have to be repeated when communicating.

Relatedly, when communicating across distances, people also have a tendency to omit context or contextual information from their messages and discussions, erroneously assuming similarities between locales. For example, one individual reported that, when he was working on a project with a team member in another country, he repeatedly asked for copies of a document to be mailed to HQ, but never received any response. After some time he discovered that there was no photocopier easily available to the foreign team member.

To make matters worse, when contextual information is communicated, it is frequently ignored or forgotten. It is difficult to imagine remote partners' contexts, and even harder to update our mental picture of their contexts as their situation changes.[11] This difficulty in understanding the other's situation also hinders our ability to identify which aspects of our own situation need to be explained. This lack of mutual knowledge frequently creates conflict, as remote partners fail to understand why others fail to honor deadlines, insist on particular points, or drop out of communication without warning.[12] For example, if we have an on-site meeting at 8:00 a.m. on a particularly bad weather day and a colleague is late, we quickly assume that our colleague must be stuck in traffic or is having difficulties arriving because of the weather. When our online colleague does not show up at the scheduled time and has no way of contacting us, however, we do not have any contextual information to make sense of the absence, and may erroneously attribute his or her absence to a lack of interest or responsibility. Similarly, while we do not expect an answer during an important local holiday, we may not be aware of other countries' holidays and may misinterpret the other side's silence.

Global virtual teams are also likely to face important cultural differences. Although a wealth of academic and practitioner literature recognizes and discusses the challenges of working abroad and working with people from different cultures (see Chapter 3), much less is known about how we deal with other cultures without the benefit of "seeing" how different things are abroad. In face-to-face cross-cultural situations, managers are advised to rely on contextual information in order to make sense of the communication. In virtual communications, however, such contextual information is not available, and we may not be looking for it, despite the fact that it is still there.

For example, if we arrive by plane in, say, South Africa, we quickly notice that it is not home. The architecture, the smells, the way the people dress and talk, the accents, and the gestures all remind us that we are in a foreign environment and therefore should suspend judgment, pay attention, and assume nothing. When we receive an e-mail from someone in South Africa, however, we are likely to be in the comfort of our own environment, we do not hear any accent, we do not see anything different, and we may fail to realize that we are in a cross-cultural situation. The chances are that our South African counterpart has been influenced by his or her culture while writing the e-mail and has embedded meaning in his or her communication that we may be unable to uncover.

Overdependence on technology

Second, an overdependence on technology can often create problems. Technology brings both beneficial and detrimental influences to virtual teams. Information technology has made virtual teams possible by allowing instantaneous information exchange regardless of geographic location. Teams transmitting information electronically may benefit from the fact that information is recorded prior to transmission, providing a record of transactions. Additionally, the ability to hand off work to teammates across time zones allows work to continue around the clock. Technological dependence for communication may lead to some problems, however, and these shortcomings curtail understanding, experimentation, and creative problem solving.

Unfortunately for all of us, e-mails sometimes fail to reach their final destinations, attachments may not go through, and different versions of documents may be erroneously circulated. Sometimes members send information to one team member but assume that everyone had access to that information. Even when messages get through, members can't control how the others will read or interpret their messages.

When communicating face to face, we indicate what we consider to be important through changes in the tone of voice, facial expressions, and nonverbal gestures. Likewise, receivers signal their understanding by nodding their heads, gesticulating, or making brief verbalizations such as "Yeah" and "M-hmmm." These signaling activities are more time- and energy-consuming in technology-mediated communication, and emoticons are of little help. Most of the time people do not write e-mails checking their understanding of message context, saying something to the effect of "I read your e-mail, and this is what I understood. Is that what you meant?"[13]

Loss of useful details

Third, virtual teams often entail a loss of useful detail. When communicating via text-based media, such as e-mail, electronic chat, and text messaging, not only is less information richness transmitted (e.g., body language or facial expressions), but less is explained as well. Writing down details tends to be laborious, so individuals do not write as much as they would say, hence oversimplifying communication and omitting important information.[14] For example, consider how much information you would provide a colleague who missed an important meeting if the request for the information came in person, a telephone call, or a text message.

One study found that, in similar circumstances, individuals communicating via text-based e-mail technology exchanged an average of 740 words, while individuals communicating verbally exchanged an average of 1,702 words.[15] Text messaging obviously leads to even shorter messages. This, of course, is understandable, as it is very difficult to know what information is important, and it takes a lot of work to write down details of our everyday reality, not knowing which parts of it may be relevant to our dispersed team members. An over-reliance on e-mails may result in a vast amount of information exchange, but little shared understanding.

Managing virtual global teams

Working with – or, indeed, managing – a virtual global team with workers distributed around the globe suggests a need to select members carefully with the right skills, abilities, and motivation to work in a highly complex and often ambiguous environment. It also suggests a need to provide these individuals with extensive training in technology use, virtual communication, virtual work, and cultural sensitivity. In addition, expectations and reward systems ought to be consistent with the goals and nature of virtual work. Managers can't control the behavior of virtual team members and members are not "seen" while at work. Clear expectations, and measurable goals, are a better way of judging employees' performance and assigning rewards.

Not all tasks can be accomplished virtually, and successful virtual managers understand this. Some tasks are very difficult to accomplish using lean media and may require members to meet face to face, at least for an initial phase, so that participants can get to know each other and negotiate ways to interact. As a rule of thumb, the higher the level of decision process or the more complex the message, the richer the communication medium required.[16] In other words, simpler tasks can easily be accomplished through lean media, while some tasks are better saved for on-site teams. In cases when insights from several regions are required, multicultural teams may be assigned temporarily to a location to work on-site in a task.

Once managers have identified the right tasks, the right people, the right technology, and the right reward systems, they must work on processes to enable coordination, shared understanding, and trust. Managers can ease the challenges caused by a lack of common context by actively working in disseminating information. For example, periodic face-to-face meetings may be arranged when possible. If it is impossible or too costly to have all members visit each other, one member of each location may visit remote locations and share information. Additionally, video- and teleconferences should be utilized for information sharing, at which each member is invited to tell how he or she is doing. This will create the conditions for contextual information to emerge, as members have the opportunity to mention things that are important parts of their reality, such as other projects or pressures they are facing.[17]

Managers also have to facilitate communication among members. They can help members' communication by making communication norms explicit, providing intercultural communication training, and developing team-building interventions that help participants to develop communication rules and build mutual understanding.[18] Managers also need to make sure that individual members do not feel isolated in remote locations. The key word here is "communicate"! Frequent short messages may go a long way to making members feel valued and feel they belong to the team. Exhibit 10.5 summarizes the key issues managers must take into consideration when managing virtual teams.

Exhibit 10.5 Strategies for managing virtual global teams

Team components	Management strategies
People	Selection of members with right skills, abilities, and motivation. Provide training on technology use, virtual communication, and cultural sensitivity. Align reward systems with nature of distributed work. Set clear expectations and measurable goals for performance appraisal purposes.
Tasks	Select tasks that are appropriate for virtual work. Use richer media for more complex problems.
Processes	Disseminate information among team members. Arrange periodic face-to-face meetings when possible. Allow time for information sharing in video- and teleconferences. Make communication norms explicit. Provide intercultural communication training. Develop team-building interventions. Make sure individuals do not feel isolated. Communicate frequently with all members.

Source: Based on Martha L. Maznevski and Nicholas Athanassiou, "Designing the knowledge-management infrastructure for virtual teams," in Cristina B. Gibson and Susan G. Cohen (eds.), *Virtual Teams that Work: Creating Conditions for Virtual Team Effectiveness.* San Francisco: Jossey-Bass, 2003, pp. 196–213.

Working virtually requires learning a new way of relating and interacting. Success in working virtually as a manager or collaborator requires learning to communicate information that maybe we would not have communicated in a face-to-face interaction. Members must communicate task-related information (details about what has to be done), social-related information (the personality, styles, and reputation of those directly or indirectly involved in the task), and context-related information (the type of support available, equipment, competing responsibilities, cultural norms, holiday schedules, office layouts, local rules, expectations, and regulations).[19]

The conundrum facing virtual teams is that, while they need more information than on-site teams, they usually share less, because members do not realize what information is important, take their own context for granted, assume similarity between locations, and have a difficult time imagining what is different for other members, and because it takes a lot of time and effort to write down or communicate everything. Nonetheless, context affects behavior in ways we may not anticipate. For example, one member may feel pressured to finish a task quickly because he or she is under pressure to tackle another task. Another member may be experiencing technological problems, however, that may be slowing him or her down. In summary, succeeding in a virtual environment requires taking the time to communicate in a variety of ways all the elements that may be affecting the work and work environment. It may include details about progress on the task, how you and other team members work, upcoming holidays, the planned construction on your building, or server shutdowns. In short, everything you know that helps you to do your job is likely to help your counterpart to do his or her job as well.

As technology continues to evolve and globalization pressures increase, it is likely that organizations around the world will continue experimenting with new work arrangements and new ways to take advantage of resources available in different locations. The challenge for global managers is to keep up with these changes and adapt their management styles accordingly.

Application 10.2   Distributed teams at Dow Chemical

Consider the example of Dow Chemical as it tries to navigate in this new world.[20] Dow expects 30 percent of its 20,000 workers to retire in the next five years. Meanwhile, enrollment in US chemical engineering schools is declining, forcing Dow to fight against deep-pocketed oil and gas companies for scarce talent. Recruitment is only the beginning of its challenges, though. The hard part is getting people to work well together, especially given that day-and-night collaboration across the globe is growing. Over the past decade many companies rushed to spread key functions, such as product development, to the far corners of the earth. The idea was to save time and money. Corporations are finding that running these new operations requires much more effort than connecting staff by phone and e-mail, however. "One problem with distributing work is that you lose the intimacy of talking things through at a local café," observes Forrester Research network innovation specialist Navi Radjou. In her view, dispersed global teams can be a real struggle.

Think about it . . .
(1) For companies such as Dow Chemical that have historically used on-site global teams effectively, how can they make the jump to using virtual global teams? In other words, do such companies need to make preparations before launching virtual teams, and, if so, what should these preparations consist of?
(2) In view of the lack of transparency of many virtual global teams, how can a manager know when the team is working effectively or when it could be more productive? Explain.

Managing tasks and team processes

A critical issue that comes to the forefront in any discussion of global teams is how they can best be organized and managed. Two factors are important here. First, managers must recognize the principal challenges facing such teams, including how to manage both tasks and processes. Second, managers need to understand what they can do to facilitate team performance. In other words, what are the key success factors here? In this endeavor, getting global teams off to a good start emerges as an essential requirement.

Recruiting and staffing global teams is only the first challenge faced by global firms. Beyond this, strategies and mechanisms must be developed to create truly effective work teams – to get members from divergent cultures to actually work together as a team. Global teams face two fundamental challenges in order to accomplish their mission: managing tasks and managing processes:

Managing tasks

First, global teams must identify their areas of responsibilities and organize their members. Managing tasks involves making sure that all team members understand why the group was formed. This includes clarifying the mission and goals of the team, setting a clear agenda and operating rules for team management, clarifying individual roles and responsibilities, clarifying how decisions will be made, and identifying who is responsible for task accomplishment.

- *Mission and goal setting*. Identifying team mission, goals, and objectives; identifying performance expectations.
- *Task structuring*. Agenda setting; creating operating rules and procedures; time management procedures.
- *Roles and responsibilities*. Division of labor; responsibility charting; team interdependencies; role of leader.
- *Decision making*. Delegation of authority; selection and role of a leader; how decisions should be made.
- *Accountability*. Identifying who is responsible for task accomplishment.

Managing processes

Second, global teams must develop productive group processes to facilitate collective efforts towards goal attainment. Managing group processes includes developing and completing team-building activities, understanding communication flows and patterns among group members, facilitating participation across team members, specifying methods of conflict resolution, and clarifying how and when performance will be assessed.[21]

- *Team building*. Team-building activities; trust building; cross-cultural understanding; opportunities for social interaction.

- *Communication patterns.* Selection of a working language; challenges of language fluency; appropriate use of information technologies.
- *Participation.* Guaranteeing everyone a voice; balancing quiet and more vocal members; getting the best from everyone.
- *Conflict resolution.* Accommodating legitimate differences of opinion; managing constructive conflict; eliminating destructive conflict; strategies for compromise.
- *Performance evaluation.* How and when to evaluate performance; one-way versus two-way evaluations; role of feedback; who evaluates performance.

Application 10.3   Global R&D teams

To see the importance of managing both tasks and processes, let's go back almost twenty years, to an oft-cited example of collaborative failure, and the ability of companies to learn from these failures. In the early 1990s three electronics giants – IBM, Siemens, and Toshiba – tried to form a strategic alliance to develop a new computer chip. Scientists from all three companies were brought to a state-of-the-art research facility in upstate New York to design the next-generation semiconductor. The idea was to pool their knowledge to beat the competition. Unfortunately, each group of scientists quickly identified problems with the joint venture. German scientists from Siemens were shocked to find their Toshiba colleagues closing their eyes and appearing to sleep during meetings. They failed to understand that such behavior is a common practice in Japan for concentrating on what is being said. At the same time, the Japanese scientists from Toshiba, who were used to working in groups, found it uncomfortable to sit in small individual offices all day and speak English. Finally, the US managers from IBM complained that the Germans planned too much and that the Japanese wouldn't make clear and decisive decisions. Intergroup trust evaporated as suspicions began to circulate that some researchers were withholding their best information from the group. Over time, the well-intentioned alliance simply melted away.[22]

Now fast-forward to the present, and we see the same three companies in the forefront of global strategic alliances – including with each other. Not only have all three companies learned the strategic importance of global teams in both R&D and marketing, but they have also seen to it that their global teams are now less insular and more multicultural in orientation (see example of IBM above). All three companies now have extensive training programs aimed at improving managers' abilities to work across cultures, including not only cross-cultural communication but also cross-cultural conflict resolution. Moreover, much of their multi-company work is now done virtually instead of face to face. Each company has learned from its past mistakes and now works to face the global economy as a partner instead of a competitor whenever possible.

Think about it...

(1) At the time Siemens, Toshiba, and IBM were having problems; what might they have done to build a more communicative and effective global team?

(2) Today Siemens, Toshiba, and IBM all have numerous successful global partnership and employee teams working around the globe. Can their recent successes be explained simply by the increase in globalization around the world or are there other factors at work here? Explain.

(3) What are the lessons in terms of managing both tasks and processes for other companies contemplating the use of multi-company global teams?

Key success factors in global teams

Working with global teams can bring important advantages. They are usually more creative and innovative than less diverse teams, and can draw on different sources of information as members bring understanding of both different locales and relationships with different stakeholders. The co-location facilitates trust development and the sharing of information. Making such teams work effectively is not an easy task, however, as noted above by Percy Barnevik.[23] It is often more difficult and requires more time to develop group cohesiveness when team members' backgrounds are highly diverse. Moreover, it often takes more time both to reach decisions and to implement them, again because of differences in how decision-making processes are viewed. Finally, people's work habits – the way they approach even simple tasks at work – not only differ significantly across cultures but can also lead to considerable misunderstandings, conflict, and mistrust.

  McGill professor Nancy Adler argues that cultural diversity in work teams provides the biggest asset for teams when team members are engaged in difficult discretionary tasks requiring innovation.[24] Under such circumstances, the differing perspectives provided by having people from different cultures around the table frequently leads to greater insights and a wider array of possible problem solutions. According to Adler, however, when teams are working on simple tasks or are working on implementation problems as opposed to creative or strategic problems, multicultural teams may be of less value. Indeed, they may slow the process. Thus, a multicultural team's greatest asset appears to be during the planning and development (or analysis) stage, not the implementation (or action) stage.

University of Michigan professor Paula Caproni suggests that teams in general achieve synergy by building on five foundations or facilitators: purpose, performance measures, people, process, and practice.[25] These same facilitators apply to a wide variety of global teams, as described in Exhibit 10.6. Global teams that make use of such techniques to manage both tasks and processes typically have an easier time completing their assigned responsibilities in a creative and productive manner. Group objectives, responsibility tasking, and ground rules are clearly understood by members. By contrast, groups that fail to manage these activities tend to do less well, because they spend needless time assessing and reassessing goals and objectives and reinventing solutions to recurring problems that could have been dealt with more easily had a structure and a process been squarely in place to guide behavior.

Exhibit 10.6 Key success factors of global teams

Goals	Key success factors
Clear, engaging purpose	Provide direction, inspiration, and motivation to team members. A clear purpose keeps the team together in difficult situations. A powerful purpose should be consistent with organizational values and missions, create a sense of urgency, be positive and inspiring, be easily understood and remembered, be performance-based, and be flexible, attainable, but challenging.
Performance goals and measures	Provide specific and measurable performance goals to evaluate the team's progress, focus the team's efforts on results, enable team members to see how they contribute to the team's goals, and create milestones that build team commitment, confidence, and competence.
People	Team members need to have complementary skills and together have all the skills needed to accomplish a task. Team members should also be committed to the team's purpose, have a specific expertise or skill set to contribute to the team, and possess problem-solving, decision-making and implementation skills. They should also have relationship skills, including the ability to develop trust, deal with conflict, and communicate effectively, be adaptive, and be aware of their own strengths and weaknesses.
Results-driven processes	To accomplish complex tasks, teams need processes in place to identify problems and opportunities, generate solutions, make trade-offs, agree on decisions, implement solutions, evaluate the consequences of their decisions, and coordinate their efforts. Teams also need relationship processes to help them deal with conflict and develop trust, a sense of cohesiveness, and commitment. These processes rest on norms of behaviors that can be implicit and well assimilated in the team's culture or explicit and well documented in a team contract.
Preparation and practice	One of the most critical aspects of team success – and one frequently neglected – is preparation and disciplined practice. High-performing teams routinely reflect on their performance, identify skills they need to succeed, and make efforts to acquire them.

Application 10.4   Global teams at Nokia

Nokia is another company that has been in the forefront of using global teams, particularly in product development and marketing. Succeeding in building successful teams places a premium on recruiting people who are globally minded from the outset, rather than being just technicians. Nokia succeeds by involving scores of people working in several countries. The company is careful to select people who have a "collaborative mindset" and a range of nationalities, ages, and education levels. Teams are made up of employees who have worked together in the past, as well as others who have never met. Members are encouraged to network online and even share their photographs and personal biographies.

Think about it . . .

(1) Nokia encourages virtual team members to build relationships through networks, as well as sharing photographs and personal biographies. How effective do you think this is compared to building face-to-face relationships between team members? Why?

(2) Is it possible that building team relationships virtually would lead to sharing different types of information from what people might share face to face? What might these differences look like?

(3) If you were selecting global team members, how would you assess whether or not applicants had a "collaborative mindset"? Explain.

Team-building strategies

Managing successful global teams also includes knowing how to build them. This is no easy task if concrete results and ultimate success are important. Successful teams are not generally constructed from whomever in the organization or division is not busy or is otherwise available. Nor are they typically constructed through a "Noah's ark" approach of appointing a member or two from every country represented. Rather, creating effective teams requires considerable thought, attention to detail, and, above all, an understanding of purpose. What is the principal goal of this team? Who can best facilitate this goal? Who is best qualified to organize and supervise this team through goal accomplishment? These are not simple questions, nor can they be resolved in an expedient way.

Building successful teams

The role of a team leader or coordinator is critical in helping global teams develop the foundations for high group cohesion and job performance. As might be expected, managers need to create the right context for teams to succeed, rather than try to intervene and manage group behavior. To this end, managers and coordinators may productively focus their efforts on the following areas (Exhibit 10.7).

- *Select members on the basis of skills.* Select members for their skills and invest in global team members' development: teams need the skills to accomplish their tasks and to work together. Team members should be carefully selected to make sure all necessary skills are available, or, if not, are developed.
- *Provide clear direction.* Provide global teams with direction, purpose, and clear performance goals: team members must believe they have a worthwhile purpose to accomplish and have common expectations regarding their performance goals.[26]

Exhibit 10.7 Leadership and team-building strategies

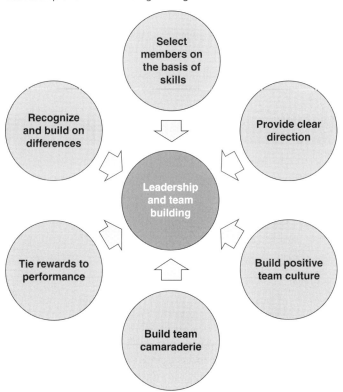

- *Build a positive team culture.* Help nurture a positive team culture: As discussed above, groups develop cultures on the basis of their first experiences and the solutions they find to the problems they encounter.[27] For this reason, the creation of a global team must be carefully managed, as members are monitoring each other and the leader's behavior carefully to infer rules that will inform future behavior. Clear rules of behavior need to be developed at the outset of team formation, with the team purpose in mind.

- *Build team camaraderie.* Encourage global teams to take time to know one another. Teams need to develop a sense of trust and camaraderie that will facilitate creative exchanges. Teams need to spend time together, not only on-task but also building relationships and getting to know each other.

- *Tie rewards to performance.* Develop milestones and provide feedback and rewards throughout the project duration, and not just at the end of it. It will help global teams to reflect on their performance, celebrate small wins, and take action to deal with shortcomings.

- *Recognize and build on differences.* Heterogeneity of cultures and points of view may be a fundamental source of advantage (more knowledge, different perspectives, better problem solving) if used properly but a major challenge if not managed (conflicts and misunderstandings). Teams that recognize their differences and use the difference to their benefit will perform better than homogeneous teams.[28]

Application 10.5   Developing collaborative skills at Accenture

Obviously, it is much easier to identify leadership and team-building skills than to actually develop them. Considerable leadership training is involved. One company that does a lot of this type of training is Accenture. Accenture is a global management consulting, technology services and outsourcing company, with approximately 236,000 people serving clients in more than 120 countries. As a global firm, it is intent primarily on making employees globally minded. It spends millions of dollars each year on employee education, mostly focused on developing collaboration skills with offshore colleagues. In addition, Accenture puts 400 of its most promising managers through a special leadership development program annually. They are assigned to groups that can include Irish, Chinese, Belgians, and Filipinos, and specialists in fields such as finance, marketing, and technology. Over ten months teams meet in different international locations. As part of the program, they select a new project and learn how to tap the company's worldwide talent pool to complete it.

Think about it...

(1) Accenture goes to great lengths and spends a considerable sum to train its managers and consultants to work across cultures. How does such a company carry out a cost–benefit analysis of such expenditures?

(2) Team-building strategies include selecting members on the basis of their skills, building a positive team culture, and building team camaraderie. What can managers do concretely to ensure that these strategies are implemented effectively in global teams?

Building mutual trust

Trust among the members of global teams is both important and elusive. Experience tells us that, without trust between members, the likelihood of long-term team success is significantly reduced. Indeed, a review of the research on successful teams reveals clearly that trust represents one of the key success factors.[29] Exhibit 10.8 compares trust levels by country. As can be seen, the belief that people can be trusted varies somewhat by region. Latin American countries in this study ranged from 7 percent for Brazil to a high of 34 percent for Mexico, while most – but not all – European countries were above this (between 23 and 68 percent). This was particularly true in the

Exhibit 10.8 Can people be trusted?

Country	Agreement (%)	Country	Agreement (%)	Country	Agreement (%)
Brazil	7	Austria	32	United Kingdom	44
Turkey	10	Mexico	34	Ireland	44
Romania	16	South Korea	35	United States	47
Slovenia	17	Spain	35	Canada	52
Latvia	18	India	35	Netherlands	54
Portugal	23	Russia	37	Denmark	58
Chile	24	Germany	38	China	60
Nigeria	24	Japan	42	Finland	64
Argentina	24	Switzerland	43	Norway	67
France	24	Iceland	44	Sweden	68

Source: Data compiled from World Values Survey Association, *World Values Survey*. Ann Arbor, MI: Institute for Social Research, 2000.

Scandinavian countries, where trust levels ranged from 58 to 68 percent. Canada and the United States were in the third quartile, fairly trusting but also cautious.

Now consider another comparison of trust levels, this time within the European Union. A 2011 study found that nearly half the people in the European Union trusted citizens from their own countries, but only 20 percent trusted citizens of other EU countries.[30] In one example of this, German farmers and politicians quickly blamed Spanish farmers for selling them diseased cucumbers, even though it was later found that the problem originated in Germany. Another example can be seen in the recent finger pointing across the EU concerning who is really to blame for the ongoing economic crisis.

Considering the disparity across countries and regions in general trust levels, the issue of trust in global teams raises two questions. First, what is the process by which trust between team members is developed? Second, what can team members do to facilitate or enhance this trust over time? To answer the first question, consider a simplified model of trust development as shown in Exhibit 10.9. As shown here, a principal ingredient in the development of trust is the foundation upon which it is based. In this regard, three "trust expectations" can be identified: competence-based trust – the degree to which members believe the others can deliver on their commitments; incentive-based trust – the extent to which each member believes the others are sufficiently motivated to deliver on their commitments; and benevolence-based trust – the extent to which each member believes the others are making a good-faith effort to meet their commitments.[31]

Following the model, team members weigh each of these three expectations and calculate an overall expectation that the other members of the team can be trusted. This "trust judgment" leads to trusting behavior (e.g., increased openness with members, fewer demands for costly control systems or oversight, etc.) and subsequent trust-related outcomes (e.g., increased efficiency, cost reductions, goal attainment, etc.). While no model can capture the entirety of a complex process such as the development of trust, this model does serve to highlight several of the key factors in the process.

As might be expected, when trust development has to occur between team members from significantly different countries and cultures, the challenges of doing business can increase exponentially. In point of fact, a number of strategies can be identified that, though simple, can nonetheless be effective. To start, team members must be open and candid in their communications with the other members. One misrepresentation of the facts can destroy months of stability and success. This is not to say that all proprietary information (e.g., trade secrets) must be shared; rather, it suggests that other members

Exhibit 10.9 Developing mutual trust

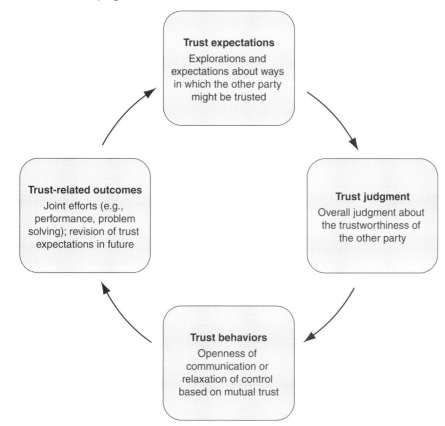

Source: Based on Nancy R. Buchan, "The complexity of trust: understanding the influence of cultural environment on the nature of trust and trust development," in Rabi S. Bhagat and Richard M. Steers (eds.), *Cambridge Handbook of Culture, Organizations, and Work*. Cambridge University Press, 2009, pp. 373–417.

must know when and why information is proprietary. If such information has little to do with the goals of the team project, there is little reason for honest members to push for answers in these confidential areas. On the other hand, when one member keeps to him- or herself confidential information relating to the operation and success of the team, the commitment of other members will likely decline.

Finally, successful teams are universally characterized by mutual benefit for the various individual members. No one likes to remain willingly in an inequitable relationship. When members see others working diligently on behalf of the collective good, however, and not just for their own personal goals, openness and trust will logically follow.

Working with global teams

The use of teams – both on-site and virtual – has increased significantly in recent years as a result of two pressures. First, the move towards increasing globalization has required companies and their managers to work more closely with people from different regions or the world in order to accomplish their goals and objectives. Second, major changes in communications and computer technologies have created new environments in which global teams can operate and new tools for them to use. It only seems logical that these two changes will continue. As such, an understanding of how global teams work, as well as how they can be successfully managed, probably represents one of the most important tools in a manager's repertoire of skills.

Global teams: assessing demands and constraints

Once again, we need to consider demands and constraints from the environment (see Exhibit 10.10). Looking at – or trying to build – teams without reference to the environment in which they operate is clearly a suboptimal management strategy. Differences in local cultures, such as individualism or collectivism or polychronic or monochronic approaches to work and time, often impact the work habits of team members. When the members come from highly diverse cultures, these differences are only exacerbated. Likewise, differences in the organizational environment, such as management style or organizational culture, help shape how teams view their jobs, as well as the extent to which they might be willing to collaborate openly with one another – or with other teams. Finally, situational differences, such as variations in personal characteristics, the location of the team, or differences in personal or subunit goals, or available technologies, can often create significant limitations on managerial action.

Global teams: developing action plans

Within this constraint set, managers clearly have room to maneuver. Their choices must be carefully considered, however. Although a number of management actions have been suggested throughout this chapter, we can distill these down to three key items (see Exhibit 10.11).

Exhibit 10.10 Assessing the global team environment (examples)

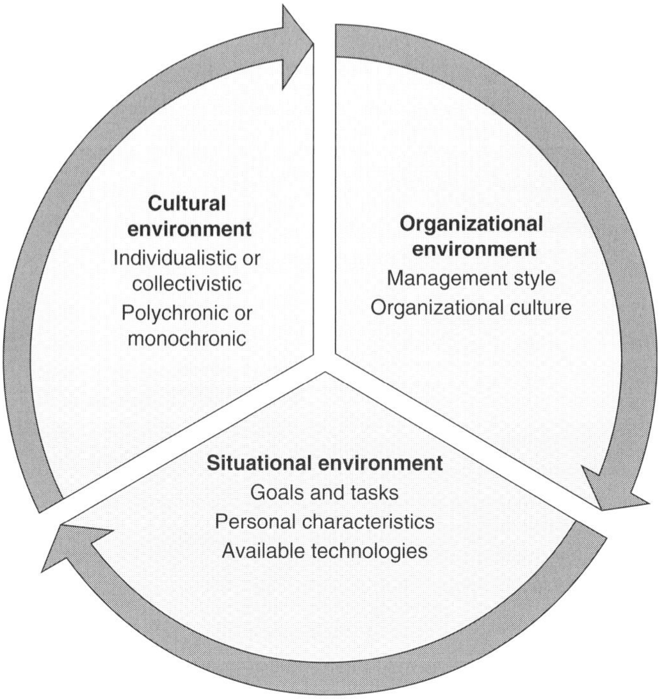

Cultural environment
Individualistic or collectivistic
Polychronic or monochronic

Organizational environment
Management style
Organizational culture

Situational environment
Goals and tasks
Personal characteristics
Available technologies

Exhibit 10.11 Action plans for managing global teams

(1) Build and develop global teams	(2) Manage on-site global teams	(3) Manage virtual global teams
• Mapping: engage differences among team members, and understand their implications. • Bridging: build effective cross-cultural communication • Integrating: use cultural differences to create new ideas, build participation, and resolve conflicts.	• Recognize the importance of managing both team goals and tasks and team progresses. • Build leadership skills in working with global teams. • Build trust among team members. • Understand and utilize conflict resolution strategies.	• Recognize the advantages and drawbacks of virtual teams compared to on-site teams. • Manage the special circumstances under which virtual teams operate (e.g., asynchronous time). • Match communication styles to the virtual team environment.

1   Build global teams

Leadership and team building were discussed above. By way of summary, IMD professor Martha Maznevski has suggested three very useful strategies for getting the most out of team efforts.[32] These are called mapping, bridging, and integrating.

Mapping is engaging the differences between people. It is literally drawing a picture of the similarities and differences in the team, and then working to understand what implications these differences have. There are several different dimensions that can be mapped by managers and team members alike. For example, we might want to map the differences in cultures among different team members. We might want to map differences in personality, in function, in different business units – all the different perspectives that people bring to the team that can be used with the team. It may appear to be somewhat odd to sit down with a team and literally put their names, strengths, and weaknesses on paper, but research has shown that teams that do this actually end up performing better, because they end up being able to use their whole selves in bringing every aspect of the team and the team members into the team, and using it for performance. Mapping – drawing a picture of the different dimensions of diversity in the team – is the first step to using it to get high performance.

The second strategy is *bridging*. In essence, bridging is communicating effectively, taking those differences into account, speaking and listening from the other person's point of view. There are three steps to bridging. The first step is approaching or preparing, really being motivated and wanting to understand other people from their points of view. The second step is "decentering," or putting ourselves in the other person's place and speaking and listening from their point of view. The third step is "re-centering," or finding commonalities, and developing common norms, common definitions of the situation, and common objectives.

The third strategy suggested by Maznevski is *integrating*. This involves using the differences between team members to create new ideas, build participation, resolve conflicts and create a more innovative work environment. Taken together, these three strategies help build well integrated teams committed both to team cohesiveness and to team performance.

2   Manage on-site global teams

As noted above, working with on-site global teams can potentially add value to corporate objectives. Such teams are often more creative and innovative than less diverse teams, and are often able to draw from a wider array of sources of opinion and information. Working on-site can help facilitate trust and the sharing of information. Building such teams can be more difficult than building monocultural teams, however, and it requires more time to develop group cohesiveness. In addition, it can take more time both to reach decisions and to implement them, on account of variations in decision-making processes. Finally, people's work habits – they way they approach even simple tasks at work – not only differ significantly across cultures but can lead to considerable misunderstanding, conflict, and mistrust. As a result, managers are advised to be sensitive to changing levels of team trust, as well as any conflicts that arise.

There are specific action strategies that managers can initiate in this regard. First, they need to recognize the importance of managing both team goals and tasks and team progress. In addition, they can work to build their leadership skills in working with global teams. They should also work to build trust among team members. Finally, managers need to develop their skills in understanding and utilizing conflict resolution strategies where needed.

3   Manage virtual global teams

Emerging electronic technologies have led to an explosion of virtual work, including virtual teams. Although such teams promise improved productivity, this can occur only when such teams are well managed and well led. Opportunities for problems proliferate. Building cohesive virtual teams is problematic in the absence of face-to-face interactions. Social loafing can be a problem, as can overwork (working 24/7). The manager's challenge is to find a productive and sustainable medium. The role of the manager is to understand when and under what circumstances virtual teams have advantages – or, potentially, disadvantages – compared to on-site teams. In many cases there is no choice, as the people we want for our team may reside in different locations.

Beyond this, as discussed above, managers must have sufficient tools to manage effectively regardless of location or technology. This includes recognizing both the advantages and the drawbacks of virtual teams compared to on-site teams. It also includes managing the special circumstances under which virtual teams operate (e.g., asynchronous time). Finally, it includes matching communication technologies to the virtual team environment. This is no easy task, but it is becoming increasingly important as we move with both speed and determination towards a more electronically based work environment.

Summary points

- A global team is a group of employees selected from two or more cultural contexts who work together to coordinate, develop, or manage some aspect of a firm's global operations. Companies usually turn to such teams either when they need specific cross-cultural expertise on some aspect of the business or when they partner with a foreign firm. Many firms prefer using global teams because they can often do a better job than homogeneous teams consisting exclusively of either home- or host-country nationals.

- To be effective, global teams must identify their areas of responsibilities and organize their members. Managing tasks involves making sure that all the team members understand why the group was formed. This includes clarifying the mission and goals of the team, setting a clear agenda and operating rules for team management, clarifying individual roles and responsibilities, clarifying how decisions will be made, and identifying who is responsible for task accomplishment. Second, global teams must develop productive group processes to facilitate collective efforts towards goal attainment. Managing group processes includes developing and completing team-building activities, understanding communication flows and patterns among group members, facilitating participation across team members, specifying methods of conflict resolution, and clarifying how and when performance will be assessed

- While cultural differences can play a role in the acceptance and use of technologies and work arrangements, technology also influences culture and norms of behavior in a reciprocal fashion. As people incorporate technologies into their lives, they develop new ways of dealing and relating to tasks and people. The way – and frequency – with which we receive information has changed. Similarly, the persistent use of technology may well shape the way individuals work and relate, changing the way cultures interact. For managers, this means great opportunities, but also challenges.

- Working virtually requires learning a new way of relating and interacting. Success as a manager or team member requires learning to communicate information that maybe we would not have communicated in a face-to-face interaction. Members have to communicate task-related information, social-related information, and context-related information.

- Trust among the members of global teams is both important and elusive. Without trust between members, the likelihood of long-term team success is significantly reduced. Indeed, a review of the research on successful teams reveals clearly that trust represents one of the key success factors.

■ Several trust-building strategies, though simple, can nonetheless be effective. Teams must be open and candid in their communications with the other members. A misrepresentation of the facts can destroy months of stability and success. This is not to say that all proprietary information must be shared; rather, it suggests that other members must know when and why information is proprietary. If such information has little to do with the goals of the team project, there is little reason for honest members to push for answers in these confidential areas. On the other hand, when one member keeps to him- or herself confidential information relating to the operation and success of the team, the commitment of other members will likely decline.

Notes

1 Personal communication, Atsushi Kagayama, Panasonic Corporation, formerly Matsushita Business Group, Osaka.
2 Cited in David Thomas, *Cross-Cultural Management: Essential Concepts*. Thousand Oaks, CA: Sage, 2009, p. 1.
3 *Bloomberg Business Week*, "The future of work: managing the new workforce," *Bloomberg Business Week*, August 20, 2007.
4 Anil Gupta and Vijay Govindarajan, *Global Strategy and Organization*. New York: Wiley, 2004.
5 Charles C. Snow, "Types of transnational teams," in Transnational Teams Project, *Transnational Teams Resources Guide*. Lexington, MA: International Consortium for Executive Development Research, 1993.
6 Snow, "Types of transnational teams."
7 Martha L. Maznevski and Nicholas Athanassiou, "Designing the knowledge-management infrastructure for virtual teams," in Cristina B. Gibson and Susan G. Cohen (eds.), *Virtual Teams that Work: Creating Conditions for Virtual Team Effectiveness*. San Francisco: Jossey-Bass, 2003, pp. 196–213.
8 Pamela J. Hinds and Suzanne P. Weisband, "Knowledge sharing and shared understanding in virtual teams," in Gibson and Cohen, *Virtual Teams that Work*, pp. 21–36.
9 Catherine D. Cramton, "The mutual knowledge problem and its consequences for dispersed collaboration," *Organization Science*, 2001, 12(3), pp. 346–71.
10 Cramton, "The mutual knowledge problem," p. 346.
11 Cramton, "The mutual knowledge problem."
12 Cramton, "The mutual knowledge problem."
13 Cramton, "The mutual knowledge problem."

14 Catherine D. Cramton and Kara L. Orvis, "Overcoming barriers to information sharing in virtual teams," in Gibson and Cohen, *Virtual Teams that Work*, pp. 214–32.

15 Susan G. Strauss, "Getting a clue: the effects of communication media and information distribution on participation and performance in computer mediated and face-to-face groups," *Small Group Research*, 1996, 27(1), pp. 115–42.

16 Martha L. Maznevski and Katherine M. Chudoba, "Bridging space over time: global virtual team dynamics and effectiveness," *Organization Science*, 2000, 11(5), pp. 473–92.

17 Cramton and Orvis, "Overcoming barriers to information sharing," p. 229.

18 Cramton and Orvis, "Overcoming barriers to information sharing."

19 Cramton and Orvis, "Overcoming barriers to information sharing."

20 John Battelle, *The Search: How Google and Its Rivals Rewrote the Rules of Business and Transformed Our Culture*. New York: Penguin Books, 2005.

21 Susan Schneider and Jean-Louis Barsoux, *Managing Across Cultures*, 2nd edn. London: Prentice Hall, 2003.

22 E. S. Browning, "Side by side: computer chip project brings rivals together, but the cultures clash," *Wall Street Journal*, May 3, 1994, p. A1.

23 Cited in Thomas, *Cross-Cultural Management*, p. 1.

24 Nancy J. Adler, *International Dimensions of Organizational Behavior*, 3rd edn. Cincinnati: South-Western College Publishing, 1997.

25 Paula Caproni, *Management Skills for Everyday Life: The Practical Coach*. Upper Saddle River, NJ: Prentice Hall, 2005, pp. 316–20.

26 Jon R. Katzenbach and Douglas K. Smith, "The discipline of teams," *Harvard Business Review*, 2005, 83(7/8), pp. 162–71.

27 Edgar H. Schein, *Organizational Culture and Leadership*. San Francisco: Jossey-Bass, 2004.

28 Martha L. Maznevski, *IMD: Leading Diverse Teams*, Financial Times video, available at http://video.ft.com/v/62063401001/IMD-Leading-diverse-teams (accessed October 7, 2011).

29 Nancy R. Buchan, "The complexity of trust: understanding the influence of cultural environment on the nature of trust and trust development," in Rabi S. Bhagat and Richard M. Steers (eds.), *Cambridge Handbook of Culture, Organizations, and Work*. Cambridge University Press, 2009, pp. 373–417.

30 Pankaj Ghemawat, "Why can't Europeans get along?," *Fortune*, December 26, 2011, p. 22.

31 Ghemawat, "Why can't Europeans get along?"

32 Mark E. Mendenhall, Joyce S. Osland, Allan Bird, Gary R. Oddou and Martha L. Maznevski, *Global Leadership: Research, Practice and Development*. London: Routledge, 2008.

CHAPTER 11

Living and working globally

MANAGEMENT CHALLENGE

Living and working globally is both exciting and routine. It is both easy and difficult. Why? Because some people initially bring more skills to global assignments than others – that is, some have less to learn – and because some foreign locations are more comfortable or familiar than others. For example, a manager from Singapore would likely have an easier time moving to the United States or United Kingdom than Ecuador or Peru, because more Singaporeans speak English than Spanish. This does not suggest that they should avoid South America; they just have to work harder, as the territory is less familiar. Moving overseas brings with it a number of challenges, including both psychological and socio-cultural adjustments. In addition, there are personal, time, family, and career considerations. There is also the problem of returning home following the assignment. All of this is doable, of course, but it is made much easier to the extent that managers can develop and enhance their multicultural competence.

Chapter outline

Applications

There are no foreign lands. It is the traveller only who is foreign.

Robert Louis Stevenson[1]
Poet and novelist, Scotland

Everyone thinks in terms of changing the world, but no one thinks in terms of changing himself.

Leo Tolstoy[2]
Poet and novelist, Russia

When travelers arrive in an airport after a long international flight, they are typically told to get in one of two lines for passport control: one says "Citizens," the other "Aliens." Have you ever thought of yourself as an alien? For that matter, have you ever thought of yourself as a foreigner? "Alien" and "foreigner" are wonderfully ambiguous terms. Technically, they refer to people who are not from the local community, region, or country. It is assumed they are somehow different. Now comes the hard question: who is an alien or foreigner – and when? When managers prepare for overseas assignments, are they preparing to go to a foreign country or are they about to become a foreigner themselves? In both cases, they are about to become an outsider.

Expatriates and frequent flyers who travel regularly to work in global operations often express the same frustration: on foreign assignments, they often feel decidedly like outsiders, yet they must find ways to "break into" the local culture simply to do their job. This is clearly no easy task, since local environments can be highly variable, often secretive, and occasionally hostile. They are, quite literally, surrounded (see Exhibit 11.1). Outsiders are often seen as having "foreign" beliefs, norms, and values. They are not members of the local society, or, in many cases, the local organization. From their standpoint, moreover, outsiders are often outside their own comfort zone. All the same, they have to adjust. Whether their assignment is to supervise local employees in an overseas operation, build or manage a global partnership, or simply fly in to check on the progress of a team project, the challenge is basically the same, although in different degrees: they are immersed in a foreign environment with unfamiliar or uncomfortable norms, and they are expected to perform. In most cases, furthermore, it is the responsibility of the singular outsider, not the multitude of insiders, to make adjustments.

Exhibit 11.1 Key relationships in living and working globally (example)

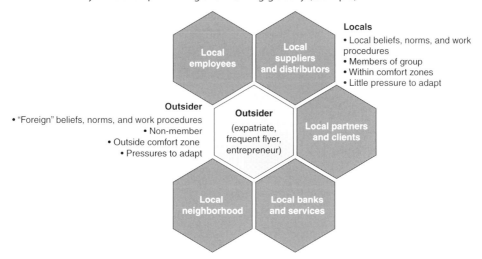

Hence the question: how can outsiders live when surrounded by insiders? This is the fundamental expatriate challenge.

To begin thinking about this question, we begin with an example. During a recent voyage through the Caribbean on the *Allure of the Seas*, the largest cruise ship ever built, two passengers discussed how much they had enjoyed the voyage. As they rode the glass elevator to the top of the ship's massive eleven-story atrium, one turned to the other and said, "I've been on this voyage for two days, and I haven't even seen the ocean yet."[3] This observation raises an interesting question: what was the purpose of the cruise? Relaxation? Adventure? A similar question can be asked about managers who seek global assignments in their companies, particularly those who want to live and work abroad. What is their motivation? What do they seek to gain from their experience? What will they actually see and learn as a result of their assignment? Is it to be a voyage of discovery, a "life experience," or a serious career move? What will their employer gain from the experience and expense, come to that? Then there is a very different question: what if the assignment abroad is the company's idea, not yours? How should you evaluate this? Must you say "Yes"?

Many managers see an international assignment as a great opportunity. It may be an opportunity to advance one's career, make more money, or learn new things. It may represent a personal challenge or a way to a more interesting life. Managers who take such global assignments report learning new managerial skills, increasing their tolerance for ambiguity, learning new ways of seeing things, and improving their ability to work with others.[4] Exciting though it may be, however, living and working abroad is also challenging, and many people fail. In most cases, it implies immersing oneself in a different environment, learning new cultural norms and rules, developing new skills and behaviors, and adjusting to unexpected situations. Clearly, foreign assignments are different and vary in how challenging they are. In some cases host and home countries share many similarities, and differences are often subtle and apparent only after careful observation or experience. In other cases differences may be overwhelming and apparent at first sight (for example, compare how different the experience would be for an Irish manager moving to France or Mexico). Either way, living in a foreign culture requires adjusting to a different cultural system.

In this chapter we look at the process of adaptation to a new cultural environment and discuss strategies to prepare for foreign assignments. While previous chapters dealt with management realities on the ground – how we communicate or negotiate a contract – this chapter is more personal. Certainly, managers require social and technical skills to succeed in foreign environments, but they also need *emotional* skills. This balance – the technical and the emotional – is the topic of this chapter.

Global assignments

To begin with, let us talk briefly about how global managers become "global" in the first place. In other words, how do they get into their new "foreign" assignments or jobs? The variety within these people is probably too large to identify any commonalities or central tendencies. They are all simply too different. Some people are assigned (or requested) by their employers to move abroad for a particular job assignment; others initiate the move themselves by accepting employment with overseas companies that offer them opportunities; and still others move abroad without a job or any concrete idea of how they will make a living. Some want to join established firms; others start their own businesses. Some go abroad for a month; others for several years; and still others emigrate permanently. Each unique combination of location, reasons for the relocation, length of assignment, and other individual characteristics create constraints and opportunities for the individual worker and his or her family, as well as the local organization employing him or her.

Employer- and self-initiated assignments

A topic that is often overlooked in discussions concerning foreign assignments is how they began. We sometimes fail to recognize that there can be major differences between employer-initiated or self-initiated assignments. People's motivations and expectations may be different, as well as their commitment to be away from their home culture for long

Exhibit 11.2 Implications of employer-initiated and self-initiated assignments

	Employer-initiated	Self-initiated
Managers (employees, entrepreneurs, global workers)	Manager may not want the assignment but feel pressed to accept in order not to jeopardize future career advancements.	Manager chooses where and when to relocate.
	Organizations vary widely in the amount of support they provide and how well they manage the expatriation process.	Manager takes the responsibility for finding a job and relocating the family.
	May not select location of the assignment.	May take a long time to establish local relationships and credentials.
	Have some relative job security while abroad.	May need to take a job below what was used to in home country.
	May negotiate financially interesting expatriate package, including trips home, foreign living allowances, support for partner and family.	In many cases, limited expatriate support provided.
	May negotiate terms of repatriation.	At times may negotiate attractive packages when organization can't find local talent, but most times must accept local standards – or less.
	Organization responsible for legal arrangements such as visas and licenses.	May need to deal with work visa and other legal requirements on own.
Organizations (employers, local support network)	Need to manage the expatriation and repatriation.	Difficulty to evaluate credentials from foreign country.
	Costly and potentially high-risk.	Need to manage multicultural workforce.
	Can select workers with knowledge of the company and technical skills.	May need to accommodate difficulties experienced by the worker due to his or her foreign status (e.g. visa restrictions, local knowledge, lack of family support).

periods of time (see Exhibit 11.2). Business organizations have long relied on organization-initiated global work assignments to develop and control organizations, divisions, and subsidiaries in different regions and countries of the world, transfer knowledge and skills across subsidiaries, and develop globally experienced managers. Such assignments vary in terms of their difficulty, complexity, opportunity, and duration.

Recently, large numbers of people have been choosing to pursue international careers and move across borders without the support of a home organization or employer. On their own accord, they relocate to a foreign country in search of new career opportunities or a more satisfying life. These are a new breed of international workers, and they vary widely in skill sets and motivations, from adventurous travelers who perform low-level jobs in exotic countries to those at the higher end of the job market, particularly coming from developing countries, in search of better career opportunities. Many are highly educated and experienced; many others are not. Most end up working in organizations of different sizes in the host country, bringing such organizations many advantages and challenges.

Exhibit 11.3 Long- and short-term global assignments

By their nature, self-initiated assignments are unique to each individual and circumstances, and the reasons for engaging in each of them and the length of the assignment vary widely. Organization-initiated assignments also vary widely, but share some important commonalities. In the remainder of this chapter we focus on organization-initiated assignments, but in many cases the challenges identified here also apply to self-initiated assignments.

Long- and short-term assignments

Business organizations routinely rely on global work assignments to develop and control organizations, divisions, and subsidiaries in different regions and countries of the world, transfer knowledge and skills across subsidiaries, and develop globally experienced managers. Such assignments come in a variety of degrees of difficulty, complexity, opportunity, and duration. On a general level, however, they can be categorized into two groupings: those managers who live overseas on relatively permanent, or long-term, assignments; and those who travel overseas on relatively short-term assignments. As shown in Exhibit 11.3, the characteristics (and developmental goals) of each of these sets of managers can be quite different. While long-term assignments require deep knowledge of a particular country or region, shorter assignments typically require broad knowledge of cultural differences and cultural processes in general. One needs to be a specialist; the other a generalist. One leads a somewhat stable life, albeit in a foreign country; the other leads a highly mobile existence. This is not to say that one approach is superior to the other, only that they are different and that each plays an important role in global commerce.

Long-term global assignments

Traditionally, the most common type of foreign duty involved long-term assignments of parent-company managers to various countries in which the parent firm did, or wanted to do, business. Firms often prefer to use expatriate managers for a number of

Exhibit 11.4 Long-term global assignments

Principal roles	Advantages	Disadvantages
Integrate local operations into parent company's global strategy.	Provides ongoing opportunities for close scrutiny and control of local operations.	Costly for parent company to pay for expatriate and family.
Enhance parent-company management and control over local operations.	Easier to instill parent-company business values and management philosophy in local operations.	Cultural similarities, friendships, and connections between expatriates and their parent company may serve to reduce any trust or confidence in local (foreign) managers by parent company (e.g., local voices may not be heard).
Fill positions or skill gaps caused by a lack of local talent (e.g., technology transfer).	Local problems can often be more easily identified and reported back to headquarters for resolution.	Local managerial talent is often developed only to the extent that expatriate managers wish, impeding local training and development efforts.
Develop experienced parent-company managers for more challenging foreign assignments or promotion to parent-company HQ.	Can facilitate more direct communications and reporting (e.g., same language, same customs) when communicating with HQ.	Expatriate assignments can be used by parent company to remove less effective managers from the home office.
Develop experienced local managers for more challenging global assignments or promotion to parent-company HQ.	Useful when local talent is in short supply.	Global assignments can cause considerable family stress, both between spouses (e.g., career conflicts) and with children.
	Provides good training ground for expatriates for promotion to future parent-company executive positions.	Work permit and taxation issues can be problematic in some locations.
	Can facilitate on-the-ground mentoring of local employees and managers for future executive responsibility.	Repatriation problems for expatriates and/or their families.

reasons, especially when they feel that they need parent-company representation in a distant location, when they want to provide developmental opportunities for parent-company managers, or when they need to fill skill gaps when locals do not have the skills to do the job themselves (see Exhibit 11.4).[5]

Although the advantages of expatriate assignments are fairly obvious, finding people who can actually succeed in expatriate assignments can be problematic. While traveling abroad (perhaps on a vacation or business trip) is often seen by people as an enjoyable experience, actually living abroad can be frustrating and stressful, and sometimes very unpleasant. For many, staying in a four-star hotel, eating in fine restaurants, seeing new sights, and knowing that soon you will be back in your own bed is far preferable to setting up a household in a strange neighborhood where few people speak your language, finding schools for the kids, shopping in local markets stocked with foods you can't identify, and using public transportation. For others, these same experiences provide a sense of adventure and learning. The challenge for managers – and their companies – is to discover which type of person they are before getting on the airplane.

Many people see an international assignment as a great opportunity. It may be an opportunity to advance one's career, to make more money, or to learn new things. It may represent a personal challenge or a way to a more interesting life. Managers who take international assignments report learning new managerial skills, increasing their tolerance for ambiguity, learning new ways of seeing things, and improving their ability to work with others.[6] Living and working abroad is not easy, however. Long-term international assignments are particularly challenging for managers with a family, when a partner may need to give up a career at home and not find suitable employment in the host country, and when children require special attention such as international schooling. A recent survey suggests that 81 percent of workers declining an expatriate assignment cited family reasons.[7]

Application 11.1   Global assignments at Shell

Royal Dutch Shell is a global petroleum company with joint headquarters in London and The Hague. The company employs over 100,000 people, approximately 5,500 of whom live and work abroad at any given point in time. Shell's expatriate managers are a highly diverse group, representing over seventy nationalities and working in more than 100 countries. The company supports this because it realizes that, as a global company, success requires the international mobility of its workforce.

Over time, however, Shell found it increasingly difficult to recruit key personnel for overseas assignments. To understand the problem, Shell interviewed 200 expatriate employees and their spouses to uncover their biggest concerns. These data were then used to create a survey, which was sent to 17,000 current and former expatriate managers, expatriates' spouses, and employees who had declined international assignments. Surprisingly, the response rate for the survey was 70 percent, clearly suggesting that many employees believed this to be an important issue. According to the survey results, five key issues had the greatest influence on the willingness of employees to accept an international assignment. In order of importance, these were: (1) separation from children during their secondary education (the children were often sent to boarding schools in their home countries while their parents were away); (2) harm done to a spouse's career and employment; (3) failure to recognize and involve spouses in the relocation decision; (4) failure to provide adequate information and assistance regarding relocation; and

Application 11.1   (cont.)

(5) health-related issues, such as access to good hospitals, or the ongoing ailment of a family member.

As a result of these findings, Shell implemented a number of programs designed to make it easier for employees to go abroad. To help with the education of children, Shell built elementary schools for employees in locations with heavy expatriate concentrations. For secondary education, they worked with local schools, often providing grants to help upgrade their facilities and educational offerings. They also offered employees an educational supplement for parents wanting to send their children to private schools in the host country. Helping spouses find suitable employment proved to be a more vexing problem. According to the survey, one-half of the spouses were employed when the international assignment was made, but only 12 percent were able to find suitable work after arriving in their new location. Shell established a spouse employment center to address the problem. The center provides career counseling and support in locating employment opportunities both during and immediately following the overseas assignment. The company also agreed to reimburse up to 80 percent of the costs associated with vocational training or reaccreditation.

Finally, Shell established a global information and advice network, known as "the Outpost," to provide support for families contemplating overseas assignments. The Outpost is headquartered in The Hague and now runs forty information centers in more than thirty countries. Staffed by spouses and fully supported by Shell, this global network has helped more than 1,000 families prepare for overseas assignments. The center recommends schools and medical facilities and provides housing advice and up-to-date information on employment, overseas study, self-employment, and volunteer work. Clearly, Shell is working hard to provide a supportive work environment for its global employees in a way that also facilitates the long-term objectives of the company.

Think about it...

(1)   How would you evaluate the actions taken by Shell to make lives easier for expatriate employees and their families?

(2)   What other actions might Shell take to improve the overseas environment for their employees?

Exhibit 11.5 Short-term global assignments

Principal roles	Advantages	Disadvantages
Initiate, monitor, or complete new projects in diverse locations.	Provides parent company with greater flexibility in matching specific managers with specific global plans or problems.	Sometimes difficult for short-term visitors to develop working relationships with local managers due to brevity of visits.
Coordinate ongoing operations and plans across multiple locations.	Flexibility; travel to overseas locations often requires little advance planning.	Parent company can lose strategic benefits on long-term on-site observations and connections.
Send troubleshooters to various locations as needed.	Frequently more cost-effective than supporting "permanent" overseas staff.	Short-term visitors may be less well equipped in terms of linguistic skills than expatriates.
Retain highly skilled talent that may wish to remain in home country (for lifestyle, dual career, etc.).	Managers can more easily maintain connections and friendships at parent company.	Scheduling conflicts with managers who are continually on the go.
Expand talent pool available for various global assignments.	Provides global developmental experience for broad array of parent-company managers.	Physical strain on managers and their families resulting from continual travel.
Facilitate global management development.		
Enhance interorganizational communication and coordination.		

Short-term global assignments

In the past, the most popular of international assignments was expatriation, or individuals moving residence from the home country to a foreign location for a significant period of time, usually between one and five years. Today, due to the increased availability of local talent in host countries, increasing cost pressures, a higher incidence of dual-career couples, and the ease of transportation and communication across countries, various forms of alternative international work arrangements, including short-term overseas assignments, are becoming popular.

Global assignments of shorter duration are usually focused on a specific task or project and, as such, provide easier-to-measure results (see Exhibit 11.5).[8] Additionally, there are many workers who would not consider uprooting the family for a long-term expatriate assignment but would be interested in a shorter international opportunity. This increases the pool of talent available for such postings, which is a major plus point, as the demand for international assignees is considerably higher than the supply.[9] It is also the case that short-term assignments are easier on employees, who feel it is easier to remain connected to the home country and career opportunities.

The main challenge facing short-term assignees is that they find themselves in a foreign country without family and friends, and with a very short time to develop relationships and get adjusted.[10] Since assignees are usually sent abroad for a short period to solve a specific problem or perform a specific task, they are not given the time to learn the ropes and adjust to the new locale, as would be the case with traditional long-term expatriate assignments. Instead, short-term assignees are expected to perform as soon as they hit the ground, which increases the challenges of the assignment. Strong pressures to perform – quickly – coupled with a limited social and family life, frequently lead assignees to work long hours and endure high levels of stress. The resulting unsatisfactory work–life balance and high stress levels may lead to unwelcome side effects, such as alcoholism and other destructive behavior.

Challenges of living and working globally

Working abroad poses a number of challenges that can affect people in very different ways depending upon their personal and organizational circumstances. These challenges emerge both prior to departure (e.g., suitability for such assignment, family considerations) and afterwards (duration of assignment, family considerations again). The nature of some of these challenges can evolve with time, while others are ever-present. We explore three of these challenges: personal considerations, family considerations, and career considerations (see Exhibit 11.6).

Personal considerations

An important question for all companies is who to select for global assignments. While many people are interested in such assignments, far fewer are usually qualified. As such,

Exhibit 11.6 Challenges of living and working globally

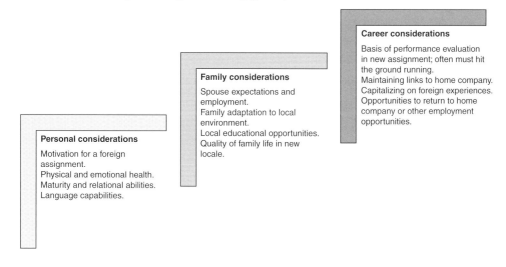

Career considerations

Basis of performance evaluation in new assignment; often must hit the ground running.
Maintaining links to home company.
Capitalizing on foreign experiences.
Opportunities to return to home company or other employment opportunities.

Family considerations

Spouse expectations and employment.
Family adaptation to local environment.
Local educational opportunities.
Quality of family life in new locale.

Personal considerations

Motivation for a foreign assignment.
Physical and emotional health.
Maturity and relational abilities.
Language capabilities.

successful companies approach overseas assignments in a systematic way, beginning with employee selection and progressing to cultural adaptation programs for those finally selected. The first issue to be addressed is what qualifications candidates for overseas positions should possess. To ensure that those selected have a reasonable chance of success, companies look for certain characteristics in job applicants.[11] Although professional and technical competencies remain prerequisites for most international assignments, other key success factors should also be considered, including the following.

- *Motivation for a foreign assignment.* Is the manager really interested in going abroad or was he or she talked into it? Why does he or she want to go? Is he or she motivated by career concerns, company commitment, or personal goals?
- *Physical and emotional health.* Many overseas assignments can be exhausting, with business meetings during the day and social obligations at night. Such assignments are not for the weak of mind or body. Companies must ensure that managers sent overseas are physically up to the challenge. They should also ensure that managers do not carry with them undue emotional baggage that could degenerate out of control in a stressful foreign environment.
- *Maturity and relational abilities.* Can the manager work independently, accept setbacks gracefully, and adapt to new and strange situations? Does the manager have good interpersonal and cross-cultural skills? Can the manager accept other people as they are or must he or she try and change them to fit a predetermined mold?
- *Language capabilities.* Learning local languages facilitates learning local cultures. It also helps develop close personal and business relationships abroad. Does the manager speak the local language? Is he or she willing to learn?

These key factors do not guarantee success in an overseas assignment, but they enhance the likelihood of success. What expatriate managers really need to succeed is a combination of these skills, a supportive family, and a supportive company. With these three mutually supportive factors, expatriate managers can focus their energies and talents on running the business for the benefit of all.

Application 11.2   Wei Hopeman, Citi Ventures

What is it like being a Chinese-American working for a US financial services company in Shanghai? Ask Wei Hopeman of Citi Ventures, a division of Citigroup.[12] As managing director for the Shanghai office of Citi Ventures, Hopeman leads a very busy life. By day, she works with entrepreneurs throughout Asia to identify their operational and financial needs. By night, she turns her focus to the other side of the world, working a full shift with her American colleagues connecting those start-ups with Citi business units. After eight years of dealing with the thirteen-hour time difference and the fifteen-hour flights between Shanghai and New York – not to mention numerous trips across China to India, Hong Kong, Singapore, and Palo Alto – she has learned to adapt.

Along the way, Hopeman has picked up a few tricks concerning the life of an on-the-go global executive. She calls them her "survival skills." First, since her working day is so long and opportunities for jet lag so frequent, she simply ignores the clock; she has learned to sleep in three-hour chunks of time. Second, she prefers to stay in hotels near her current projects instead of commuting from her home; it is easier to be close to her customers. Third, she blends her work and private life. In much of Asia, the boundary between professional and personal space is much more blurred and she must make herself available 24/7. "I make myself available. It's how business gets done."[13] Fourth, she does not ask what she is eating at business dinners, since this can be seen as rude. Finally, she uses long flights as relaxation time; they have become her sanctuary away from the never-ending demands of her job.

Think about it . . .

(1)   Would you like to have Wei Hopeman's job? Why or why not?
(2)   What is your opinion about her "survival skills"? Would these skills work for you?
(3)   What other survival skills can you identify that global managers might make good use of?

Family considerations

Family considerations are at least as important as personal considerations when deciding whether to accept a global assignment. Long- and short-term assignments both carry risks and challenges, although often of a different nature. For long-term assignments, spouses typically relocate with expatriate partner, and dual-career challenges can be accentuated. The spouse may lose contact with his or her extended family, friends, and support group. While family may reside together, considerable stress can still result from raising children in unfamiliar settings. Children typically relocate with one or both of their parents. Although they can have numerous opportunities to learn about other cultures, make new friends, learn new languages, experience new cuisine, etc., they can also experience culture shock (see below), requiring significant adjustments to the new location and changed circumstances (e.g., missing old friends, dislike of local foods, etc.). Parents who are responsible for their own parents – an increasingly common phenomenon – also face challenges. Thus, everyone in the family is affected. In view of the complexities of interpersonal relationships – even within a single family – decisions to move should not be taken lightly.

Family challenges exist for short-term assignments too. Being away from the family also places a burden on family life. On the one hand, the global manager has been immersed in a foreign location experiencing situations that are unfamiliar to his or her family, and it may be difficult for them to comprehend. As discussed above, the manager is likely to be working long hours under pressure, and may be subject to high levels of stress, straining communication. Frequently the manager retains some responsibilities back home, and after a long day at work may spend hours in an empty hotel or apartment room, answering e-mails and on the phone with the home country in a different time zone. On the other hand, the spouse at home is left with the sole responsibility for the house and family, and must pick up the slack left by the partner and assume new roles. As the family sets into a new routine it may be difficult to adapt back, creating resentments on both sides. All this may weaken family ties, and a high divorce rate is associated with this type of assignments. Of course, if the personal life of the manager crumbles, it may also jeopardize the success of the assignment (see Exhibit 11.7). The two are typically highly intertwined.

An additional problem facing short-term assignees and companies alike is that often the original assignment was conceived for a short period and a specific project, but, as the project develops, it is enriched and enlarged, or unforeseen problems can emerge, resulting in extensions of the assignment. It is estimated that more than one-half of short-term assignments get extended to eighteen months or longer,[14] and once the employee is involved in the project and in the foreign location it may be difficult to go back home. This creates a difficult situation in which the manager may feel stuck in a foreign country, and may have family problems. From the company point of view it is not necessarily better, as the costs of the position may rise quickly. Common concerns in this regard are taxes, social security payments, and work permits – issues that are frequently overlooked by managers making a decision to extend an assignment, but ones that should be taken seriously by both the assignee and the company.

Career considerations

Finally, the implications of global assignments – both long- and short-term – on careers should be considered. As illustrated in Exhibit 11.8, long-term assignments often cause

Exhibit 11.7 Family considerations in global assignments

	Long-term assignments	Short-term assignments
Managers	Some companies prefer managers with overseas experience for promotion consideration.	High levels of stress due to combined pressures from home and abroad and limited social support while abroad.
	Manager may lose friends and connections, both at parent company and in local community.	
Spouses	Spouse typically relocates with expatriate partner.	Spouse typically remains at home, while manager-partner is continually on the road.
	Dual-career challenges can be accentuated significantly.	Ongoing stress between partners can result from continual separations.
	Spouse may lose contact with extended family, friends, and support group.	
	While family may reside together, considerable stress can still result from raising children in unfamiliar settings.	
Children	Children frequently relocate with parents; keeps family together.	Children typically remain at home with one parent, friends, and extended family, but without traveling parent.
	Children have numerous opportunities to learn about other cultures, make new friends, learn new languages, experience new cuisine, etc.	Less change and potential turmoil for children.
	Like parents, children often go through culture shock, requiring significant adjustments to new location and changed circumstances (e.g., missing old friends, dislike of local foods, etc.).	No culture shock or reentry problems for children.
	Also like parents, children often go through stresses of repatriation (e.g., readjusting to old school, old friends, etc.).	May damage relationship with or lose influence over children due to repeated absences.

Exhibit 11.8 Career considerations in global assignments

Long-term assignments	Short-term assignments
Difficult to maintain connections, possibly making it more difficult to return.	Need to keep responsibilities and relationships at home office while abroad, leading to a double workload.
Difficult to keep up with home-office changes (e.g. changes in processes or technology), possibly making it more difficult to return.	Need to hit the ground running; no time to learn about the new country; must get down to work quickly.
Out of sight, out of mind. May miss out on important promotion or other opportunities.	Limited time to learn and adjust and high pressures to perform can lead to high stress and possible failure.
International experience may be an important asset for future career advancement.	Good way to gain international experience without unsettling the family or making long-term commitments.
Have more time to learn and adjust to foreign culture, but need to adjust is more acute as success depends on establishing local connections.	Breadth of knowledge acquired from various short-term international assignments may be an asset back home.

managers to lose touch with their home base and home connections. Simply put, they might become forgotten. This is true whether people work for global corporations or on their own as entrepreneurs. Even so, such assignments can lead to learning and skills development that may prove to be an asset back home. At the same time, short-term assignments also have pluses and minuses. As already noted, many managers sent on short-term assignments carry part of their home job assignments with them, causing additional work and dividing their focus and attention. Moreover, there is little time to adjust to the new culture (or cultures, in the case of frequent fliers). Short-term assignments often allow managers to experience foreign countries and meet new people without actually moving overseas, however. There are many good opportunities for personal and professional development, as well as networking. Perhaps the critical issue here is the extent to which global managers make use of their assignments for the benefit of the various parties concerned, personal and organizational alike.

Application 11.3   Preparing for global assignments

Australia has a population of over 23 million people and covers 7 million square kilometers. Its GDP is $1.5 trillion; it is a constitutional democracy; and people drive on the left-hand side of the road. It is surrounded by water on all sides, so Australian politician Kep Enderby is not wrong when he observes in jest: "Traditionally, most of Australia's imports come from overseas."[15] The service sector of the economy (e.g., tourism, education, financial services) accounts for about 70 percent of GDP. Rich in natural resources, Australia is a major exporter of agricultural products, particularly wheat and wool, minerals such as iron ore and gold, and energy in the form of liquefied natural gas and coal. Although agriculture and natural resources account for only 3 percent and 5 percent of GDP, respectively, they contribute substantially to export performance. Australia's largest export markets are Japan, China, the United States, South Korea, and New Zealand. Australia is the world's fourth largest exporter of wine, in an industry contributing $5.5 billion per annum to the nation's economy. Melbourne is the second largest city in the country and a major business center. Unfortunately, while this information may be accurate, it may not be very helpful if we are trying to understand Australia and Australians. We need something more than statistics. We need to know who the Australian people are and how we can live and work among them.

    Think about it...

(1)   You have just accepted a three-year assignment to represent your financial services company in Melbourne. You, your spouse, and your two young children leave for your assignment in ninety days. As you prepare for your

assignment, what is the most important information you will need to understand to make this assignment a success? Specifically, what are the five most
important questions you need to ask prior to your departure?

(2)   How do you plan to discover the answer to these five questions? Explain.

Adapting to local cultures

Living in a foreign country suggests that individuals are caught between two cultures. On
the one hand, there is the individual's culture of origin, which has provided him or her
with assumptions, skills, behavioral preferences, and ways of thinking that have contributed to his or her actual position in life. For example, a manager selected for a foreign
assignment is often perceived as a successful manager at home and has achieved this
position by doing things in a particular way. On the other hand, there is the foreign
culture, which may have different values, assumptions, and ways of thinking and require
different behaviors. Behaviors that have contributed to success at home may not be
appreciated – and may not be successful – in a foreign country. When two or more
cultures come into contact, *cultural friction* (see Chapter 3) can be experienced, and a
process of adjustment may be required in which new ways of relating need to be crafted.

Most people naturally and unconsciously adapt their behavior in order to adjust to
new external environments. This adaptation may or may not improve the fit between
individuals and their environment, however. Despite the widespread belief that, given
enough time, people will "go native," this is not necessarily true. While most people
change as a product of living in a foreign country, it does not necessarily mean that they
change to be more like the people in the host culture.[16] Indeed, some people may
become more attached to their original culture than they were beforehand. Expatriate
and ethnic enclaves are not uncommon, and some people spend many years in a foreign
country without ever assimilating local values or even learning the local language. For
this reason, it is often helpful to separate the process of adaptation to a foreign culture
into two related but quite different processes.[17]

- *Psychological adjustment* refers to the process of developing a way of life in the new
  country that is personally satisfying.
- *Socio-cultural adjustment* refers to the individual's ability to interact competently
  with the host culture.

Both processes are related, but they do not necessarily occur simultaneously, and in some cases only one type of adjustment may be achieved. For example, an expatriate with little cultural competence may be happy living in an enclave excluded from the local culture, while a culturally competent person may be unhappy in the foreign environment. Separating psychological and cultural adjustment helps us see why people may use different strategies to deal with foreign environments depending upon their identification with home and host cultures, their ability and willingness to modify their behavior, and the outside pressures they face. Below, we discuss the challenges associated with each type of adjustment, and strategies to deal with them.

Psychological adjustment

The challenge of *psychological adjustment* is pervasive among global residents. Immersing oneself in a new environment often results in some level of stress resulting from information overload, a breakdown in one's capacity to make sense of the environment, and the need to learn a new way to go about everyday tasks. When in a foreign environment, people frequently cannot use their past experiences to interpret and respond to cues, and their behavior does not produce the expected results, causing heightened anxiety and frustration. In addition, seemingly minor things, such as an inability to find one's favorite food or perform simple tasks such as making a phone call, using public transportation, or mailing a letter, can cause confusion and a feeling of loss of control. Individuals can face a state of internal disequilibrium created by the realities imposed by the new culture and the expectations based on the old. This disequilibrium often forces them to question their behavioral habits and can lead to emotional feelings of anxiety, stress, and confusion that are often referred to as *culture shock*.[18]

Culture shock can take many forms, from a psychological sense of frustration, anxiety, and disappointment to full-fledged chronic depression. Some individuals may experience physiological responses such as insomnia, headaches, or other psychosomatic symptoms. Even so, culture shock is not a disease. Rather, it signifies that an individual is trying to come to terms with his or her new environment – a good starting point for psychological adjustment. As such, the question is not how to avoid culture shock, but how to manage it.

Application 11.4   Dining out in Luogang

When journalist Peter Hessler was invited for lunch in the rural Chinese village of Luogang in Guangdong province he was in for a surprise.[19] After sitting down at a table in the Highest Ranking Wild Flavor Restaurant, the waitress asked him bluntly, "Do you want a big rat or a small rat?" Unsure of what to do, Hessler asked the waitress what the difference was, and was informed that the big rats eat grass while the small rats eat fruit. Both tasted good, he was assured. As he contemplated his choice, Hessler looked at the people sitting at the next table. A young boy was gnawing on a rat drumstick, but he couldn't tell whether it was from a big rat or a small one. After asking himself how he got into this predicament, he finally made a decision: a small rat. He chose an item from the menu called Simmered Mountain Rat with Black Beans. He selected this over other possibilities, including Mountain Rat Soup, Steamed Mountain Rat, Simmered Mountain Rat, Roasted Mountain Rat, Mountain Rat Curry, and Spicy and Salty Mountain Rat.

The Chinese say that people in Guangdong will eat anything. Besides rat, people at the Highest Ranking Wild Flavor Restaurant can order turtle dove, fox, cat, python, and an assortment of strange-looking local animals whose names don't translate into English. Selecting a menu item involves considerations beyond flavor and texture. You order cat not just because you enjoy the taste but also because cats are believed to impart a lively *jingshen* (or spirit). You order a snake because it makes you stronger. You order the private parts of a deer to make you more virile. Why would you eat a rat? Because it will keep you from going bald and make your white hair turn black.

After a few minutes the waitress asked Hessler to come back to the kitchen and select his rat. In the back of the kitchen, he saw several cages stacked on top of one another. Each cage contained about thirty rats. "How about this one?" the waitress asked. "Fine," Hessler replied. The waitress then put on a white glove (presumably for hygiene purposes) and grabbed the chosen rat. "Are you sure this is the one?" she asked. The rat gazed at Hessler with its little beady eyes. He nodded his approval. Then the waitress grabbed the rat by its tail and flipped her wrist, thereby launching the rat through the air until it landed on its head on the concrete floor with a soft thud. There was little blood. Hessler was told that he could return to his table; lunch would arrive shortly.

Waiting for his meal to come, Hessler had an opportunity to speak with the owner of the restaurant. The first thing he noticed was the owner's full head of thick black hair. The owner said that local people have been eating rat for more than 1,000 years. His customers insist on eating rats from the mountains, however,

Application 11.4   (cont.)

because they are clean; they won't eat city rats, he insisted. He assured Hessler that the government hygiene department came by regularly to inspect his rats and had never found anything wrong. Before walking away, the owner smiled and said that you couldn't find food like this in America. When lunch was finally served, Hessler tried to think of this as a new experience. He tried the beans first, and they tasted fine. Then he poked around at the rat meat. It was clearly well done and attractively garnished with onions, leeks, and ginger. Nestled in a light sauce were skinny rat thighs, short strips of rat flank, and delicate tiny rat ribs. He hesitantly took his first bite, and found the meat to be lean and white without a hint of gaminess. It didn't taste like anything he had had previously. It tasted like rat. Fortunately, he had lots of beer to wash it down with.

Think about it...

(1)   What would you do if you were faced with the situation that Peter Hessler experienced at the Luogang restaurant, especially if an important Chinese client had invited you to the restaurant?

(2)   Have you ever had a similar experience in another culture when you were pressured to eat or do something that was acceptable – or even required – in the local culture but that you found uncomfortable? What did you do?

(3)   Are there aspects of your own home culture that foreign visitors might find offensive or uncomfortable for some reason? What might you do to put your foreign guests at ease in this situation?

(4)   Think about your eating habits and food preferences. How easy would it be for you to live in a foreign country with drastically different cuisine?

Stages of psychological adaptation

The process of psychological adjustment to a new culture can be quite personal and can vary widely depending on individual characteristics, the cultures involved, and the particulars of the situation. Nevertheless, knowledge of common stages in the process of adaptation is helpful in coping and understanding one's feelings while abroad. One of the most popular models of adaptation to a foreign culture suggests four distinct stages: honeymoon, disillusionment, initial adaptation, and adaptation (see Exhibit 11.9).[20]

(1)   *Honeymoon.* Upon first arriving at a foreign location, expatriates may experience a great deal of excitement. Things are interesting, sometimes beautiful, and often

Exhibit 11.9 Stages in psychological adaptation to a new culture

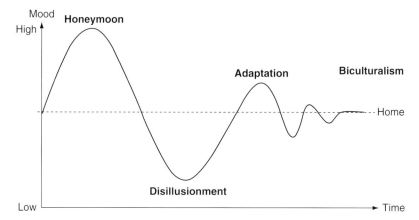

amusing. The fascination with new things makes the difficulties and differences encountered seem relatively minor, and people often overestimate the ease of adjustment to the foreign culture. This period can last from only a few days to several months, depending on the person, the nature of the assignment, and the degree of similarity between the home and host countries. Many expatriates report that the honeymoon happened before arrival at the foreign location or not at all. Some suggest that, while many individuals experience excitement upon arrival at the foreign location, these feelings may be overwhelmed by the stresses associated with settling in and coping with the differences in lifestyle.[21]

(2) *Disillusionment.* After the honeymoon period is over and the initial euphoria or excitement has faded, the differences in lifestyles, lack of comfortable food, and difficulties coping with the uncertainties of the new environment cease to be amusing and become irritating. These difficulties become magnified, and people often feel overwhelmed and psychologically exhausted. This is the most difficult stage in the cultural adaptation process. Many individuals give up at this stage and return home, while others remain in the foreign surroundings but withdraw emotionally, refusing to speak the local language or interact with locals. Some may even adopt dysfunctional coping behaviors, such as excessive drinking or drug use.

(3) *Initial adaptation.* During the third stage of initial adaptation, people begin to understand the new culture and adjust to everyday living. This stage can still be characterized by mood swings, but their magnitude or intensity is less pronounced than during the disillusionment stage.

(4)   *Adaptation and biculturalism.* Finally, expatriates begin to gain confidence in their ability to function productively in new culture and experience a sense of stability. Some people may feel better than at home, others may feel worse, but in either case there is a newfound sense of stability, comfort, and competence.

Another way to think about culture shock is to consider that the stress associated with adjusting to a new cultural environment is not unlike other types of stress caused by a mismatch between our internal capabilities and new demands of the environment (e.g. starting a new job, starting college, or having a child). As is the case with other types of stress, adapting to a new cultural environment offers a unique opportunity to change and recreate ourselves. As we strive to maintain a functional relationship with our surroundings, we make internal changes and adjustments. This process of adaptation and growth is cyclical and continual: each stressful experience leads to some adaptation on the part of the individual, which will lead to internal growth. The stress–adaptation–growth process continues as long as there are new environmental challenges, but tends to be less severe over time as the major changes are likely to be experienced in the early stages of the foreign assignment[22] (just as the first semester at university may be more emotionally challenging than later years, even if courses become harder and workload increases).

The degree and pace of adjustment to the foreign culture will vary person by person depending on many variables, including individual expectations, personal character-istics and circumstances, and the characteristics of the host environment.

First, disillusionment is often magnified by individuals' unrealistic expectations about what the experience in the foreign country is likely to be. Many people find the prospects of living in an exotic location appealing, but fail to prepare for easy-to-know realities of life such as the traffic, weather, and others features of daily life. For example, a manager may find it appealing to live surrounded by lush tropical vegetation, but fail to consider the mosquitoes that invariably come with it. Individuals may also under-estimate the cultural differences or overestimate their own abilities to cope, adjust, and learn a new language or ways to live in a new environment.

Second, people are different in how readily they adapt to new situations, how easily they develop new relationships, and how comfortable they are with ambiguity and temporary loss of control. Likewise, individual circumstances vary widely and may help or hinder adaptation. For example, individuals moving with family may have higher emotional support, but face more challenges in settling in a spouse and children than someone moving alone. Individuals with prior experience in the country and knowl-edge of the language may find it easier to adapt than someone with no knowledge of the language or experience in the culture. The expected length of the assignment may also influence how culture shock is experienced. For instance, the difficulties in practicing a favorite sport or hobby may not bring much frustration in a three-month assignment but may be a major source of concern in a permanent relocation.

Third, the external environment in which the expatriate is immersed has an important role in shaping the process and degree of adjustment. For example, some countries are more open to foreigners than others and have developed an infrastructure to support foreigners, in the form of language training, information centers, and support groups. There may also be important variation within the same country. For example, it may be relatively easy to speak English to get around in large or touristic cities, but not in smaller towns. Cultures also vary in the extent to which they tolerate difference and embrace multiculturalism. In some cultures differences are valued and appreciated and it is not expected that people will let go of their own cultures, while in others a strong emphasis is placed on fitting in. The organization hosting the expatriate also plays an important role. If a Canadian manager is in Thailand working for a Canadian organization the experience is likely to be different from the situation if the same manager were working for a Thai firm.

A key question surrounding the ease of adaptation is whether expatriates can improve their adaptation skills after multiple assignments. On the one hand, experience is helpful, because individuals learn how to cope with culture shock, gain confidence, and may not feel as stressed by the prospects of settling in a foreign environment. On the other hand, however, overconfidence may be a hindrance, because one overlooks important details and may fail to prepare appropriately. Additionally, some expatriates report fatigue after several international assignments, and lose interest in learning yet another language and culture and taking the time to develop relationships in a foreign country they expect to leave soon.

Coping with culture shock

Culture shock cannot be avoided, but it can be alleviated to some degree through proper advanced preparation.[23] This preparation includes aligning expectations by understanding both the host environment and oneself. The more that expatriates understand about the local environment, including the local culture and organizational demands, the easier the transition is likely to be. Likewise, the more that expatriates understand about the challenges posed by their own personal preferences, the more prepared they will be to address those needs. Below we offer some suggestions to better prepare for an international assignment (see Exhibit 11.10).

Exhibit 11.10 Strategies for coping with culture shock

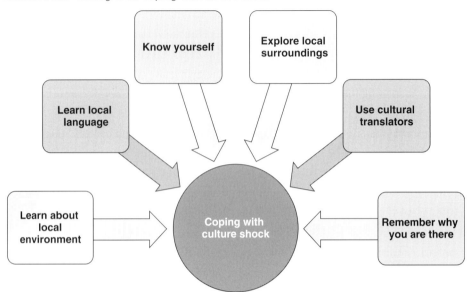

- *Learn about the local environment.* Cultures are complex, fragmented, dynamic, and idiosyncratic. Cultural knowledge is often useful to explain behavior but seldom to predict it. Each situation is unique, and it is impossible to predict the cultural conflicts that one is likely to experience. In spite of these challenges, learning about the local culture, history, and geography can help people make sense of the new environment and situations they encounter and will facilitate conversations with locals. At a minimum, it helps expatriates to know what to look for. When possible, it is often a good idea to visit the host country for a short period prior to moving there. A quick visit goes a long way to shape expectations and help expatriates to be better prepared psychologically for what is to come. If nothing else, expatriates get a feel for what the immediate challenges will be – traffic, pollution, language, or food. Indeed, many firms send expatriates and their families to the worksite for a brief visit prior to the assignment, so that they can decide if the assignment is suitable for themselves and their families. Talking with previous expatriates or others with experience in the foreign country is also helpful for knowing what to expect. It is important not to rely excessively on others' accounts, however. People and situations are unique, and it is likely that your experience will be different.
- *Learn the local language.* As discussed in Chapter 6, language is a key channel of cultural information. Learning the local language can facilitate the process of

cultural adaptation immensely. Learning the host language can provide a sense of being in control and facilitate communication with locals. In addition, locals are often more receptive to foreign visitors if they speak the local language, even if only in a rudimentary way. Interestingly, research has shown that learning new languages facilitates cognitive flexibility – a critical asset for managers who work and move around the globe.[24] One should not underestimate the challenges involved in learning a new language, however. Particularly for short-term assignments, learning the language may not be possible given the short time available and the high work demands. Some managers have several expatriate assignments throughout their careers; how many languages can one realistically master?

- *Know yourself.* Given the challenges of knowing the host country a priori, the best knowledge expatriates can take on a foreign assignment is knowledge about their own culture and themselves. First, foreigners are likely to ask you questions about your country and culture you may have never thought about. Many expatriates report learning about their own country when they were abroad. Second, knowing how your own culture has influenced you will help you to look at situations more neutrally. When we recognize that our ways of thinking are a product of our culture just as someone else's ways of thinking are a product of his or her culture, it is easier to look at conflict neutrally and not expect that everyone will agree with our notions of what should be a universally agreed best way of doing things. When we know our culturally imposed limitations (e.g., believing that meetings should start promptly) we are also better able to look for information and deal with situations. Finally, knowing yourself also helps with the more practical aspects of the relocation. It may sound silly, but packing some goods "you can't live without" may go a long way to making your first days abroad go more smoothly. For example, one student reported an "addiction to peanut butter" and how helpful it was to take some on her journey to Europe (no, peanut butter is not available everywhere).

- *Explore the local surroundings.* Upon arrival in a foreign location it is possible to take measures that will ease the process of culture shock. As a starting point, it is important to get to know your environment quickly and establish a sense of control over your surroundings. Simple things such as getting your place to feel comfortable and walking around the neighborhood will help to establish some confidence and reduce anxiety. Venturing out is the only way to learn about the foreign environment and start a process of adjustment. While at a distance this may seem non-problematic, it can be more challenging than it seems. As one student summarized it: "It is very tempting to stay home watching YouTube videos [from home] rather than venturing out feeling lost when you don't know anyone and do not have a particular place to go to."

- *Use cultural translators.* After getting settled in a new country, it is often a good idea to look for mentors or cultural translators. These are individuals who have a good understanding of both cultures and can help new arrivals make sense of what they are experiencing. The best cultural translators usually have international experience of their own, allowing them to recognize and interpret cultural differences as well as the reasons behind them. They may also prove an important source of basic information locals may not realize you need to know (e.g., not being allowed to throw toilet paper in the toilet). It also helps to join clubs or social groups in different areas of interest, as this is a good way to integrate into the community and know people who may become an important source of support.

- *Remember why you are there.* It also helps not to lose track of your reasons for embarking on the foreign assignment in the first place. Whether it was a professional opportunity, a lifestyle choice, or just an adventure, keeping in mind how the experience will help you grow may make things a little more bearable. Some individuals report benefiting from writing a personal journal (or blog) as a way to keep track of their experiences and observe their progress.

A key thing to keep in mind is that the process of adjustment is about finding ways to resolve conflicts about internal and external demands in ways that are both comfortable and helpful. In some cases, it may mean recreating aspects of the home culture in the foreign environment (e.g., cooking your favorite meal) and making choices about how involved one becomes with the new surroundings (e.g., avoiding religious ceremonies). There are many options between "going native" and "not changing at all." Dealing with culture shock is about finding the balance that works for each individual.

Socio-cultural adjustment

A second major challenge to global residents is called *socio-cultural adjustment*. The process of adapting to a new cultural environment may involve both *acculturation* (the acquisition of new cultural practices in wide-ranging areas, including the learning of a new language) and *deculturation* (the unlearning of at least some of the old cultural practices, at least in the sense that new responses are needed in situations that previously would have evoked old ones).[25] Through trial and error, people adjust their behaviors so as to fit the new environment better, either by learning how to behave like the locals or finding an alternative behavior that is both comfortable and acceptable. For example, at home the individual may be used to speaking bluntly, but the culture of the new environment may be one that praises subtle and indirect communication. Although he or she may find it difficult to speak indirectly, he or she may learn to look for contexts within the foreign environment in which direct comments are more appropriate, such as outside the office environment or in one-on-one conversations.

Acculturation strategies

Acculturation is seldom absolute. Even after many years people may incorporate practices of the host culture and fit in perfectly in the work environment and public spheres but retain social values and or assumptions from their own culture in more private realms. For example, it is not uncommon that perfectly adjusted professionals will choose to marry within their own culture and retain some aspects of their original culture at home. As discussed previously, culture has many components, and, while adjusting superficial behaviors at the public level is relatively unproblematic and mastered by most (e.g., bowing, kissing or shaking hands), some assumptions are hard to accept or let go of (e.g., accepting polygamy). In situations in which cultural conflict becomes unavoidable because the new behavior or assumption is neither acceptable to the individual nor possible to replicate, alternative acculturation strategies are in order.

For the purposes of simplicity, we identify three main types of strategies of acculturation available to managers (see Exhibit 11.11). In reality, individuals probably navigate between those strategies depending on specific situations.[26]

Exhibit 11.11 Acculturation strategies to local cultures

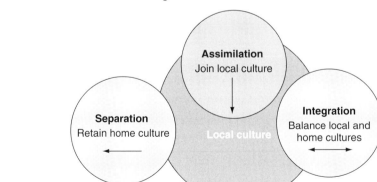

- *Separation.* At the one extreme, managers can try to hold on to their home culture and refuse to adopt practices and interact with the local culture, limiting their interaction with locals to the minimum necessary. These are expatriates who prefer to live in expatriate enclaves, do not learn the local language, and reconstruct a life that resembles the life they would have at home. Managers adopting this strategy may have a difficult time building rapport with the local workforce and community. Depending on their job requirements, however, they may very well be able to perform their duties satisfactorily (e.g., an English teacher working for an American college abroad).

- *Assimilation.* At the other extreme, managers can work to assimilate in the local environment and "go native." They let go of their original cultural habits and assumptions and incorporate the habits and assumptions of the new cultural milieu. Managers moving permanently to a foreign location may find this strategy appealing, as it decreases the opportunities for cross-cultural conflicts. On the other hand, it may prove challenging to return home if needed. Sometimes completely letting go of the home culture may not be possible, and, depending on the reason for the assignment, it may be counterproductive. Often managers are sent abroad to promote changes in the foreign location, and excessive assimilation of the local culture may be seen as an obstacle.

- *Integration.* In between assimilation and separation, managers employing an integration strategy work to integrate both cultures. They are able to retain important aspects of their home culture while at the same time building successful relationships in the local environment. An undervalued aspect of cultural adaptation is that an individual's original culture can be an important resource. Within each culture, people develop skills and habits that can be useful in other circumstances and constitute an important advantage in the host environment. For example, a Brazilian manager who is used to a polychromic environment in which he or she is expected to perform many tasks simultaneously may prove a useful resource in highly dynamic situations. Integration is only possible, however, with the participation and collaboration of the host culture. If individuals in the host culture are unable to accept and value the behaviors of the foreign culture, integration may be difficult to achieve. Although at first glance it may seem that integration is the best strategy and should be chosen by all managers, host cultures vary in the degree to which it is possible. Some cultures are open to multiculturalism (e.g., that in Canada) and make this option possible, while in other environments the pressures to fit in are higher and managers who fail to assimilate tend to be separated from the environment.

Influences on acculturation success

The process of socio-cultural adaptation depends on several variables, including cultural knowledge, cultural distance, intergroup attitudes (i.e., how the cultural groups involved perceive each other), multicultural competence,[27] and the role one plays in the new environment.

- *Cultural knowledge.* Operating successfully within a new cultural environment requires understanding the norms, rules, and expectations of the local culture. Previous exposure to the culture and the availability of cultural translators are likely to speed up the process of adaptation by helping individuals make sense of new situations quickly and minimizing the number of trials and errors needed to identify suitable behaviors (see below for a discussion on acquiring cultural knowledge).

- *Cultural distance.* The degree and type of cultural differences between the home and host cultures is an important determinant in how difficult or easy it will be to master and accept new cultural elements. In some cases cultural differences are relatively unproblematic and can be mastered easily, while in others the differences are too great and adaptation is very challenging, or even impossible.

- *Intergroup attitudes.* The stereotypes and perceptions held by people from home and host cultures about each other may ease or hinder adaptation. For example, if the host culture is admired by the people in the home culture, becoming more like the host culture may be perceived as desirable. On the other hand, if the host culture is perceived as "inferior" or "backward," adapting may be perceived more negatively. At the same time, if one is admired for being from the foreign culture and is granted privileges for belonging to that group, there may be no incentives to let go of the home culture.

- *Multicultural competence.* Successfully interacting with other cultures is a learnable competence that will help individuals to find a comfortable place within the local environment. As discussed in Chapter 2, multicultural competence represents the capacity to work successfully across cultures by developing a flexible way of thinking and behaving that embraces diversity and accepts complexity.

- *Individual roles.* The role the foreign individual plays in the host culture will influence not only how important and desirable it is to adapt to the host environment but also how much exposure one has to local individuals and, as a consequence, local cultural knowledge. For example, an expatriate working in a home-based organization primarily with other expatriates may have little exposure to the local culture, and as a consequence experience a very slow process of acculturation.

Application 11.5   Mr. Smith and Mr. Zhang

Consider the socio-cultural challenges facing two expatriates ostensibly doing much the same kind of job: a British expat working in Shanghai (Mr. Smith) and a Chinese expat working in London (Mr. Zhang). Note how the cultural, organizational, and situational environment of each differs. We begin with the context in which Mr. Smith works. "The rules in China are not always transparent," observes Smith, an executive at a Western firm that sells beauty products in China. His firm operates through a network of local individuals who knock on doors and attempt to convince their acquaintances to buy lipstick and shampoo. These salespeople also recruit other salespeople. This direct selling is controversial in many countries, including China. Some officials think it poses a threat to the harmonious society. Direct marketing companies are allowed to operate only under tight conditions designed to keep out scammers. For example, they must maintain a physical presence in the neighborhoods where they do business, so that disgruntled staff and customers have somewhere to go to make complaints.

Smith says his firm is happy to abide by the rules, but this is not as simple as it would be in the West. China's commercial law is sometimes an unreliable guide to what is allowed. For example, is it legal to recruit students to work as part-time salespeople? As far as Smith knows, it is. When some of his employees started recruiting on a university campus, however, the students' parents complained and the government took their side, making it plain that Smith's firm had crossed an invisible line. "I think it's a Confucian thing," he muses. "Chinese people place an immense value on education, and abhor anything that might distract students from their books." His firm now steers clear of students. Despite his challenges, Smith says that he enjoys working in China. He admires his Chinese sales force. In the United Kingdom, direct selling is typically someone's second job; in China, it is a full-time occupation. Chinese people tend to have large networks of family, friends, and classmates, and they do not hesitate to use them. "It's embedded in the culture," he says. They are not embarrassed to ask for favors or tout business propositions at family dinners. "That really helps us."

The context in which Mr. Zhang works is quite different. English meat pies "are dry and have no flavor," he observes. Moreover, British food is very expensive. Chinese expatriates who are posted abroad do not enjoy the same lavish pay and perks that Western expatriates in China do, especially if they work for state-owned firms. Back home, Chinese managers have housemaids. "They are not used to

Application 11.5   (cont.)

cooking for themselves," says Zhang, a telecoms executive. When sent to work in rich countries, "they even have to clean their own toilets," he chuckles. All the same, Zhang finds life in London easier than many other Chinese expatriates, because he speaks English well. His pay is low, however, and he was posted to England without his spouse or family. "We don't have the kind of expat package that pays for family expenses, housing, or the kids' education." This can make for a lonely, gloomy time. Western expatriates in China are typically there because they want to be. Some find the culture fascinating. Most expect to make good money and burnish their résumé. Western multinationals feel obliged to have a presence in China, and since the country is so potentially lucrative they often send their most capable staff there. Wal-Mart's global head of procurement is based in Shenzhen. HSBC's boss moved from London to Hong Kong last year. A spell in China helps a Western executive rise to the top. The converse is not true, though. Chinese executives, especially at state-owned firms, win promotion by cultivating the right people, and those people live in China. Even a few years away from your connections can mean they go cold, threatening your chances of promotion. If you are a senior Chinese manager and you get posted abroad, it may mean you are not doing very well at home, says Zhang; and if you work for a state-owned firm, you cannot refuse to go, he adds.

According to Zhang, an advantage of working in Europe is that the rules governing business are relatively straightforward. "Everything is transparent," he says. Relationships between companies are simpler, too. In China, he says, firms assume that customers will buy only from someone they know or have a relationship with. They therefore spend vast amounts of time catering to clients. Western firms do this too, but not to the same degree. Finally, differences in corporate etiquette can also be significant. If a Chinese vendor gives a presentation and the customer asks him lots of questions he can't answer or raises lots of potential problems, the vendor will be distraught, says Zhang. He will assume that the customer does not like him. If the customer is Western, however, it probably just means that he wants to be given more information. "People here look at the facts, not the person."

Ostensibly, Mr. Smith and Mr. Zhang have identical jobs; they are both expatriates in each other's country and are both are working in marketing and sales. Obviously, though, the jobs are not the same.

Application 11.5   (cont.)

Think about it...

(1) From what you know, how would you describe the cultural differences between the two countries involved (China and the United Kingdom)? How might these differences influence the behaviors of Smith and Zhang?

(2) Based on your assessment, do both Smith and Zhang actually have the same jobs? Explain.

(3) Finally, and recognizing that you have only limited information here, what strategies would you suggest to Smith and Zhang to facilitate their cultural adjustment to their host countries? Would you suggest the same or different strategies to the two men? Why or why not?

Managing repatriation

Repatriation refers to the process of returning expatriates to their home countries. Repatriation may occur because the assignment has been completed, family reasons, failure, or dissatisfaction. Even though repatriation can at times cause as much culture shock as expatriation, organizations and managers alike often overlook the effects. When going home, managers can face *reverse culture shock*.

Reverse culture shock may result from dissatisfaction with the job or old way of life in the home country. The excitement of foreign travel is gone. Sometimes an expatriate returns to his or her previous jobs and feels demoted or bored. At other times the employer may have undergone major changes and the expatriate's skills are no longer useful or valued. In addition, superiors and colleagues may not value the international experience or the skills acquired abroad. Reentry can also be challenging on a personal level. Family and friends may have moved, made new friends, or acquired new interests, and are no longer as available as they were before departure. Finally, sometimes the expatriates themselves have changed. They have incorporated new values, habits, and world views that may be at odds with their old friends at home. At the extreme, they can become foreigners in their own land.

Returning expatriates tend to adopt one of three coping strategies.

- *Resocialized returnees.* Resocialized returnees are people who attempt to fit in back in the home culture by ignoring or rejecting what they learned in their foreign assignment. Such returnees typically failed to assimilate into the foreign culture during their overseas assignment, often living in expat communities and minimizing their interactions with the locals. As a result, they tend to find it relatively easy to return psychologically to their home culture.

- *Alienated returnees.* Alienated returnees are at the other end of the spectrum. While abroad they tended to "go native," and over time began to reject the values of their home country in favor of the values of their host country. When they return home they feel alienated. They find it difficult to apply their foreign experiences in meaningful ways now that they have returned. For many, they simply wish to return to their adopted home.
- *Proactive returnees.* Proactive returnees represent an optimistic breed of traveler. They return home with a conviction that they can succeed in melding the two cultures in positive or productive ways. They realize that they have changed personally as a result of their overseas assignment and want to make use of what they have learned. They often seek out new friends or colleagues with similar experiences or they launch new projects or adventures. Above all, they want to make use of what they have learned abroad.

To reduce the difficulties associated with reentry, many companies create various mechanisms by which expatriates can keep in touch with their colleagues back home at company headquarters. These mechanisms can include special newsletters, regularly scheduled home visits, special web pages focusing on expatriate concerns, and assigning HRM specialists to oversee both overseas assignments and repatriation activities. The key for most major multinational firms (and most expatriates) is to ensure that expatriates do not get lost or forgotten when they are out of their home country. The old adage "Out of sight, out of mind" is pertinent here, and responsibility often falls on the expatriates themselves to guarantee that this does not occur.

Application 11.6   Andrea Walker, returning home

Examples like the following have occurred in many companies in many countries. While the details may vary, all these stories have one thing in common: they are all problematic. Consider: after working as an entry-level marketing representative for a US consumer products company for three years, Andrea Walker was offered a promotion and an overseas assignment to Belize as the local marketing manager. She readily accepted the opportunity, in order to gain both global business experience and greater corporate recognition. She spent three years in Belize, developing good contacts and building markets for her employer. When she determined that it was time to return home for her daughter's schooling, however, her employer seemed less than enthusiastic. The executive who had originally hired her was no longer with the company, and other managers at the home office preferred to work with their own protégés. Some managers observed that they couldn't remember Andrea except through her periodic market summary reports. Even so, Andrea had a written contract guaranteeing that she could return to corporate headquarters following her three-year assignment.

Think about it . . .

(1)   If you were Andrea and concluded that there was little enthusiasm for your return to corporate headquarters, what would you do? Why?

(2)   If you were company management, and recognized that few people were enthusiastic about Andrea's return, what would you do? Why?

(3)   What might the company have done differently to take full advantage of Andrea's work experience abroad?

(4)   What might Andrea have done differently to retain contacts and communications with the home office?

MANAGER'S NOTEBOOK

Living and working globally

Wei Hopeman, Peter Hessler, Mr. Zhang, Mr. Smith, and Andrea Walker all share a common experience. They need to cope – and, hopefully, prosper – in very different environments from the ones in which they grew up. They are all global travellers. While they may share relatively common goals, however, there are sizable differences in the environments to which they must adapt.

Living and working globally: assessing demands and constraints

As noted throughout this book, one of the first challenges in preparing for new assignments is to understand the cultural, organizational, and situational environments that characterize one's future home and workplace (see Exhibit 11.12). For example, if a manager is used to an individualistic and egalitarian environment, moving to an

Exhibit 11.12 Assessing the living/working environment (examples)

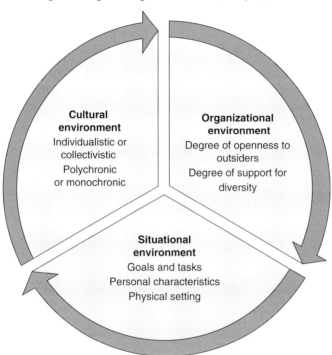

environment characterized by collectivism and hierarchy can be a shock. Likewise, moving from an organization characterized by openness to "strangers" and significant corporate support (like the Shell example discussed above) to one characterized by a more closed and perhaps hostile environment with little corporate support (not unlike that faced by Mr. Zhang above) can also create tension to would-be travelers (see discussion on culture shock). Finally, situations and the people within them are always different. What are the traveler's goals in a foreign assignment and what are his or her skills, including multicultural competence? What family responsibilities must be considered in such moves?

Assessing the living and working environment (both before and after a move) is not an easy task, but it is nevertheless necessary, or at least prudent, in order to prepare adequately for new ventures. As an English football player and coach noted, "To me the bottom line is the more education you can give yourself, and the more preparation you can do, the less chance of failing."[28]

Living and working globally: developing action plans

In *Alice's Adventures in Wonderland*, British author and Oxford professor Lewis Carroll made an important observation: To paraphrase, "If you don't know where you are going, any road will take you there."[29] So it is with international travel, living, and working. Goals and plans are essential in order to succeed. This requires advance preparation, obviously, but it also requires continual on-the-job skills development and some degree of self-confidence. The challenge for global managers is to find a workable balance between task accomplishment on behalf of the company and personal growth and development on behalf of themselves. Ideally, these two goals should be mutually complementary, but this seldom occurs without planning. What, therefore, should managers do? Here are three suggestions (see Exhibit 11.13).

1   Understand your new environment

There are many things that individuals – and families – can do to prepare themselves for an easier transition. Most of these are not difficult, though some can be challenging (e.g., learning the local language). Nevertheless, the more that people can learn about their new environment prior to arrival, the more prepared they will be to get settled and get down to work. Consider the following strategies.

- Learn about the new location and its culture.
- Search for local contacts.
- Research local associations and clubs and other interests before arriving.
- Plan to have time for enjoyment before work begins.

Exhibit 11.13 Action plans for living and working globally

(1) Understand your new environment	(2) Continue to develop multicultural competence	(3) Make yourself at home
• Begin learning about your new environment prior to departure. • If you have a spouse or family, get them involved. • Reach out to prospective contacts in the new location prior to departure. • Build a home base of support to retain contacts back home.	• Continue to develop your self-awareness and empathy skills.. • Reflect on your new experiences; look for patterns. • Build your capacity for behavioral flexibility. • Think before you act.	• Be yourself, with skill. • Find your place or role in new environment. • Facilitate your integration into local environment through information sharing. • Most cultures are patient with "foreigners." • Don't take yourself too seriously.

- If there is something you "must have," take it with you or make arrangements to have it shipped.
- Talk to friends and family and find ways to keep in touch; build a support network at home.
- Think about your goals for the experience abroad.
- Learn the local language.

2   Continue to develop multicultural competence

A second strategy for living and working globally involves continued self-development. In other words, as discussed earlier in this book, successful managers are the ones who can develop *multicultural competence*. This involves ongoing learning – both about oneself and others – and personal and managerial development. Several key strategies are identified here.

- *Develop greater self-awareness*. Self-awareness refers to an understanding of one's identity, values, and beliefs about one's social position and social interactions. It allows one to preserve one's own identity when faced with experiences that contradict existing beliefs and values. Develop awareness of your own culture and how it has shaped your values, beliefs, and worldviews.
- *Develop greater empathy*. Empathy refers to the ability to identify and understand others' feelings and motives. It allows one to assist the other party in preserving his or her identity. Understand that others are also complex cultural beings whose actions are a product of deep-seated cultural values and beliefs. When misunderstandings occur, search for cultural explanations of confusing or offensive behavior, before judging it.
- *Gather and analyze information*. Gathering and analyzing information refers to the ability to observe context, body language, facial expressions, and behavioral cues; actively listen and summarize information, and ask questions in a manner and timing that is apposite. Ask questions when appropriate, observe others, test your assumptions, and stretch frames of reference.
- *Integrate and transform information*. Integrating and transforming information refers to developing a coherent theory of action on the basis of the information collected in the negotiating meaning stage. As this theory is tested and the behaviors are practiced, new rules are created and fine-tuned. Reflect on intercultural experiences and look for patterns. Test your conclusions.
- *Develop more behavioral flexibility*. Behavioral flexibility refers to the ability to engage in different behaviors, to switch styles, and to accomplish tasks in more than one way.

Look for opportunities to increase your behavioral repertoire by engaging in different activities and practicing doing things in different ways. For example, if you are a direct communicator, practice communicating indirectly. In addition, recognize those behaviors that are challenging to you and compensate with other behaviors. For example, preface a direct statement with an apology.

- *Develop greater mindfulness.* Mindfulness refers to the ability of paying close attention to one's own feelings and actions and others' actions and reactions. Make the effort to focus on your actions and reactions. Think before you act.

3   Make yourself at home

Finally, living and working globally can be a great opportunity to learn new things and advance one's career. Foreign assignments provide a chance to develop new managerial skills, increase tolerance for ambiguity, develop new perspectives and ways of thinking, and improve one's ability to work with others. Taking advantage of this opportunity requires flexibility and high levels of self-awareness, however. In the final analysis, perhaps the principal key to success is a manager's ability to make him- or herself at home in their new environment.

- *Be yourself, with skill.* While abroad, managers can still can be themselves – but with skill. In other words, they will have to adapt and change, but they do not need to become someone they are not. They do not necessarily have to convert to the local religion or develop an appetite for fried ants (even though they are tasty) to be accepted and have a fruitful experience. They will have to be flexible in some important things, however, and learn to accept that others may not agree with them (or even like them). The key here is balance: what is really important to people and can't be compromised, and what can people live with? Revisit this question often, as the answer may change.

- *Find a place or role in the new environment.* Even though individuals are the same person, they may need to occupy a different role in the new environment. For example, at home they may be the best manager in their unit and the one helping others to succeed. Abroad, however, these same people may be the ones needing help with their assignments. People working abroad should expect that they will play different roles, and should actively look for roles that will make them feel part of the new environment.

- *Actively look for and provide information to facilitate integration.* Two communication tools may be helpful here: inquiry and advocacy. *Inquiry* refers to exploring and questioning one's own reasoning and the reasoning of others. In other words, ask yourself the following questions any time you are confronted with a cross-cultural conflict: how do you and I perceive the situation? What do you and I wish to achieve in this situation? Which actions are you and I willing to take to achieve this goal? Inquiry requires suspending judgment, letting go of a previous understanding, and tolerating uncertainty until a new understanding may be created. We like to be right, but in a cross-cultural situation what is right is relative. *Advocacy* refers to expressing and standing for what one thinks and desires. Advocacy suggests stating clearly what you think and want, and explaining the reasoning behind your view. In other words, it requires knowing yourself and understanding what your assumptions and points of view are. It also requires taking responsibility for how you feel about things. For example, if you are frustrated because your counterpart always comes late to meetings – something perhaps acceptable in his or her culture – you may say, "I prefer it when I do not have to wait for you, because for me it is very stressful not knowing what time you will arrive." This is very different from saying, "I am a busy person and it is inconsiderate when you fail to keep your appointments." The first statement is about you and how you feel about the interaction, and opens up the possibility for the other person to understand your point of view and to respond. The second can easily be construed as a specific attack on the individual that is likely to be taken personally. After all, he or she will likely provide a reason for his or her tardiness, and the problem will remain unresolved.

- *Do not take yourself too seriously.* Remember that culture shock is usually temporary, and that everyone experiences it to one degree or another. People must acknowledge that they do not have to be right all the time, and that making mistakes is part of life. Most cultures are patient with "foreigners." Be patient with yourself and others, and remember to have fun.

Summary points

■ Many managers see a global assignment as a great opportunity to advance their careers, make more money, or learn new things. It may represent a personal challenge or a way to a more interesting life. Managers who take such assignments typically report learning new managerial skills, increasing their tolerance for ambiguity, learning new ways of seeing things, and improving their ability to work with others.

■ Expatriates and frequent flyers who travel regularly to work in global operations often express the same frustration that they feel decidedly like outsiders, yet must find ways to break into the local culture simply to do their job. This is clearly no easy task, since local environments can be highly variable, often secretive, and occasionally hostile.

- There can be major differences between organizationally initiated or self-initiated global assignments. People's motivations and expectations may be different, as well as their commitment to be away from their home culture for long periods of time. Both involve expatriation.

- Working abroad often poses a number of challenges that can affect people in very different ways depending upon their personal and organizational circumstances. These challenges emerge both prior to departure and afterwards. The nature of some of these challenges can evolve with time, while others are ever-present. We have explored three of these challenges: personal considerations, time considerations, and family and career considerations.

- Although most people change as a result of living in a foreign culture, this does not necessarily mean that they change to be more like the people in the foreign culture. Indeed, some people may become more attached to their original culture than they were beforehand. Expatriate and ethnic enclaves are not uncommon, and some people spend many years in a foreign country without ever assimilating local values or even learning the local language. It is therefore often helpful to separate the process of adaptation to a foreign culture into two related but quite different processes: psychological adjustment refers to the process of developing a way of life in the new country that is personally satisfying. socio-cultural adjustment refers to the individual's ability to interact competently with the host culture.

- In order to minimize the problems of reentry after working abroad, companies often create various mechanisms by which expatriates can keep in touch with their colleagues back home at company headquarters, including special newsletters, regularly-scheduled home visits, special web pages focusing on expatriate concerns, and appointing HRM specialists to oversee both overseas assignments and repatriation activities. The key for most major multinational firms (and most expatriates) is to ensure that expatriates do not get lost or forgotten when they are out of their home country.

Notes

1 Robert Louis Stevenson, *Travels with a Donkey in the Cévennes*. Oxford University Press, 1993 [1879].
2 Leo Tolstoy, "Three methods of reform," in *Pamphlets* (trans. Aylmer Maude). Christchurch: Free Age Press, 1900, pp. 25–32, p. 29.

3 Bill Newcott, "Big boat, little boat," *AARP The Magazine*, January 2012, p. 26.

4 Nancy J. Adler, *International Dimensions of Organizational Behavior*, 5th edn. Mason, OH: Thompson, 2008.

5 Marja Tahvanainen, Denice Welch, and Verner Worm, 2005, "Implications of short-term international assignments," *European Management Journal*, 23(6), pp. 663–73.

6 Nancy J. Adler, *International Dimensions of Organizational Behavior*, 3rd edn. Cincinnati: South-Western College Publishing, 1997.

7 Martha J. Frase, "International commuters: are your overseas assignments creating risky 'stealth-pats'?," *HR Magazine*, 2007, 52(3), pp. 91–5.

8 Carla, Joinson, "Cutting down the days: HR can make expat assignments short and sweet," *HR Magazine*, 2000, 45(4), pp. 92–7.

9 *The Economist*, "Travelling more lightly," *The Economist*, June 22, 2006, pp. 99–101.

10 Helene Mayerhofer, Linley C. Hartmann, Gabriela Michelitsch-Riedl, and Iris Kollinger, "Flexpatriate assignments: a neglected issue in global staffing," *International Journal of Human Resource Management*, 2004, 15(8), pp. 1371–89.

11 Richard Hodgetts and Fred Luthans, *International Management: Culture, Strategy, and Behavior*, 5th edn. New York: McGraw-Hill-Irwin, 2003.

12 Scott Gummer, "Citigroup's Wei Hopeman transcends time zones,"*Fortune*, January 16, 2012, p. 21.

13 Gummer, "Citigroup's Wei Hopeman."

14 Sue Shellenbarger, "Separation anxiety: job transfers create problems for families," *Wall Street Journal*, October 27, 2005, p. D1.

15 Kep Enderby, "Biographies," New South Wales Council for Civil Liberties, available at www. nswccl.org.au/about/biographies.php#ke (accessed 2008).

16 John W. Berry, "Acculturation: living successfully in two cultures," *International Journal of Intercultural Relations*, 2005, 29(6), pp. 697–712.

17 Colleen Ward, Yutaka Okura, Antony Kennedy, and Takahiro Kojima, "The U-curve on trial: a longitudinal study of psychological and sociocultural adjustment during cross-cultural transition," *International Journal of Intercultural Relations*, 1998, 22(3), pp. 277–91; Berry, "Acculturation."

18 Young Yun Kim, "Intercultural personhood: globalization and a way of being," *International Journal of Intercultural Relations*, 2008, 32(4), pp. 359–68.

19 Peter Hessler, "A rat in my soup," *The New Yorker*, July 24, 2000, p. 38.

20 Adapted from Lillian H. Chaney and Jeanette S. Martin, *Intercultural Business Communication*. Upper Saddle River, NJ: Prentice Hall, 1995.

21 Lorraine Brown and Immy Holloway, "The adjustment journey of international postgraduate students at an English university: an ethnographic study," *Journal of Research in International Education*, 2008, 7(2), pp. 232–49.

22 Kim, "Intercultural personhood."

23 Harry C. Triandis, *Culture and Social Behavior*. New York: McGraw-Hill, 1994.

24 Triandis, *Culture and Social Behavior*.

25 Kim, "Intercultural personhood."

26 This framework builds on the work of Berry, "Acculturation," on the acculturation strategies of ethnocultural groups. In the original framework, Berry identified a fourth strategy, marginalization, when ethnocultural groups let go of their original culture but fail to integrate with dominant groups. We find that this strategy is less likely to be used successfully by managers given their job requirements.

27 Ward *et al.*, "The U-curve on trial"; Berry, "Acculturation."

28 Stuart Pearce, *Wikipedia*, 2012

29 Lewis Carroll, *Alice's Adventures in Wonderland*. London: Penguin Books, 1960 [1865]. This "quotation" is paraphrased here because, while this is the message Carroll was trying to convey, and while it is often cited as being his, he never actually wrote this. Instead, he wrote a longer dialog between two characters that yields this conclusion. Moreover, Lewis Carroll is his pen name; his real name was Charles Lutwidge Dodgson, and he was an author, mathematician, logician, Anglican deacon, and photographer.

CHAPTER 12

Epilogue: the journey continues

MANAGEMENT CHALLENGE

We have now come full circle in this book. We have argued that in today's economy all managers are global managers, and that they all face similar challenges regardless of where or how they work. We have discussed three types of managerial assignments – expatriates, frequent flyers, and virtual managers – and looked at both the similarities and differences in these assignments. We have examined three major aspects of the work environment – cultures, organizations, and situations – that can affect managerial success or failure. On the basis of this, we have explored six specific mechanisms for developing global management skills. The challenge for managers, then, is to integrate these factors into a unified approach to global management. This is a difficult, but nonetheless necessary, task for future success. We close with a summary of our discoveries, as well as several reflective thoughts on the future of management and what managers might consider as they go forward into uncharted waters.

Chapter outline

Your time is limited; so don't waste it living someone else's life. Don't be trapped by dogma – which is living with the results of other people's thinking. Don't let the noise of others' opinions drown out your own inner voice. And most important, have the courage to follow your heart and intuition. They somehow already know what you truly want to become. Everything else is secondary.

Steven Jobs[1]
Former chairman, Apple Computers, United States

The most dangerous thing is to be successful. You then think every decision is the right one.

Wong Wai Ming[2]
Chief financial officer, Lenovo, China

Futurists and their closely watched predictions abound in these changing times, and nowhere is this trend more prominent than with regard to future economic trends and the future of global business. Some experts predict that past competitors will become future partners, while other experts predict just the opposite. Some predict increased economic integration brought on by globalization, while others predict increased economic fragmentation and turmoil, also brought on by globalization. Even the opinions of great philosophers of the past apparently disagree. The eleventh-century Persian mathematician, astronomer, and poet Omar Khayyám suggested that, in order to see the future, we must study the past. "When I want to understand what is happening today or try to decide what will happen tomorrow, I look back." Learn from history; the past is prologue. At the same time, the fifth-century BCE Hindu prince and founder of Buddhism, Siddhārtha Gautama (also known as Śākyamuni), suggested that, if we want to see the future (indeed, if we want to be part of the future), we should step forward. If we are facing in the right direction, he noted, all we have to do is keep walking. Keep your eye on the ball; the future belongs to those who search it out and are prepared to capitalize on it. Two philosophers and two different opinions – again. Once more, our challenge is to learn from such contradictions, past and present.

What have we learned?

For managers, advice is easy to get, but getting good advice is a bit more difficult. We have tried throughout this volume to summarize what we consider to be good advice for managers in the field. We have approached this topic in three parts.

Management challenges

In the first part, we examined the new global realities, considering the changing nature of both global business and global managers.

- *Global business.* Globalization has become a fact, but it is much more than this. Business changes include increased globalization, a globalized workforce, techno-logical revolutions, political and regulatory volatility, and economic opportunities and turmoil. We need to ask ourselves what this means for contemporary global

Exhibit 12.1 Global managers and cultural embeddedness

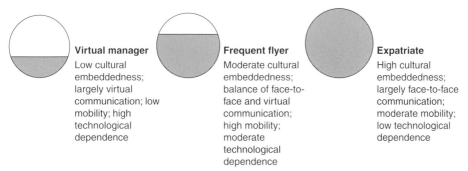

Virtual manager
Low cultural
embeddedness;
largely virtual
communication; low
mobility; high
technological
dependence

Frequent flyer
Moderate cultural
embeddedness;
balance of face-to-
face and virtual
communication;
high mobility;
moderate
technological
dependence

Expatriate
High cultural
embeddedness;
largely face-to-face
communication;
moderate mobility;
low technological
dependence

business. We introduced the concept of multicultural competence as a framework for understanding what skills managers must develop in this uncertain global economy.

- *Global managers.* We explored how the responsibilities of today's managers differ from those in the past. Global awareness and understanding have become the litmus test of successful managers. We identified three general types of global managers – expatriates, frequent flyers, and virtual managers – and how the global responsibilities and qualifications can differ for each (see Exhibit 12.1).

Developing global understanding

In the second part of the book, we focused on better understanding the environment in which managers work. We broke this environment down into three categories: cultural, organizational, and situational (see Exhibit 12.2).

- *Cultures.* We discussed the various meanings of culture as a concept. We also noted that cultures affect managerial actions through prevailing work values and social normative beliefs. We introduced the concept of core cultural dimensions as a means of building thumbnail portraits of various peoples and cultures (see Exhibit 12.3). For example, compared to people in individualistic cultures, people working in collectivistic cultures may be more likely to value working in groups, share information, and strive for group success over individual performance. Like thumbnails, however, these portraits lack details, which need to be fleshed out through further investigation. We also pointed out that all cultures exist in environments characterized by complexities and contradictions. Generalizations are difficult. Finally, we discussed institutional environments as a subset of culture but still an important factor for managers to understand.

Exhibit 12.2 Cultural, organizational, and situational environments

Exhibit 12.3 Core cultural dimensions

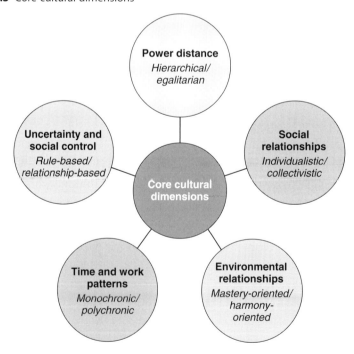

- *Organizations.* People working in organizations with manifestly different structures, values, and processes, such as centralized or collaborative decision making, may approach negotiation, leadership, and workforce management in very different ways. Because of this, it is important to understand the relationships between global strategy, organization design, and structure. Moreover, when and where are we likely to see autocratic or collaborative decision making? How do different cultures define the concept of employee participation? How do organizational cultures influence employee and managerial behavior?

- *Situations.* Each unique situation that managers find themselves in can influence both behaviors and managerial success. For example, negotiating a contract or managing people in a location where the manager does not understand the local language changes the work environment equation significantly. Interpreters must be used, and considerable information can easily be lost. This is just one example of how situations can vary. We discussed differences among people – particular cognitions and cognitive schemas – as well as roles and responsibilities, locations, and goals and tasks. Understanding factors such as these frames the managerial task environment in ways that illuminate potential suitable actions. We ended this chapter by presenting a model for managers for use throughout the remainder of the book.

Developing global management skills

Finally, in the third part of the book, we explored how variations across environments can create both demands and constraints on managerial action (see Exhibit 12.4) – that is, managers in the field are advised to understand local cultures (including their own), organizational or corporate realities, and the specific nature of situations before determining a course of action. In other words, managerial options for behavior in cross-cultural settings are not unlimited, and behaviors outside these parameters risk managers losing face as well as opportunities. We focused in this part on exploring six concrete managerial actions.

- *Communicating across cultures.* A model of cross-cultural communication was introduced and used to analyze how various environmental factors can influence success in interpersonal relations. Cultural screens on interpersonal communication were discussed, including cognitive limitations on communication and communication protocols. Content and context were explored as key factors influencing verbal, as well as nonverbal, behavior. Strategies for understanding and managing first encounters were also discussed.

Exhibit 12.4 Choices for the manager

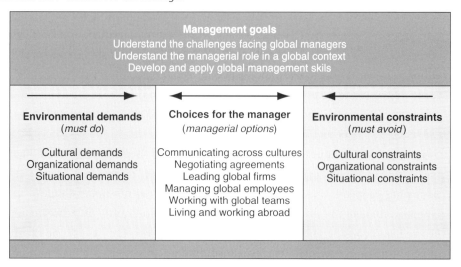

Management goals
Understand the challenges facing global managers
Understand the managerial role in a global context
Develop and apply global management skils

Environmental demands (*must do*)	Choices for the manager (*managerial options*)	Environmental constraints (*must avoid*)
Cultural demands Organizational demands Situational demands	Communicating across cultures Negotiating agreements Leading global firms Managing global employees Working with global teams Living and working abroad	Cultural constraints Organizational constraints Situational constraints

- *Negotiating global agreements.* Negotiation and bargaining across borders are no easy task, because so many of the variables involved are culture-based. In many cases, they are even hidden from view, leaving managers to work partially blind-folded in a very high-stakes game. The discussion in this chapter ranged from making preparations for negotiations all the way through to managing final contracts once made. Ethics and the importance of building mutual trust – and even mutual benefit – emerge as key considerations when seeking partners, negotiating agreements, and managing the subsequent partnerships.

- *Leading global organizations.* Leadership in a global context is something that everyone agrees is important, but few know how to implement. It remains an ambiguous concept largely because its implementation relies heavily on leaders understanding (and being able to leverage) local environments in ways that direct collective energies towards the accomplishment of specific tangible goals. Without understanding cultures, organizations, and variations in situations, this endeavor becomes largely a hopeless task. The GLOBE study was introduced here as one framework for understanding and then applying leadership behaviors within cultural constraints.

- *Managing a global workforce.* Managing and motivating people across borders must be one of the most challenging jobs facing managers. It can also be one of the most stressful. In this chapter we explored the management and motivational environment. We looked at how work values can affect employee behaviors, and how managerial roles can change with different environments. We examined the psychology of work, as well as psychological contracts. Finally, incentives and rewards were discussed as potential motivational strategies.

- *Working with global teams.* Working with teams, global or otherwise, can be both exhilarating and threatening for managers. It can be exhilarating to the extent that positive group dynamics leads to creative and collaborative efforts that may have been impossible working individually. It can also be threatening, though, to the extent that the manager and the team are working from different scripts, don't like each other, don't trust each other, or simply have opposing objectives. Accordingly, team management becomes an important skill. In this regard, we explored different types of global teams, as well as key success factors. We explored the role of leadership in team building and the importance of building mutual trust among members. Finally, we examined strategies for resolving – or at least living with – team conflicts. Throughout, it was suggested that highly diverse teams, including global teams, can bring much to the table and create truly creative solutions to the extent that such endeavors are managed, nurtured, and rewarded.

- *Living and working abroad.* Finally, we explored the challenges of living and work-ing abroad. We examined the advantages and disadvantages of global assignments, as well as potential differences between self-initiated and organizationally initiated assignments. The two concepts of psychological and socio-cultural adjustment were discussed, as were strategies and techniques for managing the acculturation – and repatriation – processes.

Where do we go from here?

Throughout this volume, an effort has been made to integrate issues of culture with those of management, in the belief that success in the global economy requires a detailed understanding of both. Successful global managers move with ease across international borders and adapt readily to local changes and challenges. They look for a competitive edge wherever they can find it. Most of all, however, they continually learn from their surroundings and apply these lessons to their work.

Learning from the past

In this regard, perhaps a good place to begin this learning process is with history. Spanish philosopher George Santayana once observed, "Those who fail to learn from the mistakes of their predecessors are destined to repeat them."[3] This may be true, but it is equally correct that one of the benefits of studying history – learning from the past – is that it alleviates the need to start from scratch. History provides lessons as building blocks upon which to build our own approach to management, as well as our own careers. In this spirit, we offer three lessons from three very different time periods and involving very different people and circumstances. The first two examples, Christopher Columbus and Mahatma Gandhi, come from earlier generations, while the third comes from the very recent past. All speak to business managers, locally and globally.

Christopher Columbus is widely credited with being the first European explorer to "discover" America. (Many Scandinavians disagree, and point out that the Vikings landed and actually colonized the northeastern tip of Canada centuries earlier. Many Native Americans and Inuits also disagree, and point out that they were actually there first; indeed, some of them met Columbus on the shore of Hispaniola when he arrived in the "New World," and paid a heavy price.) Columbus is also widely, if incorrectly, credited with proving that the world was round instead of flat. The controversies surrounding Columbus aside, what many scholars have overlooked in this story is that Columbus succeeded in his quest of discovery because he was wrong, not because he was right.

Consider: ancient Greek mathematicians demonstrated long before Columbus that the world was round. They even estimated with amazing accuracy that the earth was approximately 25,000 miles in circumference. Columbus and his maritime contemporaries understood this, even if many peasants and less educated people did not. Most explorers of the time reasoned with moderate accuracy that India and the Spice Islands – their targeted objective – were roughly 8,000 miles to the west of Spain. They also reasoned, correctly, that, in view of this distance, such a voyage was impossible. Given the prevailing technology of the time, no ship could travel so far without running out of water and supplies. Columbus studied available maps and charts of the time and concluded, incorrectly, that his contemporaries were wrong and that India was only about 3,000 miles away – a journey he considered possible, if difficult. Off he sailed in 1492. After his long voyage at sea and, ironically, just over 3,000 miles from Spain, Columbus sailed into the undiscovered Caribbean and concluded, again incorrectly, that he had reached India.

The useful lesson from Columbus's voyage is simple. If Columbus had had more accurate information or had listened to local experts about the true distance to India, he might never have attempted the voyage. He believed he was right, however, and he initiated action on the basis of his belief. As he continued his journey, he adapted his strategies and tried to learn from his mistakes. Indeed, many of today's managers have learned this same lesson: Some of life's greatest successes result from accidents, hunches, or simple luck. All managers make mistakes and miscalculate – some more than others.

Managerial success is seldom linear; there are many bumps and detours along the way. What differentiates winners from losers, however, is both their steadfastness and determination and their ability to learn, adapt, and, when possible, capitalize on their mistakes.

The second lesson is more direct, and comes from the nonviolent Indian peace activist of the twentieth century, Mahatma Gandhi. Gandhi was fond of saying: "We must be the change we wish to see in others." In other words, the real challenge for global managers is leadership, not followership. The challenge is how to build both a more prosperous company and a more prosperous world. To accomplish this, successful global managers must bring people together in collaborative and symbiotic ways that create value for the organization and its surroundings. In this endeavor, an understanding of how cultures differ and how they influence organizational and managerial processes alike emerges as an essential ingredient in a successful global manager's toolkit.

A final example comes from the global economic turmoil of the past several years. We have heard much recently about economic downturns, financial exigencies, bankruptcies, corporate bailouts, recessions, and unemployment. We have also seen a number of people and institutions being blamed, including bankers, investors, mortgage lenders, manufacturers, offshore companies, and politicians. We see leaders from entire continents collectively blaming leaders from other continents. The finger of blame is pointing in an almost infinite number of directions. Finally, we have seen individual and collective greed as never before. In the world of business, regardless of geographic location, we have witnessed entrepreneurs and managers alike desperately trying to find a quick fix, a short-term competitive advantage that will allow them to become wealthier than their competitors and colleagues. Wealth is celebrated, even worshipped, in places. Meanwhile, millions of people around the world in both developing and industrialized countries lose their homes, jobs, security, health, and even education for their children.

What has been lost in all this chaos is a fundamental premise of successful global (and local) business: mutual exchange and mutual benefit. Researchers and managers alike see successful global negotiations as being based on people and companies coming together to achieve their common objectives. Even in countries where legal contracts reign supreme, the role of personal relationships is not undervalued. Likewise, successful communication is typically seen as being best facilitated when all parties share a common understanding – and a common cause. Leaders are seen to be more effective when they strive to see that everyone involved wins. Work motivation and performance are best facilitated when employees at all levels see a reason for buy-in. Equity, fairness, and stewardship are seen by most people to be the most effective way to create a more ethical and sustainable world order.

Certainly, these management processes get more complex and challenging when managers and their companies cross borders, yet the fundamental principles hold. The individual and corporate selfishness of the past few years has demonstrated quite clearly that greed is a short-term and nonsustainable strategy for future development and security, both at home and abroad. Breaking faith with one's stakeholders – whether they are customers, investors, or employees – is invariably suboptimal in the long run. Instead, global managers and their firms would be better advised to seek long-term global strategies and partnerships and to incorporate a genuine stakeholder model as part of their business plan (see Exhibit 12.5): inclusion rather than exclusion; partnerships rather than lethal competition.

Looking to the future

We suggested earlier in this book that culture and cultural differences represented major keys to understanding managerial thought and action, although they are certainly not the only key. We also suggested that a productive way to discover the utility of these keys is to approach intellectual discovery and management development as part of an overall learning strategy. To understand how individuals learn, we introduced experiential learning theory, one of the most influential models of managerial development.[4] As will be remembered, following this theory, the learning process is composed of four stages: concrete experiences, observation and reflection, abstract concepts and generalizations, and testing the implications of concepts.

Exhibit 12.5 Learning from the past, looking to the future

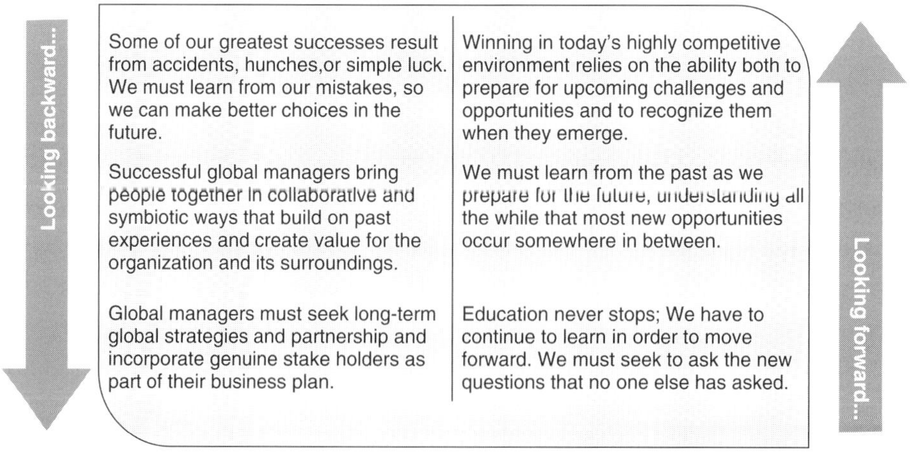

Looking backward...

Some of our greatest successes result from accidents, hunches, or simple luck. We must learn from our mistakes, so we can make better choices in the future.

Successful global managers bring people together in collaborative and symbiotic ways that build on past experiences and create value for the organization and its surroundings.

Global managers must seek long-term global strategies and partnership and incorporate genuine stake holders as part of their business plan.

Winning in today's highly competitive environment relies on the ability both to prepare for upcoming challenges and opportunities and to recognize them when they emerge.

We must learn from the past as we prepare for the future, understanding all the while that most new opportunities occur somewhere in between.

Education never stops; We have to continue to learn in order to move forward. We must seek to ask the new questions that no one else has asked.

Looking forward...

By using this approach, managers still may not have the power to see into the future, but they do have an ability to prepare themselves for it better. Chung Mong Koo, chairman of the Hyundai Motor Group, observed that the difference between winners and losers in a highly competitive business environment is the ability both to prepare for upcoming challenges and opportunities and to recognize such opportunities when they emerge.[5] Preparation *and* recognition: both are required. Seeing opportunities for the future without adequate preparation or preparing for the future without adequate study of emerging opportunities are both recipes for coming in second or third place.

In the same manner, many have noted that the word *weiji* means "crisis" in Chinese and is typically expressed using two characters: one for danger and one for opportunity.[6] This interpretation of the concept suggests that crises are often related to two other variables: threats and opportunities. In many cases, threats and opportunities can indeed lead to productive changes in organizations to make them more nimble, quicker to respond, and more competitive. Again, however, this occurs only if and when managers realize what is happening and understand the surrounding environment to the extent that they are in a position to capitalize on the events as they unfold.

When the business environment is viewed in this manner, it may be that Omar Khayyàm and Siddhārtha Gautama are actually giving the same advice to global managers in the twenty-first century. Yes, the past is prologue, and we must understand the "How?s" and "Why?s" about how we got to this point; but also, yes, if we believe that we are headed in the right direction (that we can "see" the future, at least metaphorically), all we need to do is to pursue it. Perhaps the focus of our principal attention right now, therefore, should be on the present, so long as we see this present in dynamic or continuous terms: past > present > future. Most business opportunities are here now, not in the past and not in the future. Maybe the wisest thing global managers can do is to understand this dynamic. What can we learn from the past that can help us in the future, and what can we do in the present that can help guarantee this success in the future?

To accomplish this, as we have discussed throughout this book, global managers must develop proficiencies in working across cultures, because this is where most future opportunities will be found. They must develop an ability to distinguish between cultural differences and similarities across borders, as well as differences within single countries. They must develop an ability to tease out the subtle contradictions and dualities that are rooted in various cultures, and not look for easy answers when none may exist. They must also develop an ability to adapt traditional management skills, such as leadership, motivation, negotiation, and communication, to fit cross-cultural or multicultural venues. Herein lies the essence of effective global management.

The prospects of dealing with people from different cultural backgrounds can be very challenging, but potentially it can also be very rewarding. For many managers, though, it doesn't happen easily. Remember Percy Barnevik's dictum "Global managers are made, not born. This is not a natural process."[7] Remember, too, Thomas Stewart's observation that "a global manager is set apart by more than a worn suitcase and a dog-eared passport."[8] To the extent that these observations are correct, the onus is clearly on managers to prepare themselves for success in the future. Engaging with managers and entrepreneurs from different cultures opens up considerable opportunities to learn more about ourselves, discover new ways of doing things, and find creative solutions to problems both old and new. It is clearly part of the developmental process for most managers; and, in this pursuit, continual cognitive, analytical, and experiential learning play a significant – and often underappreciated – role.

Notes

1 Steven Jobs, commencement address, Stanford University, California, June 12, 2005.
2 Chuck Salter, "Protect and attach: Lenovo," *Fast Company*, January 2012, pp. 116–20.
3 George Santayana, *The Life of Reason or the Phases of Human Progress: Reason in Common Sense*. New York: Charles Scribner & Sons, 1924, p. 284.
4 David A. Kolb, "Management and the learning process," *California Management Review*, 1976, 18(3), pp. 21–31; David A. Kolb, *Experiential Learning: Experience as the Source of Learning and Development*. Englewood Cliffs, NJ: Prentice Hall, 1984.
5 Personal communication from Chung Mong Koo.
6 The Chinese word *weiji*, in traditional Chinese, is typically translated as "crisis" in much of the world, and is said to be composed of the characters for "danger" and "opportunity," the implication being that, in Chinese culture, a crisis is regarded not merely as a danger but also as an opportunity. This translation is open to question, however. In fact, *wei* can mean many things, including "danger"; "dangerous"; "endanger"; "jeopardize"; "perilous"; "precipitous"; "precarious"; "high"; "fear"; and "afraid." The polysemous *ji* can mean "machine"; "mechanical"; "airplane"; "suitable occasion"; "crucial point"; "pivot"; "incipient moment"; "opportune", "opportunity"; "chance"; "key link"; "secret"; and "cunning." Thus, while the word *jihui* can mean "opportune" or "opportunity" in modern Chinese, its *ji* component has many meanings, of which "opportunity" is only one. In *weiji*, *ji* means "crucial point," not necessarily "opportunity."
7 Percy Barnevik, cited in Philip R. Harris, Robert T. Moran, and Sarah V. Moran, *Managing Cultural Differences: Global Leadership Strategies for the 21st Century*, 6th edn. Amsterdam: Elsevier, 2004, p. 25.
8 Thomas Stewart, cited in Harris, Moran, and Moran, *Managing Cultural Differences*, p. 1.

Models of national cultures

For many managers, the study of culture often begins with a comparison of different cultures or countries using several cultural dimensions (e.g., individualism/collectivism). For example, if a manager from France is traveling to Prague in the Czech Republic, it can be quite helpful to understand differences in cultural trends between the two locales prior to arrival. While such models clearly do not explain everything managers need to know to succeed, they can be a useful starting point.

A number of such models are available and have been widely adopted. These include the works of Clyde and Florence Kluckhohn and Fred Strodtbeck, Geert Hofstede, Edward T. Hall, Fons Trompenaars, Shalom Schwartz, and Robert House and his GLOBE project associates. Each attempts to capture the essence of cultural differences through the use of multiple dimensions or measures. In doing so, each model highlights different aspects of societal beliefs, norms, and/or values, and, as such, convergence across the models has been seen as being very limited. This may not be the case, however. Below, we briefly summarize each of the six models. This is followed by a brief comparison between the models in search of commonalities.[1]

Models of national culture

Based on the initial research by Clyde Kluckhohn, cultural anthropologists Florence Kluckhohn and Fred Strodtbeck suggested one of the earliest models of culture, which has served as a principal foundation for several later models.[2] They proposed a theory of culture based on value orientations, arguing that there are a limited number of problems that are common to all human groups and for which there are a limited number of solutions. They further suggested that values in any given society are distributed in a way that creates a dominant value system. They used anthropological theories to identify five value orientations, four of which were later tested in five subcultures of the American southwest: two Native American tribes, a Hispanic village, a Mormon village, and a farming village of Anglo-American homesteaders. The five dimensions

Exhibit A.1 Kluckhohn and Strodtbecks' cultural dimensions

Relationship with nature: beliefs about the need or responsibility to control nature	*Mastery:* belief that people have a need or responsibility to control nature.	*Harmony:* belief that people should work with nature to maintain harmony or balance.	*Subjugation:* belief that individuals must submit to nature.
Relationship with people: beliefs about social structure	*Individualistic:* belief that social structure should be arranged on basis of individuals.	*Collateral:* belief that social structure should be based on groups of individuals with relatively equal status.	*Lineal:* belief that social structure should be based on groups with clear and rigid hierarchical relationships.
Human activities: beliefs about appropriate goals	*Being:* belief that people should concentrate on living for the moment.	*Becoming:* belief that people should strive to develop themselves into an integrated whole.	*Doing:* belief in striving for goals and accomplishments.
Relationship with time: extent to which past, present, and future influence decisions	*Past:* in making decisions, people are principally influenced by past events or traditions.	*Present:* in making decisions, people are principally influenced by present circumstances.	*Future:* in making decisions, people are principally influenced by future prospects.
Human nature: beliefs about good, neutral, or evil human nature	*Good:* belief that people are inherently good.	*Neutral:* belief that people are inherently neutral.	*Evil:* belief that people are inherently evil.

are identified in Exhibit A.1. Each dimension is represented on a three-point continuum.

Dutch management researcher Geert Hofstede has advanced the most widely used model of cultural differences in the organizations literature.[3] His model was derived from a study of employees from various countries working for major multinational corporations and was based on the assumption that different cultures can be distinguished on the basis of differences in what they value. In other words, some cultures place a high value on equality among individuals, while others place a high value on hierarchies or power distances between people. Likewise, some cultures value certainty in everyday life and have difficulty coping with unanticipated events, while others have a greater tolerance for ambiguity and seem to relish change. Taken together, Hofstede argued that it is possible to gain considerable insight into organized behavior across cultures on the basis of these value dimensions. Initially, Hofstede asserted that cultures could be distinguished along four dimensions, but later he added a fifth dimension based on his research with Michael Bond.[4] The final five dimensions are illustrated in Exhibit A.2.

Edward T. Hall, a noted American cultural anthropologist, has proposed a model of culture based on his ethnographic research in several societies, notably Germany, France, the United States, and Japan.[5] His research focused primarily on how cultures vary in interpersonal communication, but also included work on personal space and time. These three cultural dimensions are summarized in Exhibit A.3. Many of the terms used today in the field of cross-cultural management (e.g., monochronic and polychronic) are derived from his work.

Exhibit A.2 Hofstede's cultural dimensions

Cultural dimensions	Scale anchors	
Power distance: beliefs about the appropriate distribution of power in society	*Low power distance:* belief that effective leaders do not need to have substantial amounts of power compared to their subordinates.	*High power distance:* belief that people in positions of authority should have considerable power compared to their subordinates.
Uncertainty avoidance: degree of uncertainty that can be tolerated and its impact on rule making	*Low uncertainty avoidance:* tolerance of ambiguity; little need for rules to constrain uncertainty.	*High uncertainty avoidance:* intolerance of ambiguity; need for many rules to constrain uncertainty.
Individualism/collectivism: relative importance of individual versus group interests	*Collectivism:* group interests generally take precedence over individual interests.	*Individualism:* individual interests generally take precedence over group interests.
Masculinity/femininity: assertiveness versus passivity; material possessions versus quality of life	*Masculinity:* values material possessions, money, and the pursuit of personal goals.	*Femininity:* values strong social relevance, quality of life, and the welfare of others.
Long-term versus short-term orientation: outlook on work, life, and relationships	*Short-term orientation:* past and present orientation; values traditions and social obligations.	*Long-term orientation:* future orientation; values dedication, hard work, and thrift.

Exhibit A.3 Hall's cultural dimensions

Cultural dimensions	Scale anchors	
Context: extent to which the context of a message is as important as the message itself	*Low context:* direct and frank communication; message itself conveys its own meaning.	*High context:* much of the meaning in communication is conveyed indirectly through the context surrounding a message.
Space: extent to which people are comfortable sharing physical space with others	*Center of power:* territorial; need for clearly delineated personal space between themselves and others.	*Center of community:* communal; comfortable sharing personal space with others.
Time: extent to which people approach one task at a time or multiple tasks simultaneously	*Monochronic:* sequential attention to individual goals; separation of work and personal life; precise concept of time.	*Polychronic:* simultaneous attention to multiple goals; integration of work and personal life; relative concept of time.

Building on the work of Hofstede, Dutch management researcher Fons Trompenaars has presented a somewhat different model of culture based on his study of Shell and other managers over a ten-year period.[6] His model is based on the early work of Harvard sociologists Talcott Parsons and Edward Shils and focuses on variations in both values and personal relationships across cultures.[7] It consists of seven dimensions, as shown in Exhibit A.4. The first five dimensions focus on relationships among people, while the last two focus on time management and society's relationship with nature.

Taking a decidedly more psychological view, Shalom Schwartz and his associates asserted that the essential distinction between societal values is the motivational goals they express.[8] He identified ten universal human values that reflect needs, social motives, and social institutional demands.[9] These values are purportedly found in all cultures and represent universal needs of human existence. The human values identified are: power;

Exhibit A.4 Trompenaars' cultural dimensions

Cultural dimensions	Scale anchors	
Universalism/particularism: relative importance of applying standardized rules and policies across societal members; role of exceptions in rule enforcement	*Universalism:* reliance on formal rules and policies that are applied equally to everyone.	*Particularism:* rules must be tempered by the nature of the situation and the people involved.
Individualism/collectivism: extent to which people derive their identity from within themselves or their group	*Individualism:* focus on individual achievement and independence.	*Collectivism:* focus on group achievement and welfare.
Specific/diffuse: extent to which people's various roles are compartmentalized or integrated	*Specific:* clear separation of a person's various roles.	*Diffuse:* clear integration of a person's various roles.
Neutral/affective: extent to which people are free to express their emotions in public	*Neutral:* refrain from showing emotions; hide feelings.	*Affective:* emotional expressions acceptable or encouraged.
Achievement/ascription: manner in which respect and social status are accorded to people	*Achievement:* respect for earned accomplishments.	*Ascription:* respect for ascribed or inherited status.
Time perspective: relative focus on the past or the future in daily activities	*Past-/present-oriented:* emphasis on past events and glory.	*Future-oriented:* emphasis on planning and future possibilities.
Relationship with environment: extent to which people believe they control the environment or it controls them	*Inner-directed:* focus on controlling the environment.	*Outer-directed:* focus on living in harmony with nature.

Exhibit A.5 Schwartz's cultural dimensions

Cultural dimensions	Scale anchors	
Conservatism/autonomy: extent to which individuals are integrated in groups	*Conservatism:* individuals are embedded in a collectivity, finding meaning through participation and identification with a group that shares their way of life.	*Autonomy:* individuals are autonomous from groups, finding meaning in their own uniqueness. Two types of autonomy: intellectual autonomy (independent pursuit of ideas and rights) and effective autonomy (independent pursuit of affectively positive experiences).
Hierarchy/egalitarianism: extent to which equality is valued and expected	*Hierarchy:* cultures are organized hierarchically; individuals are socialized to comply with their roles and are sanctioned if they do not.	*Egalitarianism:* individuals are seen as moral equals who share basic interests as human beings.
Mastery/harmony: extent to which people seek to change the natural and social world to advance personal or group interests	*Mastery:* individuals value getting ahead through self-assertion and seek to change the natural and social world to advance personal or group interests.	*Harmony:* individuals accept the world as it is and try to preserve it rather than exploit it.

achievement; hedonism; stimulation; self-direction; universalism; benevolence; tradition; conformity; and security. Schwartz argued that individual and cultural levels of analysis are conceptually independent.[10] Individual-level dimensions reflect the psychological dynamics that individuals experience when acting on their values in their everyday life, while cultural-level dimensions reflect the solutions that societies find to regulate human actions. At the cultural level of analysis, Schwartz identified three dimensions: conservatism versus autonomy, hierarchy versus egalitarianism, and mastery versus harmony, summarized in Exhibit A.5. Based on this model, he studied school teachers and college students in fifty-four countries. His model has been applied to basic areas of social behavior, but its application to organizational studies has been limited.[11]

Finally, in one of the most ambitious efforts to study cultural dimensions, Robert House led an international team of researchers that focused primarily on understanding the influence of cultural differences on leadership processes.[12] Their investigation was called the GLOBE study, for Global Leadership and Organizational Behavior Effectiveness. In their research, the GLOBE researchers identified nine cultural dimensions, as summarized in Exhibit A.6. While several of these dimensions have been identified previously (e.g., individualism/collectivism, power distance, and uncertainty avoidance), others are unique (e.g., gender egalitarianism and performance orientation).

Based on this assessment, the GLOBE researchers collected data in sixty-two countries and compared the results. Systematic differences were found in leader behavior across the cultures. For example, participatory leadership styles that are often accepted in the individualistic West are of questionable effectiveness in the more collectivistic East. Asian managers place a heavy emphasis on paternalistic leadership and group maintenance activities. Charismatic leaders can be found in most cultures, although they may be highly assertive in some cultures and passive in others. A leader who listens carefully to his or her subordinates is more valued in the United States than in China. Malaysian leaders are expected to behave in a manner that is humble, dignified, and modest, while American leaders seldom behave in this manner. Indians prefer leaders who are assertive, morally principled, ideological, bold, and proactive. Family and tribal norms support highly autocratic leaders in many Arab countries.[13] Clearly, one of the principal contributions of the GLOBE project has been to systematically study not just cultural dimensions but also how variations in such dimensions affect leadership behavior and effectiveness.

Common themes across models

Taken together, these six culture models attempt to accomplish two things. First, each model offers a well-reasoned set of dimensions along which various cultures can be compared. In this regard, they offer a form of intellectual shorthand for cultural analysis, allowing researchers to break down assessments of various cultures into power distance, uncertainty avoidance, and so forth, and thus organize their thoughts and focus attention on what otherwise would be a monumental task. Second, four of the models offer numeric scores for rating various cultures. For example, we can use

Exhibit A.6 GLOBE project's cultural dimensions

Cultural dimensions	Scale anchors	
Power distance: degree to which people expect power to be distributed equally	*High:* society divided into classes; power bases are stable and scarce; power is seen as providing social order; limited upward mobility.	*Low:* society has large middle class; power bases are transient and sharable; power often seen as a source of corruption, coercion, and dominance; high upward mobility.
Uncertainty avoidance: extent to which people rely on norms, rules, and procedures to reduce the unpredictability of future events	*High:* tendency to formalize social interactions; document agreements in legal contracts; be orderly and maintain meticulous records; rely on rules and formal policies.	*Low:* tendency to be more informal in social interactions; reliance on word of people they trust; less concerned with orderliness and record keeping; reliance on informal norms of behavior.
Humane orientation: extent to which people reward fairness, altruism, and generosity	*High:* interests of others important; values altruism, benevolence, kindness, and generosity; high need for belonging and affiliation; fewer psychological and pathological problems.	*Low:* self-interest important; values pleasure, comfort, and self-enjoyment; high need for power and possessions; more psychological and pathological problems.
Institutional collectivism: extent to which society encourages collective distribution of resources and collective action	*High:* individuals integrated into strong cohesive groups; self viewed as interdependent with groups; societal goals often take precedence over individual goals.	*Low:* individuals largely responsible for themselves; self viewed as autonomous; individual goals often take precedence over societal or group goals.
In-group collectivism: extent to which individuals express pride, loyalty, and cohesiveness in their organizations and families	*High:* members assume they are interdependent and seek to make important personal contributions to the group or organization; long-term employer–employee relationships; organizations assume major responsibility of employee welfare; important decisions made by groups.	*Low:* members assume they are independent of the organization and seek to stand out by making individual contributions; short-term employer–employee relationships; organizations primarily interested in the work performed by employees over their personal welfare.
Assertiveness: degree to which people are assertive, confrontational, and aggressive in relationships with others	*High:* value assertiveness, dominance, and tough behavior for all members of society; sympathy for the strong; value competition; belief in success through hard work; values direct and unambiguous communication.	*Low:* prefers modesty and tenderness to assertiveness; sympathy for the weak; values cooperation; often associates competition with defeat and punishment; values face saving in communication and action.
Gender egalitarianism: degree to which gender differences are minimized	*High:* high participation of women in the workforce; more women in positions of authority; women accorded equal status in society.	*Low:* low participation of women in the workforce; fewer women in positions of authority; women not accorded equal status in society.
Future orientation: extent to which people engage in future-oriented behaviors, such as planning, investing, and delayed gratification	*High:* greater emphasis on economic success; propensity to save for the future; values intrinsic motivation; organizations tend to be flexible and adaptive.	*Low:* less emphasis on economic success; propensity for instant gratification; values extrinsic motivation; organizations tend to be bureaucratic and inflexible.
Performance orientation: degree to which high performance is encouraged and rewarded	*High:* belief that individuals are in control of their destiny; values assertiveness, competitiveness, and materialism; emphasizes performance over people.	*Low:* values harmony with environment over control; emphasizes seniority, loyalty, social relationships, and belongingness; values who people are more than what they do.

Hofstede's model to say that Germany is a thirty-five while France is a sixty-eight on power distance, suggesting that Germany is more egalitarian than France. Regardless of whether these ratings are highly precise or only generally indicative of these countries, they nonetheless provide one indication of how these countries might vary culturally.

As is evident from this review, there are many different ways to represent cultural differences. Unfortunately, the six cultural models available frequently focus on different aspects of societal beliefs, norms, or values, and, as such, convergence across the models seems at first glance to be limited. This lack of convergence presents important challenges both for researchers attempting to study cultural influences on management and for managers trying to understand new cultural settings.

Instead of advocating one model over another, we suggest that all the models have important factors to contribute to our understanding of culture as it relates to management practices (see Chapter 3).[14] In order to navigate this culture theory jungle, we argue that the most productive approach is to integrate and adapt the various models on the basis of their utility for better understanding business and management in cross-cultural settings. In doing so, we seek common themes that collectively represent the principal differences between cultures. While no single model can cover all aspects of a culture, we believe it is possible to tease out the principal cultural characteristics through such a comparative analysis.

In our view, five relatively distinct common themes emerge from this comparison (see Exhibit A.7).

Exhibit A.7 Core cultural dimensions

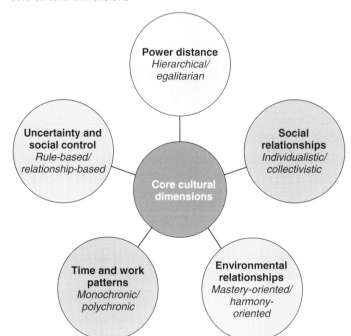

- *Power distribution.* How are power and authority distributed in a society? Is this distribution based on concepts of hierarchy or egalitarianism? What are societal beliefs concerning equality or privilege?
- *Social organization.* What is the fundamental building block of a society: individuals or groups? How does a society organize for collective action?
- *Environmental relationships.* On a societal level, how do people view the world around them and their relationship with the natural and social environment? Is their goal to control the environment and events around them or to live in harmony with these external realities?
- *Time/work patterns.* How do people in a society organize and manage their time to carry out their work and nonwork activities? Do people approach work in a linear or nonlinear fashion?
- *Uncertainty and social control.* How do societies try to ensure predictability in the behavior of their members? Do they work to control people through uniformly applied rules, policies, laws, and social norms or do they rely more on personal ties or unique circumstances?

To achieve this clustering, we must recognize that, in a few cases, multiple dimensions in the original models can be merged into a single more general or unifying cultural dimension (e.g., institutional and in-group collectivism in the GLOBE model), as discussed below. In addition, we need to look beyond the simple adjectives often used by the various researchers and seek deeper meaning in the various concepts themselves, also as discussed below.

At first glance, these five themes seem to replicate Hofstede's five dimensions, but closer analysis suggests that the other models serve to amplify, clarify, and, in some cases, reposition dimensions so that they are more relevant for the contemporary workplace. Indeed, we believe the commonality across these models reinforces their utility (and possible validity) as critical evaluative components in better understanding global management and the world of international business. As such, each model thus adds something of value to this endeavor.

Core cultural dimensions

Power distribution: hierarchical versus egalitarian

All societies have normative beliefs governing how power and influence should be distributed and used. Typically, these norms are expressed in terms of whether power should be clustered at or near the top of a hierarchy or distributed in a more egalitarian fashion. In other words, is the culture more *hierarchical* or *egalitarian*? Questions pertaining to this dimension include the following. Should authority ultimately reside in strong centralized governments or in the people themselves? Should organizations be structured vertically (e.g., tall organization structures) or horizontally (e.g., flat organization structures, or even networked structures)? Is decision making largely autocratic or participatory? Are leaders chosen because they are the most qualified for a job or because they already have standing in the community? Are leaders elected or appointed? Are people willing or reluctant to question authority?

Social relationships: individualistic versus collectivistic

The nature of social organization and perceptions of self-identity have been widely identified in various models of culture as representing a key variable in understanding what differentiates one society from another. This is usually expressed in terms of cultures being more *individualistic* or *collectivistic*. At issue here is whether members of a society see themselves first and foremost as individuals or as members of a group. Do they achieve self-identity through their own efforts or through group endeavors? Are individual goals or group goals more important? Do group sanctions reinforce personal responsibility or conformity to group norms? Is individual or group decision making preferred? Is business done primarily on the basis of written contracts or personal relationships? Is communication characterized primarily by low context (when the message contains all or almost all the intended message) or by high context (when the context surrounding the message also carries significant information – see Chapter 6)?

An understanding of this dimension is critical for managers to succeed overseas. For example, initiating performance-based incentive systems that reward individual performance will likely have a difficult time succeeding in highly collectivistic cultures. Group-based rewards and incentives will probably be more successful in such circumstances. Likewise, overemphasizing participatory decision making in a highly individualistic culture may also be problematic (see Chapter 4). Again, the challenge for global managers is to develop administrative practices that support, rather than contradict, local customs and social norms.

Environmental relationships: mastery versus harmony

Most societies have a reasonably widely shared view with respect to their relationship to their surroundings. We refer to this as the distinction between *mastery-oriented* and *harmony-oriented*. This relationship often represents an underlying motive structure or goal for the society. In other words, on a fundamental level some societies seek to control their surrounding environment, while others seek to live in relative harmony with it. Does a society emphasize competition in the pursuit of personal or group goals or striving for social progress, quality of life, and the welfare of others? Does a society attempt to bend nature to its will or conform to nature as much as possible? Is a society assertive, proactive, and "masculine" (to use Hofstede's term) or passive, reactive, and "feminine"? Does a society tend to emphasize extrinsic rewards on the basis of job performance or intrinsic rewards based on seniority or on one's position in the organization? Is there an emphasis on material possessions as symbols of achievement or on economy, harmony, and societal sustainability? Finally, do people tend to engage in conspicuous consumption or do they tend to be more modest and unpretentious?

An understanding of this dimension can help managers determine how to structure work plans and incentive plans, and may even influence leadership style. For example, most employees in a mastery-oriented culture will respond to challenges and personal incentives; they will strive for success. Employees in more harmony-oriented cultures will more likely focus their attention on building or maintaining group welfare, personal relationships, and environmental sustainability. They tend to be more committed to social progress. As such, they will likely be more responsive to participative leadership and be more skeptical of proposed change. Managers who understand this are in a position to tailor their leadership style to fit the situation.

Time and work patterns: monochronic versus polychronic

A fourth major difference across cultures is people's approaches to time and tasks. Here we distinguish between *monochronic* and *polychronic*. People in more monochronic cultures tend to be somewhat methodical in their use of time and their approaches to tasks. They see time as a commodity that can be measured, used, and sometimes sold. They often approach work as a series of tasks or goals that should be tackled sequentially, or one at a time. By contrast, people in more polychronic cultures tend to be more flexible, addressing several problems simultaneously. They are often oblivious to time and resist firm deadlines. They also tend to mix work and personal lives in a more fluid fashion than their monochronic counterparts, who stress a clear separation between work and family.

Logical questions to ask here include the following. Do people have a precise concept of time and tend to be very punctual or do they have a relative concept and tend to be late? Are people more committed to their jobs or to family and friends? Do they separate work and family life or see them as an integrated whole? Do they take a linear or nonlinear approach to planning? Finally, are they focused and impatient or unfocused and patient?

Uncertainty and social control: rules versus relationships

A final dimension used by managers to differentiate across cultures involves the issue of rules versus relationships as a means of reducing uncertainty in society. In other words, how is social behavior best controlled? This distinction is referred to here as *rule-based* and *relationship-based*, although it is also referred to as *universalistic* and *particularistic* (see also Chapter 3).[15] In essence, this issue focuses on the means of social control.

Rule-based (or universalistic) cultures believe that social values and standards take precedence over individual needs or claims by friends and relations; rules are intended to apply equally to the whole "universe" of members. Exceptions serve only to weaken the rule of law. For example, a rule that people should bear truthful witness in a court of law, or give their honest judgment to an insurance company concerning a payment it is about to make, is more important than particular family or friendship ties. This is not to say that "particular" ties are unimportant in universalistic cultures; rather, universal truth as embodied in the law is believed to be more important than these relationships. By contrast, particularistic cultures see the ideal culture in terms of human friendship, extraordinary achievement, unique situations, and close personal relationships. The spirit of the law is deemed to be more important than the letter of the law. Clearly, there are rules and laws in particularistic cultures, but these are designed simply to codify how people relate to one another. Rules are needed (if only to be able to make exceptions to them for particular cases), but people need to be able to count on their friends.

As a result, in rule-based cultures there is a tendency to promulgate a multitude of laws, rules, regulations, bureaucratic procedures, and strict social norms in an attempt to control as many unanticipated events or behaviors as possible. People tend to conform to officially sanctioned constraints because of a moral belief in the virtue of the rule of law, and will often obey directives even if they know violations will not be detected. Waiting for a red light in the absence of any traffic is a good example here. Rules and laws are universally applied (at least in theory), with few exceptions for extenuating circumstances or personal connections. There is a strong belief in the use of formal contracts and rigorous record keeping in business dealings. Things are typically done "by the book," and infractions often bring immediate sanctions or consequences. Finally, decisions tend to be made on the basis of objective criteria to the extent possible. All this is aimed at creating a society with no surprises.

By contrast, relationship-based (or particularistic) cultures tend to use influential people more than abstract or objective rules and regulations as a means of social control.[16] This personal control can come from parents, peers, superiors, supervisors, government officials, and so forth – anyone with influence over the individual. In this sense, relationship-based cultures tend to be particularistic, and individual circumstances often influence the manner in which formal rules are applied. In addition, greater emphasis is placed on developing mutually beneficial interpersonal relationships and trust as a substitute for strict rules and procedures. There is generally less record keeping, and things tend to be done on an informal basis. There is also greater tolerance for noncompliance with bureaucratic rules, in the belief that formal rules cannot cover all contingencies and that some flexibility is often required. Finally, decisions tend to be made on the basis of a combination of objective and subjective criteria and with less formality.

This is not to say that relationship-based cultures do not value laws and official procedures; they do. Rather, laws and procedures are often followed only to the extent that one's social network embraces them and sees either the virtue or necessity of following them, not because of some innate belief in their moral correctness, as is the case with universalistic cultures. When predictability of behavior is important, it is motivated largely through contacts, not contracts, and interpersonal trust and mutual support between partners is critical.

Notes

1 Luciara Nardon and Richard M. Steers, "The culture theory jungle: divergence and convergence in models of national culture," in Rabi S. Bhagat and Richard M. Steers (eds.), *Cambridge Handbook of Culture, Work, and Organizations*. Cambridge University Press, 2009, pp. 3–22.

2 Clyde Kluckhohn, "Values and value orientations in the theory of action," in Talcott Parsons and Edward A. Shils (eds.), *Towards a General Theory of Action*. Cambridge, MA: Harvard University Press, 1951; Florence Kluckhohn and Fred Strodtbeck, *Variations in Value Orientations*. Evanston, IL: Row, Peterson, 1961.

3 Geert Hofstede, *Culture's Consequences: Comparing Values, Behaviors, Institutions, and Organizations across Nations*. Thousand Oaks, CA: Sage, 1980.

4 Michael Bond and Peter Smith, "Cross-cultural social and organizational psychology," *Annual Review of Psychology*, 1996, 17, pp. 205 35.

5 Edward T. Hall, *The Silent Language*. New York: Doubleday, 1959; Edward T. Hall and Mildred Reed Hall, *Understanding Cultural Differences: Germans, French and Americans*. Yarmouth, ME: Intercultural Press, 2000.

6 Fons Trompenaars, *Riding the Waves of Culture: Understanding Cultural Diversity in Business*. London: Economist Books, 1993; Fons Trompenaars and Charles Hampden-Turner, *Riding the Waves of Culture: Understanding Diversity in Global Business*. New York: McGraw-Hill, 1998.

7 Parsons and Shils, *Towards a General Theory of Action*.

8 Shalom Schwartz, "Universals in the content and structure of values: theoretical advances and empirical tests in 20 countries," in Mark Zanna (ed.), *Advances in Experimental Social Psychology*, vol. XXV. New York: Academic Press, 1992, pp. 1–65.

9 Cigdem Kagitçibasi, "Individualism and collectivism," in Marshall Segal and Cigdem Kagitçibasi (eds.), *Handbook of Cross-Cultural Psychology*, vol. III. Boston: Allyn & Bacon, 1997, pp. 1–49.

10 Shalom Schwartz, "Beyond individualism/collectivism: new cultural dimensions of values," in Uichol Kim, Harry C. Triandis, Cigdem Kagitçibasi, Sang-Chin Choi, and Gene Yoon (eds.), *Individualism and Collectivism: Theory, Methods and Applications*. Thousand Oaks, CA: Sage, 1994, pp. 85–122.

11 Bond and Smith, "Cross-cultural social and organizational psychology."

12 Robert J. House, Paul J. Hanges, Mansour Javidan, Peter W. Dorfman, and Vipin Gupta, *Culture, Leadership and Organizations: The GLOBE Study of 62 Societies*. Thousand Oaks, CA: Sage, 2004.

13 House *et al.*, *Culture, Leadership and Organizations*.

14 Nardon and Steers, "The culture theory jungle."

15 John Hooker, *Working across Cultures*. Stanford Business Books, 2003.

16 Hooker, *Working across Cultures*.

Name and company index

Subject index